LIBERTARIANISM

A Political Philosophy for Tomorrow

BOOKS BY JOHN HOSPERS

Human Conduct (1961)
Introduction to Philosophical Analysis (2nd edition 1967)
Meaning and Truth in the Arts (paperback edition 1967)
Readings in Introductory Philosophical Analysis (1968)
Introductory Readings in Aesthetics (1969)
Readings in Ethical Theory (2nd edition 1970; with Wilfrid Sellars)
Artistic Expression (1971)

LIBERTARIANISM

A Political Philosophy for Tomorrow

BY
JOHN HOSPERS

Nash Publishing / Los Angeles

Library of Congress Catalog Card Number: 71-127482
Standard Book Number: 8402-1163-5

Published simultaneously in the United States and
Canada by Nash Publishing, 9255 Sunset Boulevard,
Los Angeles, California 90069.

Printed in the United States of America.

Second Printing

Contents

Introduction

"It was those early morning hours that we learned to dread." The little Latvian woman trembled and tried to keep back the tears, but she continued to speak with quiet dignity. "That was when the secret police would knock on the door and take people away. Usually we never heard from them again. Sometimes we heard that they had been shot, and sometimes that they were still alive somewhere in Siberia—but we never knew. Whole families would be taken, separated, their houses would be occupied by the Soviet authorities. During the Russian occupation of the Baltic countries, almost half the populations of Latvia, Lithuania, and Estonia were taken away. Sometimes the whole family would be sent to Siberian prison camps—but that was a death sentence too, usually within a year, from cold and starvation and overwork. Others were told to get out of their homes with just the possessions they could carry on their backs—they were told to migrate east, wherever they could find a place—but of course there weren't any places, and they tried to live off the land, but mostly they just starved along the way, the aged and crippled first. But in the end there was no chance for any of them, and the Russian authorities knew it. I guess they wanted to get rid of all of us Latvians, and they didn't care how."

"What about you?" I asked her.

"I was lucky. When they came to get some members of my family I was hiding in the woods. I saw them put my uncle on a truck—it was already overcrowded, with people from four months old to eighty-four years. The gardener who lived next door was killed. He wasn't rich but he had employed six people, and this according to the Soviets made him an 'exploiter.' My uncle was arrested, and his whole family with him, because he had owned a lake-front cottage. He used to have boats and rent them out to people who wanted to fish. This made him an 'exploiter' too, and he was shot as soon as they captured him. My aunt and uncle owned a flour mill. It was nationalized, of course. But the government let them stay on as workers—in their own mill. In fact they were forced to work there until they had taught the new workers how to operate it. They weren't killed till after they had taught the others."

She paused, trying to keep her composure. "I wasn't on their June 14 [1941] list, but I heard that I was on the next one. But in the meanwhile the Germans came, in the invasion of Russia. Naturally we ran to them as if they were saviors. But they were no better. Still, two from our family managed to get through to the West—my brother and I. As far as we know, all the rest died. We never heard from them again. I don't know how they died—I do know there was a big purge. The best Latvian army officers, including one of my brothers, were ordered by the Russians to some 'field maneuvers'—and then they were all killed by the Russians, with bullets in the back of the head, and dumped into a mass grave."

I thought of the student who had sat in that same chair in my office just a week before and told me that the Soviet way was the wave of the future, and that "the Czechs had it coming." And of the professor who had broadcast a speech that evening saying that "the United States has become so bad that it must now be liberated by Soviet Russia." I wondered how many mass graves for Americans he was planning as the price for American "liberation."

The second scene is perhaps less dramatic. It takes place in Chile, 1970. Salvador Allende has become President of Chile, and many farmers and businessmen who are able simply leave the country, fearing what is about to come. But the government makes no immediate moves and many people choose to stay in the land they have settled. Arthur Lewis, who came to Chile in 1915, was one who elected to remain. He had cleared the land, planted crops, built a large pleasant house. It was not easy to make ends meet, but when he turned a profit he reinvested it all in the land. Then, in December 1970, before dawn, his ten hired workers seized his farm. Some of these workers had been with the family for years; relations between them had always been pleasant, and Lewis' wages were higher than those on most other farms. But one worker, a Communist candidate for alderman, took charge and made sure that his men stuck by their seizure of Lewis' land. When Lewis, already 82 years old, awoke one morning in December 1970, he found his farm occupied and guarded by armed peasants who were strangers to him. He and his family were imprisoned on the farm. When his grandson tried to move some of these strangers away from the family swimming pool, the worker in charge threatened to cripple him for life.

The family plans to emigrate to Australia, if they can find the money. The $100,000 investment in their land, the years of work and effort, are all gone. They will not be reimbursed.

As for the farm itself, the workers have already sold off most of the produce and the poultry. The work on the farm has ground to a halt. When planting time comes, there may be little left to plant. The workers, having stripped the farm of its salable resources, spend their time sleeping beside the swimming pool. (See *Newsweek*, Feb. 1, 1971, p. 40.)

The third example is still less dramatic. It takes place in the United States. The Amish, a peace-loving religious sect residing chiefly on farms in the hill country of Pennsylvania, have for generations lived in peace with their neighbors, taking care of their own, asking nothing from anyone, making their living thriftily and efficiently, though without tractors and other machine tools since the possession of these is against their religious creed. Not wishing to be a part of the federal Social Security program or any similar federal programs, they declined to pay into them—nor, of course, did they wish any benefits from them. They simply wanted to be left alone. Then federal agents swooped down upon the Amish farms, demanding payment. When the farmers again declined, explaining their reasons, the agents took their horses and plows away from them, selling them and confiscating the money in order to pay the alleged debts. In the absence of farm machinery, these horses were the farmers' source of livelihood: without them they could not till the soil. But this of course did not matter to the agents: they simply took them away.

This last story may strike the reader as too low-keyed to be memorable. It never made headlines in the newspapers, nor much of an impression on the public. But all three have something in common: they all have to do with the taking away by force of human life or property, and in each case the act or removal is performed by government. And it is the use of force against individuals, particularly by government, that is considered the ultimate evil by the proponents of the political philosophy which is the subject of this book. This philosophy is called *libertarianism*. As the name implies, it is a philosophy of personal liberty—the liberty of each person to live according to his own choices, provided that he does not attempt to coerce others and thus prevent them from living according to their choices. Libertarians hold this to be an inalienable right of man; thus, libertarianism represents a total commitment to the concept of individual rights.

Individuals often try to use force against others: murderers, rapists, robbers, burglars, and sundry other criminals. So do groups of individuals like the Mafia. But by far the most numerous and most flagrant violations of personal liberty and individual rights are performed by *governments*. Governments in virtually every country of the world plunder the most productive people to support various projects dreamed up by politicians, and to keep those same politicians in power. Governments in most countries initiate aggression against their own people—in some cases forcing people to work at jobs they do not choose, in places to which they do not want to go, coercing them in virtually the whole conduct of their lives, including their amusements—and in extreme cases, forcing them to die in gas chambers and slave labor camps. The major crimes throughout history, the ones executed on the largest scale, have been committed not by individuals or bands of individuals, but by governments, as a deliberate policy of those governments—that is, by the official representatives of governments, acting in their official capacity.

Libertarianism is not yet well known to the general public. In the eyes of the average American citizen, the only choice is between "liberals" ("the left") and "conservatives" ("the right"). The "liberals," when confronted by a social problem, regularly turn toward government for a solution. Whether it is the problem of the cities, the problem of integration, the prob-

lem of poverty, the problem of housing, the problem of underdeveloped nations, and so on ad infinitum, they invoke
government for solutions, at the expense of the citizenry. The
problems have not been solved, but the cry is for more, more,
all from government, that is, the taxpayer. I refer of course to
the twentieth-century variety of those who call themselves
"liberals"; the doctrine of political liberalism in the nineteenth
century came much closer to deserving its name, which is of
course derived from the French word *libre*, free. Liberals of
our century are adept in advocating grand designs hatched
from their brains—that is, the plans are to be thought of
by them, and the bill for carrying them out is to be paid by
everyone else.

In most respects, the conservatives are much to be preferred. The word "conservative" does not always carry the
same meaning, depending on what things at the given time
and place its advocates desire to conserve. As a rule they have
a much more realistic picture of the economic facts of life than
do the liberals, who seem to imagine that endless quantities of
money will fall from heaven to fulfill their plans. The conservatives are usually aware that "you can't get something for
nothing" and that when people's liberty is tampered with they
will not produce as successfully and the standard of living will
decline as a result. Yet the conservatives are (typically at least)
not averse to using government to force their plans on others;
yes, there should be censorship, they say—that is, the moral
convictions of one group (the one in political power) should be
forced on everyone else; yes, there should be compulsory
prayers in public schools; yes, there should be foreign aid to
some nations, though perhaps not as indiscriminate as the liberals would have. They would still undertake to decide these
questions—such as what one shall read—not only for themselves but *for others* via the coercive machinery of the law.

Libertarians oppose both of these alternatives, and for the same reason. Each approves, to varying degrees, the use of force by government to make an individual act contrary to his voluntary choice. Both tend to curb the freedom of an individual to act in accordance with his choices even when it does not interfere with the equal freedom of others to do the same.

What libertarianism is, what it recommends in detail and why, and what would be its consequences if adopted, will be the subject of this book.

1
Liberty
and
Government

Everyone is in favor of liberty—at least everyone pays it lip service. Yet many of those who pose as eager champions of liberty agitate for measures that would destroy it in one segment of man's life after another. In the name of liberty, social reformers have supported legislation which has led to totalitarian dictatorships. Sometimes they have done this knowingly, being so anxious to interfere forcibly in the lives of other people that they have advocated the most hairbrained utopias (to be managed by themselves or those friendly to their ideas) and called them bastions of freedom. But more often they have done it unknowingly, with a real interest in justice and motivated by various kinds of idealism and humanitarianism; but nonetheless they have advocated policies which, not by their intention but by the operation of natural laws, have led to the very negation of liberty. In this book, I shall endeavor to show the lines of connection between these policies and their ultimate results.

9

What, then, is liberty? In its most fundamental sense, the sense from which the other senses stem, and the sense which is also historically the earliest, liberty (or freedom) is the *absence of coercion by other human beings.* To the extent that a person is forced against his will to do something, he is not free. A slave is not free, for the activities of his life are undertaken at the whim of others who are his masters. A person who is being robbed by a gunman is not free in that episode of his life, for he is forced to surrender his money against his will, though of course he is free in other aspects of his life. A people under the grip of a tyrannical dictator and secret police are not free in most of the activities of their lives, for they are forced by threat of death or loss of livelihood to do things they would not willingly do and to refrain from countless activities in which they would prefer to engage.

This sense of liberty should be distinguished from a second one that is dependent on it. A compulsive gambler may say in a reflective moment, "I am a slave to my desire to gamble." In one sense he is not free, because he cannot control his desires —it is just *as if* some inner demon were forcing him to gamble, even knowing that obeying the demon's dictates will lead to his own destruction. This sense of freedom or liberty is of great importance for the therapeutic psychologist, who attempts to remove the psychological stumbling-blocks to the realization of the person's rational desires. Nevertheless, it *is* a different sense: the word "slave" here is a metaphor. The literal slave has his life and work subject to the commands of another human being, external to himself; such a person is not free in the first and fundamental sense, no matter how psychologically well-adjusted he may be. The "slave to his own desires" need be no slave in this first sense at all; he just can't make himself stop doing things he knows will injure him, and the outcome may be much the same as if someone else were forcing him to do them. This similarity of outcome, plus the inner sense of "feeling enslaved and powerless," probably accounts for the use of the same word for both situations. But the second sense is a metaphor only; the victim of powerful destructive inner drives is not a literal slave such as existed on Southern plantations before the Civil War. And it is this literal sense which concerns us in political philosophy. Southern Negroes were quite literally slaves; the compulsive gambler who flies to Las Vegas every weekend is not, for no *other* human will intervenes to prevent him from acting in accordance with his voluntary choices. Whatever problem he may have in altering the trend of his choices is a problem between him and his psychiatrist, and does not affect his enjoyment of political freedom or rights.

There is still a third sense of the term "liberty" which is much more easily confused with the first and original sense: liberty, or freedom, in the sense of *power* or *ability*. I am free to walk; that is, I can do so if I choose; but I am not free to fly in the air like a bird, or to make myself fifty feet tall, or to change myself into an ostrich. Doubtless the range of my choices is limited because I cannot do all these things; but I am still free in the first sense as long as no one is coercing me. Similarly, I may have few choices open to me, or even just one at a given time: if I have undertaken a dangerous river trip and find myself in the rapids, I may be quite helpless to do anything and have no choice but to continue downstream, but I am still free in the first sense as long as I voluntarily decided to embark on the journey and no one forced me to make it. My finding myself in this position, as well as my failure to fly, is not the result of the imposition of any other human will upon mine. The distinction is an important one because much confusion results from the failure to observe it: those who say, for example, that "a poor man is not free," may be speaking truly in the third sense, in that the range of a poor man's choices is much more limited than that of a wealthy man; but he is not speaking truly if he is using the word "free" in the first sense, for a man may be poor and yet coerced by no one (a humble fisherman, for example). For the sake of clarity, the word "liberty" will be used in this book in the first and fundamental sense, the sense with which political philosophy is primarily concerned.[1]

Now, what shall we say of freedom in this first sense? One's first thought might well be that the ideal of liberty would be that there should be no coercion whatever by anyone on anyone else—no limitation through the use of force on anyone's actions. And if no one ever used force against anyone else, this would indeed be true: there would be no interference by anyone with anyone else's choices, hence no need to defend one's liberty against the one who would take it away. But people do sometimes use force against others, and hence one must be permitted to retaliate. Suppose, for example, that I commit multiple murders, or hold up others at gunpoint and take away their possessions. I would then be using my freedom to deprive other people of theirs. If I were permitted to do this, my freedom to act thus would be bought at the price of the freedom of others, indeed of their very lives. My freedom would be considered so valuable that the extinction of the freedom of others would weigh nothing against it. But if *everyone* should have freedom, then the freedom of one person to violate the freedom of others must be inhibited, in order to preserve the equal freedom of those others.

If everyone were permitted the liberty to infringe on the liberty of others, some people would soon be murdered, and countless others would be the slaves of the strongest. Clearly in such a situation the freedom of the victims would be violated. If each human being is to have liberty, he cannot also have the liberty to deprive others of *their* liberty.

It appears reasonable, then, to conclude that in any society there must be a set of rules in operation, designed to protect people from infringement on their freedom. The prohibition of killing, robbing, assaulting, maiming, and otherwise inflicting damage on others, including taking away by force the products of their labor, would be rules of first importance, for only if such rules are operative can citizens live free from coercive acts or attempts.

Not only do such rules have to be conceived of, they must be enforced. And here government enters the picture. If no one ever attempted to interfere with the liberty of another, government would not be necessary. But once some individual or group does interfere, or attempts to do so, government comes in to punish the offender after a trial according to prescribed rules.

Why not leave it up to the individual? For one thing, an individual who had to be constantly protecting himself would be unable to engage in many more activities than self-defense; when the government takes over that function for him, he is to a large measure relieved of this responsibility. Secondly, a criminal is also entitled to protection of his rights by impartial judgment. A theft of ten dollars, for example, is not justly punishable by death. When government exists, and its laws are enforced by uncorrupted officials, the punishments attaching to various offenses are known in advance and carried out according to previously enacted laws.

Most of the social relations into which we enter, and the organizations to which we belong, are voluntary: clubs, churches, fraternities, professional societies. We choose to join them, and we can pull out if we no longer wish to be associated with them. The exception to this is government. If we are born in a certain country, we are subject to its laws and restrictions even though we did not consent to be, or ever choose to live in that nation. We can, if we live in the United States (but not as a rule if we live in Soviet Russia) emigrate to another country—but then of course we are subject to *its* laws and restrictions.

Nor can we plausibly say that our continued residence in a country implies consent to its laws. It would be perfectly absurd to say that a person born into a dictatorship, whose life is beset by harsh laws at every turn, who is hounded by the secret police and shot if he tries to leave the country, has tacitly consented to live under its government. Membership in such a government is far from a matter of choice; and, if the government under which we live is one under which we would have chosen to live in any case, we can consider ourselves fabulously fortunate.

The feature that distinguishes government from all other institutions, which is obvious on reflection but comes as a surprise to those who have not considered the matter, is that *it operates by the use of force and threat of force*—that is, by coercion, and that this system of coercion includes everyone in the land. (It is, of course, legalized coercion: the Mafia also operates by force, but illegal force—and one is not compelled to belong to the Mafia.) The government of a nation has a *monopoly of legalized physical force* within the defined boundaries of that nation. (A nation in which there are two competing armies within the same nation is in a state of civil war.) Government's distinctive function, within the geographical boundaries of the nation, is to pass laws that will be binding on everyone and to enforce them.

The use of force by government is not always obvious to everyone because the threat usually lies in the background; but it is always ready to be used if the citizen does not conform. If you receive a letter "advising" you to pay your income tax, and you write back to Washington that you have thought the matter over and decided not to accept the advice, you will soon see the iron fist which lies concealed under the velvet glove. The government does not operate through advisement, preachment, moralizing, persuasion, or exhortation; it operates through coercion. Therein lies its power and its efficacy—and also its tremendous danger.

The only government tolerated by libertarians is one that exercises only *retaliatory* use of force on anyone who initiates the use of force against anyone else within its borders. Such a government removes the need for the individual to provide his own defense by taking to itself the protection of the individual's "inalienable right of self-defense." The danger of government is that it may exceed this function—that instead of (or in addition to) the exercise of retaliatory force it itself will initiate force against its own citizens. The former government is a protector of the individual: the citizen is free to engage in his chosen activities without constantly having to defend himself, for the government takes over that function. The latter government is not a protector, but an aggressor—an aggressor far worse than any criminal or even a band of criminals; for the criminal at least wishes to escape detection and the law is constantly working against him, whereas if the government becomes the initiator of force against you, there is nowhere else to turn: for it has the guns and you are the disarmed victim. Unfortunately most of the governments in the history of the world have belonged to the latter class.

Should an individual or a government use force at all, even in retaliation? Clearly yes; complete pacifism is self-defeating. If a person were not permitted to protect himself against those who would harm him, he would be a victim at the hands of any aggressor; and an announced policy of not resisting would be an open invitation to anyone who wanted to harm him. If such a policy were known in advance, the peaceful people would soon be eliminated in favor of the aggressive ones. It is surely a deterrent to the use of force for the aggressor to know that his efforts will be resisted. "It is only as retaliation that force may be used and only against the man who starts its use. No, I do not share his evil or sink to his concept of morality: I merely grant him his choice, destruction, the only destruction he had the right to choose: his own. He uses force to seize a value; I use it only to destroy destruction. A holdup man seeks to gain wealth by killing me; I do not grow richer by killing a holdup man."[2]

If each individual had constantly to defend himself against possible aggressors, he would have to spend a considerable portion of his life in target practice, karate exercises, and other means of self-defense, and even so he would probably be help-less against groups of individuals who might try to kill, maim, or rob him. He would have little time for cultivating those qualities which are essential to civilized life, nor would im-provements in science, medicine, and the arts be likely to occur. The function of government is to take this responsibility off his shoulders: the government undertakes to defend him against aggressors and to punish them if they attack him. When the government is effective in doing this, it enables the citizen to go about his business unmolested and without con-stant fear for his life. To do this, of course, government must have physical power—the police, to protect the citizen from aggression within its borders, and the armed forces, to protect him from aggressors outside. Beyond that, the government should not intrude upon his life, either to run his business, or adjust his daily activities, or prescribe his personal moral code.

Government, then, undertakes to be the individual's protector; but historically governments have gone far beyond this function. Since they already have the physical power, they have not hesitated to use it for purposes far beyond that which was entrusted to them in the first place. Undertaking initially to protect its citizens against aggression, it has often itself become an aggressor—a far greater aggressor, indeed, than the criminals against whom it was supposed to protect its citizens. Governments have done what no private citizens can do: arrest and imprison individuals without a trial and send them to slave labor camps. Government must have power in order to be effective—and yet the very means by which alone it can be effective make it vulnerable to the abuse of power, leading to managing the lives of individuals and even inflicting terror upon them.

Governments would not exist everywhere if they did not answer to some need. But since they do possess the physical force to implement their commands, it is all too easy for them to get out of hand and to aim the force they have garnered for legitimate purposes toward illegitimate purposes. Since they have the force at their disposal anyway, who is to stop them? The signs we see on bumper stickers are tragically true: "Beware: the Government Is Armed and Dangerous."

Libertarianism and Law

Government passes laws and enforces compliance with them upon every member of the population. What is the attitude of the libertarian toward law?

First, the libertarian believes in government by law as opposed to government by men. What this means is not that the laws are not made and administered by men, but that they must be passed and enforced according to a previously agreed on procedure (embedded in a constitution), that they be publicized and written (so that everyone can know what the law is), that they can never be made retroactive, and that they cannot be selectively enforced at the whim of a judge or policeman. This point is admirably illustrated in Henry Hazlitt's novel, *Time Will Run Back,* in which the Soviet dictator, Stalenin, dies suddenly and his son, Peter, who has some ideas about how to run a government, replaces him. In the following passage, Peter is trying with one of his assistants to work out a just system of laws:[3]

"Where do we begin? That is the question that has been bothering me for some time," said Peter. "There are so many places to begin. . . . But the first thing that needs to be done is to free the people from terror, to free them from servility and grovelling. . . . We must give them freedom from fear."

"From fear of what?"

"From fear of us, of course. From fear of the government."

"But fear is the only thing that keeps people in line! If people didn't fear the government, if they didn't fear the police, how would we be able to keep them from committing every sort of crime?"

"Crime would continue to be made illegal," said Peter, "and people would be punished for it by penalties graded according to the seriousness of the crime. But crime must be carefully defined by law."

"It already is."

"Maybe. But we should change the laws so that nobody can be arrested until he is charged with a definite crime. He should be told what that crime is. He should be allowed to confront his accusers and to answer them. These accusers should present real evidence. The man accused should be assumed to be innocent until he is proved guilty and not, as now, the other way around. And maybe—I haven't yet thought this out—the accused ought to be entitled, if he wants, to have someone else who knows the law better than he does, and who knows better than he does what his rights are, to defend him. Maybe the government itself ought to provide him with such a defender."

"I shudder to think what would happen, chief, if the cards were stacked so much in favour of the criminals. You would practically never be able to find anyone guilty. The criminals would certainly be freed from fear. . . ."

"I think it can be made to work," Peter said. "Anyway I'm going to try. . . . Don't misunderstand me. Crime will continue to be illegalised. But each crime will be carefully defined, and nobody will be punished unless he is guilty of an act that had already been defined as a crime before he did it. We are no longer going to have acts declared to be crimes retroactively."

"But suppose somebody does something that is clearly anti-social, that is clearly against the interests of the State, and we have merely neglected beforehand to define that act as a crime?"

"Then that will be our fault, Adams, and we will have to define it as a crime so that we can punish it as such in the future. But we will not punish anybody for having done it before it was defined as a crime. If I may invent a term, we will not pass any ex post facto laws."

"It seems to me, chief, that you have thought of a most ingenious way of tying the government's hands in advance. How can we guess ahead of time every crime that anyone can think of committing? And what's the use of having prosecutors and judges if we are not going to allow them to exercise any discretion?"

"The discretion of the judges will be exercised," replied Peter, "in interpreting and applying the existing body of law. The judge will have to decide whether the evidence presented by the prosecutor or the plaintiff is substantial enough to show that the accused actually did the act with which he is charged. But first the judge will have to decide whether the act with which a man is charged would fall within the pre-existing definition of a crime."

"How are you going to get a judge to act with all this impartiality and self-restraint?"

"We'll remove any judge who doesn't."

"In other words, chief, we'll remove any judge who doesn't act the way we should like him to act. Stalenin has been doing that already."

"But the government, until now, Adams, has been removing judges for being too merciful or too impartial. I will remove them for being too harsh or too biased."

"This arrangement then, chief, will last only as long as your own power lasts—certainly no longer than there is someone in power who feels exactly as you do."

"Well then," Peter said reconsidering, "we will have to make the judiciary independent of the whims of the government?"

"Won't the judges be part of the government?"

"Well, independent of the executive arm of the government."

"Pardon me, chief, but aren't you contradicting what you just said a minute ago? You were going to remove any judge who did not act with impartiality and self-restraint, and did not conscientiously apply the law as it stood. If you make your judge independent of you, how are you going to discipline them and make them carry out their duties and powers with abuse?"

Peter lit a cigarette.

"You're right, I'll have to give all this more thought. . . . But what I am trying to do is to establish what we might call a rule of law. The only way, as I see it, in which we can free the people from constant fear of their own government is to set up a definite code of rules, a definite set of laws, and then say to them: 'As long as you live in accordance with these rules, as long as you stay within these laws, you are free to do whatever else you wish without fear. You need no longer be in terror of being sent to a concentration camp or being shot just because you have incurred the personal displeasure of the judge, or of some government official, or of someone higher up than yourself. If you are accused, your accusers must definitely prove your guilt, instead of forcing you to try to prove your innocence. And, above all, no so-called "confession" will be wrung from you by threats or fatigue or force or torture. As long as you stay within the pre-established code of laws, you are free to do as you like.' Such a rule of law, as I see it, is the only thing that will free the people from terror and from the arbitrary decisions of those in power."

Second, and most important, what should be the *scope* of law, according to libertarianism? What should laws be about, and why? On this matter the libertarian agrees with the principle set down by John Stuart Mill, in Chapter 1 of his *On Liberty*:

The sole end for which mankind are warranted, individually or collectively, in interfering with the liberty of action of any of their number, is self-protection. The only purpose for which power can be rightfully exercised over any member of a civilized community, against his will, is to prevent harm to others. His own good, either physical or moral, is not a sufficient warrant. He cannot rightfully be compelled to do or forbear because it will be better for him to do so, because it will make him happier, because, in the opinions of others, to do so would be wise, or even right. These are good reasons for remonstrating with him, or reasoning with him, or persuading him, or entreating him, but not for compelling him, or visiting him with any evil in case he do otherwise.[4]

Thus, (1) there should be no laws to protect people from themselves. Each person is the owner of his own life, and no one should be permitted to use force against him to make him change it: he can, as Mill says, use persuasion, entreaty, argument, but not compulsion. (2) Nor should there be laws which force him to help others; helping others is something an individual is free to do or not to do, as he chooses. In some cases helping your neighbor when he is in a jam might be the morally right and proper thing to do, but it is one thing to assent to this, and another to say that you should be forced *by law* to do it. (3) The sole province of law is to prevent people from harming one another. If I am permitted to kill you, then your liberty is extinguished along with your life. If I assault or maim you, your freedom is also compromised—there are things you would have done which you can no longer do. If I am free to rob you, you are no longer free to spend the money which I took from you. It is for this reason that the libertarian approves of laws, and only those laws, which proscribe the interference of one person with the liberty of another. It is for an individual to decide whether or not to become intoxicated, and there should be no penalty for his becoming so; but if he drives while intoxicated, he is a threat to every other motorist on the highway, and the law may quite properly arrest him for thus endangering the lives of others.

And how can one person restrict the freedom of another? "By harming him," one might say; but "harm" is a vague word. I may in some way harm you if I tell you dirty stories, but if you are a willing listener you have no cause to complain. (This doesn't mean, of course, that it is necessarily a good thing for me to do so.) You, for your part, are free not to listen, or to tell me to stop, or to leave the room, or to ask me to leave. What I should not be free to do—and what the law is empowered to prevent me from doing—is to *use force* against you. Your liberty is violated by the use of force, or *threat* of force. (If I threaten to kill you, I can force you to give up things you otherwise would not have parted with.) Sex between consenting parties should be no business of the law, but this does not include rape, for rape is the use of *force* against another for sexual purposes.

But when is one using force? If I see a man beating a woman, I may conclude that he is using force against her; but once I learn that she is a masochist who wanted the beating and asked for it, that she is a willing partner to the transaction and not an unwilling victim, I can no longer conclude that he forced her. It is the *unwillingness* that makes it force. If I make you an unwilling participant, I am using force ("forcing you against your will"). Of course you may not *like* to wash the dishes, but if I tell you it is your duty as my wife to do it and you believe me, or if I make a bargain with you that if you do the dishes I'll sweep the floor, I am not forcing you; you consented to my order or suggestion, even though you may not have liked it. (One does plenty of things one doesn't like, but as long as one consented to do it then one is not the victim of force.) It is making you do something against your own judgment that makes it force; it is not enough that I led you into making a wrong or false or unwise judgment, for as long as you made it, I have not used force—only persuasion and perhaps flattery, insult, etc. If I play recordings of advertising or propaganda during your sleep and they influence your subse-

quent behavior, I have not forced you as long as you consented to what I did; but if I did it to you against your will or even
without your consent, I could be said to have used force in
that you were an unwilling or unknowing victim of my actions:
your *will* was in no way involved.

Force is behavior which requires the unwilling involvement
of another person or persons. Force is a violation of liberty, for
if I use force (or threat of force) against you, I thereby prevent
you from using *your* judgment in the matter and am substitut-
ing my judgment for yours in a matter that concerns you. You
are free, of course, not to *use* your judgment, or not to use it
wisely if you use it at all; but if I use force against you I am
preventing you from exercising that choice, and thereby preventing you from acting on *your own* judgment.

It is sometimes said that television commercials should be
banned because they force people to buy the products advertised; but of course they do no such thing. Whether a person
buys the product advertised is still his own decision; the ad
may influence him, but he may still decide against buying for
whatever reason he chooses—he is still not being forced. He
may indeed be weak-willed and rush out to buy the first product he hears about; but then it is time that he trained himself
to be a bit more strong-willed in the future: the fault lies with
him, not with the commercial.

Of course, if the commercial misrepresents a product, or
states that it has properties which in fact it does not have, then
the advertiser is guilty of *fraud*: the practice of deceit, trick-
ery, or breach of confidence, by which it is sought to gain
some unfair or dishonest advantage. Fraud can and should be
brought under the category of force, for the following reason:
a product that is sold via fraud is not a voluntary exchange.
Ordinarily when you buy an article from a merchant you agree
to exchange the money for the product sold—you would rath-

er have the product than the money and he would rather have
the money than the product. If you later decide that the product isn't worth it, you will not buy it again, but as long as the
merchant has not misrepresented it to you, you have no valid
complaint against him. However, if he misrepresented the
product, for example if he sold you an imitation rather than a
genuine diamond, or said that this was genuine whipped
cream when in fact it was only an indigestible grease called
"topping," then he has defrauded you—and fraud is a proper
cause for court action. The reason is that if you had known
what the product really was you would not have bought it voluntarily. He has, in that sense, not physically but via misrepresentation, used force in getting you to buy it, and you were an
unwilling victim of his machinations.

The concept of force can be extended to include moral or
spiritual matters as well as material. If someone spreads lies
about you, so that you lose your reputation and your job, you
can sue him for slander; and if the lies are in written form, you
can sue him for libel. Your reputation and your job, which
may mean more to you than money or possessions, have been
taken away from you by means of misrepresentation, just as
your money was taken away from you (in the former example) by misrepresentation of the product you bought. In
both cases you are an unwilling victim of someone else's actions; you were harmed against your will by the voluntary acts
of others. Even if you were harmed by his *non-voluntary* acts,
you may have cause to invoke the law against him: this includes all cases of negligence. If you negligently left unlighted
at night an exit from your house where there was a sharp drop-
off without steps, so that your visitor fell and broke his arm, he
has been an unwilling victim of your action even if you did not
intend that he should fall and break his arm.

The matter is admittedly different with infants and children, who cannot yet be said to possess responsibility for their own existence or the ability to make their own decisions with any insight into the consequences. The parents (or parent-surrogates) are the guardians of children until they reach the "age of discretion"—and what this age is, is admittedly somewhat vague, since a youngster can be mature in some ways and not in others, and some individuals mature intellectually and emotionally at an earlier age than others do. Parents may quite properly forbid their children from doing certain things (whether or not they harm others), or from witnessing certain things (books or movies), and may even use physical coercion on them—but not without limit. It is one thing to pick a child off the street who is playing too near the traffic, but it is quite another for sadistic parents to beat the child black and blue; and in this latter case, the parents can quite properly be taken to court on criminal charges.

Another example of deprivation of liberty is *censorship,* the suppression of all or parts of books, plays, news reports, motion pictures, TV and radio programs, etc., deemed objectionable on moral, political, military, or other grounds.

The government should not inhibit individual freedom by imposing censorship of any kind. Censorship consists in one group of people, political appointees, deciding that the rest of the people shall not be permitted to read certain books or see certain films, etc. A person should be free to decide *for himself* whether he wishes to read the book in question; but the error lies in giving the censor the jurisdiction to make that decision *for others.* When a book or a film is censored, the people are not permitted even to decide whether they would prefer to read it or not, because it is not permitted to enter the country (or to be printed within the country) in the first place. Liberty is lost because people are not permitted a choice. Perhaps the censor thinks it would be harmful for everyone, but the cit-

izen may not find it so at all. The political appointee is deciding not only what would (in his opinion) be good for himself,
but what would be good *for everyone else*. Even if he were
omniscient (which he is not), and even if it would in some way
harm everyone else, it should still be *their* decision whether
they wish to have it available to them—not his. His interference is merely meddlesome. He is depriving you against your
will of access to something you might have valued; and this is
still true even if you decide not to avail yourself of the material
offered—the decision now rests with *you,* not with him, as to
whether you should have it.

Censorship is particularly insidious when it suppresses ideas
—particularly those ideas which the government does not like
to have spread about because they are in disagreement with
the government's own position. It is precisely this form of censorship, however, that has been most typical of the history of
governments. Indeed, the best single test to be put to any government is: Does it suppress ideas contrary to the official ones?
If the answer is yes, then that government is an enemy of liberty no matter how much it may mouth words praising liberty in
its official propaganda.

"But can't other organizations than government censor material?" Not in the same meaning of the term. You may form
the John Jones Society and not admit into the society anyone
who disagrees even in the slightest degree with your views; and
this is perfectly permissible because no one is forced to belong
to that society. Most people will simply not join, or leave when
the society is seen in its true colors, and there is nothing you
can do about it. The Catholic Church can "censor" a film—
that is, the cardinal or archbishop can declare that any church
member within his diocese will be excommunicated or otherwise penalized if he goes to see it. But membership in the
Catholic Church is not compulsory, and the edict is not bind-

ing on those who are not members—indeed, in practice such edicts are constantly violated by members without the Church being any the wiser. The Church has no army or police by means of which it could use force against any of its members who see the film; if Church officials did start to beat up members who saw it, the members could appeal to the law and sue in the courts. The Church can use only moral suasion on its members, as any private citizen can do, but it cannot employ the strong arm of the law against dissenting members. It was not always so, of course—once the Church could torture men on the rack and burn them for heresy, but that was when the Church *was also* the state.[5]

The concept of liberty will be further amplified in Chapter 2, where it will be seen in the context of human rights. Meanwhile, we shall consider the nature of governments in relation to the question of human liberty.

Types of Government

Apart from having no government at all, there are many ideals of what the function of government should be, ranging from *libertarianism* (or liberalism in the nineteenth-century sense of that term), according to which the function of government should be limited to the protection of individuals against aggression by others or by government, to *totalitarianism* (or *statism*), in which the life of the individual is regulated and dominated by government. Between these two, all existing governments occupy various positions, depending on the degree to which the individual can conduct his life and work independently of government.

The nearest approach to a libertarian government was the government of the United States at the time of its inception.

The Founding Fathers were extremely sensitive to government tyranny of all kinds, and their experiences in Europe led them to make very sure that no such thing would recur in the United States. Even after the Constitution had been submitted to the thirteen colonies, there were still not sufficient guarantees against government power, and the final ratification took place only after the Bill of Rights (the first ten amendments to the Constitution) had been added. There were still defects in the Constitution, primarily the lack of prohibition against slavery (without which the southern states would never have ratified); it took a civil war to iron out that flaw in the Constitution. Also, some things which were virtually taken for granted by the Founding Fathers, such as economic freedom, were scarcely mentioned at all; and several passing references, such as to "the general welfare," were so distorted from the original intentions of the founders in later history (as we shall see in subsequent chapters) that they opened the way to a tremendous degree of government control, which made the United States into something considerably less than "the land of the free." Nevertheless, the Constitution of the United States is without doubt the greatest political document in the history of the world, and the first century of the history of the United States exemplifies the nearest approach to political libertarianism in operation—with the government serving only as the protector of the citizens.

Many governments stand at or near the very opposite extreme on this continuum of individual liberty vs. government control. Most governments in the course of history have not hesitated to exert increasing control over their populations, and the citizens, far from being protected by their government, have been in terror of their government and what it might do to them next. History is one long record of governments infringing on the liberty of individual citizens. The totalitarian government of Nazi Germany is of course a prime example: non-Aryans and political dissenters were not only persecuted but sent to the gas chambers by the millions; but every citizen was in constant danger, even members of the Nazi Party if they were suspected of disloyalty or dissent. Any citizen could be taken from his house by the storm troopers on trumped-up charges, and either jailed, sent to work camps and not be heard from for long periods, or killed.

The record of Hitler's Germany is now well known. That government perished with the downfall of the Nazi war machine in 1945, and has been replaced by a far more benevolent government, at least in West Germany. The government of Soviet Russia, by contrast, began much earlier, with the victory of the Bolsheviks in 1918 over the Kerensky government (the only democratic government that Russia ever had); in its total control by terror over the lives of its citizens, it is perhaps the most tyrannical in all history; and in spite of certain precarious leniencies that have taken place since the death of Stalin, it continues its virtually total control over the life of the Soviet citizen to this day.

Today's haters of the United States who speak favorably of Lenin (even though they may not go so far as to revere Stalin), should remember some of Lenin's main contributions to world history. Lenin seized power in November of 1917, overthrowing not the Czarist regime (which was also totalitarian in most respects) but a government of democratic socialists and liberals; on November 17 there was established a more rigid censorship than had ever existed in Russia; on December 20 was organized one of the most efficient terroristic secret police that ever existed anywhere; and on January 20, 1918, "government by the people" ended with the eviction of a Constituent Assembly in which the majority of deputies disagreed with Lenin. Terror began at once with the assassination on that same day of two former republican ministers (Shingarev and Kokoshkin), and continued in a bloodbath which makes the terror of the French Revolution look like a child's game. During that same year concentration camps for dissenters were set up. All these measures were "temporary," of course, to keep the new "people's republic" from collapsing. But after more than fifty years, all of them are still there: censorship, despotism, terrorism, total control over the lives and destinies of every individual in the land.

The regime of Stalin is better known to the general public, though the younger generation of today, not having lived while these events were happening, have little sense of their real horror. The slave-labor camps instituted in the Stalinist era; the systematic starvation, by government policy, of five million peasants for the "crime" of resisting the forced collectivization of agriculture; the extermination or exile of everyone who opposed the regime or was even vaguely suspected by some bureaucrat of opposing it; the terror of the secret police under Beria, with whom torture and judicial murder were daily occurrences—all these are facts of history, of which the present generation is largely ignorant, and which certain "liberals" in the Western world, who believed that the Soviet experiment was a great piece of "social engineering," condoned even at the time with far less excuse than ignorance.

Czarist Russia was also a dictatorship, often a very harsh one, yet it was positively benign in comparison with the Soviet dictatorship which has ruled Russia since 1918. The Soviet dictatorship attempts to control virtually all the aspects of human life, including some that no czar or sultan of past centuries would have dreamed of controlling. Everything that the Soviet tyranny wishes to discourage becomes "a crime against the state."[6]

Dissent against the government? In the United States we

take it for granted. Many people make their living by doing nothing else. But in Soviet Russia the government has a stranglehold on the life of every citizen, and the citizen is afraid to say anything for fear of invoking the wrath of the all-powerful government against him. The government appoints him to his job (and if he lives on a farm he is not permitted even to go to the city without a special pass), which he cannot change without the permission of the government; to go on strike is illegal, and punishable by fine and imprisonment; and even to complain about conditions of work is to run the risk of being charged with disloyalty. Novelists and social critics who suggest government reforms, even in the most constructive spirit, are often sent to Siberian slave-labor camps or to insane asylums, where they are declared "mentally ill" and incarcerated until their "illness" is cured, i.e., until they recant and say, in effect, that "Big Brother is good."

Privacy? It almost doesn't exist in Soviet Russia. The citizen's mail is read, and if he has a phone it is tapped; places of meeting are bugged and if two people converse on the street, particularly with foreigners, they may be followed by the secret police and arrested. The result is that the citizen hardly dares to say anything to anyone, never knowing who might be an informer for the police. Even the relations between parishioner and pastor, husband and wife, defendant and his lawyer, are not private. In America the lawyer and psychiatrist are agents of their client; in Soviet Russia they are agents of the government. The state constantly intrudes itself into all of these areas. The citizen of course knows this, and must live in terror if he dares speak or hint of ill about the regime to anyone.

Freedom of travel? Only a few receive passports to travel abroad, and then only if one leaves one's family behind as hostages. But there is also a domestic passport system, and no one may travel without a passport within the country. Those who live in the cities and near a few of the largest cities (Moscow, Leningrad, Kiev) are permitted limited travel at the discretion of the government. Those who live in the rest of the country are not granted a passport at all. (Farmers may come to the city to bring produce to the collective farm market, and shop for items they need, but may not remain in an urban area more than five days.) A member of a collective farm is not permitted even to move from one farm to another without government permission. The peasants—half the population—are tied to the land just as surely as when they were serfs more than a century ago.

The American dissidents who deplore the evils of our system, and wish they could be transported to eastern Europe for better conditions, should note that everyone is required to work, even if he prefers to beg or panhandle or live off the land. No one is permitted housing without being employed; and since the government dispenses all housing, this means that such persons would be homeless. Those who have no visible means of support are considered "antisocial" and are often banished to remote areas, where they are subjected to backbreaking toil.

Wages are determined by the government, and no recourse in the form of strikes or bargaining is permitted. Nor are savings of one's earnings permitted and no one may have a checking account. Investment in business is of course impossible, since all business is owned and operated by the government. The money earned is meant to be spent, so that the individual may remain perpetually dependent on government, and can be forced to starve if he does not conform. Besides, earnings are far too low as a rule to permit savings.

There are a few private markets in which food grown on the small private plots still permitted to citizens (2 percent of the land area) may be traded. But apart from this, government decides what goods are to be produced and how much. Prices are set by the government, with the result that huge shortages develop of things not produced in sufficient quantity, or excesses of things no one is willing to buy at the state-set prices.

Living conditions? The average Russian family lives in a single room, sharing bath and kitchen facilities with one or more other families. Sometimes two unrelated families occupy the same room, which is divided by a curtain. The citizen cannot complain, for the government assigns all living quarters, and no one can choose who will live next to him, nor is he permitted to move.

Ten years ago 90 percent of the urban population of Russia had electricity in their homes, 34 percent had running water, 31 percent plumbing, 22 percent central heating, 9 percent a bath, and 2 percent hot water. Even in the cities, most streets are unpaved. Only a small percentage of the streets have sewage lines, and the sewage is untreated before entering the polluted rivers. In the villages, water is drawn from a well, the toilet is an outhouse, and the heat comes from a stove or hearth. In short, conditions among the peasantry are much the same as they were a hundred years ago.

Freedom of the press? Every printing establishment is owned by the government, and everyone working there must get his job through the government. No one is permitted to operate any equipment designed for reproduction of pages— not even a duplicating machine. All manuscripts submitted to a printer must be censored by government agents, who decide whether or not they should be published. There is no appeal from this decision—there are no other publishers to whom one can turn. And even if a work was passed by the censor and published, it may later be removed from circulation by government order, and all copies burned. Not only books, but printed materials of all kinds, can be sold, and given away only through state channels.

The court system is hardly calculated to determine guilt or innocence with an impartial eye. There is no presumption that a defendant is innocent until proven guilty. There is a pretrial hearing, during which defendants are not entitled to counsel. For ten days after their arrest, defendants need not be informed of the charges against them, and they may be detained for nine months without the right to contact anyone. A lawyer, whether prosecution or defense, must remain in the good graces of the Party, and his performance is surely influenced by this consideration. There are no trials by jury: a case is heard by a judge and two laymen, who are chosen from a panel that has been approved by the Party (the implications for impartiality here are obvious). Laws do not emanate from a legislature but are decrees later ratified by the legislature. An enormous number of administrative regulations (unknown to most citizens) carry the full force of law. In both cases, however, the law is not written down, so as to be available to the ordinary citizen. In most cases he has no sure way of knowing what the law is on any given issue. Moreover, the secret police are established as an independent judicial body empowered to try and sentence people suspected of crimes against the state. The Soviet secret police makes extensive use of every known form of physical and mental torture. As a result of such methods, many innocent men have confessed crimes in public and been sentenced or executed; millions of others were tried by special boards in secret, then executed in secret or sent to Siberian slave-labor camps and never heard of again.

The Soviet government can and does assign people to various national projects, forcing them to relocate under whatever conditions it dictates—with vast indifference to how many people are killed along the way. In 1940 the Soviet government took over the three Baltic nations of Latvia, Lithuania, and Estonia; these countries no longer exist as separate nations; they are a part of the Soviet empire. What happened to the inhabitants? Some were killed outright, and millions of others were dispersed to the far corners of the Soviet slave empire—forced to emigrate to uninhabited regions of Siberia where it was virtually impossible to live and absolutely impossible to make a living. In the late 1930s when the peasants resisted the forced collectivization of the farms, Stalin simply had them systematically starved; at least six million, and in all probability more, were starved to death as a deliberate policy of their own government.

When gold was found in large quantities in the barren wastes of eastern Siberia, and there was no capital for the extraction of this gold (which was nevertheless badly needed by the Soviet government), the government sent thousands of its own citizens—political prisoners, and peasants who had opposed the government in some way, such as by resisting collectivization—to this inhospitable region, without provisions for clothing or shelter, without proper equipment for mining and road-building, under the supervision of sadistic guards with trained dogs ready to tear them to bits if they resisted. Shipload after shipload of these citizens, now slave laborers, were sent to these virtually uninhabited Arctic regions to build roads and dredge harbors without equipment and in temperatures up to −90° F. Half of them died the first winter, but the supply of manpower was virtually endless, so more were sent the next year and the next, until after many years and the loss of thousands of lives through exposure, frost, starvation, disease, or torture, the job was finally completed, at the cost of one thousand human lives for every metric ton of gold. Anyone who thinks that the Soviet system is one whit better than

Nazi Germany, or is in any way a humane system of government with respect for human liberty, should read Professor
David Dallin's *Forced Labor in Soviet Russia*.[7]

When the government has unlimited powers, it can do as it
likes with its people. Nazi Germany and the Soviet Union
committed no more horrible atrocities on other nations in
World War II than they had already inflicted on their own
populations—killing, torturing, reducing them to the level of
slaves and beasts of burden. Projects such as the Kolyma gold
fields in Siberia could (if the rewards were large enough)
sooner or later have been conducted through private enterprise—or else they would have been worth no one's time and
effort, even for enormous wages, and then the gold fields
would not have been developed. But the Soviet government
forbade any dabbling in private enterprise. There was not
enough capital available to the government to absorb the cost
of laborers and machines. The cheapest commodity in Soviet
Russia, available in plentiful supply, was human beings.
These were used by the millions—between ten and twenty millions each year; they built the roads and harbors and mines,
and died after the government had used them for its purposes.
When the government has unlimited powers, what else can one
expect?

Most of the governments in the world today are, as they
have been throughout history, of a totalitarian (statist) variety
to varying degrees. These governments have gone by a variety
of names: fascist, communist, socialist. They are totalitarian to
the extent that the state governs the individual's life; the more
sectors of life in the hands of the government (and correspondingly, the less left to individual liberty), the more totalitarian or statist that government is. The government of Soviet
Russia and the misnamed "People's Republic" of China are

surely the most rigidly totalitarian of all; ruled by totalitarian governments also, to varying degrees, are the "satellite nations" which they have conquered: Bulgaria, Albania, Rumania, and other Balkan nations which are as much "terror states" as the large ones, because the totalitarian control is imposed on them by their Soviet masters. Yugoslavia, which broke off from the Soviet orbit and got away with it, is somewhat freer than the other "captive nations." Franco's Spain and Salazar's Portugal were once nearly as totalitarian in concept as the Soviet Union, though they have moderated considerably and the feeling of constant terror in the face of the government is much less apparent than it once was, except perhaps for small groups of political dissidents. Most of the "newly emerging" African nations seem more inclined to follow the totalitarian lead of Soviet Russia and China than the liberalism of the Western democracies, but this may change in time. The Union of South Africa is a bastion of liberty compared with other countries, though individual liberty is far more restricted and economic opportunity far less open to certain groups within the country, such as people with black or brown skin.

Less totalitarian are the "democratic socialist" countries such as Great Britain, Finland, and Sweden; these retain certain sectors of individual liberty, such as freedom of speech and of the press (to varying degrees), but the government holds a tight control over the economy, and in the economic sphere the individual enjoys much less liberty than in nonsocialist countries: socialism is, after all, the imposition of a central economic system upon the entire population, usually with a central planning board which imposes its will by force whether a given citizen wants it that way or not. We shall discuss the socialist economic system in greater detail in later chapters.

Fascism and communism (more accurately, Soviet socialism) are often presented to the public as if they were opposites; but of course they are not—they are two very similar systems of government control over the lives and property of individuals. They are natural allies, since both adhere to the totalitarian view of government, and both do not hesitate to use the enormous coercive powers of government to encroach upon any aspect of the lives of individuals. They differ only in details. Spain, Portugal, Bulgaria, and Soviet Russia are all totalitarian nations, differing in the degree of totality with which the state governs the lives and destinies of the individuals within them. World War Two was essentially a war of Nazi totalitarianism against Soviet totalitarianism, with the freer nations (such as the United States and Great Britain) thrown in to achieve the victory of Soviet totalitarianism.

It is popular for student groups today to label every government or individual who opposes them as "fascist." A bit of terminological housecleaning is in order here. The term "fascist" was first applied to the Mussolini government of Italy, which did indeed exert considerable control over the life and liberty of every Italian citizen. The same term was later extended to the government of Mussolini's ally, Nazi Germany, in which the economic and other controls over individual liberty were even greater. Individuals still held private property under the Nazi regime (unlike the Soviet), but the government dictated what the factories were to produce, and how much, and what profit if any they could keep. If the term is thus circumscribed, "fascist" is too favorable to be extended to include the Soviet Union and Communist China, for in these countries there is not even such nominal ownership. The interference of these governments in virtually every aspect of the lives of their citizens is far greater even than that of Nazi Germany or fascist Italy.

If one wants to extend the term "fascism" to *all* forcible interference with the liberty of individuals (by other individuals or by government), then in all consistency one should say that

A fascist is anybody who, seeing someone else succeed where he failed, says, "Send the dirty Jew to a concentration camp!"

A fascist is a sailor who, seeing long hair of which he doesn't approve, says, "What that guy needs is thirteen weeks in bootcamp."

A fascist is a citizen who, seeing someone else read a book of which he doesn't approve, says, "Ban it! Send the publisher to jail!"

A fascist is anyone who, seeing a man working hard and earning money, says, "He's getting more than we are—let's pass a law to take it away from him!"

A fascist is a student who, seeing the representatives of a chemical industry recruiting on campus, cries, "Let's chase the bastard off! We have the right to free speech but he doesn't!"

The common denominator for all these cases is not difficult to discern: *they all advocate interference by force* (usually interference by the government) with the lives of individuals. They don't want force used against themselves—they will cry "Fascist!" loudly enough if this is attempted; but they don't at all mind using force (or getting the representatives of the government to use force) against those whom they dislike or disapprove. Many of the students who cry "Fascist!" whenever their wishes are crossed are themselves fascists who would force their will upon others. And many of the people who would never take a gun and rob another individual, such as a neighbor, have no objection to using the coercive force of government to take away a neighbor's liberty. One might say that this last move is a far cry from the fascists who immolated non-Aryans in concentration camps; but the principle of the two is the same: the advocacy of force, used by themselves or by government, to inhibit in others the same freedom which they demand for themselves.

We have discussed the two opposite concepts of what government should be—the totalitarian ideal of the individual as the pawn of government, and the libertarian ideal of government as the hired servant of the citizen. But it is important to keep this distinction clearly separated from another one, having to do with the *methods* by which these ideals can be implemented. Again we have two polar opposites: the *autocratic* method, in which one person or group of persons governs the entire populace without being subject to elections or other regularized methods of retaining or releasing power; and the *democratic* method, in which the citizens themselves participate in the political decision-making processes and can unseat or retain their political leaders through the election process.[8]

Now, there is little doubt that a government with totalitarian aims is likely to be a dictatorship. When one man (such as Hitler or Franco) or a small group (such as Kosygin and Brezhnev) rule an entire nation, and their word is law, they are likely to set no limits to what the powers of government should be. Their authoritarian rule, however, is simply the method or procedure by which their totalitarian aims are achieved—and usually totalitarian aims *are* most efficiently achieved (and with the least interference from the victims) by autocratic government.

But it is also possible for totalitarian aims to be achieved by the rule of many, even by a democracy. People may be stupid, uneducated, unenlightened, or uninformed about the issues involved or about the men for whom they are to vote; or they may be simply inert and indifferent. It is possible for a people, wittingly or unwittingly, to vote themselves into slavery. Usually they do so unwittingly, and don't realize until afterward the true nature of the men they have elected: when a coup or a military takeover occurs, it is too late for them to correct the situation. The evidence suggests that Hitler had the approval of the majority of the German people. While it is true they had no chance to unseat him by vote after he assumed power, it is probable that he was, at least for a long time, approved by an even larger majority than before. If the majority of the people themselves "put their trust in the Fatherland" and tend to leave political decisions to "those who know more about such things," they may easily bring into being a government whose aims are as totalitarian as any dictatorship. In the long run, if democracy persists, the authoritarian rule will usually be dissolved, for the people will see in their own lives the consequences of their former vote. But by that time, of course, the nation will probably no longer be a democracy, and the reins of government will no longer be in their hands.

Just as the totalitarian ideal of government will typically be implemented by an authoritarian procedure, so a libertarian ideal of government will typically be implemented by a democratic procedure. People do not usually—though as we have seen they do sometimes—vote themselves into servitude. But democracy by itself constitutes no guarantee that a libertarian aim of government will exist or, if it exists, will continue. It is also possible that a dictator will be so enlightened and so concerned for the liberty of his people that he will actually promote a libertarian philosophy of government by non-democratic means: while not permitting free elections, he would leave the people alone, permit them maximum freedom, not interfere with their activities unless they tried to encroach upon the freedom of others. But if he is a libertarian, what is he doing as a dictator?

In any case, the rule of a "benevolent despot" is most unstable: even if it endured for a time, it would end with the death of the "benevolent despot," whose descendants (or usurpers) would probably be less benevolent and use the governmental machinery of coercion to gang up on the disarmed subjects.

The tendency is always for dictatorships to be totalitarian in their aims—that is why people aspire to become dictators, and why they remain in office in spite of public hostility and assassination attempts. The power impulse which leads a man to become a dictator and take all the risks necessary to get to that position and retain it in the face of competition from other would-be dictators, is not usually worth the trouble if anything less than total control accrues to him at the end of it. It does not matter whether the dictatorship is of the "left" or the "right"; the distinction between political "left" and "right" is a specious one, since both are subtypes or varieties of totalitarianism.

A further distinction must now be made. Democracies may be "pure"—that is, every citizen may vote on every piece of legislation, as in a New England town meeting or in the ancient Athenian assembly (though female citizens and slaves were excluded). Democracies may also be—and in modern times always are—*representative*: the citizens themselves do not make the laws, but they elect the people (members of Congress or Parliament) who do. What becomes law is decided not by the majority of the citizens, but the majority of the members of these legislative bodies. In a representative democracy, a law may be passed which is not approved by the majority of the citizens—it need only be approved by a majority of their elected representatives at the time of its passage; but of course if many such laws are passed, the electorate will see to it that the elected representatives who violated their wishes so many times will be unseated at the next election.

Whether the democracy is pure or representative, democracy is no guarantee of the liberty of the citizens. Democracy is essentially government by the majority, and a majority may be stupid, unenlightened, foolish, misled, and corrupt. If one person can make a mistake, fifty million can make the same mistake. If one person can be ignorant of the issues, so can fifty million of them. The laws passed in a democracy may even be worse on the whole than the decrees of an enlightened despot.

Most specifically, in a democracy a majority may gang up on a minority: a majority may vote to inhibit the freedom of a minority or even a group of minorities. A majority may vote to prohibit everyone (not just themselves) from consuming alcoholic beverages. A majority may vote to ban Negroes from public places. A majority may vote to persecute a minority for its religion or its moral code or any other thing. A majority may even vote to send a minority to death camps and gas chambers. The tyranny of a majority can be just as cruel as the tyranny of a single dictator—depending on the degree of enlightenment or stupidity of the voting majority.

Louis XIV was a monarch, and the government of France was certainly a dictatorship, with totalitarian aims ("The state? I am the state"). After the Revolution, the monarchy was replaced by "democracy"—the rule of the majority, a majority that was inflamed with passion and hatred, a majority that approved of beheading the members of the old order and taking away the property of those they allowed to live. The tyranny of the post-Revolution era was far bloodier than that of the one that preceded it. The supremacy of the monarch was replaced by the supremacy of the mob.

Unlimited democracy affords no protection of the minority against the reigning majority. As the whims of the majority change, so may the fortunes and the lives of these minorities suffer. (Consider the fate of the Jews throughout history.)

Indeed, what would give the majority (any more than a

king) the right to rule over a minority and interfere with their free decisions? On this point the English philosopher Herbert Spencer spoke eloquently almost a century ago:

. . . The hypothesis of a social contract, either under the shape assumed by Hobbes or under the shape assumed by Rousseau, is baseless. Nay more, it must be admitted that even had such a contract once been formed, it could not be binding on the posterity of those who formed it. . . .

This will at once draw forth the rejoinder: "Of course, in the absence of any agreement, with its implied limitations, the rule of the majority is unlimited; because it is more just that the majority should have its way than that the minority should have its way." A very reasonable rejoinder this seems until there comes the re-rejoinder. We may oppose to it the equally tenable proposition that, in the absence of an agreement, the supremacy of a majority over a minority does not exist at all. It is cooperation of some kind, from which there arises these powers and obligations of majority and minority; and in the absence of any agreement to cooperate, such powers and obligations are also absent. . . . Had social cooperation to be commenced by ourselves, and had its purposes to be specified before consent to cooperate could be obtained, there would be large parts of human conduct in respect of which cooperation would be declined; and in respect of which, consequently, no authority by the majority over the minority could be rightly exercised.[9]

. . . Turn now to the converse question— For what ends would all men agree to cooperate? None will deny that for resisting invasion the agreement would be practically unanimous. Excepting only the Quakers, who, having done highly useful work in their time, are now dying out, all would unite for defensive war (not, however, for offensive war); and they would, by so doing, tacitly bind themselves to conform to the will of the majority in respect of measures directed to that end. There would be practical unanimity, also, in the agreement to cooperate for defense against internal enemies as against external enemies. Omitting criminals, all must wish to have person and property adequately protected. Each citizen desires to preserve his life, to preserve things which conduce to maintenance and enjoyment of his life, and to preserve intact his liberties both of using these things and getting further such. It is obvious to him that he cannot do all this if he acts alone. Against foreign invaders he is powerless unless he combines with his fellows; and the business of protecting himself against domestic invaders, if he did not similarly combine, would be alike onerous, dangerous, and inefficient. In one other cooperation all are interested—use of the territory they inhabit.[10]

In any organization, the right of the majority is a delegated one, for a specific and limited purpose.

. . . The right of a majority is a purely conditional right, valid only within specific limits. Let us take a few. Suppose that at the general meeting of some philanthropic association, it was resolved that in addition to relieving distress the association should employ home-missionaries to preach down popery. Might the subscriptions of Catholics, who had joined the body with charitable views, be rightfully used for this end? Suppose that of the members of a book-club, the greater number, thinking that under existing circumstances rifle-practice was more important than reading, should decide to change the purpose of their union, and to apply the funds in hand for the purchase of powder, ball, and targets. Would the rest be bound by this decision? Suppose that under the excitement of news from Australia, the majority of a Freehold Land Society should determine, not simply to start in a body for the gold-diggings, but to use their accumulated capital to provide outfits. Would this appropriation of property be just to the minority? and must these join the expedition? Scarcely anyone would venture an affirmative answer even to the first of these questions; much less to the others. And why? Because everyone must perceive that by uniting himself with others, no man can equitably be betrayed into acts utterly foreign to the purpose for which he joined them. Each of these supposed minorities would properly reply to those seeking to coerce them: "We combined with you for a defined object; we gave money and time for the furtherance of that object; on all questions thence arising we tacitly agreed to conform to the will of the greater number; but we did not agree to conform on any other questions. If you induce us to join you by professing a certain end, and then undertake some other end of which we were not apprised, you obtain our support under false pretenses; you exceed the expressed or understood compact to which we committed ourselves; and we are no longer

bound by your decisions." Clearly this is the only rational interpretation of the matter. The general principle underlying the right government of every incorporated body, is, that its members contract with
one another severally to submit to the will of the majority in all matters concerning the fulfilment of the objects for which they are incorporated; but in no others. To this extent only can the contract hold.
For as it is implied in the very nature of a contract, that those entering
into it must know what they contract to do; and as those who unite
with others for a specified object, cannot contemplate all the unspecified objects which it is hypothetically possible for the union to undertake; it follows that the contract entered into cannot extend to such
unspecified objects. And if there exists no expressed or understood
contract between the union and its members respecting unspecified objects, then for the majority to coerce the minority into undertaking
them, is nothing less than gross tyranny.[11]   ·

How, then, is the individual to be protected? Only by the
recognition of individual *rights*; only if the minority, even that
smallest minority which is the single individual holding out
against the mob, is protected by the government in his freedom to conduct his life in accordance with his choices. But the
government of a democracy may not do this, and if passions
are running high it certainly will not do this. If a government
protects every individual, and has such protection written into
its constitution *and* abides by it, it is the government of a
republic.

The government of the United States is the government of a
republic, not an unlimited democracy. Its procedure—in
electing people to office and so on—is democratic, but it is not
an unlimited democracy, for in the Constitution of the United
States there are *limitations placed upon what the majority may
do*. The government shall not abridge freedom of speech or of
the press, says the First Amendment to the Constitution—and
it does not add, "unless the majority vote that it shall." There
are no ifs, ands, or buts—the government shall not abridge

this freedom, period. Also, a defendant has a right to *habeas corpus* (to be tried by a body of his peers)—not "unless the majority vote to suspend this right," but he is guaranteed this protection, period. And so on. What distinguishes the American republic from most other nations of the world, including democracies, is the constitutional guarantee of individual rights against the violation of them by other individuals, by the majority, and by the government itself.

It must be added at once that the United States is not fully a republic in this sense, for it does not always protect the liberty of its residents: not only does it not do so in practice, but it does not do so in law. Many "Jim Crow" laws violated the rights of Negroes (and prior to the Civil War, violated them even more through the institution of slavery). The anti-trust laws, as we shall see in Chapter 4, violate the liberty of the manufacturer to conduct his business as he sees fit. The income tax law (which was once held unconstitutional by the Supreme Court before it was passed by the same body by a 5–4 vote) violates the liberty of each wage-earner to dispose of the fruits of his labor in accordance with his own judgment.

The Constitution of the United States, then, partly in its original conception and partly in its subsequent interpretation, is not purely a republican constitution. The United States has tended through the years to become more like an unlimited democracy, in which some citizens can use the force of the law to prey upon other citizens. The ways in which this has come to operate will be discussed in Chapters 4–8.

Why all this emphasis upon liberty? Why should every citizen possess it? The libertarian's answer is: Because every individual has a *right* to liberty. What man's rights consist of, and what implications this has for government, will be the subject of Chapter 2.

2
Rights and Government

The function of government, says the libertarian, is the protection of human rights. What then is a right? And to what things do human beings have rights?

Let us make a simple but important distinction at the outset. The word "right" is used in English as various parts of speech, with very different meanings. "Would it be right for me to break a promise to my neighbor in an emergency?" we ask, and here of course we use the word "right" as an adjective, to question a particular choice of action. But the question "What have I *a right* to?" is very different; if you have a right to something, you have a claim upon others for it—a right to X implies a duty on the part of others. The difference, of course, is considerable: it may be right (adjective) for me to give to a person who needs help, but that is a very different thing from saying that he has a right (noun) to it: i.e., that he has a moral claim upon my beneficence. Whether it is right to give to him, or wrong not to, is a moral question which I shall not discuss in this book; but whether he has a right to it, one that should be enforced by law and the coercive power of government, is a question of supreme importance for political philosophy.

In one perfectly ordinary sense, a right of somebody to something is brought about by contract. A man lends a hundred dollars to his neighbor, and the neighbor promises to repay it at a specified time; the lender has a right to the money at the agreed-upon time. A man voluntarily undertakes to support a wife and family, and his family has a right to his support. Contractual obligations generate these rights: because a person has voluntarily agreed to do a certain thing, the other person has a right to the performance of it. The promise of the return of a loan would be valueless if the lender had no right to the return of the borrowed money.

But we also speak of rights in a wider sense, not limited to that of contractual obligations voluntarily entered upon. We speak of "*natural* rights" or "*human* rights"—rights that human beings have "because of their very nature as human beings": for example, the right to life, the right to liberty and the pursuit of happiness. What specifically do these rights involve? What are their limitations, if any? What, if anything, justifies us in saying they are human rights?

When a man claims that he has a certain right, he is making a large claim: for there is a logical relation between the rights of A and the duties of others (B, C, D, etc.); and similarly, if B has a right, then A, C, D, etc. have a duty. If A has a right to something, then others have a duty not to behave in such a way as to violate that right. Nor can B have a right to violate A's right: A cannot have a right to your life or liberty if B has the right to take them away whenever he pleases.

The libertarian account of rights can be stated simply: "Every man has the right to be free." What this means was stated by Herbert Spencer: "Every man may claim the fullest liberty to exercise his faculties compatible with the possession of like liberty by every other man."[1] And again, "Every man has freedom to do all that he wills, provided he infringes not on the equal freedom of any other man."[2]

It has also been stated in our time by Professor H. L. A. Hart: "Any adult human being capable of choice (1) has the right to forbearance on the part of all others from the use of coercion or restraint against him, save to hinder coercion or restraint, and (2) is at liberty to do (i.e. is under no obligation to abstain from) any action which is not one coercing or restraining or designed to injure other persons." (He adds: "*Coercion* includes, besides preventing a person from doing what he chooses, making his choice less eligible by threats. *Restraint* includes any action designed to make the exercise of choice impossible and so includes killing or enslaving a person. But neither coercion nor restraint includes *competition*. . . . In terms of the distinction between having a right to and being at liberty to . . . all men may have, consistently with the obligation to forbear from coercion, the *liberty* to satisfy if they can such at least of their desires as are not designed to coerce or injure others, even though in fact, owing to scarcity, one man's satisfaction causes another's frustration.")[3] And "to have a right entails having a moral justification for limiting the freedom of another person and for determining how he should act."

The above account does not yet tell us precisely what are the limits beyond which a right has been violated. Does a person not have the right to cause pain to another? A man marries the girl he loves, but his parents disapprove and are caused intense pain over a prolonged period. Has he violated their rights? Surely not, one is inclined to say; the marriage may be ill-advised, but if the parties to it voluntarily consent, they have not violated the rights of anyone else. Does a person have a right to harm another? The word "harm" is extremely vague. I may harm you emotionally by something I say to you; but don't I have a right to say it? (Not that I am necessarily right—correct—in saying it.) The same vagueness pervades the word "injury." It all depends on what activities are grouped together under that term.

For this reason it has been suggested that, in defining infringement of rights, " . . . the vague, question-begging term 'injury' must not be used. Instead, infringement can be defined as 'direct physical interference with another man's person or property, or the threat of such physical interference.' . . . The important point to remember is never to use such vague expressions as 'injury,' 'harm,' or 'control,' but specific terms, such as 'physical interference' or 'threats of physical violence.'[4]

Thus I can violate your rights by using *physical force* against you, or by using the *threat* of such physical force (e.g. threatening to beat you up—assuming that I am in a position to back up this threat, and you know it).

I can also violate your rights by physical interference with your *property*, such as stealing your car or taking anything that belongs to you without your permission. Why it is so important to include property will be apparent as the chapter proceeds. But anyone who initiates force against a man's property is (though somewhat less directly than by attacking his person) initiating force against that man himself. Your house, your books, the car you have worked to own, are the products of your effort and of your choice to live in a certain way (without coercing others). Thus, if I steal a book from you I am violating your rights, but not if I take the book with your permission. If I regularly swim in your swimming pool and you don't mind, I am not violating your rights, but I am if you do not wish me to swim there and I do anyway. How you should run your life or dispose of your property (as conditions of living by your own judgment) is a matter for you to decide; it is not for me to preempt that decision by taking it from you.

Why is the ability to act on one's own judgment a matter of such importance? Because man is a volitional being who, to survive and prosper, must live and plan in accordance with his own decisions—or those of others only if they are voluntarily accepted by him, in which case they become his. Let us note some facts about man's nature and the world in which he lives, which are relevant to the concept of man's rights:

What are the conditions of man's existence? Under what conditions can he live and prosper? Let us note some facts:

(1) Each form of organic life populating this planet has its own distinctive kind of existence and survives in its own distinctive way. Plants, incapable of locomotion, do not survive by the same means as animals do; and among the animals, fish do not survive as worms do, or either of them as lions do. In every one of these cases, however, the means of survival of the organism depends on features which are "built in," in which the creature has no choice, but acts for its survival by means implanted in it by nature.

(2) Man too has a distinctive means of survival, and that is the use of his mind. He is not as fully equipped with instincts as are the other animals, which "program" his response to most life-situations; if left to these alone, he would long since have vanished from the scene. But alone among the animals, what happens in man's life is the result of *choices,* choices which he consciously makes. Man alone can promote his life through thought, and man alone can act so as to destroy himself. But whichever he does, he does it by virtue of his distinctive nature as a rational animal, that is, an animal capable of reason. Virtually everything that distinguishes man's life from that of the animals is a result of his ability to think: he has

learned to grow crops and harvest them, to build fires and harness rivers, to find cures for diseases, and to read books and write them—the most important of all, since books allow the knowledge laboriously gained by one man to be transmitted from one generation to another, with each generation being able to stand on the shoulders of the one before. In this way man has been able to master virtually the entire animal creation, and to acquire knowledge extending back aeons in time and millions of light-years in space.

(3) One of the very first lessons that reality teaches man is that to live he must produce and that to produce he must work. He can't sit by and do nothing and yet live.

(4) The effects of his acts are largely *on himself*. If a person drinks poison, it is his digestive tract, not his neighbor's that absorbs the effect. If he is to support himself, it is he who must work—except in unusual cases, another's work will not help him. He is himself the principal beneficiary or the maleficiary of his own actions.

(5) To live, he must plan long-range. He cannot rely on instincts to store nuts for the winter, and if he fails to make the conscious choice of doing so he will place his life in jeopardy. He who is caught without preparation by each successive winter will probably not survive many winters.

(6) In working and planning long-range, he cannot place upon his own shoulders the survival of a large group of others, else he will himself be borne down in the process. He may keep himself and his family going, but if he undertakes much more he will not be able to succeed. He may want to but he cannot. Reality makes it impossible.

(7) One of the things that makes human survival possible —not merely his biological survival, but his survival as a civilized being—is the possibility of *transmission* of knowledge and techniques (art, applied science, medicine) from one gen-

eration to the next. If each generation had to start from zero, then the vicissitudes of a single generation could wipe man out. But man's knowledge is a cumulative thing: in one generation he discovers an herb that will cure a certain disease; in ˙ another generation he discovers still more, and applies the knowledge to wider areas; in another generation he delves into chemistry and discovers the physical explanation underlying the cure—such as the germ theory of transmission of disease; and this permits him in a still later generation to devise complex medication, anesthetics, surgery, and the taking of precautions against the communication of disease. The non-human animals, relying chiefly on instincts, do not have this power, and their lives, except insofar as affected by human beings, are pretty much the same from one generation to another. Man's survival *qua* man—that is, as a being of intelligence, volition, and feeling—depends upon this accumulation of knowledge from generation to generation.

That which is required for man's survival *qua* man does not mean a *momentary* or merely a *physical* survival. It does not mean the momentary physical survival of a mindless brute, waiting for another brute to crush his skull. It does not mean the momentary physical survival of a crawling aggregate of muscles who is willing to accept any terms, obey any thug and surrender any values, for the sake of what is known as "survival at any price," which may or may not last a week or a year. "Man's survival *qua* man" means the terms, methods, conditions and goals required for the survival of a rational being through the whole of his lifespan—in all those aspects of existence which are open to his choice.[5]

The right to property is not the right to grab what I can from whoever has worked to secure it—that would violate *his* right to it; it is the right only to an activity; to work for it, to direct my actions in such a way that I may secure the property (clothes, a house, books) through my labor. The right to freedom is the right to conduct my life in whatever way I please as long as I do not thereby violate *your* right to live your life as *you* please.

I have the right to life, being the owner of my life. I may willingly give up my life for another if I so choose, but no one has the right to *take* my life from me. (If he did, what would have happened to my right to life?) I may speak freely: liberty is of such inestimable importance to man's life that no one is entitled to deprive me of it unless I have first attempted to deprive someone else of it. I may say what I please to others, but they do not have to listen or even be present. The watch I crave is not mine until I can produce the money to buy it (or whatever the seller wants in return for it)—I have no right to the product (the watch) *per se*, I have only the right to work for it and then obtain it if I can through a voluntary arrangement with the person who is willing to part with it. (If I had a right to take it from him by force, what would happen to *his* right to the products of his labor?)

Indeed, it would seem that I can violate the rights of others only by the use of force—to take his life, to deprive him of some aspect of his liberty of speech or action. If he voluntarily stops speaking or voluntarily parts with his watch, there is no violation of rights; the violation occurs when force is used to keep him from doing what he would have done through his own free decisions. (Of course, if he freely decides to kill me or rob me, he is violating my rights to life and/or property, and then my action against him is only a *retaliation* against the use of force initiated by him.)

Since a man must determine the course of his life by means of his own free decisions, the use of force against him represents the ultimate negation of his status as a human being:

To interpose the threat of physical destruction between a man and his perception of reality, is to negate and paralyze his means of survival; to force him to act against his own judgment, is like forcing him to act against his own sight. Whoever, to whatever purpose or extent, initiates the use of force, is a killer acting on the premise of death in a manner wider than murder: the premise of destroying man's capacity to live. . . .

To force a man to drop his own mind and to accept your will as a substitute, with a gun in place of a syllogism, with terror in place of proof, and death as the final argument—is to attempt to exist in defiance of reality. Reality demands of man that he act for his own rational interest; your gun demands of him that he act against it. Reality threatens man with death if he does not act on his rational judgment; you threaten him with death if he does.[6]

But other than the use of force a man has complete liberty of action in the entire realm of voluntary action which is coercive against no one.

. . . All that which an individual possesses by right (including his life and property) are morally his to use, dispose of and even destroy, as he sees fit. If I own my life, then it follows that I am free to associate with whom I please and *not to* associate with whom I please. If I own my knowledge and services it follows that I may *ask* any compensation I wish for providing them for another, or I may abstain from providing them at all, if I so choose. If I own my house, it follows that I may decorate it as I please and live in it with whom I please. If I control my own business, it follows that I may charge what I please for my products or services, hire whom I please and *not hire* whom I please. All that which I own in fact, I may dispose of as I choose to in reality. For anyone to attempt to limit my freedom to do so is to violate my rights.

Where do my rights end? Where yours begin. I may do *anything* I wish with my own life, liberty and property without your consent; but I may do *nothing* with your life, liberty and property without your consent. If we recognize the principle of man's rights, it follows that the individual is sovereign of the domain of *his own* life and property, and is sovereign of no other domain. To attempt to interfere forcibly with another's use, disposal or destruction of his own property is to initiate force against him and to violate his rights.[7]

I have no right to decide how *you* should spend your time or your money. I can make that decision for myself, but not for you, my neighbor. I may deplore your choice of life-style, and I may talk with you about it provided you are willing to listen to me. But I have no right to use force to change it. Nor have I the right to decide how you should spend the money you have earned. I may appeal to you to give it to the Red Cross, and you may prefer to go to prizefights. But that is your decision, and however much I may chafe about it I do not have the right to interfere forcibly with it, for example by robbing you in order to use the money in accordance with *my* choices. (If I have the right to rob you, have you also the right to rob me?)

When I claim a right, I carve out a niche, as it were, in my life, saying in effect, "This activity I must be able to perform without interference from others. For you and everyone else, this is off limits." And so I put up a "no trespassing" sign, which marks off the area of my right. Each individual's right is his "no trespassing" sign in relation to me and others. I may not encroach upon his domain any more than he upon mine, without my consent. Every right entails a duty, true—but the duty is only that of *forbearance*—that is, of *refraining* from violating the other person's right. If you have a right to life, I have no right to take your life; if you have a right to the products of your labor (property), I have no right to take it from you without your consent. The non-violation of these rights will not guarantee you protection against natural catastrophes such as floods and earthquakes, but it will protect you against the aggressive activities *of other men*. And rights, after all, have to do with one's relations to other human beings, not with one's relations to physical nature.

Nor were these rights created by government; governments—some governments, obviously not all—*recognize* and *protect* the rights that individuals already have. Governments regularly forbid homicide and theft; and, at a more advanced stage, protect individuals against such things as libel and breach of contract.

It cannot be by chance that they thus agree. They agree because the alleged creating of rights [by government] was nothing else than giving formal sanction and better definition to those assertions of claims and recognitions of claims which naturally originate from the individual desires of men who have to live in presence of one another.[8]

. . . Those who hold that life is valuable, hold, by implication, that men ought not to be prevented from carrying on life-sustaining activities. . . . Clearly the conception of "natural rights" originates in recognition of the truth that if life is justifiable, *there must be a justification for the performance of acts essential to its preservation;* and, therefore, *a justification of those liberties and claims which make such acts possible.*[9]

. . . To recognize and enforce the rights of individuals, is at the same time to recognize and enforce the conditions to a normal social life.[10]

We have not yet described the boundary lines of these rights, but we can see this most clearly if we consider the relation of rights to government. A proper government is one that protects the rights of its citizens from violation. If someone attempts to assault or maim you, the government (a) steps in to protect you if there is any foreknowledge that you are in danger and (b) attempts to seek out, try, and punish the assailant afterward, so as to keep him (and others) from doing similar deeds in the future. (More frequently the government does only the second, because the time and place of assaults on a person can seldom be predicted; however, by keeping "law and order," it can create a climate unfavorable to crime, thus minimizing the danger to each individual.) If someone takes away your belongings, the government intervenes to catch the culprit and, if possible, makes restitution to you through the courts.

But few, if any, governments are "proper" governments Since governments possess a virtual monopoly on physical force, those in power tend to use it. Governments have been the principal violators of man's rights. They make thieves, murderers, and rapists look saintly by comparison. Government and government alone foments wars, sends men to death camps and labor camps, devises and uses nuclear bombs, arrests individuals in the dead of night and takes them to where they are never heard from again, and—most frequently of all —systematically plunders them of what they have labored to earn. Never mind that that which they rob men of are the very things man needs to survive; historically governments have taken it away just the same, systematically and ruthlessly. This has been the history of governments—such a sordid history that one might well be skeptical of *all* governments. (Of this, more in the final chapter.) Judged by the standard of protection of the rights of individuals, no government has a perfect record and most governments have very bad records. The United States has a better record than most, but this is not to ignore or excuse its mistakes, and its record is not improving.

A man has the right to conduct his life as he sees fit, compatible with the right of other men to conduct their lives as *they* see fit. But when the government drafts him to fight and perhaps die in some foreign jungle, it is surely tampering with his right to life. *He* as the owner of his life has a right to live it according to his choice—if he values what freedom he has and volunteers to fight for it, that is his privilege; but no individual or collection of individuals has the right to force you to risk your life against your will. Sometimes medical researchers who have made experiments on guinea pigs and rats feel the need of trying out a new serum or vaccine on human beings, and they ask the inmates of prisons for volunteers with promise of a lightened sentence if they cooperate. But even a "lifer" in a prison is not forced: he is left free to choose whether to be inoculated or not. This, however, is not an option the draftee has with regard to his life.

The Right to Property

The right to property is the most misunderstood and unappreciated of human rights, and it is one most constantly violated by governments. "Property" of course does not mean only real estate; it includes anything you can call your own—your clothing, your car, your jewelry, your books and papers.

The right of property is not the right to just *take* it from others, for this would interfere with *their* property rights. It is rather the right to work for it, to obtain non-coercively, the money or services which you can present in voluntary exchange.

The right to property is consistently underplayed by intellectuals today, sometimes even frowned upon, as if we should feel guilty for upholding such a right in view of all the poverty in the world. But the right to property is absolutely basic. It is your hedge against the future. It is your assurance that what you have worked to earn will still be there, and be yours, when you wish or need to use it, especially when you are too old to work any longer.

Government has always been the chief enemy of the right to property. The officials of government, wishing to increase their power, and finding an increase of wealth an effective way to bring this about, seize some or all of what a person has earned—and since government has a monopoly of physical force within the geographical area of the nation, it has the power (but not the right) to do this. When this happens, of course, every citizen of that country is insecure: he knows that no matter how hard he works the government can swoop down on him at any time and confiscate his earnings and possessions. A person sees his life savings wiped out in a moment when the tax-collectors descend to deprive him of the fruits of his work; or, an industry which has been fifty years in the making and cost millions of dollars and millions of hours of

time and planning, is nationalized overnight. Or the government, via inflation, cheapens the currency, so that hard-won
dollars aren't worth anything any more. The effect of such
actions, of course, is that people lose hope and incentive: if no
matter how hard they work the government agents can take it
all away, why bother to work at all, for more than today's
needs? Depriving people of property is *depriving them of the
means by which they live*—the freedom of the individual citizen to do what he wishes with his own life and to plan for the
future. Indeed, only if property rights are respected is there
any point to planning for the future and working to achieve
one's goals. *Property rights are what makes long-range planning possible*—the kind of planning which is a distinctively
human endeavor, as opposed to the day-by-day activity of the
lion who hunts, who depends on the supply of game tomorrow
but has no real insurance against starvation in a day or a
week. Without the right to property, the right to life itself
amounts to little: how can you sustain your life if you cannot
plan ahead? and how can you plan ahead if the fruits of your
labor can at any moment be confiscated by government?

Without property rights, no other rights are possible. If one is not
free to use that which one has produced, one does not possess the right
of liberty. If one is not free to make the products of one's work serve
one's chosen goals, one does not possess the right to the pursuit of happiness. And—since man is not a ghost who exists in some non-material
manner—if one is not free to keep and to consume the products of
one's work, one does not possess the right of life. In a society where
men are not free privately to own the material means of production,
their position is that of slaves whose lives are at the absolute mercy of
their rulers. It is relevant here to remember the statement of Trotsky:
"Who does not obey shall not eat."[11]

Indeed, the right to property may well be considered second
only to the right to life. Even the freedom of speech is limited
by considerations of property. If a person visiting in your

home behaves in a way undesired by you, you have every right to evict him; he can scream or agitate elsewhere if he wishes, but not in your home without your consent. Does a person have a right to shout obscenities in a cathedral? No, for the owners of the cathedral (presumably the Church) have not allowed others on their property for that purpose; one may go there to worship or to visit, but not just for any purpose one wishes. Their property right is prior to your or my wish to scream or expectorate or write graffiti on their building. Or, to take the stock example, does a person have a right to shout "Fire!" falsely in a crowded theater? No, for the theater owner has permitted others to enter and use his property only for a specific purpose, that of seeing a film or watching a stage show. If a person heckles or otherwise disturbs other members of the audience, he can be thrown out. (In fact, he can be removed for any reason the owner chooses, provided his admission money is returned.) And if he shouts "Fire!" when there is no fire, he may be endangering other lives by causing a panic or a stampede. The right to free speech doesn't give one the right to say anything anywhere; it is circumscribed by property rights.

Again, some people seem to assume that the right to free speech (including written speech) means that they can go to a newspaper publisher and demand that he print in his newspaper some propaganda or policy statement for their political party (or other group). But of course they have no right to the use of his newspaper. Ownership of the newspaper is the product of his labor, and he has a right to put into his newspaper whatever he wants, for whatever reason. If he excludes material which many readers would like to have in, perhaps they can find it in another newspaper or persuade him to print it himself (if there are enough of them, they will usually do just that). Perhaps they can even cause his newspaper to fail. But as long as he owns it, he has the right to put in it what he wishes; what would a property right be if he could not do this? They have no right to place their material in his newspaper without his consent—not for free, nor even for a fee. Perhaps other newspapers will include it, or perhaps they can start their own newspaper (in which case they have a right to put in it what they like). If not, an option open to them would be to mimeograph and distribute some handbills.

In exactly the same way, no one has a right to "free television time" unless the owner of the television station consents to give it; it is his station, he has the property rights over it, and it is for him to decide how to dispose of his time. He may not decide wisely, but it is his right to decide as he wishes. If he makes enough unwise decisions, and courts enough unpopularity with the viewing public or the sponsors, he may have to go out of business; but as he is free to make his own decisions, so is he free to face their consequences. (If the government owns the television station, then government officials will make the decisions, and there is no guarantee of *their* superior wisdom. The difference is that when "the government" owns the station, you are forced to help pay for its upkeep through your taxes, whether the bureaucrat in charge decides to give you television time or not.)

"But why have *individual* property rights? Why not have lands and houses owned by everybody together?" Yes, this involves no violation of individual rights, as long as everybody consents to this arrangement and no one is forced to join it. The parties to it may enjoy the communal living enough (at least for a time) to overcome certain inevitable problems: that some will work and some not, that some will achieve more in an hour than others can do in a day, and still they will all get the same income. The few who do the most will in the end consider themselves "workhorses" who do the work of two or three or twelve, while the others will be "freeloaders" on the efforts of these few. But as long as they can get out of the arrangement if they no longer like it, no violation of rights is involved. They got in voluntarily, and they can get out voluntarily; no one has used force.[12]

"But why not say that everybody owns everything? That we *all* own everything there is?"

To some this may have a pleasant ring—but let us try to analyze what it means. If everybody owns everything, then everyone has an equal right to go everywhere, do what he pleases, take what he likes, destroy if he wishes, grow crops or burn them, trample them under, and so on. Consider what it would be like in practice. Suppose you have saved money to buy a house for yourself and your family. Now suppose that the principle, "everybody owns everything," becomes adopted. Well then, why shouldn't every itinerant hippie just come in and take over, sleeping in your beds and eating in your kitchen and not bothering to replace the food supply or clean up the mess? After all, it belongs to all of us, doesn't it? So we have just as much right to it as you, the buyer, have. What happens if we *all* want to sleep in the bedroom and there's not room for all of us? Is it the strongest who wins?

What would be the result? Since no one would be responsible for anything, the property would soon be destroyed, the food used up, the facilities nonfunctional. Beginning as a house that *one* family could use, it would end up as a house that *no one* could use. And if the principle continued to be adopted, no one would build houses any more—or anything else. What for? They would only be occupied and used by others, without remuneration.

Suppose two men are cast ashore on an island, and they agree that each will cultivate half of it. The first man is industrious and grows crops and builds a shelter, making the most of the situation with which he is confronted. The second man, perhaps thinking that the warm days will last forever, lies in the sun, picks coconuts while they last, and does a minimum of work to sustain himself. At the time of harvest, the second man has nothing to harvest, nor does he assist the first man in his labors. But later when there is a dearth of food on the island, the second man comes to the first man and demands half of the harvest as his right. But of course he has no right to the product of the first man's labors. The first man may freely choose to give part of his harvest to the second out of charity rather than see him starve; but that is just what it is—charity, not the second man's right.

A medical researcher spends evening after evening in his laboratory doing medical research, while another man wastes his time. One day the first man comes up with a cure for a disease—and the second man, who later contracts the disease, now claims the cure as his right. "You may have it for a price," says the first man; "I deserve something for all the years of work I put in to perfect it." But the second man insists that he should have it for nothing. "Free medical care is a human right," he says, "so fork it over."

But of course the second man has no such right. If he had a right to the product of the first man's labor (without the first man's consent), then to that extent the first man would be his slave. But, because each has rights, neither is the slave of the other. Of course the first man may decide that if the other one can't pay for it, he'll give it to him for nothing. Physicians often do this, charging more to patients who are able to pay more, to make up for those patients who are unable to pay. They do this, and perhaps it is right (adjective)—probably sometimes it is and sometimes it isn't, depending on the particular circumstances of the case—but the would-be recipient cannot claim the product of another person's effort as his right (noun). If it were his right, does A's cure become B's property the moment B needs it? (And what if A had decided not to expend the effort to invent the cure in the first place? Then there would be nothing for B to claim as his right!) And how far is this to go? Suppose B later claims half of A's income as his right "because he needs it"?

Someone has violently assaulted you. Should he be legally liable? Of course. He has violated one of your rights. He has knowingly injured you, and since he has initiated aggression against you he should be made to expiate.

Someone has negligently left his bicycle on the sidewalk where you trip over it in the dark and injure yourself. He didn't do it intentionally; he didn't mean you any harm. Should he be legally liable? Of course; he has, however unwittingly, injured you, and since the injury is caused by him and you are the victim, he should pay.

Someone across the street is unemployed. Should you be taxed extra to pay for his expenses? Not at all. You have not injured him, you are not responsible for the fact that he is unemployed (unless you are a senator or bureaucrat who agitated for further curtailing of business, which legislation passed, with the result that your neighbor was laid off by the curtailed business). You may voluntarily wish to help him out, or better still, try to get him a job to put him on his feet again; but since you have initiated no aggressive act against him, and neither purposely nor accidentally injured him in any way, you should not be legally penalized for the fact of his unemployment. (As we shall see in Chapter 4, it is just such penalties that increase unemployment.)

One man, A, works hard for years and finally earns a high salary as a professional man. A second man, B, prefers not to work at all, and to spend wastefully what money he has (through inheritance), so that after a year or two he has nothing left. At the end of this time he has a long siege of illness and lots of medical bills to pay. He demands that the bills be paid by the government—that is, by the taxpayers of the land, including Mr. A.

But of course B has no such right. He chose to lead his life in a certain way—that was his voluntary decision. One consequence of that choice is that he must depend on charity in case of later need. Mr. A chose not to live that way. (And if everyone lived like Mr. B, on whom would he depend in case of later need?) Each has a right to live in the way he pleases, but each must live with the consequences of his own decision (which, as always, fall primarily on himself). He cannot, in time of need, claim A's beneficence as his right.

If a house-guest of yours starts to carve his initials in your walls and break up your furniture, you have a right to evict him, and call the police if he makes trouble. If someone starts to destroy the machinery in a factory, the factory-owner is also entitled to evict him and call the police. In both cases, persons other than the owner are permitted on the property only under certain conditions, at the pleasure of the owner. If those conditions are violated, the owner is entitled to use force to set things straight. The case is exactly the same on a college or university campus: if a campus demonstrator starts breaking windows, occupying the president's office, and setting fire to a dean, the college authorities are certainly within their rights to evict him forcibly; one is permitted on the college grounds only under specific conditions, set by the administration: study, peaceful student activity, even political activity if those in charge choose to permit it. If they do not choose to permit peaceful political activity on campus, they may be unwise, since a campus is after all a place where all sides of every issue should get discussed, and the college that doesn't permit this may soon lose its reputation and its students. All the same, the college official who does not permit it is quite within his rights; the students do not own the campus, nor do the hired trouble-makers imported from elsewhere. In the case of a privately owned college, the owners, or whoever they have delegated to administer it, have the right to make the decisions as to who shall be permitted on the campus and under what conditions. In the case of a state university or college, the ownership problem is more complex: one could say that the "government" owns the campus or that "the people" do since they are the taxpayers who support it; but in either case, the university administration has the delegated task of keeping order, and until they are removed by the state administration or the taxpayers, it is theirs to decide who shall be permitted on campus, and what non-academic activities will be permitted to their students on the premises.

Property rights can be violated by physical trespass, of course, or by anyone entering on your property for any reason without your consent. (If you *do* consent to having your neighbor dump garbage on your yard, there is no violation of your rights.) But the physical trespass of a person is only a special case of violation of property rights. Property rights can be violated by sound-waves, in the form of a loud noise, or the sounds of your neighbor's hi-fi set while you are trying to sleep. Such violations of property rights are of course the subject of action in the courts.

But there is another violation of property rights that has not thus far been honored by the courts; this has to do with the effects of *pollution* of the atmosphere.

From the beginnings of modern air pollution, the courts made a conscious decision not to protect, for example, the orchards of farmers from the smoke of nearby factories or locomotives. They said, in effect, to the farmers: yes, your private property is being invaded by this smoke, but we hold that "public policy" is more important than private property, and public policy holds factories and locomotives to be good things. These goods were allowed to override the defense of property rights—with our consequent headlong rush into pollution disaster. The remedy is both "radical" and crystal clear, and it has nothing to do with multi-billion dollar palliative programs at the expense of the tax-payers which do not even meet the real issue. The remedy is simply to enjoin anyone from injecting pollutants into the air, and thereby invad-ing the rights of persons and property. Period. The argument that such an injunction prohibition would add to the costs of industrial produc-tion is as reprehensible as the pre-Civil War argument that the aboli-tion of slavery would add the costs of growing cotton, and therefore should not take place. For this means that the polluters are able to im-pose the high costs of pollution upon those whose property rights they are allowed to invade with impunity.[13]

What about automobiles, the chief polluters of the air? One can hardly sue every automobile owner. But one can sue the manufacturers of automobiles who do not install anti-smog de-vices on the cars which they distribute—and later (though this is more difficult), owners of individual automobiles if they discard the equipment or do not keep it functional.

The violation of rights does not apply only to air-pollution. If someone with a factory upstream on a river pollutes the river, anyone living downstream from him, finding his water polluted, should be able to sue the owner of the factory. In this way the price of adding the anti-pollutant devices will be the owner's responsibility, and will probably be added to the cost of the products which the factory produces and thus spread around among all consumers, rather than the entire cost being borne by the users of the river in the form of polluted water, with the consequent impossibility of fishing, swimming, and so on. In each case, pollution would be stopped at the source rather than having its ill effects spread around to numerous members of the population.

What about property which you do not work to earn, but which you *inherit* from someone else? Do you have a right to that? You have no right to it until someone decides to give it to you. Consider the man who willed it to you: it was his, he had the right to use and dispose of it as *he* saw fit; and if he decided to give it to you, this is a windfall for you, but it was only the exercise of *his* right. Had the property been seized by the government at the man's death, or distributed among numerous other people designated by the government, it *would* have been a violation of his rights: for he, who worked to earn and sustain it, would not have been able to dispose of it according to his own judgment. If he doesn't have the right to determine who shall have it, who does?[14]

What about the property status of your intellectual activity, such as inventions you may devise and books you write? These, of course, are your property also; they are the products of your mind; you worked at them, you created them. Prior to that, they did not exist. If you worked five years to write a book, and someone stole it and published it as his own, receiving royalties from its sales, he would have stolen your property just as surely as if he had robbed your home. The same is true if someone used and sold without your permission an invention which was the product of your labor and ingenuity.

The role of government with respect to this issue, at least most governments of the Western world, is a proper one: government protects the products of your labor from the moment they materialize. Copyright law protects your writings from piracy. In the United States, one's writings are protected for a period of twenty-seven years, and another twenty-seven if one applies for renewal of the copyright. In most other countries, they are protected for a period of fifty years after the author's death, permitting both himself and his surviving heirs to reap the fruits of his labor. After that they enter the "public domain"—that is, anyone may reprint them without your or your heirs' permission. Patent law protects your inventions for a limited period, which varies according to the type of invention. In no case are you forced to avail yourself of this protection; you need not apply for patent or copyright coverage if you do not wish to do so. But the protection of your intellectual property is there, in case you wish to use it.[15]

What about the property status of the airwaves? Here the government's position is far more questionable. The government now claims ownership of the airwaves, leasing them to individuals and corporations. The government renews leases or refuses them depending on whether the programs satisfy authorities in the Federal Communications Commission. The official position is that "we all own the airwaves"; but since only one party can broadcast on a certain frequency at a certain time without causing chaos, it is simply a fact of reality that "everyone" cannot use it. In fact the government decides who shall use the airwaves, and one courts its displeasure only at the price of a revoked license. One can write without government, but one cannot use the airwaves without the approval of government.

What policy should have been observed with regard to the airwaves? Much the same as the policy that was followed in the case of the Homestead Act, when the lands of the American West were opening up for settlement. There was a policy of "first come, first served," with the government parcelling out a certain acreage for each individual who wanted to claim the land as his own. There was no charge for the land, but if a man had not used it and built a dwelling during the first two-year period, it was assumed that he was not homesteading and the land was given to the next man in line. The airwaves too could have been given out on a "first come, first served" basis. The first man who used a given frequency would be its owner, and the government would protect him in the use of it against trespassers. If others wanted to use the same frequency, they would have to buy it from the first man, if he was willing to sell, or try to buy another, just as one now does with land.[16]

There are several corollaries to our principle of rights, which will be stated separately although they are implicit in what has already been said.

1. In any activity involving more than one person, the consent of *every person* who is a party to it is required; the alternative to voluntary membership in a group is force, and if a person is forced to be a member, his rights are being violated.

A person who joins a club, a church, a fraternity, does so voluntarily, and he can resign from it voluntarily. No rights have been violated. A person who is a stockholder in a corporation, or a member of any other group, may voluntarily have assented to the acceptance of majority vote on all policy decisions. If then he is outvoted in a particular case, his rights have not been violated.

In the case of government, one did not have that decision— one was born into the system. From this some libertarians have concluded that all government is a violation of human rights. But other libertarians have advocated government (or tolerated it), arguing that the limited government they espouse is restricted to the protection of man's rights; and any government that goes beyond this role is indeed violating rights. Thus, if a person is not guilty of any crime, he would have nothing to fear from a limited government; indeed, he could go about his business as if it did not exist—unless his rights were violated, in which case the government would (if it fulfilled its function) step in to protect him.

2. *No man need sacrifice himself to others, but neither should he sacrifice others to himself.*

This is another way of viewing the libertarian principle of individual rights. It is more unique than it first appears; for ethical theories have historically been divided between those exhorting a person to sacrifice himself for others (altruism) and those exhorting him to sacrifice others to himself (egoism, in what is unfortunately its most popular form).[17] But if we adhere to the principle of human rights, we shall adopt neither of these alternatives. I respect your rights, and you respect mine. I can lead my life as I wish, limited only by the choices available (no one has infinite choices); and so can you. I do not attempt to use force to change your voluntary decisions, except in retaliation if you use force against me first; nor do you use force against me, unless I initiate it first against you. I do not take the fruits of your labor without your consent, nor do you take mine without my consent. Not I alone or any group to which I belong may kill, injure, or rob you; nor may you, alone or in any group however large, kill, injure or rob me. The principle of individual rights is basic to all a person's relations with other human beings.

3. *No man's life is a non-voluntary mortgage on the life of another.* I cannot claim your life, your work, the products of your effort as mine. In order to give someone a blood transfusion, you do not cause another to die of anemia. The fruit of one man's labor is not fair game for every freeloader who comes along and demands it as his own. The orchard that has been carefully grown, nurtured, and harvested by its owner is not "ripe for the plucking" for any bypasser who has a yen for ripe fruit.

A cannibal in the physical sense is a person who lives off the flesh of other human beings. A *moral* cannibal is one who believes he has a right to live off the "spirit" of other human beings—who believes that he has a moral claim on the productive capacity, time, and effort expended by others.

It has become fashionable to claim virtually everything that one needs or desires as one's *right*. Thus, many people claim that they have a right to a job, the right to free medical care, to free food and clothing, to a decent home, and so on. Now if one asks, apart from any specific context, whether it would be desirable if everyone had these things, one might well say yes. But there is a gimmick attached to each of them: *At whose expense?* Jobs, medical care, education, and so on, don't grow on trees. These are goods and services *produced only by men*. Who, then, is to provide them, and under what conditions?

If some men are entitled *by right* to the products of the work of others, it means that those others are deprived of rights and condemned to slave labor.

Any alleged "right" of one man, which necessitates the violation of the rights of another, is not and cannot be a right.

No man can have a right to impose an unchosen obligation, an unrewarded duty, or an involuntary servitude on another man. There can be no such thing as *"the right to enslave."*[18]

If you have a right to a job, who is to supply it? Must an employer supply it even if he doesn't want to hire you? What if you are unemployable, or incurably lazy? (If you say "the government must supply it," does that mean that a job must be created for you which no employer needs done, and that you must be kept in it regardless of how much or little you work?) If the employer is forced to supply it at his expense even if he doesn't need you, then isn't *he* being enslaved to that extent? What ever happened to *his* right to conduct his life and his affairs in accordance with his choices?

If you have a right to free medical care, then, since medical care doesn't exist in nature as wild apples do, some people will have to supply it to you for free: that is, they will have to spend their time and money and energy taking care of you whether they want to or not. What ever happened to *their* right to conduct their lives as they see fit? Or do you have a right to violate theirs? Can there be a right to violate rights?

All those who demand this or that as a "free service" are consciously or unconsciously evading the fact that there are in reality no such thing as free services. All man-made goods and services are the result of human expenditure of time and effort. There is no such thing as "something for nothing" in this world. If you demand something free, you are demanding that other men give their time and effort to you without compensation. If they voluntarily choose to do this, there is no problem; but if you demand that they be *forced* to do it, you are interfering with their right not to do it if they so choose. "Swimming in this pool ought to be free!" says the indignant passerby. What he means is that others should build a pool, others should provide the materials, and still others should run it and keep it in functioning order, so that *he* can use it without fee. But what right has he to the expenditure of *their* time and effort? To expect something "for free" is to expect it *to be paid for by others* whether they choose to or not.

Here, then, is the importance of saying (as we said earlier) that you have a right to an activity. You have the right to earn property, if you can—not the right to simply take it over. "A right does not include the material implementation of that right by other men; it includes only the freedom to earn that implementation by one's own effort."

Observe, in this context, the intellectual precision of the Founding Fathers: they spoke of the right to *the pursuit* of happiness—*not* of the right to happiness. It means that a man has the right to take the actions he deems necessary to achieve his happiness; it does *not* mean that others must make him happy.

The right to life means that a man has the right to support his life by his own work (on any economic level, as high as his ability will carry him); it does *not* mean that others must provide him with the necessities of life.

The right to property means that a man has the right to take the economic actions necessary to earn property, to use it, and dispose of it; it does *not* mean that others must provide him with property.

The right of free speech means that a man has the right to express his ideas without danger of suppression, interference or punitive action by the government. It does *not* mean that others must provide him with a lecture hall, a radio station or a printing press through which to express his ideas.

Any undertaking that involves more than one man, requires the *voluntary* consent of every participant, but none has the right to force his decision on the others.

There is no such thing as "a right to a job"—there is only the right of free trade, that is: a man's right to take a job if another man chooses to hire him. There is no "right to a home," only the right of free trade: the right to build a home or to buy it. There are no "rights to a 'fair' wage or a 'fair' price" if no one chooses to pay it, to hire a man or to buy his product. There are no "rights of consumers" to milk, shoes, movies or champagne if no producers choose to manufacture such items (there is only the right to manufacture them oneself). There are no "rights" of special groups, there are no "rights of farmers, of workers, of businessmen, of employees, of employers, of the old, of the young, of the unborn." There are only *the Rights of Man*—rights possessed by every individual man and by *all* men as individuals.

Property rights and right of free trade are man's only "economic rights" (they are, in fact, *political* rights)—and there can be no such thing as "an *economic* bill of rights." But observe that the advocates of the latter have all but destroyed the former.[19]

But aren't food, shelter, and so on human *needs?* And isn't your doctrine of rights based on human needs? That is, on what is necessary for man's survival as man?

Indeed these are human needs. But (1) how are they best fulfilled? By an economic system of freedom, or by one which would take from some to give to others? I shall endeavor to show in the coming chapters that the first and not the second is

the type of economic system that can fulfill these needs; and
that a system not grounded in economic liberty will lead to a
lowering of the standard of living and bring on the very poverty it was (sometimes) designed to prevent. (2) In any case, a
need is not the same as a right. A man has a right to work to
earn and thus fulfill his needs, and those of any others he
wishes. But a need of one man does not mean he has a right to
tap the earned income of others to fulfill it; if it did, the second man would be (to that extent) deprived of *his* rights. No
man's life constitutes a non-voluntary mortgage on the lives of
other human beings. No man may claim the fruits of another's
labor as his right, although the other man may voluntarily give
it. If it were otherwise, others would always have an open-
ended claim on your life and work, and no one's life and work
would be secure.

Many people want a guarantee of "security": they say that
they have "a right to security." Since they do not want to (or
cannot) con Mr. X next door into giving them a weekly handout for the rest of their lives, they say, "The government must
do it." But "the government" means every taxpayer in the
land, and particularly those people who have produced the
most and thus are taxed the most. Now, the businessman or
industrialist on whom one primarily depends for this "security" (since most of it comes out of his taxes) has no guarantee of
security himself: one bad business decision, or one crop failure, or one failure by a supplier on whose materials he depends for his products, and his whole business (his entire life's
work) may be wiped out. His security depends on his continued business acumen, on the correctness of his judgments.
How, then, can those who depend on him for their "security"
possibly be guaranteed security if he is not? Should they, who
depend on him, have a guarantee which the nature of reality

denies him? And *can* they have it, if he on whom they depend goes bankrupt?

I enjoy seeing operas; but operas are expensive to produce. Opera-lovers often say, "The state (or the city, etc.) should subsidize opera, so that we can all see it." Also it would be for people's betterment, cultural benefit, etc." But what they are advocating is nothing more or less than legalized plunder. They can't pay for the productions themselves, and yet they want to see opera, which involves a large number of people and their labor; so what they are saying in effect is, "Get the money through legalized force. Take a little bit more out of every worker's paycheck every week to pay for the operas we want to see." But I have no right to take by force from the workers' pockets to pay for what I want.

Perhaps it would be better if he *did* go to see opera—then I should try to convince him to go voluntarily. But to take the money from him forcibly, because in my opinion it would be good for *him,* is still seizure of his earnings, which is plunder.

Besides, if I have the right to force him to help pay for my pet projects, hasn't he equally the right to force me to help pay for his? Perhaps he in turn wants the government to subsidize rock-and-roll, or his new car, or a house in the country? If I have the right to milk him, why hasn't he the right to milk me? If I can be a moral cannibal, why can't he too?

We should beware of the inventors of utopias. They would remake the world according to their vision—with the lives and fruits of the labor of *other* human beings. Is it someone's utopian vision that others should build pyramids to beautify the landscape? Very well, then other men should provide the labor; and if he is in a position of political power, and he can't get men to do it voluntarily, then he must compel them to "cooperate"—i.e. he must enslave them. Or perhaps he

. . . looks with envy at the achievements of industrialists and dreams of what beautiful parks *he* could create if only everyone's lives, efforts and resources were turned over to *him*. . . .

The next time you encounter one of those "public-spirited" dreamers who tells you rancorously that "some very desirable goals cannot be achieved without *everybody's* participation," tell him that if he cannot obtain everybody's *voluntary* participation, his goals had jolly well better remain unachieved—and that men's lives are not his to dispose of.[20]

4. *Other men's lives are not yours to dispose of.* A hundred men might gain great pleasure from beating up or killing just one insignificant human being; but other men's lives are not theirs to dispose of. The principle of rights protects that one lone individual. "In order to achieve the worthy goals of the next five-year-plan, we must forcibly collectivize the peasants . . ."; but other men's lives are not theirs to dispose of. Do you want to occupy, rent-free, the mansion that another man has worked for twenty years to buy? But other men's lives are not yours to dispose of. Do you want operas so badly that everyone is forced to work harder to pay for their subsidization through taxes? But other men's lives are not yours to dispose of. Do you want to have free medical care at the expense of other people, whether they wish to provide it or not? But this would require them to work longer for you whether they want to or not, and other men's lives are not yours to dispose of.

The freedom to engage in any type of enterprise, to produce, to own and control property, to buy and sell on the free market, is derived from the rights to life, liberty, and property . . . which are stated in the Declaration of Independence. . . . [but] when a government guarantees a "right" to an education or parity on farm products or a guaranteed annual income, *it is staking a claim on the property of one group of citizens for the sake of another group.* In short, it is violating one of the fundamental rights it was instituted to protect.[21]

Individualism vs. Collectivism

Human rights are the rights of *individuals*. When we say that all men have certain rights, we mean that *each individual* who exists has certain rights. "Society" has no rights; only the individual has rights. If by "society" we mean each individual (all together exchanging goods and services with one another), then we can say, misleadingly, that society has rights. But except in this individualistic sense, there *is* no such entity as "society"; there are only individual human beings.

If people would stop talking about "society" as if it were some separate entity, much confusion would be avoided. For example, it is said that when a felony is committed and the guilty man is put in prison, "society" is exacting its punishment due from the criminal. But what does each member of "society," including those thousands of miles away who have never heard of the crime or the criminal or even the country in which it was committed, have to do with the matter? There is a criminal, who owes a debt to those he has harmed; there is also the aggrieved party, to whom the restitution is owed. If the aggrieved party has been robbed, he is owed what he was robbed of plus whatever other inconveniences (including pain and suffering) were inflicted on him; if he was murdered, no restitution can be made to him, but his family and perhaps others near to him, particularly those economically dependent on him, are owed a great deal. But all the members of the human race, or even of the nation in which the incident occurred? Surely not.

A variant of the word "society" that is often used is the phrase, "the people." It has a noble sound: "the people." "Power to the people!" is a popular student chant just now; but who are the people? All the individuals in the nation? (And could they all agree on any matter of public policy?) Does it

mean the majority—sanctioned to persecute a minority? And
if it is only some people out of the total population, by what
means are they to be selected to rule over others? Whatever we
might be able to distill from this confusion, the fact is that
most of the time when national leaders speak of "the people"
they mean themselves, the government officials. "The People's
Republic of China" is a viciously totalitarian nation in which
the vast majority of the people have no say about anything at
all—their lives are ruled coercively from the cradle to the
grave by a comparative handful of officials who will brook no
dissent and crack down even on strikes for higher wages.

"We should take the property away from the rich capitalist
and give it back to the people!" (All the people? Did they ever
have it, seeing that the filthy capitalist created the product in
the first place?) "But we all own it!" What does that mean?
"The people should own the airwaves" means, in practice,
that a few government officials decide who shall operate which
airwave—the rest of the people have nothing to say about it at
all. And aren't private owners people too? When they own it,
at least things are managed more efficiently. But the slogan
carries great popular appeal to those who fail to consider its
implications.

The most popular argument in favor of nationalization of
private property, one that is extremely persuasive to those who
do not think through its implications, is what I shall call "the
people argument": "But if we take it away from the individual, or the corporation, it will belong to all of us—to the people!" We have the magic word "the people" waved before us,
and we are supposed to have the delicious feeling of sharing
some benefits. But what does it mean to say that something
"belongs to the people?" If "the people"—all two hundred million of us—own a house that has been taken over by the government, does this mean that we all have the right to sleep in

the bedroom and eat in the kitchen? Of course not—the thing would be impossible. Even if only a few of us used the house on any given day, we would get in each other's way and fall to quarreling about the use of "our" kitchen and bathroom. What it means is that a few people (bureaucrats and police) have effective use of it, while all of us pay for it. One is reminded of the account of an American visitor to a government-owned factory in the Soviet Union. "Who owns the factory?" the visitor asks. "The people," says the Russian. "Who owns the land?" "The people." The visitor espies a few cars. "Who owns the cars?" "The people. But they are used for the time being by the Secret Police." Later the Russian visits a car factory near Detroit. "Who owns the factory?" "Henry Ford." "Selfish exploiter," mutters the Russian, but he continues, "Who owns the land?" "Henry Ford." "Capitalistic greed," says the Russian, but asks, seeing thousands of cars all about, "Who owns the cars?" "Why, the workers, of course!"

"The fiction of public ownership" should be exposed for what it is, a fiction.[22] If you think you own something that is said to be owned by "the people" (of whom you are one), ask yourself what power you individually have over it. If you own stock in a corporation, you are genuinely part-owner: you can cast your vote on the corporation's policy decisions, and (more important) you can take out your stock at any time that you care to dissociate yourself from the corporation, and collect the value of the shares you own. But try the same with any government-owned enterprise. If you say, "The Post Office Department belongs to the people, and since I don't care to have anything to do with that department, I think I'll write to Washington and collect my share of what it's worth." You can imagine how far you would get in such an endeavor. Or, "Since I own part of the car that is used by the secret police, I think I'll cash in on the part that I own." You would soon find that you own none of it— you pay taxes to support it, whether you want to or not, but there is no part of it that you can call yours. What is "owned by the people" is only paid for by the people, and used by government officials at the people's expense—and occasionally by you, under conditions laid down by them. Or in other words, what is owned by "the collective" is paid for by one group and used by another.

People speak of "the public interest." But what is the public interest? Strictly speaking, there is no such thing. There is only the interest of each individual human being. There are interests that many or all people share, but these are still the interests of individuals. When politicians say that something is "to the public interest," they usually mean that it serves the interests of some people but goes against the interests of others—and usually the interests of the people with the most political pull win out. Is it to the public interest for some to be forced to die so that others may be saved? Is it to the public interest for a hundred crazed men to lynch one man in the public square? Is it to the public interest for all the citizens of the nation to be taxed to pay for a federal dam in one section of it? In Sweden it takes a couple eight to ten years on the average before they can obtain an apartment of their own (owned by the government, rented by them); but they are not supposed to complain, because "it's in the public interest."

Just as there are only individual rights, so there are only individual interests.

It seems too obvious to mention, and yet constantly needs mentioning, that each person should be judged as an *individual*, on the basis of his individual characteristics (and qualifications, if he is an applicant for a job or graduate status in a university). He is not to be judged more highly because he had a distinguished father, or less highly because he had an undistinguished father. It is his individual characteristics that make him worthy or unworthy, not his membership in a group. If the group is one which he voluntarily joined, then one can judge him for the voluntary act of joining it; if he joined the Ku Klux Klan, one can reasonably make certain judgments about him. But if one judges him on the basis of characteristics which he doesn't have (which his father had, for example) or on the basis of characteristics that he had nothing to do with (such as his race), one is not really judging or evaluating *him* as an individual, but only invoking a stereotype of a race or nationality and evaluating the person on the basis of that class membership (which he inherited). It is, of course, a naive assumption that every member of a particular class is alike.

The respectable family that supports worthless relatives or covers up their crimes in order to "protect the family name" (as if the moral stature of one man could be damaged by the actions of another); the bum who boasts that his great-grandfather was an empire-builder, or the small-town spinster who boasts that her maternal great-uncle was a state senator and her third cousin gave a concert at Carnegie Hall (as if the achievements of one man could rub off on the mediocrity of another); the parents who search genealogical trees in order to evaluate their prospective sons-in-law; the celebrity who starts his autobiography with a detailed account of his family history; all these are samples of racism, the atavistic manifestations of a doctrine whose full expression is the tribal warfare of prehistorical savages, the wholesale slaughter of Nazi Germany, the atrocities of today's so-called "newly emerging nations."[23]

Racism is a particularly crude form of collectivism. The man who will not hire a black candidate for a position even though his qualifications for the job are better than a white candidate's, is guilty of racism; he is not judging the man on the basis of his individual qualifications for the job, but on the basis of the record that (he thinks) other people of the same race have, or perhaps just on the basis of pure unreasoned prejudice; if there are five black applicants and five white ones and he automatically eliminates the black ones from consideration, he may well be eliminating some or all of the persons with the best qualifications for the job—and the success of his enterprise will suffer as a result.

It is sometimes said that some races are "genetically inferior" to others, that there are fewer intelligent people in a certain racial group than there are in others. So far as I know there is no evidence for this. But even if there were, the point is irrelevant: if this man of race X is intelligent and adaptable, then he has these qualities regardless of how many *other* persons of his race do not have them.

A genius is a genius, regardless of the number of morons who belong to the same race—and a moron is a moron, regardless of the number of geniuses who share his racial origin. It is hard to say which is the more outrageous injustice: the claim of Southern racists that a Negro genius should be treated as an inferior because his race has "produced" some brutes, or the claim of a German brute to the status of a superior because his race has "produced" Goethe, Schiller, and Brahms.[24]

Today one often encounters the phenomenon of "racism in reverse"—giving special consideration to individual members of races which were discriminated against in the past. Very frequently letters cross my desk saying in effect, "We want to hire a Negro philosopher. Can you recommend one? We don't care about his qualifications for the job as long as he's black." But this is just as much an example of racism as the previous illustrations. If the man is not a good teacher or scholar, on what basis can one recommend *him* as an individual? He had nothing to do with his racial origin. And what could one think of oneself for recommending an inferior teacher to inflict on students when a superior teacher (of whatever race) is available? How does the fact that he belongs to a certain race constitute either a recommendation or a condemnation of *him*?

Many labor unions have discriminated, and some still do,

against blacks, and will not even admit them to membership regardless of qualifications. This of course is as blatant an example of racism as one could encounter. But equally so is the demand of certain black leaders that, because white men held black men as slaves in the past, black men should now receive preferential treatment by employers regardless of qualification—or, sometimes, that there should be a racial quota system for hiring employees, a certain fixed percentage of blacks employed in each profession, regardless of how many are available or what their qualifications are.

Consider the implications of that statement. It does not merely demand special privileges on racial grounds—it demands that white men be penalized *for the sins of their ancestors.* It demands that a white laborer be refused a job because his grandfather may have practiced racial discrimination. But perhaps his grandfather had *not* practiced it. Or perhaps his grandfather had not even lived in this country. Since these questions are not to be considered, it means that that white laborer is to be charged with *collective racial guilt,* the guilt consisting merely of the color of his skin.[25]

When students receive grades for a course, each is supposed to receive a grade based on his achievement in the course. Those individuals who have achieved the most receive the highest grades. This is an example of *individualism*—each person being rewarded in proportion to his merit.

But suppose the teacher said, "Now we don't want any student to get D's or F's, do we? So those of you who have the A's and B's should give these higher points to the students with lower grades. We will take the average of the whole class and give everybody a C." Though this plan would indeed eliminate the D's and F's, it would not be a very revealing grading system: no graduate school or future employer could discover whether any student's record was a good one. It would, however, be an example of *collectivism*: of taking the average of an entire group and assigning that value to each person in the group by virtue of his membership in the group.

Our penal code is individualistic with regard to punishment. Those individuals who have committed the most serious crimes are supposed (though it doesn't always work out that way) to receive the most serious punishments, and no one is punished for crimes his neighbor or cousin committed. But there are tribes in which this system of penal individualism does not operate: if a member of tribe A kills a member of tribe B, any member of tribe A is taken at random and killed by the members of tribe B—or somethimes a depredation is made on the entire tribe A, even though all its members but the guilty man are innocent and may have known nothing about the commission of the crime. This is collectivism in the realm of penal justice.

In the realm of economic matters, collectivism is entirely analogous to what it would be in the grading system if everyone's grades were averaged out and all the students received the same grade. Suppose that some citizens work very hard, some average, some very little, and some do not work at all—and that the work of some (such as physicians) is exacting and requires long special training while the work of others (such as ditchdiggers) does not require such qualifications; but everyone, regardless of these differences, receives the same income. When this is entered into as a voluntary system, and each member can enter when he chooses and leave when he chooses, then *politically* there is nothing to be said against it—they are living as they choose to live, and so be it. The worst one could say of it is that it is inefficient and usually unproductive, because it "goes against human nature," and that if one person must carry a huge load of work because there are a number of freeloaders who prefer not to work at all, then sooner or later that person will break down, physically or psychologically. Many colonies organized on such principles have begun with high hopes and ended in bitterness and rancor. The Pilgrim Fathers tried it the first winter at Plymouth Rock, and they were nearly wiped out by starvation from lack of provisions. When a hard worker sees someone not working, or malingering, he says or thinks to himself, "Why should I work for him too? Why should he get just as much as I from the common pot when I work hard and he works hardly at all? Let him work for himself, and I for myself, and we'll soon see who is better off!" And thus, inevitably, economic individualism asserts itself.

When a collectivistic system is not voluntary but compulsorily imposed on every citizen in the land, it becomes a monster. It penalizes the productive people for the sake of the unproductive, and it increases the ranks of the unproductive because they see no advantage to themselves in being productive. Such a system can land a nation in economic ruin. This is such a plain empirical fact that even the collectivistic nations, such as Soviet Russia, though certainly not operating on a free market, do devise special benefits for certain types of jobs as an incentive for the individual who wishes to contribute more.

Such a system does not exist in the United States, but we are approaching it more and more closely every time we guarantee one group of people an income out of work done by another group. Whenever this happens, the incentive to produce work at all is reduced. It has been proposed, for example, that everyone in the U.S. should receive a minimum income of $3,000 regardless of whether or not he works to earn it. As long as people can get *more* by working, of course many if not most will do so: they won't care to live on only $3,000. But the amount would tend to increase to $4,000, and then $5,000—politicians would scream for it in the name of humanity (votes?)—and finally the load on the worker would become unbearable. He would go off the producer-list and enter the parasite-list—he'd get his $3,000 anyway, wouldn't he? and in any case, he wouldn't have much more than that left after taxes—and so production would tend to come to a halt, as before.

Capitalism, of course, is individualism in the realm of economics. An individual trades his product or services for the products and services provided by others. And the amount he earns bears a close relation to his effort and his achievement. His efforts may, of course, misfire, as the result of bad luck or miscalculation: he might spend years marketing a product that the public wouldn't want, at least not in sufficient quantity to make it worth his while. It is also possible that he wouldn't particularly care to earn a lot of money—that he would go into some occupation he likes which would pay him less than a more lucrative occupation which he dislikes—and this too is his right, as long as he doesn't later demand as a right a higher income which he voluntarily forswore through his choice of profession. But in a capitalist system, that decision is *his*—it is not made for him by a bureaucrat or a National Labor Board or any other association of government bureaucrats. The efforts are his as an individual, the choice of profession is his as an individual, and the rewards come back to him as an individual—provided his activities are not interfered with at any point along the line by government.

The influence of collectivism is enormous, however, and in thousands of popular books it is simply taken for granted. Readers seldom question the collectivistic assumptions contained in them. For example: writers constantly talk of the allocation of our "national resources," as if these resources belonged to everybody, and it was only for a group of assorted Washington bureaucrats to decide who shall get which of the benefits (from them). But these economic resources were created and developed and distributed by *individuals,* and the income from these labors belonged to and were the right of individuals.

Capitalism is not, indeed, as some writers have held, the economic system that distributes "our national assets" through private means. (Capitalism is not a system of distribution at all, but a system of production.) There are no "national assets," there are only the assets earned by *individuals.*

It is morally obscene to regard wealth as an anonymous tribal product and to talk about "redistributing" it. The view that wealth is the result of some indifferentiated, collective process, that we all did something and it's impossible to tell who did what, therefore some sort of equalitarian "distribution" is necessary—might have been appropriate in a primordial jungle with a savage horde moving boulders by physical labor (though even there someone had to initiate and organize the moving). To hold that view in an industrial society—where individual achievements are a matter of public record—is so crass an evasion that even to give it the benefit of the doubt is an obscenity.

Anyone who has ever been an employer or an employee or has observed men working, or has done an honest day's work himself, knows the crucial role of ability, of intelligence, of a focused, competent mind —in any and all lines of work, from the lowest to the highest. He knows that ability or the lack of it . . . makes a difference of life or death in any productive process. The evidence is so overwhelming . . . in the events of history and in anyone's own daily grind—that no one can claim ignorance of it. Mistakes of this size are not made innocently. When great industrialists made fortunes on a *free* market (i.e., without the use of force, without government assistance or interference), they *created* new wealth—they did not take it from those who had *not* created it. If you doubt it, take a look at the "total social product"— and the standard of living—of those countries where such men are not permitted to exist.[26]

There is no one "national wealth pie" for the bureaucrats to cut up and distribute according to their whims. There is only the wealth produced through labor by a large number of individuals.

Those who are constantly judging the progress of the nation by the annual "Gross National Product" often forget, in their constant concern with *aggregates*, that the production of wealth is the work of *individuals*. Some individuals produce much and some little; and some nothing at all, being parasitical on others; but all these diverse achievements are lumped together as if matters of individual achievement and initiative did not count.

There is no end of social planners who would gladly use the wealth and productivity of other individuals (even though they themselves are incapable of producing it) for their pet projects. According to their plan, this or that is needed for "the collective good" (as seen by the planner, of course) or "the people" (all the people? most of them? some of them at the expense of others?).

The examples of such projects are innumerable: "Isn't it desirable to clean up the slums?" (dropping the context of what happens to those in the next income bracket); "Isn't it desirable to have beautiful, planned cities, all of one harmonious style?" (dropping the context of *whose* choice of style is to be forced on the home builders); "Isn't it desirable to have an educated public?" (dropping the context of *who* will do the educating, *what* will be taught, and *what* will happen to dissenters); "Isn't it desirable to liberate the artists, the writers, the composers from the burden of financial problems and leave them free to create?" (dropping the context of such questions as: *which* artists, writers, and composers?—chosen by whom?—at whose expense?—at the expense of the artists, writers, and composers who have no political pull and whose miserably precarious incomes will be taxed to "liberate" that privileged elite?)[27]

The view that we must sacrifice for the sake of "society" is indeed a very dangerous one. You want to speak freely? To write? To engage in the work you choose? But no, "society has demands on you, and society comes first." How many collectivists who want your services (but probably wouldn't do a thing for you) have used this timeworn stratagem to control your life, and make you feel guilty if you don't voluntarily submit?

Once you admit that the individual is merely a means to serve the ends of the higher entity called society or the nation, most of those features of totalitarian regimes which horrify us follow of necessity. From the collectivist standpoint, intolerance and brutal suppression of dissent, the complete disregard of the life and happiness of the individual, are essential and unavoidable consequences of this basic premise; and the collectivist can admit this and at the same time claim that his system is superior to one in which the "selfish" interests of the individual are allowed to obstruct the full realization of the ends the community pursues. . . .[28]

Once a man has decided that only the final end matters and is so important that any means one takes to achieve it is justifiable, and once such a man has come into power, then the most ruthless totalitarianism will come into existence, bearing the moral cloak of "we [collectively] must sacrifice all now for the sake of a glorious future."

Once Lenin had decided that all means were permissible to bring about the dictatorship of the proletariat, with himself ruling in the name of the proletariat, he had committed Russia to intolerable deprivations of human freedom. His power was naked power; his weapon was extermination; his aim the prolongation of his own dictatorship. He could write, "Put Europe to the flames"—and think nothing of it. He could decree the deaths of thousands of men, and their deaths were immaterial, because they were only statistics impeding the progress of his theory. The butchery in the cellars of the Lubyanka did not concern him. He captured the Russian Revolution and then betrayed it, and at that moment he made Stalin inevitable.[29]

In Soviet Russia, and more recently in Red China, millions of men have worked and died, sacrificing their personal goals (with a gun at their backs in case they preferred not to) in

order to achieve the "public good," the good of "the collective." They have waited in vain for this good to arrive.

That waiting has no end. The unborn profiteers of that wholesale
sacrificial slaughter will never be born. The sacrificial animals will
merely breed new hordes of sacrificial animals—as the history of all
tyrannies has demonstrated—while the unfocused eyes of a collectivized brain will stare on, undeterred, and speak of his vision of service
to mankind, mixing interchangeably the corpses of the present with the
ghosts of the future, but seeing no *men*.[30]

In the United States, free men worked to achieve their own
personal goals. And the result? Railroads that span the continent; an industrial plant that can mass-produce half the goods
that are made by men in the entire world; mass-production of
millions of items, necessities and luxuries, available in super-
markets and department stores; medical and dental expertise
second to none; a standard of living far higher than the world
has ever seen before, and such as could not even have been
dreamt of in ages past. And all of it the work of *individual*
men, working for their own *individual* goals—sometimes personal profit, sometimes love of challenge, sometimes love of
their country and the freedom one could enjoy in it, sometimes the satisfaction of seeing human beings released from
poverty and pain.

3
Economic
Liberty

For sixty known centuries, this planet that we call Earth has been inhabited by human beings not much different from ourselves. Their desire to live has been just as strong as ours. They have had at least as much physical strength as the average person of today, and among them have been men and women of great intelligence. But down through the ages, most human beings have gone hungry, and many have always starved.

The ancient Assyrians, Persians, Egyptians, and Greeks were intelligent people; but in spite of their intelligence and their fertile lands, they were never able to get enough to eat. They often killed their babies because they couldn't feed them.

The Roman Empire collapsed in famine. The French were dying of hunger when Thomas Jefferson was President of the United States. As late as 1846, the Irish were starving to death; and no one was particularly surprised because famines in the Old World were the rule rather than the exception. It is only within the last century that western Europeans have had enough food to keep them alive—soup and bread in France, fish in Scandinavia, beef in England.

Hunger has always been normal. Even to this day, famines kill multitudes in China, India, Africa; and in the 1930's, thousands upon thousands starved to death on the richest farmlands of the Soviet Union.

Down through the ages, countless millions, struggling unsuccessfully to keep bare life in wretched bodies, have died young in misery and squalor. Then suddenly, in one spot on this planet, people eat so abundantly that the pangs of hunger are forgotten.

Why did men die of starvation for 6,000 years? Why is it that we in America have never had a famine?

Why did men walk and carry goods (and other men) on their straining backs for 6,000 years—then suddenly, on only a small part of the earth's surface, the forces of nature are harnessed to do the bidding of the humblest citizen?

Why did families live for 6,000 years in caves and floorless hovels, without windows or chimneys—then within a few generations, we in America take floors, rugs, chairs, tables, windows, and chimneys for granted and regard electric lights, refrigerators, running water, porcelain baths, and toilets as common necessities?

Why did men, women, and children eke out their meager existence for 6,000 years, toiling desperately from dawn to dark—barefoot, half-naked, unwashed, unshaved, uncombed, with lousy hair, mangy skins, and rotting teeth—then suddenly, in one place on earth there is an abundance of such things as rayon underwear, nylon hose, shower baths, safety razors, ice cream sodas, lipsticks, and permanent waves.[1]

The world of today, which would be unrecognizable to anyone entering it from any previous era of history—what made it possible? In a phrase, one might answer: *the miracle of production*. There is an enormous variety of articles which technology has made possible, many of which had never been conceived of even a generation ago. And even with things that would have been familiar three centuries ago, such as houses and clothing, there is such a vast proliferation of kinds and brands and quantities of these things that our pre-industrial ancestors would have been utterly amazed. At the same time there is far less drudgery, less back-breaking toil from dawn to dusk, at least in the industrialized nations today, than there was in centuries past. *Production* has made the difference—

the enormous quantity and variety of production, to fill every material need.

But what has made this vast production take place now? Why was it not possible in the thousands of years past? There has of course always been a certain amount of production of material goods to fulfill man's needs for clothing and shelter. But the conveniences that virtually every laborer has today are greater than that which was possessed in any pre-industrial age by anyone except kings and emperors; and some things available to everyone now, such as vaccines and electricity, were not available then even to emperors. What has made them available now?

The amount of labor performed per person is no greater now—on the whole it is less. A farmer who used a hand-plow fourteen hours a day can now do the same job in an hour with a tractor. Grain that used to be threshed by hand can now be done several thousands times faster with a combine. Instead of the muscles of human beings doing the work, *the machine* now does the work, and the man has only to operate the machine. The heart of the answer is to be found in the substitution of machines for human labor, the chief function of the human beings being to design and then operate the machine. The difference between today and the other ages is the *amount that can be produced per man-hour of work*—and it is the machine which has made this production possible. Before the Industrial Revolution it took many hours of labor to produce one suit of clothes, and to buy one would take the wages of many months. Today the racks of dresses and suits in clothing stores have been made largely by machinery, and a dress can usually be bought for much less than a day's pay. It is a far cry from the days when a man could afford only one suit of clothes, and that suit was passed down from father to son; and it could not often be washed, for the use of soap would weaken the fabric and shorten the life of the suit—besides, soap was prohibitively expensive. In Hollywood movies, historical dramas are presented in which thousands of people in machine-made togas and gowns move about on highly polished marble floors amid indescribable splendor, giving audiences the impression that these things were always available; but in historical fact no such opulence was ever possible to the masses of mankind, and the few kings and pharaohs who enjoyed these luxuries required the services of hundreds or thousands of laborers or slaves to do the work that today could be performed in a small fraction of the time.

If one wants to know the degree of affluence in any society, one must ask how much goods can be produced per man-hour of work. If thousands of items can be produced today, whereas only one could be produced in the same time in previous eras, one can be sure that very few people in previous eras had them. If they were fortunate, a long day's toil could provide barely enough to keep body and soul together—with no guarantees at all for tomorrow.

Today we take this vast industrial production for granted, never having lived through a period in which it did not exist. Some of us, repelled by factory chimneys and the sight of railroad yards, like to imagine a happier age in which these things did not exist. And of course, in all but the most recent times, they didn't exist—but neither did the vast profusion of consumer goods which they make possible. People imagine that once upon a time everyone lived in an agrarian paradise, happily tilling the fields and reading by pleasant lamplight at night. But such a paradise exists solely in the imagination of wishful thinkers. The average life span was half what it is today; the labor was long and wearing and demeaning to the spirit; there was seldom enough to eat, even on the farms, never enough protection against the cold, and almost none against disease. About half the babies born did not live to maturity. Not one of us, even from the slums of a twentieth-century city, would exchange the quality of our life for that if we actually had to live it; even the poorest persons in the United States today take for granted products and services which were unknown and undreamt of during this so-called golden age.

It is important to be clear, at this point, that neither legislation nor labor unions could have produced such a change. If there had been a law two or more centuries ago forbidding anyone to work more than forty hours a week, the greater part of the human race would have starved. Why? Because the machine had not yet been developed to the point where it could relieve human beings of that much labor. If such a law had been enforced, it would have meant mass suicide. In the same way, if there had been labor unions requiring men to stop working when they had worked for forty hours that week, either the union would have had to collapse or its members would have had to starve—for no one could eke out a living by working so little. It was not the imposition of some human wills upon others, to limit their working hours, that led to the vastly improved workers' conditions of today; it was the fact that, thanks to the machine, a smaller amount of work can now turn out a vastly greater amount of production. How could such legislation, and such unions, have improved the standard of living of the medieval worker, without power tools, without electricity, without anything but a few crude implements and the work of his hands and his body? "The power capacity already being exerted by the steam engines of the world in existence and working in the year 1887 has been estimated by the Bureau of Statistics at Berlin as equivalent to that of 200 million horses, representing approximately one billion men; or at least three times the working population of the earth."[2] How many hours of toil of how many donkeys around a treadmill do you think it would take to provide the energy provided by the electricity used in one day in one American city?

It is true that life was grim in the early stages of the Industrial Revolution. Hours were long and wages small—they could be nothing else, for the employers in the new factories had so little reserve against disaster that if they had doubled the wages they paid they would have had to close down. Yet grim as conditions were then, people voluntarily came in large numbers from the farms to the factories because they could make a better living in the factories. Young children labored in these factories, true; but parents made them do this to earn extra money to keep the family ahead. It was not legislation which put an end to these conditions, but the gradually increasing *capital accumulation* of the employers' enterprises; year by year, decade by decade, the reserve of capital increased, labor-saving machinery was devised, and it was possible to pay higher wages—higher not merely in money but in the things that the money would buy. And gradually a life became possible even for the most humble worker, which while poor by the standards of twentieth-century America, was paradise compared with what it had been in centuries past.[3]

In all centuries prior to the Industrial Revolution, the population of the world increased very little. It is not that people had sexual relations less frequently than now; it is simply that many more people were born than could survive. The excess people born died through disease, malnutrition, and starvation. There was not enough production of life's essential goods to support them, so they died—it was as simple as that. But between the beginning of the nineteenth century and the end of it, the population of the world doubled; and it has doubled again since that time. How was this enormous increase possible? How could they live, these thousands who in every preceding generation would have died? Only because more production was achieved per man-hour of labor, thanks to the machine; only because of the gains in production made possible by the Industrial Revolution, and which continue to this day. There are more American Indians today than there were when the first settlers came. But with fewer than a million Indians in the seventeenth century, there was already an overpopulation problem. They had no machinery, of course, and in many cases no agricultural production at all. Most of them survived by hunting with simple weapons, and the vast land mass of the United States could sustain only that small population. Consider any metropolitan area in the U.S. today, such as Los Angeles. Here are millions of people in a few square miles. If they had to scrounge off the land, which is a desert, almost all of them would starve, if they did not first die of thirst from the lack of water in the area. Those today who scoff at our present economy and repudiate all these advances would be not only dead wrong, but dead. In a pre-industrial economy, the entire area of the United States would be insufficient to keep a million people alive.

It is enlarged production, then, that is the key, providing people with the vast quantity of produce they want and need, and which relieves life of much of its drudgery. But now let us go back a step further: how did this vast production by machines come about? Obviously someone had to invent the machines; invention is required before we can enjoy the benefits of mass production. And invention is something that takes place only in the minds of creative men.

Now as long as mankind has existed there have been creative men. There has been no lack of human inventiveness. But in most ages of mankind's history the genius of these men has fallen on barren soil. The conditions required for bringing about an improvement in man's life did not prevail. What were these conditions?

First an atmosphere of *liberty* was essential, in which people could investigate any areas they wished—to work, experiment, and compare notes with other men, without interference from their governments or the Church, when the Church was identical with the government. During the time that the Church permitted no dissection of cadavers, very little advance in medical science was possible. Untold millions of lives were lost through pestilence, plague, and disease, until such time as men could devote their inventive talents to a study of the body. Similarly, modern engineering would have been impossible without the prior development of physics. And this occurred through the creative thinking of men such as Galileo, who usually suffered condemnation, excommunication, sometimes torture and death for their efforts. But slowly, through a handful of men, working in an increasing atmosphere of freedom to think and to experiment, modern science and its resultant technology became a reality.

But it is one thing to invent something, and another to make it available to masses of men. Between the invention of the steam engine, and the existence of railroads spanning a continent, there is an enormous gap. Between the invention of a process for the manufacture of steel, and the actual use of that process in factories around the world, there is a gap. The gap is filled by many hundreds or thousands of men who (though perhaps not geniuses) are inventive and productive in other ways—those who can take the ideas of others and put them to commercial use through the facilities of mass-production. After someone has devised a method for extracting aluminum from bauxite, someone else starts a factory for the mass-production of aluminum products and millions of people consequently can buy aluminum products. After Eli Whitney invented the cotton gin, thousands of them were manufactured, and the cost of cotton goods came within reach of even the poorest individuals in the land.

But to start a factory and to install large and complex machines takes much planning and a great deal of capital. It may be years before the man who initiates these moves is out of debt, and still more years before he turns a penny of profit. Besides, countless things may go wrong: the demand for the product may not be what he anticipated, or someone else may think of it first and outsell him, or the process of mass-producing the item may not be as foolproof as he thought, so that the products cannot be made, or made as cheaply, as he thought. The entrepreneur who undertakes these jobs is the *risk-taker* of a society, laying all his capital on the line and borrowing more in the hopes that the enterprise will succeed. Moreover, once factories are built they cannot easily be moved; so before he will take such risks, of course, he wants to be quite sure that he will not be taxed to death once he breaks even, and that his property will not be expropriated by the government after all his capital expenditures and years of planning.

If the risks are to be worth taking, the entrepreneur must live in a country that is politically stable; his property rights must be secure, so that he can start a major enterprise without fear of losing all he has through nationalization or excessive taxation. Only then can he go ahead with confidence and begin to be economically productive. Then he can borrow money with some fair chance of his enterprise turning a profit so that he can return the money with interest; then he can start up a factory or a processing plant or a chain of stores. Then he can produce steel for buildings and mechanical equipment, or wood for houses and paper, or any of a million other products. Then he can mass-produce his products so that thousands or millions of them can come into existence where few or none existed before—lowering the prices through mass-production, so that great masses of people can afford to buy them. The person who sells the product uses the money he gets from this transaction to buy other things from other individuals, and this in turn requires the work of other producers similar to himself in other areas of productive activity. Each producer —both managers and workers—trades his goods or services on the free market, that is, the market regulated not by bureaucratic decisions but by the natural law of supply and demand. Thus the free-enterprise system, or capitalism, is born.

Capitalism is the economic system of freedom to produce and freedom to trade the products of one's labor on the free (open) market. Freedom of *production* and *trade* is the essence of the capitalistic system. Equally important is the freedom of individuals to keep the fruits of their labor: if people were free to produce and trade, but not free to keep what they had earned, there would be no incentive to produce and the system of economic liberty (capitalism) would not function.

In the capitalist system, the supply of a product tends to meet the demand. If there is not enough of product X to meet the demand for it, those who are producing X will expand their facilities and hire additional workers; and other would-be producers would enter the arena and produce it as well. Once they are competing with each other, the supply of the product increases and the price comes down, which usually means that more people will buy product X. When the demand is satisfied and more of X is produced than the buying public wants, the price comes down below the point at which it is profitable to produce it, and production of it tapers off until the demand and the supply are in equilibrium.

Capitalism might also be called a system of *economic democracy*. Every time a housewife goes to the supermarket and buys, let us say, twenty products from the shelves, she is casting a vote for these products. The plebiscite is going on every day in every store in the land. The products that receive the most votes are the ones whose producers reap the most profits, with the result that more of these products get produced in order to meet the demand. Competitors who are less efficient either make less profit or are forced to get out of the business entirely for lack of profit. And thus inefficient production gives way to efficient production.

The efficient producer is the gainer in all this, of course, but so is the *consumer*, for because of this efficiency the manufacturer can get the product to him at a lower price (or a higher price for one of higher quality). In the free market the consumer is king. This does not mean that the manufacturer is his slave, for the manufacturer freely undertakes to go into his enterprise with a hope of turning a profit, but that the consumer is the *final arbiter* of what products get produced and in what quantity. If enough Mrs. Jonses don't like Drudge Soap, they won't buy it, and for lack of profit Drudge Soap will no longer be made; but if enough Mrs. Joneses prefer Sludge Soap to any other, more of it will get made in order to meet the demand and turn a profit for the Sludge Soap Company. The manufacturer cannot make a profit without the cooperation of the consumer, for it is the consumer who lays down the money from which the manufacturer must glean his profit. If most of them do not want product X, in vain will the manufacturer remonstrate that product X is the best one. Even if X is really superior to Y, but Y is more attractively packaged or more convincingly sold, the manufacturers of X will give way to the manufacturers of Y. In an economic democracy there is no appeal from the decision of the consumers.

Under the conditions of peace that would prevail if government performed its proper offices, every consumer is a king, of sorts. All those who have anything to sell court his favor; each vies with the other to

give greater quantity and higher quality at lower cost. The legend that
the customer is always right might well be rendered "the consumer is
always right," for the great cater to his whims, and the mighty are
brought low by his adverse decisions. There is daily evidence of this in
our lives in America. The daily mail brings its catalogs or circulars de-
scribing a vast variety of merchandise available at my command; the
merchants have stocked their shelves in anticipation of my wishes; the
salesmen may even beset me with persuasive arguments, so eager are
they to satisfy my desires and have my custom. Indeed, advertisers wax
poetic in the description of their wares thinking by some means to lure
my trade their way. The business which does not serve the desires of its
customers will lose out and fail, no matter how great the name of its
founder, how far-flung its establishments, or how numerous its salesmen. If men may not use fraud and violence, the consumer is king.[4]

There is a great deal of misunderstanding about this point.
People often talk as if there were some conspiracy among
manufacturers to sell one kind of product while the consumers
want a different kind. At the present moment consumers are
busy blaming automobile manufacturers for not providing
them with safer cars. But the fact is that car-buyers get pretty
much what they are willing to pay for. If most consumers
wanted safer cars, and were willing to pay a somewhat higher
price to get them (since it costs more to make them), that is
what the car-manufacturers would produce. People sometimes
talk as if the manufacturers could make enormous amounts of
money manufacturing safer cars but that out of sheer perversi-
ty they refuse to do so. But this is a delusion. If cars now are
not as safe as they could be made, this is because the vast majority of the buying public does not want them safer—when
the chips are down they prefer the lower price and less safety.
In fact, for many years the sales have gone to the fastest cars
with the highest horsepower and the most streamlined design
rather than the ones with more safety features—and the car-

manufacturers, responding to the public demand, make them the way the public wants them.

There are many kinds and qualities of cars, some cheaper, some less so; some more safe, some less safe; some with much chrome, some with little or none, and so on—each one appealing to a different segment of the market. When the market is as huge as it is in America, the manufacturer can mass-produce each of these kinds and still make a profit on them. But when he miscalculates the public taste, as with the Edsel, he loses heavily, for once again, the consumer is king. If most buyers wanted their cars yellow, manufacturers would make them yellow; and if most consumers wanted collapsible steering-wheels and non-protruding dashboards, the manufacturers would do this also. If it is technically possible for the manufacturer to produce a specific product, and there is good reason to believe that enough people will buy it, there is no reason for the manufacturer *not* to produce it.

The situation is, of course, quite different in government-controlled economies where factories are government-owned and the decision as to what products are to be made is determined not by market conditions but by government-employed bureaucrats. The bureaucrats need pay no attention to the consumers' demands at all. Most consumers may want product A, and yet it may not be made; and product B, which they don't much care for, will be made instead—and since they are prohibited from entering into production themselves, there is nothing they can do about it. Since no manufacturer in such an economy stands to lose his own money if his product doesn't sell, it doesn't matter if the product doesn't meet with consumer approval; the consumer is just out of luck: there is no competing producer to whom he can turn, for the government controls all production and has a monopoly on it. If the product is shoddily made and falls apart after a few uses (as is typically the case in a government-controlled economy), again it is no skin off the producer's back—the product is financed by the government, that is, by increased taxation upon everyone. And thus the consumer pays twice over—once for a shoddy product that he wouldn't have chosen to buy on the free market in the first place, and again, in taxes to help recoup the losses to the government in making it.

On the free market, by contrast, any manufacturer who offers a shoddy product is in danger. He may deceive his customers for a while, particularly if he has developed a good reputation in the past, but as more and more customers become dissatisfied with his product they will cease to buy it. The manufacturers and store-owners who fare best in the long run are those who offer the best products at the lowest price, and who are willing to stand by the products that they sell, repairing or replacing them if they are defective. Only in this way can they develop a reputation that will endure through the years, and keep customers coming back again and again to buy. How, for example, could Sears Roebuck have grown into a multi-billion dollar company if it regularly sold shoddy or defective products and refused to replace them? The company has doubtless shortchanged some customers and left others unsatisfied, but if it had done this on a large scale in comparison with other companies, it would gradually have lost out to them in competition, even if it had established a good reputation at the beginning.

We have, then, in the capitalistic system of production and trade, a marvelous automatic machine for causing supply to meet demand.

The private enterprise system might be compared to thousands of machines, each regulated by its own quasi-automatic governor, yet with these machines and their governors all interconnected and influencing each other, so that they act in effect like one great machine. Most of us must have noticed the automatic "governor" on a steam engine. It usually consists of two balls or weights which work by centrifugal force. As the speed of the engine increases, these balls fly away from the rod to which they are attached and so automatically narrow or close off a throttle valve which regulates the intake of steam and thus slows down the engine. If the engine goes too slowly, on the other hand, the balls drop, widen the throttle valve, and increase the engine's speed. Thus every departure from the desired speed itself sets in motion the forces that tend to correct that departure.

It is precisely in this way that the relative supply of thousands of different commodities is regulated under the system of competitive private enterprise. When people want more of a commodity, their competitive bidding raises its price. This increases the profits of the producers who make that product. This stimulates them to increase their production. It leads others to stop making some of the products they previously made, and turn to making the product that offers them the better return. But this increases the supply of that commodity at the same time that it reduces the supply of some other commodities. The price of that product therefore falls in relation to the price of other products, and the stimulus to the relative increase in its production disappears.[5]

The free market—freedom in exchange, with prices freely responsive to changing supply and demand—is, in fact, an enormous computer, far superior to any electronic computer man has ever devised or ever will. Data from all over the world, of the most varied and complex nature—only fragments of which any one man or set of men can even be aware of, let alone assemble and feed into it—are automatically and quickly processed, answers coming out as prices. These prices are, in effect, stop and go signals which clearly say to all would-be enterprisers: "Go into this activity at once, the supply is comparatively short and the demand is comparatively heavy" or "Get out of this activity now, the supply is comparatively bountiful and the demand is comparatively negligible. . . ."

Tomatoes, let us say, are suddenly in "short supply." Millions of people relish this fruit, and, thus, the demand continues high. The few growers fortunate enough to have escaped the destructive blight discover that they can sell their small supply for two dollars per pound—and they do! Salad lovers who cannot afford to pay this "exorbitant" price

are inclined to think unfavorably of these growers: "Why, they're highway robbers." Yet these fortunate few are only adhering closely to the
computer's instructions; they are behaving precisely as you and I act
when we accept an increase in our wages. . . .

Assuming the market to be free, what would happen in this situation? Several corrective forces would automatically and immediately go
to work. First, the high price, with promises of exceptional profit,
would entice others to grow tomatoes; and even more important, it
would lead to the development of blight-resistant strains. In the shortest
possible time, there would be tomatoes galore, perhaps at a dollar a
bushel—within the reach of all.

For contrast, imagine the other extreme: a law to keep the price at
its old level. What would be the probable results? At that price there
would be little incentive for new tomato growers to enter the field.
And, thus, *favoritism* instead of prices would necessarily determine the
allocation of the reduced supply of tomatoes.[6]

The price of products on the free market is not the result of
an arbitrary decision by bureaucrats. It is the result of the laws
of supply and demand, which operate impersonally and to the
benefit of consumers, supplying them with the products they
want, or at least the products they want most, given their ability to buy. It is the only economic system geared to the satisfaction of men's wants.

To read most newspapers these days, one would think that
the history of the United States is nothing but a series of dismal failures. We are constantly reminded of our failures at
home—many of which, of course, stem from the very government intervention which these same editorial writers advocate.

Failure at home indeed. Is it failure to have converted an empty continent in two centuries into the most prosperous and thriving area in
the world? Is it failure to have absorbed the "poor" of Europe by the
teeming millions and to have converted them into affluent middle-class
citizens? Is it failure to have produced the most extensive network of
private eleemosynary [charitable] institutions in the world? The most

extensive system of higher education? To have a larger fraction of the population go to college than any other nation?

Seldom if ever has there been a success story like ours. Consider the third of a century from 1880 to 1914. Population doubled from 50 million to 100 million, as more than 22 million immigrants came to our shores. Most came with little besides the clothes on their backs—plus two hands and the urge to improve their lot and the lot of their children. Not only were they absorbed but their level of living as well as that of the rest of the population rose by leaps and bounds. And all this —let present-day liberals note—without any governmental wars on poverty, graduated income taxes, and burgeoning bureaucracies. This was a triumph of participatory democracy—the right kind, voluntary cooperation coordinated by a free market.[7]

Capitalism and Selfishness

But capitalism, it is said, is an economic system dedicated to selfishness. This charge, more than anything else, is the reason for the opprobrium popularly attached to it, and the reason why "social engineers" get by with dismissing it so casually without ever going into specific detail about how it functions.

The word "selfish" is popularly employed as a term of abuse, in which the evil of selfishness is something taken for granted without question. The present work is on political philosophy and not on moral philosophy; nevertheless it is worth pointing out that the person who hurls the charge very seldom considers what forms or kinds of selfishness there may be. If being selfish is being concerned with the needs and interests of one's self, then no one who is *not* thus concerned could remain alive for a single day, unless he could count on others to minister to his interests as well as their own. Normally a person must see to it that *he* has food and clothing and shelter, and such of the other goods of life as he is able to procure; once this is done, it is difficult or impossible for him to provide for the needs of others beyond a very limited few, such as his family, unless, like the owner of a business enterprise with hundreds of employees, he receives some return (profits from the industry) for providing them with a livelihood. Unlimited beneficence, even the attempt to care for (without return) a large number of others, must inevitably result in the poverty or bankruptcy of the benefactor. Each person's concern is and must be first and foremost a selfish one—one whose goal is the continued existence and well-being of himself and his family —if he and his family are to remain alive; this is simply a fact of reality, the nature of the "human condition." People who advocate anything other than this are living in a realm of floating abstractions unconnected with man's actual situation on this planet and the choices actually open to him in real-life situations.

Capitalism is a selfish system in the sense that it is the one socio-economic system that recognizes each individual's right to pursue his own self-interest. To produce for profit, and trade one's product or service non-coercively on a free market, is the means to greater wealth than any other economic system ever designed by man—this is a lesson that history teaches beyond the slightest shadow of a doubt. Nor is it true that capitalism is necessarily "materialistic": an individual is free to spend the money he has earned on symphony concerts just as much as on yachts; he can even build and sustain a concert hall or a cathedral if he has the money. What he does with the money he earns is up to him; it can be put to a "spiritual" as well as a "material" use if he so chooses.

But the most important point, one that is constantly ignored by capitalism's critics, is that he cannot obtain his money on the free market unless he has a product or service that other people will pay for because the product serves *their* needs or desires. If he amassed a million dollars by inventing a beauty aid for aging women, well, then he served them in providing for them what they wanted—they wouldn't have given him the money for just doing nothing; he clearly provided them with something they were willing to pay for. Maybe they *shouldn't* have wanted it, but what bureaucrat has the right to dictate what they *should* want? Anyway, they *did* want it, and they wanted it enough to pay him for the product he offered them. There is all the difference in the world between the robber who takes property from people by force, and the entrepreneur who exchanges goods and services for money on the free market— and who stands to lose his skin if people don't buy the product he may have spent a fortune producing. Yet both of these men are popularly lumped together under the heading of "selfish."

Very well, we say, the entrepreneur is selfish—he wants to make a living—he *has* to make a living—and his concept of how to do it involves much expenditure of time, effort, and money, and, incidentally, the employment of numerous other people, who earn their living as a result. If he fails, he loses everything; if he succeeds, he makes a profit; and if he succeeds spectacularly, he makes a spectacular profit. And why not? It was his time, his money, his effort—so who has the right to take it away from him? He is entitled to every bit of his selfish reward. But he doesn't get one penny of this selfish reward unless he has placed on the market a product or service for which the consuming public will pay. He cannot earn a dime without their voluntary purchase of whatever it is he has to offer. In other words, on the free market he cannot serve himself without first serving others.

What I say applies to the man who obtains his fortunes on the free (uncoerced) market—without any help from the gov-

ernment. The businessman who can't make it on his own, who
lobbies or bribes the legislature into subsidizing him, is forcing
every taxpayer in the land to give up a portion of his income to
pay for something that he wouldn't willingly buy on the open
market. To the extent that a businessman does this, he is morally no different from the gunman who steals your wallet or
your jewelry. Both have taken from you a portion of your
earnings which you would not have given them voluntarily.

But now suppose you are not an egoist, but an ethical altruist, believing you should live entirely to serve others. The altruist typically despises the man who has a large income; but
in all consistency he shouldn't. It isn't merely that the man
with a large income has more that he can give to others (if he
earned nothing, he would have nothing to give, so the chances
of the needy are greater with him if he earns a lot). The main
point is that in order to get the large income on a free market,
he has already had to serve the interests of others. If Vanderbilt earned a million dollars by building his railroad, he had to
serve others in order to get the million dollars: they would
have paid him nothing if he had provided no service. His possession of the million is already evidence of his socially important deed—not necessarily intention, but deed. In fact, as
Murray Rothbard has pointed out,[8] if a well-paid coal-miner
decides to take a lower-paying but more pleasant job as a grocery clerk, the consistent altruist ought to condemn him for
depriving his fellow men of the benefit he was conferring on
them by mining coal. The fact that he got more money for
mining coal shows that his services as a coal-miner were worth
more to consumers than are his present services as a grocery
clerk. And his purpose in life is to serve others in the best
possible way, isn't it?

Capitalism and the Jungle

The free market, many critics claim, is "the rule of the jungle," where "the survival of the fittest" is the only law.

But the free market is the very opposite of the "jungle." When not involved with government, it is characterized by peaceful competition. If a man miscalculates and starts a second grocery store in a village where one grocery store is all that the market will bear, the second one goes under—that is true. The failure is a result of the man's miscalculation, based on his own free decision. Either he must bear the consequences of the failure himself (as capitalism requires), or every taxpayer in the land must be called upon to pay a few cents more in taxes to protect him against the loss (as the welfare state requires—and if a man is thus cushioned against loss, there will be many more losing enterprises). In the real, literal jungle, there is a struggle for survival in which the stronger crushes his weaker foe, but in the free market one man gains wealth only through serving the consumers best, as determined by the opinion of those very consumers themselves.

"Survival of the fittest." Is this equivocation to be foisted on us forever? Fitness for what? "The 'fit' in the jungle are those [who are] most adept at the exercise of brute force. The 'fit' on the market are those most adept in the service of society [consumers]."[9] In the jungle, "some seize from others and all live at the starvation level; the market is a peaceful and productive place where all serve themselves *and* others at the same time and live at infinitely higher levels of consumption. On the market, the charitable can provide a luxury that cannot exist in the jungle.

"The free market . . . transmutes the jungle's destructive competition for meager subsistence into a peaceful *cooperative* competition in the service of one's self *and* others. In the jungle, some gain only at the expense of others. On the market, everyone gains. It is the market—the contractual society—that wrests order out of chaos, that subdues natures and *eradicates* the jungle, that permits the 'weak' to live productively, or out of gifts from production, and in a regal style compared to the life of the 'strong' in the jungle. Furthermore, the market, by raising living standards, permits man the leisure to cultivate the very qualities of civilization that distinguish him from the brutes."[10]

No, it is the rise of government control over ever increasing sectors of the lives of individuals that is bringing back the jungle. We shall examine some varieties of government control in the next chapter.

4
Economic Liberty and Government

In most nations of the world, there is what is called the "public sector" and the "private sector." More accurate labels would be the *coerced* sector and the *uncoerced* or *free* sector. In the uncoerced sector—that is, the free market—we have only voluntary exchange. In the coerced sector, conditions are imposed on the free market by government which distort the market and impede its efficiency.

In the capitalistic system of the free market, all economic relations between people are in the form of voluntary exchange. Capitalism is a system of *voluntary exchange*—of goods or products, for other goods or products or money. Ordinarily at least, the exchange is to the benefit of both parties, else they would not effect it. The wages are worth more to the grocery clerk than the labor he gives in exchange; and the labor the grocer receives from his clerk is worth more to him, in his situation, than the wages he expends. But the intervention of government has the effect of inhibiting and impeding these voluntary exchanges.

There is no subject on which there is more popular misunderstanding than the consequences of government intervention in the free market. One could spend years dispelling one confusion and fallacy after another, and others arise to replace those that were eliminated. Yet nothing is more important for our conception of a free society than that we try to eliminate these confusions and fallacies.

Of all the insights into the functioning of an economy, the most important is the distinction between *what is seen* and *what is not seen*. In fact, one might say that the science of economics is a study of what happens vs. what would have happened *if* certain conditions had been met. The distinction is admirably illustrated by the "broken window fallacy" in the writings of the great nineteenth-century French economist Frédéric Bastiat, whose discussion of the issue is so simple and lucid that it would be impossible to improve on his presentation of it.

Suppose that a boy hurls a brick through a pane of glass in someone's house. One would think, and quite rightly, that the broken pane is a loss, for it will cost something to have it replaced. But now someone comes up with the bright idea that the event is not a loss but a gain. "Such accidents keep industry going. Everybody has to make a living. What would become of the glaziers if no one ever broke a window?"[1] Now, says Bastiat,

Suppose that it will cost six francs to repair the damage. If you mean that the accident gives six francs' worth of encouragement to the glazier, I agree. . . . The glazier will come, do his job, receive six francs, congratulate himself, and bless in his heart the careless child. *That is what is seen.*

But if you conclude . . . that it is good to break windows, that it helps to circulate money, that it results in encouraging industry in general, I am obliged to cry out: That will never do! Your theory stops at *what is seen*. It does not take account of *what is not seen*.

It is not seen that, since our citizen has spent six francs for one thing, he will not be able to spend them for another. *It is not seen* that if he had not had a windowpane to replace, he would have replaced, for example, his worn-out shoes or added another book to his library. In brief, he would have put his six francs to some use or other for which he will not now have them.

Let us next consider industry *in general.* The window having been broken, the glass industry gets six francs' worth of encouragement; *that is what is seen.*

If the window had not been broken, the shoe industry (or some other) would have received six francs' worth of encouragement; *that is what is not seen.*

And if we were to take into consideration *what is not seen,* because it is a negative factor, as well as *what is seen* because it is a positive factor, we should understand that there is no benefit to industry *in general* or to *national employment* as a whole, whether windows are broken or not broken.

Now let us consider James Goodfellow.

On the first hypothesis, that of the broken window, he spends six francs and has, neither more nor less than before, the enjoyment of one window.

On the second, that in which the accident did not happen, he would have spent six francs for new shoes and would have had the enjoyment of a pair of shoes *as well as* of a window. . . .

There are not only two people, but three, in the little drama that I have presented. The one, James Goodfellow, represents the consumer, reduced by destruction to one enjoyment instead of two. The other, under the figure of the glazier, shows us the producer whose industry the accident encourages. The third is the shoemaker (or any other manufacturer) whose industry is correspondingly discouraged by the same cause. It is this third person who is always in the shadow, and who, personifying *what is not seen,* is an essential element of the problem. It is he who makes us understand how absurd it is to see a profit in destruction.[2]

P. S.: If the loss of one window is an economic gain, why not break every window in the entire city—wouldn't that then be more of a gain? Why not applaud at the approach of hurricanes, tornadoes, and bombing raids? But the fact is too obvious: these are losses, not gains—they may be a temporary gain to a special group, such as the building industry, but the level of wealth in the community is lower, not higher, as a result. With the money that was used to replace the glass, other things could have been purchased that now cannot be purchased; and the merchants who would have gained by these purchases will now not see these gains.

Second example: A nation raises, at the taxpayers' expense, an army to meet an emergency. But now the emergency is over, and the army, or most of it, can disband. And now someone will present an argument that will sound persuasive to the economically unwary:

"Discharge a hundred thousand men! What are you thinking of? What will become of them? What will they live on? On their earnings? But do you not know that there is unemployment everywhere? That all occupations are oversupplied? Do you wish to throw them on the market to increase the competition and to depress wage rates? Just at the moment when it is difficult to earn a meager living, is it not fortunate that the state is giving bread to a hundred thousand individuals? Consider further that the army consumes wine, clothes, and weapons, that it thus spreads business to the factories and the garrison towns, and that it is nothing less than a godsend to its innumerable suppliers. Do you not tremble at the idea of bringing this immense industrial activity to an end?" . . .

A hundred thousand men, costing the taxpayers a hundred million francs, live as well and provide as good a living for their suppliers as a hundred million francs will allow: *that is what is seen.*

But a hundred million francs, coming from the pockets of the taxpayers, ceases to provide a living for these taxpayers and *their* suppliers, to the extent of a hundred million francs; *that is what is not seen.* Calculate, figure, and tell me where there is any profit for the mass of the people.

I will, for my part tell you where the *loss* is, and to simplify things, instead of speaking of a hundred thousand men and a hundred million francs, let us talk about one man and a thousand francs.

Here we are in the village of A. The recruiters make the rounds and muster one man. The tax collectors make their rounds also and raise a thousand francs. The man and the sum are transported to Metz, the one destined to keep the other alive for a year without doing anything. If you look only at Metz, yes, you are right a hundred times; the procedure is very advantageous. But if you turn your eyes to the village of A, you will judge otherwise, for, unless you are blind, you will see that this village has lost a laborer and the thousand francs that would remunerate his labor, and the business which, through the spending of these thousand francs, he would spread about him.

At first glance it seems as if the loss is compensated. What took place at the village now takes place at Metz, and that is all there is to it. But here is where the loss is. In the village a man dug and labored: he was a worker; at Metz he goes through 'Right dress!' and 'Left dress!': he is a soldier. The money involved and its circulation are the same in both cases: but in one there were three hundred days of productive labor; in the other there are three hundred days of unproductive labor, on the supposition, of course, that a part of the army is not indispensable to public security.

Now comes demobilization. You point out to me a surplus of a hundred thousand workers, intensified competition, and the pressure that it exerts on wage rates. That is what you see.

But here is what you do not see. You do not see that to send home a hundred thousand soldiers is not to do away with a hundred million francs, but to return that money to the taxpayers. You do not see that to throw a hundred thousand workers on the market in this way is to throw in at the same time the hundred million francs destined to pay for their labor; that, as a consequence, the same measure that increases the supply of workers also increases the demand; from which it follows that your lowering of wages is illusory. You do not see that before, as well as after, the demobilization there are a hundred million francs corresponding to the hundred thousand men; that the whole difference consists in this: that before, the country gives the hundred million francs to the hundred thousand men for doing nothing; afterwards, it gives them the money for working. Finally, you do not see that when a taxpayer gives his money, whether to a soldier in exchange for nothing or to a worker in exchange for something, all the more remote consequences of the circulation of this money are the same in both cases: only in the second case the taxpayer receives something; in the first he receives nothing. Result: a dead loss for the nation.

The sophism that I am attacking here cannot withstand the test of extended application, which is the touchstone of all theoretical principles. If, all things considered, there is a national profit in increasing the size of the army, why not call the whole male population of the country to the colors?[3]

Third example: Taxes

Have you ever heard anyone say: "Taxes are the best investment; they are a life-giving dew. See how many families they keep alive, and follow in imagination their indirect effects on industry; they are infinite, as extensive as life itself."

The advantages that government officials enjoy in drawing their salaries are what is seen. The benefits that result for their suppliers are also what is seen. They are right under your nose.

But the disadvantage that the taxpayers try to free themselves from is *what is not seen,* and the distress that results from it for the merchants who supply them is *something further that is not seen,* although it should stand out plainly enough to be seen intellectually.

When a government official spends on his own behalf one hundred sous more, this implies that a taxpayer spends on his own behalf one hundred sous the less. But the spending of the government official *is seen,* because it is done; while that of the taxpayer *is not seen,* because —alas!—he is prevented from doing it.

You compare the nation to a parched piece of land and the tax to a life-giving rain. So be it. But you should also ask yourself where this rain comes from, and whether it is not precisely the tax that draws the moisture from the soil and dries it up.

You should ask yourself further whether the soil receives more of this precious water from the rain than it loses by the evaporation?

When James Goodfellow gives a hundred sous to a government official for a really useful service, this is exactly the same as when he gives a hundred sous to a shoemaker for a pair of shoes. It's a case of give-and-take, and the score is even. But when James Goodfellow hands over a hundred sous to a government official to receive no service for it or even to be subjected to inconveniences, it is as if he were to give his money to a thief. It serves no purpose to say that the official will spend these hundred sous for the great profit of our *national industry;*

the more the thief can do with them, the more James Goodfellow could have done with them if he had not met on his way either the extralegal or the legal parasite.

Let us accustom ourselves, then, not to judge things solely by *what is seen,* but rather by *what is not seen.*[4]

Fourth example: Public works

Nothing is more natural than that a nation, after making sure that a great enterprise will profit the community, should have such an enterprise carried out with funds collected from the citizenry. But I lose patience completely, I confess, when I hear alleged in support of such a resolution this economic fallacy: "Besides, it is a way of creating jobs for the workers."

The state opens a road, builds a palace, repairs a street, digs a canal; with these projects it gives jobs to certain workers. *That is what is seen.* But it deprives certain other laborers of employment. *That is what is not seen.*

Suppose a road is under construction. A thousand laborers arrive every morning, go home every evening, and receive their wages; that is certain. If the road had not been authorized, if funds for it had not been voted, these good people would have neither found this work nor earned these wages; that again is certain.

But is that all? Taken all together, does not the operation involve something else? At the moment when M. Dupin pronounces the sacramental words: "The Assembly has adopted, ..." do millions of francs descend miraculously on a moonbeam into the coffers of M. Fould and M. Bineau? For the process to be complete, does not the state have to organize the collection of funds as well as their expenditure? Does it not have to get its tax collectors into the country and its taxpayers to make their contribution?

Study the question, then, from its two aspects. In noting what the state is going to do with the millions of francs voted, do not neglect to note also what the taxpayers would have done—and can no longer do —with these same millions. You see, then, that a public enterprise is a coin with two sides. On one, the figure of a busy worker, with this device: *What is seen;* on the other, an unemployed worker, with this device: *What is not seen. . . .*[5]

Fifth example: Machines

James Goodfellow had two francs that he let two workers earn.

But now suppose that he devises an arrangement of ropes and weights that will shorten the work by half.

Then he obtains the same satisfaction, saves a franc, and discharges a worker.

He discharges a worker: *that is what is seen.*

Seeing only this, people say: "See how misery follows civilization! See how freedom is fatal to equality! The human mind has made a conquest, and immediately another worker has forever fallen into the abyss of poverty. Perhaps James Goodfellow can still continue to have both men work for him, but he cannot give them more than ten sous each, for they will compete with one another and will offer their services at a lower rate. This is how the rich get richer and the poor become poorer. We must remake society."

A fine conclusion, and one worthy of the initial premise!

Fortunately, both premise and conclusion are false, because behind the half of the phenomenon *that is seen* is the other half *that is not seen.*

The franc saved by James Goodfellow and the necessary effects of this saving are not seen.

Since, as a result of his own invention, James Goodfellow no longer spends more than one franc for manual labor in the pursuit of a given satisfaction, he has another franc left over.

If, then, there is somewhere an idle worker who offers his labor on the market, there is also somewhere a capitalist who offers his idle franc. These two elements meet and combine.

And it is clear as day that between the supply of and the demand for labor, between the supply of and the demand for wages, the relationship has in no way changed.

The invention and the worker, paid with the first franc, now do the work previously accomplished by two workers.

The second worker, paid with the second franc, performs some new work.

What has then been changed in the world? There is one national satisfaction the more; in other words, the invention is a gratuitous conquest, a gratuitous profit for mankind.

From the form in which I have given my demonstration we could draw this conclusion:

"It is the capitalist who derives all the benefits flowing from the invention of machines. The laboring class, even though it suffers from them only temporarily, never profits from them, since, according to what you yourself say, they *reallocate* a portion of the nation's industry without *diminishing* it, it is true, but also without *increasing* it."

It is not within the province of this essay to answer all objections. Its only object is to combat an ignorant prejudice, very dangerous and extremely widespread. I wished to prove that a new machine, in making a certain number of workers available for jobs, *necessarily* makes available at the same time the money that pays them. These workers and this money get together eventually to produce something that was impossible to produce before the invention; from which it follows that *the final result of the invention is an increase in satisfactions with the same amount of labor.*

Who reaps this excess of satisfactions?

Yes, at first it is the capitalist, the inventor, the first one who uses the machine successfully, and this is the reward for his genius and daring. In this case, as we have just seen, he realizes a saving on the costs of production, which, no matter how it is spent (and it always is), gives employment to just as many hands as the machine has made idle.

But soon competition forces him to lower his selling price by the amount of this saving itself.

And then it is no longer the inventor who reaps the benefits of the invention; it is the buyer of the product, the consumer, the public, including the worker—in a word, it is mankind.

And *what is not seen* is that the saving, thus procured for all the consumers, forms a fund from which wages can be drawn, replacing what the machine has drained off.

Thus (taking up again the foregoing example), James Goodfellow obtains a product by spending two francs for wages.

Thanks to his invention, the manual labor now costs him only one franc.

As long as he sells the product at the same price, there is one worker the fewer employed in making this special product: *that is what is seen;* but there is one worker the more employed by the franc James Goodfellow has saved: *that is what is not seen.*[6]

And so it goes. The theme could be repeated ad infinitum. The point is simple, yet politicians never seem to learn it, or when they do, they usually ignore it for political reasons.

"Raise taxes and spend money on Project X!" Now, Project
X, considered in itself, may or may not be a worthwhile one—
that depends on what it is, and each one must be examined on
its merits. But one argument that will *not* hold water is, "Raise
taxes and spend money on Project X, because this will give
people more work!" The government can give to some only by
taking it away from others. Specifically, before the man who
has earned it can glean any satisfaction from it, the state intervenes to take it away from him—and give it to someone else,
(retaining a percentage for handling the operation). And, as if
to pour salt into the wound, the apologists for the state then
argue, "With this money we will put more men to work!" Let
us listen to Bastiat once more:

"The state gives a detestable reason when it says, 'With these hundred
sous I am going to put some men to work,' for James Goodfellow (as
soon as he has seen the light) will not fail to respond: 'Good Lord! With
a hundred sous I could have put them to work myself!' "[7]

The next time that a senator wants to take ten billion dollars
in tax money for the construction of a dam in his home state,
and points to the benefits of the completed dam and the work
that will be given out to construction workers along the way,
reflect:

1. Is it a project to which I would willingly have contributed my money? No? Then by what right does the government
take it away from me by force?

2. If the dam is needed in the economy of the nation, why
haven't private enterprisers seen this? Why haven't individuals,
who do seek projects, banded together to construct it themselves?

3. If it is not needed, then no one should spend money on
it—not those who are financing its construction if it is privately financed, and surely not the hapless taxpayers if it is being
financed from public funds.

4. The dam is what is seen, when it is completed. Consider all the millions that are taken away from the taxpayers for this project. Consider the things each one of them might have done with his share of those millions. The project takes away his *freedom* to choose how he shall spend the money he has earned.

"Oh, it's all paid for by the government!" people say, unthinkingly. But where does the government get its money? The government cannot allocate money for any project unless it has first taken that money away, by force or threat of force, from the taxpayer. If the government had some magic source of supply, such as manna falling from heaven, the situation would be different; but, of course, the government can only give out what it has first taken away. What the government—that is, the bureaucrats who are in charge of the details of these functions—gives to people in "its" great generosity, it has first taken away. The presence of the money in government hands gives the bureaucrats freedom of decision as to what to do with it; but this freedom is dearly bought, for it involves the lessening of freedom on the part of those who earned the money in the first place: their free choice to spend it as they wish has been taken away from them by the government.

There may indeed be government functions for which it is justifiable to take away this choice—for example, having an efficient police force and being protected from murder and robbery is to everyone's interest. But in the case of most things for which government takes your tax dollar, you can be quite sure that the government administrators are no better able or more qualified to spend your dollars for you than you are to spend them for yourself. (And even if they are sometimes more qualified, and sometimes decide more wisely, does that justify taking it away from you? After all, you have worked to earn

the money; don't you have a right to spend it as you see fit—
even to make some mistakes?)

The intervention of government in economic affairs, even
when it is justified (if it ever is—more of this later), is almost
always wasteful and inefficient. Owners of private businesses
and corporations who have put their own money into the enterprise will be careful as to how it is spent; but the government bureaucrat who administers public funds (taken from
the taxpayer) is not spending what he himself has earned—he
is spending money that the taxpayer has earned; and one is seldom if ever so careful of other people's money as of one's
own—particularly when no matter how badly it is spent, and
how great the losses are, one never faces personal backruptcy
because of it: one simply passes the loss on to the taxpayer,
who is forced to absorb it.

Consider that government monopoly, the post office. The
collection and distribution of mail is a large job, but not a particularly complex one; but the government cannot administer
even that bit of routine without an annual deficit of millions of
dollars, which is passed on to the citizen in the form of higher
taxes. Private organizations would long since have taken it
over, did not federal law explicitly forbid anyone but the government from carrying first-class mail. But now there is an organization distributing third class or "junk" mail at a smaller
fee than the government charges, and which is already making
a profit. The entire postal organization should be turned over
at once to private enterprise, which could handle it efficiently
without exerting anything like the effort it requires for more
complex enterprises.

But government functions are monopolies; private organizations are not permitted to enter. If you have ever stood at the
post office with a dozen people in line and one man working
behind the counter and fifteen postal employees moving about

doing nothing in particular and not caring whether the customers are served or not, or if you have ever waited half an hour at the Bureau of Motor Vehicles while the clerks who were supposed to be serving you telephoned their girlfriends, sublimely unperturbed by the line of waiting people, you have seen the typical government agency at work. The government knows that you have to deal with it—it doesn't permit any competition; if you want a driver's license or a package weighed, there is no place else you can go. You have no choice but to wait, and chafe in helpless fury. If Macy's did that to you (and once in a while it does) you would probably march out of the store and go to Gimbels or Saks or one of the other competitors, threatening never to bring your business to Macy's again. But in the case of the government agency, there is no one else to whom you can turn.

But, of course, there isn't merely the post office. Consider the telephone company. Consider the thousands of technological decisions that have had to be made each year, each week, by the engineers in Bell Telephone throughout the decades—with the result that we can now pick up a phone and direct-dial someone thousands of miles away, usually in a matter of a few seconds. I find it difficult to pick up a telephone even now without marveling at the science and engineering that made such a feat possible. But when the government takes over the telephone service, it casts a blight upon the entire system. One can usually guess, when he visits foreign countries, in which ones the telephone service is operated by the government; in those countries the service is inefficiently operated, insensitive to consumer complaints, rife with shortages and red tape. In some European countries, long after wartime shortages were over, it took two or more years after one ordered a telephone before one could have it installed. The reason was patent: the government bureaucrats didn't care—it was no skin off their backs if you didn't get service. When the telephone is in the hands of a private corporation that profits from installing new telephones, service is greatly improved. Even in the United States, where the technological improvements connected with the telephone have been most spectacular, telephone service has been considerably less than spectacular because the telephone company is operated as a government franchise, with rules and rates specified and regulated by government and competition prohibited by government. The result, as always when government creates a monopoly, is deteriorating service and constant annoyances.

Now add to the post office and telephone countless other things: roads; utilities; interference with the production and distribution of agricultural products; the construction and operation of dams and electrification projects; housing; the regulation of airwaves; sustenance and regulation of education; and most of all, the maintenance of a vast series of interlocking systems of welfare and poverty relief. Whatever the government manages is infiltrated with waste, inefficiency, and usually bribery and corruption of all kinds. Costs of a service operated by government are normally double or treble what they would be when private enterprise does it.

Let us suppose you had lived in 1900 and somehow were confronted with the problem of seeking a solution to any *one* of the following problems: (1) to build and maintain roads adequate for use of conveyances, their operators, and passengers; (2) to increase the average span of life by thirty years; (3) to convey instantly the sound of a voice speaking at one place to any other point or any number of points around the world; (4) to convey instantly the visual replica of an action, such as a presidential inauguration, to men and women in their living rooms all over America; (5) to develop a medical preventive against death from pneumonia; (6) to transport physically a person from Los Angeles to New York in less than four hours; (7) to build a horseless carriage of the qualities and capabilities described in the latest advertising folder of any automobile manufacturer.

Without much doubt you would have selected the first problem as the one easiest of solution. In fact, the other problems would have seemed fantastic and quite likely would have been rejected as the figments of someone's wild imagination.

Now, let us see which of these problems has been solved. Has the easiest problem been solved? No. Have the seemingly fantastic problems been solved? Yes, and we hardly give them a second thought.

It is not accidental that solutions have been found wherever the atmosphere of freedom and private ownership has prevailed wherein men could try out their ideas and succeed or fail on their own worthiness. Nor is it accidental that the coercive force of government—when hooked up to a creative field such as transportation has been slow, plodding, and unimaginative in maintaining and replacing its facilities.[8]

Everywhere that the free market has been permitted to flourish, prosperity for the masses of the people has followed. To the extent that the government has interfered with the functioning of the free market, the economy is plagued with shortages, inefficiency, and a lower standard of living. Consider West and East Germany—the same geography, the same conditions of soil and climate, the same ethnic group, so habituated to work that the East Germans have become the model of production in the controlled economies although much of their produce is expropriated by Soviet Russia. But the difference is enormous: in West Germany, a high standard of living, reward for individual effort, high wages, continually increasing production; in East Germany—and even more in other Soviet-dominated nations—a controlled economy, collectivism, little reward for effort and achievement and ingenuity, and consequent lowering of the standard of living, everything and everyone looking tacky at the seams.

An even more interesting comparison is between India and Japan. India has many times more natural resources than does Japan; the British left India with many industrial advances such as a functioning railroad system, factories, and equipment;

and a tremendous amount of foreign aid after World War Two. But after India became independent in 1948, it followed a collectivistic course, with a centrally controlled economy. The result has been poverty, starvation, shortages, an abysmal standard of living. Japan had few of India's advantages —it has few natural resources, it was for generations out of touch with the Western world, and later it lost World War Two. Yet Japan is today (after the U.S. and West Germany) the world's third most prosperous nation. Why the difference? It has been said that the Indians are lazy and unenterprising, as opposed to the Japanese; but while it is true that the Japanese are an enterprising people, so are Indians when they are given a chance: those who have migrated to Africa or Southeast Asia have been among the most economically successful people there; but in their home country the bureaucracy is so huge, unwieldy, and inept that individual enterprise is not given a chance. The fact is that, during the past century, even when Japan was under dictatorial control, the Japanese economy was left pretty much alone (at least compared with India and most other nations). The Japanese government did not at any time try to control production, trade, and investment. The result has been a truly amazing degree of prosperity considering the overpopulation of the tiny islands and their lack of natural resources. Japan followed a free-market policy. The future for Japan at this moment seems very bright indeed; for India, very dismal unless it turns to a free-market economy.[9]

The nations of Africa are at this moment in a condition of the most dismal poverty; even the Greek nation is prosperous by comparison. We cannot help be grieved and appalled by the spectacle there confronting us, but most of us do not perceive the cause-and-effect relations in operation. The World Council of Churches does not see it, for it has issued a statement saying: "Justice demands that the inhabitants of Asia

and Africa should have the benefit of more machine production." But how are they going to get this? Only by having an
industrial economy which uses many machines and gives employment to the men operating them. And how is this in turn
to be brought about? Only by capital investment; and is it any
wonder that capital investment lags when the conditions which
make it possible are so unfavorable?—e.g., when there are not
enough trained men to make a factory workable? when the
government itself is so unstable that no one knows what it will
do next? Why should the investor go into Africa to start a
plant only to have his own head chopped off? or only to have
his own factory destroyed, or taken over in some new act of
nationalization? Africa will remain in poverty until it has
created a favorable climate for capital production. When this
happens, capital investment will stream in and the standard of
living will increase by leaps and bounds, as it has always done
when the conditions that make possible stable capital investment have been created.

It is not that Africa lacks natural resources; indeed, it has
many more untapped resources than the United States. Nor
does it lack intelligent people—people who *could* be trained in
industrial jobs. What it lacks is a capitalistic economy, and
this it can never have until it creates the conditions of freedom
and the protection of human rights, including property rights,
which make capitalism possible. It has everything except the
right economic system. And until it has this system, millions
and billions of dollars' worth of loans from America are not
going to help. The dollars will only go down into a bottomless
pit. We can feed the hungry now, but they will only be hungry
again tomorrow; indeed there will be many more millions of
people tomorrow than today, and so they will be even hungrier.
We shall only impoverish ourselves by these devices without
really helping them. Indeed, our endless loans to them will

only perpetuate the status quo; they will only continue in existence the kind of economy—socialistic or feudalistic, as the
case may be—which makes their continued poverty inevitable.
Let us not be misled by a short-sighted humanitarianism. We
don't like to see people starve, and we want to do all we can to
help them. But pouring out our tax dollars to them is not
going to help them for more than a very brief time; what we
should do is to try to create there the type of economic system
under which *they will not starve again because they will be
self-sufficient*. Giving a beggar money is not nearly as effective
as giving him a job, for if we give him a job we shall not have
to help him any more—he will be able to help himself. Giving
him alms only drains ourselves while he is back in the same
condition of poverty the next day as he was the day before we
helped him.

And so it is: the materials are there; the natural resources
are there; the human potential is there; what is not there is the
economic system which will make their rise to wealth possible.
After all, the United States did it; our country was once an un-
tracked wilderness, and we converted it into the most prosperous nation that has ever existed on the face of the earth. We
did not have conspicuously more natural resources than other
countries; nor did we have a monopoly on human brain-power.
What we did have was an economic system, capitalism,
which made it possible for that brain-power to be used, to
flower, and to put great ideas into practice by means of capital
investment. Africa could do the same. But it will not do the
same as long as it does not have the economic system which
alone makes this possible, and especially as long as other nations, via financial aid, help to perpetuate the very system
which makes it impossible.

Economic liberty—the freedom of production and trade,
and the freedom to control the fruits of one's production—is

the principal ingredient in every nation with a high standard of living. But after people have become accustomed to having the fruits of the productive process, they tend to take that process for granted, assuming without question that "we have now licked the problem of production" and that this process will continue indefinitely, no matter what. But this is far indeed from being the case: there are many conditions, easily fulfilled, which would interfere seriously, and sometimes fatally, with the productive process that is needed to keep three or more billion people alive on our planet.

People often take electricity for granted: when the child sees a dark room in which the light won't go on because the wiring is defective, he says simply, "Turn it on!" as if electricity were something always "there," and all anyone had to do was flick a switch. Most adults, of course, are aware that without a power plant and wires and so on there will be no electricity available in their houses. They are aware of this because they have personal experience with malfunctioning electrical appliances. But suppose that in all your experience no electrical appliance had ever failed to work—no power had ever been shut off, no wires or plugs or fuses had ever misbehaved. You would then tend, like the child, to take electricity for granted. Decades might go by, and people would even forget where the underground conduits were; they would be so accustomed to having electricity that it would never occur to them that it might suddenly become unavailable.

Many millions of people in the industrialized nations are in a similar position. They are so accustomed to the fruits of production in great abundance that they never question the factors on which production depends. It does not occur to them that economic abundance can be assured only by capitalism and the free market—and that to the extent to which the free market is tampered with, the abundance that they take for granted is jeopardized. They assume without question that the products will always "keep coming"; but of course this assumption is false and dangerous, for it will lead them, and has led many people in our own generation, to tamper more and more with the elements which make production possible. Writers of the liberal press are always excoriating the corporations and businesses that produce the goods on which they depend, for their "selfishness," contriving countless ways of taking away from these producers the fruit of their production—while assuming that the same producing people will continue to produce as before, obediently and without question.

When a tree has grown to maturity and is already healthy and vigorous, it can endure a great deal: it can survive storm, drought, flood, and blight—but there is nevertheless a limit to its strength; there are combinations of circumstances which will kill it. In exactly the same way, there are combinations of circumstances which will kill off the productive process, at least in the amount in which it is needed in today's populous world. But the advocates of government interference in the economy act as if they were bent on destroying the economic processes on which they themselves depend for their continued existence.

There are many ways in which this phenomenon of interference is manifested. In the remainder of this chapter we shall consider a few; in the following chapter we shall consider the most crucial ones. All of these measures are introduced under the banner of "humanitarianism": sometimes their proponents acutally believe them to be humanitarian, and sometimes they simply find them politically expedient; but in either case they are passed, and the electorate approves them because it believes that they are indeed "for the good of people." This belief is in every case false; for anything that tampers with the productive process can only lessen production, lower the standard of living, and create poverty for some or for all.

The vast mass of people are, however, ignorant of economics: the consequences of economic actions are often long in coming, and when things go wrong people look for immediate causes and not at the long-term policies which led to the catastrophes. They vote for a policy, or place in office congressmen who will support it, and then complain bitterly when the consequences of these same policies occur. Let us observe, in a few examples, how this operates.

1. Rent Controls

One example of a "humanitarian" measure is a law fixing a maximum that landlords may charge on rents, or freezing rents at a certain level. Landlords are popularly branded as greedy profiteers, and tenants for their own personal reasons often agitate for such legislation—and in this they are often successful, since they outnumber landlords at the polls.

What is the result of such legislation? First, landlords are not able to make as much profit on rentals. Fine, we say. Sometimes they are not able to make any profit at all. Fine, some say; serves them right. In fact sometimes they have to operate the apartment building at a loss, and they often prefer not to rent their units at all rather than rent at a price at which they must lose money. Well, not quite so fine—that means that fewer people are housed than before, whereas it was the "tight" housing situation that pushed up rents in the first place.

But this is not all. Little or no new housing will be constructed. Who wants to do so, when the owner knows in advance that with rent control he won't be able to make a profit on his investment? Or even perhaps to make the payments on his loans? So whatever housing shortage there was in the first place is not eased; and if the population increases and still no new housing is built, the shortage worsens. Competitive bidding for apartments increases, thus tending to increase rental rates further (on the black market, of course). Again the result: the problem is worsened, not eased.

How then does one obtain lower rents for everyone in a free-market situation? Let there be incentive—profit—for building apartment units and private enterprise will build them. Let private enterprise be free to build more and more apartment buildings until the supply exceeds the demand, and landlords must compete with one another for rentals. Then we will have a buyer's market in rentals and the rates will come down, since buildings in which extravagant rents are charged will remain vacant on the open market. The only remedy for a housing shortage is more houses; and private enterprise, if left alone, will build them.

In France, where there has been rent control since World War I, almost no residential building has gone on for fifty years; it is next to impossible to obtain, without political pull, any houses and apartments for rent; the whole building industry has been stagnated by the controls. But in Germany, where more than half the dwellings were destroyed or damaged by bombings in World War II, an intelligent free-enterprise policy was begun under Erhard after the war (against the objections of the planners from the American occupation), with the result that by the end of the 1950s there was ample housing for everyone's needs. Again, in the long run there is no solution save abundance—in this case, abundance of available housing; but you cannot achieve abundance unless there is an incentive to produce the commodity of which you desire to have the abundance.

2. Federal Housing Projects

In the last few decades vast urban-renewal housing projects have mushroomed in every large city. Tenement houses and apartments were condemned by the city and razed to the ground, and until such time as new housing is erected on the site, the tenants are forced to relocate elsewhere (to date, more people have been thrown out of their homes by urban renewal projects than have ever been housed by them). When the new buildings are finally constructed, at the taxpayers' expense, the new tenants are sustained there also at the taxpayers' expense, because the rents charged are less than the cost of the upkeep of the buildings. (When a tenant earns more than a certain amount per week, he is forced to live elsewhere, thus ensuring the result that those who remain are among the least enterprising groups of citizens.)

The liberal press reserves its greatest fury for the owners of private housing units, calling them exploiters, slumlords, racketeers, and so on. Some of them are doubtless deserving of these names. But for the most part it is the system, not the individual apartment-owner, which deserves the blame—the system of constant interference and harassment by government with the business of ownership. Typically the owner is subjected to taxation so prohibitive that he is forced to cut corners on expenses if he is to make a financial success of the building he owns—and among the projects for which he must help to pay via taxes are the tax-free government housing projects, his own competition. The expense of maintaining a building is also considerable, as is the cost of making improvements. When an owner does try to improve the quality of his housing, making it adequate or even elegant, he finds the next year that his real estate and property taxes have doubled or trebled. In addition, he often finds the Housing Commission and the Building Codes (which may once have had some utility, but have run quite wild) breathing down his neck, requiring him to make innovations which have been passed into law but which he cannot afford: for example, his thirty-inch-wide doors must now be increased to thirty-six inches, his eight-inch-tread stairways must be reduced to six inches, and so on for countless changes he is forced to make at the cost of many thousands of dollars, or his apartment building will be closed down. In the end, the cards are so stacked against him that he decides to make no more improvements and let the place become a slum, thus decreasing his tax burden. But the moment he does that, an army of preachers and do-gooders cry out, "Look at this filthy profiteer! See under what conditions these tenants must live! What we need is to take housing out of the hands of these exploiters and turn it over to the government!" And so in the course of time the owner's property is condemned, the buildings are torn down, and more public housing is erected on its site, thus creating another piece of real estate that operates at a loss, that cannot be taxed (thus increasing the tax burden on all the others), and usually in the course of a few years or months becomes a worse slum than the one it replaced.

Everyone who has owned houses and apartments for rental purposes is acquainted with situations of this kind. If the intellectuals and assorted do-gooders continue to agitate as they do, it is because they have completely lost touch with the facts of economic reality. Meanwhile, they fail entirely to see how much better things could be in housing if conditions were left up to the free market. Much more housing would exist; and with landlords in competition for tenants, the quality of the rental apartments would have to improve. If owners didn't have to bear the load of property tax, housing could be built and maintained at much less than its present costs, and hence could be rented at much less than its present cost.

The do-gooders are only worsening by their actions the very

conditions they wish to correct. The damage that one unit of government interference has brought about, they think can be corrected by two units of government interference. So they agitate for an increased role of government, instead of working for the abolition of such interference.[10]

There are, of course, problems in housing that would exist even under a free-market system. There are, and probably always will be, people whose habits will turn any neat and clean apartment into a pigsty. What can one do when the tenants leave their apartment dirty, to be taken over by rats and vermin? When they write obscene graffiti on the walls and urinate in the elevators? When they throw their garbage out of windows into the street instead of putting it into the garbage pails? But the fault here of course lies with the tenants. Wouldn't you think twice about repainting an apartment and putting new conveniences in it for tenants if you knew that they would turn it into a garbage dump within a month? And that you would have to spend three thousand dollars on it before you could rent it again? Here the task is one of re-education—economics alone cannot solve such a problem.

3. Price Fixing

Suppose people say, "Everyone is entitled to milk at less than 25¢ a quart." So the price of milk is reduced by government decree, and it becomes illegal to sell milk at more than 20¢ a quart. Many more people can now afford milk, and many children who may have done without, or with less than their need, will be benefited. Certainly this appears to be a humanitarian measure. But wait. What is the effect of such a law? Milk producers will have to operate at a smaller profit, some with no profit, some at a loss; these will be forced out of business entirely, and will turn to a more profitable line of endeavor. What is the result? The available supply of milk will be smaller, not greater.

Now the next step: in order to save the milk-producers from great loss and keep them in business the government decides to subsidize them; in that case, money is taken out of the pockets of all taxpayers in order to underwrite one industry at the expense of the others—another clear case of robbing Peter to pay Paul without Peter's consent. The milk producers can then stay in business, at the expense of everyone else in the nation.

Perhaps the government will not subsidize the milk-producers but will force a reduction of prices on those who supply the milk-producers, e.g., the manufacturers of dairy equipment. That way the milk-producers' expenses will be less and more of them can stay in business in spite of the low price they are forced to charge. But the same problem arises at a new level now: either the supplier himself will go out of business or he must be subsidized in turn. And so on for the other industries. But if everyone who produces is subsidized, who gains? No one: in fact everyone loses in paying taxes for the subsidies plus the considerable cost of the governmental machinery required to keep them going.

The tendency of this government tampering is to go further and further, fixing the prices of all the factors of production (both human labor and material) and forcing every producer and every worker to continue to work at these wages and prices. "No branch of production can be omitted from this all round fixing of prices and wages and this general order to continue production. If some branches of production were left free, the result would be a shifting of capital and labor to them and a corresponding fall of the supply of the goods whose prices the government considers as especially important for the satisfaction of the needs of the masses."[11]

4. Guaranteed Jobs

"Well, if private enterprise doesn't have enough jobs for all these people, let the government guarantee them jobs!"

Of course, if private enterprise weren't shackled by an ever-increasing burden of taxation, there *would* be lots more jobs available. The government tax bite makes it impossible or unfeasible for a business to expand—sometimes even for it to exist any longer—and then one wonders why unemployment has increased. The advocates of government-guaranteed jobs are trying to make government cure a disease which (to a large extent at least) is government-caused in the first place.

But even assuming that there would be unemployment under capitalism—though more likely there would be jobs, not people, going begging—the suggestion that everyone have a job guaranteed by the government is a particularly hair-brained one, which sounds nice in the mouths of legislators, and can be counted on to get votes, but from whose consequences the legislators themselves would surely shirk, if they only thought them through.

What kind of jobs would the government offer the people whom private enterprise didn't find it worth its while to employ? If offered worse conditions, the recipients probably would refuse them. (Even now, it is difficult to get people to take the dirty and smelly jobs, though they command higher wages.) The government would then presumably offer easier jobs, attracting workers from private industry as a result. But the government jobs would on the whole be economically useless—jobs that no private enterprise found it economically feasible to hire anyone to perform (such as sweeping by hand when a machine could do the job). But if everyone were to have a guaranteed job, the government bureaucrats would have to invent "busy work" like digging ditches only to fill them again (already done by the army). Moreover, it would, in many cases, have to move the people (at government expense) to where the jobs were.

There would be further problems: "Suppose the workers with guaranteed jobs were incapable of learning to perform them, or created far more spoilage than usable production? Suppose they habitually showed up an hour or two late, or took three hours for lunch, or came in only to collect their pay, or ignored all instructions, or were unruly, or committed acts of sabotage and vandalism, or kicked the boss downstairs? Their jobs would be guaranteed, wouldn't they?"[12]

In truth, this is the kind of insanity that would be proposed only by people who knew they wouldn't have to be around to observe the consequences of their scheme.

5. Minimum Wage Laws

A favorite humanitarian measure, always favored by "liberals," is a law requiring every employer to give each employee not less than a certain hourly wage. Some people are underpaid, aren't they? Well, why not solve it by legislation—force the nasty employer to give them more, and the thing is done. One can then go home with the consoling thought that one has done a lot of good in the world—and without sacrificing anything oneself.

But the matter is not so simple. The self-styled humanitarians who advocate such measures do not know—or perhaps some of them do know—that the legislation they favor harms the very people it was supposed to help.

The fact is that there are certain jobs which are not worth $1.75 per hour (or whatever the minimum wage is at the time) to the employer. After the big tax bite, he doesn't have enough left in profits to pay these employees the legal minimum wage. So he lets them go. Now they are unemployed, roaming the streets, idle. Is this better? At least they would have been doing something, receiving something, and would have had a chance to rise! It is usually easier to get a second job if you are already holding a first one.

So, the employer, a corner restaurant-owner, doesn't hire that extra dishwasher, or he fires the current one and does the dishes himself, or he buys an automatic dishwasher on time. The result of the legislation is that a man is out of a job—and all across the country, thousands are unemployed because of the minimum-wage law. Let us note in passing that the group hit hardest by this legislation is the Negro teenager. "In 1952, the unemployment rate among white teenagers and non-white teenagers was the same—9 percent. But year by year, as the minimum wage has been jacked higher and higher, a disparity has grown and increased. In February 1968, the unemployment rate among white teenagers was 11.6 percent, but among non-white teenagers it had soared to 26.6 percent."[13]

"Well, pass a law that not only requires minimum wages but prohibits the employer from firing any of his employees! That way, no unemployment could be caused by the law." No? The employer can't fire them, even if they do slovenly work or refuse to work at all? And what if their jobs are no longer needed, if the industry is going downhill? And even if it isn't, by what right is that kind of coercion exercised upon the employer? And what happens if he has to hold on to numerous employees at a minimum wage that he can't afford, and he goes bankrupt as a result, with his life's savings going down the drain together with the business he started twenty years ago and the labor of all those years? Not only he is ruined, but since he is bankrupt his employees are now out of jobs; he can't keep the plant going any more, so *all* of them must be let go. And thus greater unemployment is created than before.

It is not commonly realized that an employer has very little elasticity in the matter of how much of a wage to give for a certain kind of job. If he pays much less than the going wage, he will lose his employees and those that remain will do less efficient work. If he pays much more than the going wage, he will have such a large overhead that he will have to charge the public more for his products, and the public will then buy from his competitors instead, and soon he will be out of business. It simply is not true that the "good-hearted employer" will pay double the going wage and is a Scrooge if he doesn't. If he paid double the going wage to all his employees, he would soon be bankrupt. Even if General Motors did this, they might be able to absorb the losses for a while, but in a comparatively short time they would be priced out of the market and their employees would have to be discharged. The open market is the only guideline for wages, and any departure from it for any length of time results in disaster for the employer and the employee.

After the minimum-wage law was passed, the owner of a food store in Michigan wrote:

For thirty-eight years I have been in the retail grocery business. I have trained hundreds of young fellows sixteen to twenty years old as stock boys, retail clerks, produce managers, meat managers, assistant managers, and finally managers. It was a real pleasure to work with these kids. About three years ago Congress passed a bill making it impossible to hire more than 10 percent of your total payroll-in-hours at a figure of 80 percent of the minimum wage. Some of the sixteen-year-old boys in our state area are just not worth wages of $1.40 per hour. We . . . eliminated the part-time students. . . .

A laundry in Utah reported:

We have some choice and loyal employees but we have some who are not able to produce to the necessary capacity, so we are forced to replace them. This is a most difficult thing to do to an old employee, but the dollars just won't reach.

The owner of a plant in Wisconsin reported,

The minimum wage and hour law keeps me from employing high school and college students. Many students seek work in this area but have no experience. An employer like myself cannot train the students and pay $1.40 per hour. We could use them for clean-up personnel and they would be happy to work for less but it puts our cost too great.[14]

Milton Friedman wrote as follows about the fate of the migrant workers in the face of minimum wage legislation and legislation forcing employers to provide them with certain types of housing:

Migrant workers are clearly hurt. It is small comfort to an unemployed migrant worker to know that, if he could get a job, he would have better housing. True, the housing formerly available may have been most unsatisfactory by our standards. However, the migrant workers clearly regarded it, plus the accompanying jobs, as the best alternative available to them, else why did they flock to Michigan? It is certainly desirable that they have better alternatives available to them, but until they do, how are they helped by eliminating alternatives, however unsatisfactory, that are now available? That is simply biting off their noses to save our faces.

Farmers are clearly hurt. The cost of migrant labor has been raised. That is why they are mechanizing. The machines limit the rise in cost but do not eliminate it. Costs would be lower if farmers could hire migrant labor on terms that would be mutually satisfactory to them and the laborers. But they are not permitted to do so.

Consumers are clearly hurt. At the higher costs, less food will be harvested, so making food prices higher than they otherwise would be.

Producers of mechanized farm equipment are helped by having a larger market. But in the main, they simply produce harvesting equipment instead of other equipment.

The only other people who are helped are the do-gooders responsible for this type of legislation and for these effects. They have the high-minded satisfaction of promoting a noble cause. The good intention is emblazoned forth for all to see. The harm is far less visible, much more indirect, much harder to connect with the good-hearted action. Besides, the harm is mostly to someone else.

. . . I know hardly any do-gooder legislation of this kind—whether it be minimum-wage laws or rent control or urban renewal or public housing or fair-employment legislation—which, on examination of its full consequences, does not do more harm than good—and more harm as judged by the intentions of the well-meaning people who sponsor such legislation.

Will the liberals ever learn this lesson of experience? So far, the clear failure of government program after government program to achieve its objective has simply led to a clamor for still larger, still more expensive, still more far-reaching programs—to do still more harm. It is about time that the liberals asked themselves whether the fault may not be in the system they favor—doing good at other people's expense— rather than in the way the system is operated. It is about time that they appealed to their heads as well as their hearts.[15]

Let us put the liberals to the test: if they really mean what they say, if they are not just bleeding-hearts but really are concerned with the fate of the young members of minority groups, and wish to avoid unemployment as well as riots, let them agitate to have all minimum-wage laws stricken from the books. Then and only then can we be assured that they mean what they say.

6. Government Credit

Suppose that there is only one plow in the world and that two farmers want it.

Peter is the owner of the only plow available in France. John and James wish to borrow it. John, with his honesty, his property, and his good name, offers guarantees. One *believes* in him; he has *credit*. James does not inspire confidence or at any rate seems less reliable. Naturally, Peter lends his plow to John.

But now, under socialist inspiration, the state intervenes and says to

Peter: "Lend your plow to James. We will guarantee you reimburse-
ment, and this guarantee is worth more than John's, for he is the only
one responsible for himself, and we, though it is true we have nothing,
dispose of the wealth of all the taxpayers; if necessary, we will pay
back the principal and the interest with their money."

So Peter lends his plow to James; *this is what is seen.*

And the socialists congratulate themselves, saying, "See how our
plan has succeeded. Thanks to the intervention of the state, poor James
has a plow. He no longer has to spade by hand; he is on the way to
making his fortune. It is a benefit for him and a profit for the nation as
a whole."

Oh no, gentlemen, it is not a profit for the nation, for here is *what is
not seen.*

It is not seen that the plow goes to James because it did not go to
John.

It is not seen that if James pushes a plow instead of spading, John
will be reduced to spading instead of plowing.

Consequently, what one would like to think of as an *additional* loan
is only the *reallocation* of a loan.

Furthermore, *it is not seen* that this reallocation involves two profound injustices: injustice to John, who, after having merited and won
credit by his honesty and his energy, sees himself deprived; injustice to
the taxpayers, obligated to pay a debt that does not concern them.[16]

There are many people who need loans who are unable to
get them from bankers, loan companies, and other private
lenders. It is not that these lenders are necessarily "greedy" or
"stingy"; they would be glad to lend money, the more the better, since this is their business and their source of income. If
they refuse to lend to some people, it is because they consider
these people to be bad risks, who may never return the money
loaned. They are simply being realistic in their estimate of the
potential borrower (more realistic than the would-be borrower
usually is about himself). The would-be borrower, seeing only
his own need and not the reasons for suspicion by the would-
be lender, responds with anger and resentment. Then, as often
as not, he agitates for the government to lend him the money.

And thus a hue and cry begins among the "humanitarians": "Let the government lend him the money! If the banks lose business, they deserve to—see how the Scrooges refuse to lend to this needy person!" and so on.

Private bankers and loan companies and other businessmen make loans all the time, of course—even to people without collateral, if they have a record of being reliable and trustworthy. If government entered the lending business in order to lend money to these same people, its activities would be completely superfluous. But these people of course are not the ones to whom the government lends money: government lends to poorer risks, those who could not obtain loans on the free market. So instead of the banker risking his (the bank's) money on these poorer risks, the government's money (yours and mine and all other taxpayers') is being risked. A government bureaucrat is placed in charge to "administer the loan"; but usually he is less careful about the conditions of the loan than the banker who stands to lose personally if the loan is not repaid. The bureaucrat doesn't have to pay the defaulter's loan out of his own pocket; he simply throws the liability on the taxpayer, who then has to foot the bill.

Let us say that Mr. A is a man who would get the loan if the government did not enter the picture; he would get it because he is honest, reliable, and hard-working.

. . . But the government goes into the lending business in a charitable frame of mind because . . . it is worried about B. B cannot get a mortgage or other loans from private lenders because he does not have credit with them. He has no savings; he has no impressive record as a good farmer; he is perhaps at the moment on relief. Why not . . . make him a useful and productive member of society by lending him enough for a farm and a mule or tractor and setting him up in business?

Perhaps in an individual case it may work out all right. But it is obvious that in general the people selected by these government standards will be poorer risks than the people selected by private standards. More

money will be lost by loans to them. There will be a much higher percentage of failures among them. They will be less efficient. More resources will be wasted by them. Yet the recipients of government credit
will get their farms and tractors at the expense of what otherwise
would have been the recipients of private credit. Because B has a farm,
A will be deprived of a farm. A may be squeezed out either because interest rates have gone up as a result of the government operations, or
because farm prices have been forced up as a result of them, or because there is no other farm to be had in the neighborhood. In any case
the net result of government credit has not been to increase the amount
of wealth produced by the community but to reduce it, because the
available real capital (consisting of actual farms, tractors, etc.) has
been placed in the hands of the less efficient borrowers rather than in
the hands of the more efficient and trustworthy. . . . The bureaucrats
[are to be] permitted to take risks with the taxpayers' money that no
one is willing to take with his own.

There are several consequences of such a policy:

It would lead to favoritism: to the making of loans to friends, or in
return for bribes. It would inevitably lead to scandals. It would lead to
recriminations whenever taxpayers' money was thrown away on enterprises that failed. . . . But [the most important consequence] of loans
of this type . . . is that they will waste capital and reduce production.
They will throw the available capital into bad or dubious projects. They
will throw it into the hands of persons who are less competent or less
trustworthy than those who would otherwise have got it. For the
amount of real capital at any moment (as distinguished from monetary
tokens run off on a printing press) is limited. What is put into the
hands of B cannot be put into the hands of A.[17]

What people don't seem to realize is that credit is something
one *earns,* not something he receives as a gift.

Someone says to you as you pay a bill at a restaurant with a
credit card, "You're lucky. Why can't I get one of those
things? I'm broke all the time."

Many thoughts occur to one at such a moment. First: perhaps the reason that he can't get a credit card is that he is

broke all the time; and perhaps he is broke all the time because
he can't manage his financial affairs well—he overspends in
relation to what he takes in. Such people are not good risks for
credit; would *you* extend credit to such a person, with such an
uncertain payoff? Second: he, and many like him, act as if
"you don't have to pay it at all" if you just sign a card. They
don't realize that the billing date is once per month and all
payments are delinquent if made more than ten days thereafter. If one does not pay promptly, one soon loses one's credit
rating. A person who buys beyond his means on credit, soon
finds the bills piling up on him, and then he tends to curse the
credit company which demands payment of him, condemning
it as a "set of filthy-rich exploiters." If the company offering
credit *is* rich, it got that way (on a free market) from satisfying the demands of many customers; it didn't get rich by
having the money fall from heaven. In any case, when he accepted the credit card he signed an agreement to pay at the required time; if he can't do that he shouldn't have accepted the
card. Most important of all, credit is not just given to a fortunate number selected by lot, it is *earned* by those who have
shown that they can handle it responsibly, by paying bills regularly; those who cannot handle it responsibly, if they do per-
chance get a card, soon forfeit their title to it. But it is easier to
curse the company than it is to mend one's financial ways. The
question to ask oneself is: Would *you* lend your money to
someone with that record of financial responsibility?

7. Social Security

If there is anything that looks to many people like benefi-
cent government intervention, it is social security. Many people live under the delusion that "the government is providing

for us in our old age." According to some reports, Barry Goldwater lost the New Hampshire primary in 1964 because the people thought that "he's trying to take away our social security payments."

But of course, nothing is *provided* by government; government has no source of income but the very people whom it taxes to pay for its so-called benefits. Government can only give what it has first taken away—less its handling fee which sometimes amounts to several hundred percent. If millions of dollars are "provided" by government in social security payments, it is only because millions of dollars have first been extracted from the taxpaying public.

In pre-social-security days, people planned for their old age; they would set aside so much every month, so that they would have it when they retired. Some people did not, and then were left to the charity of others when they grew old. But today almost everyone who works for a living in America is required by law to pay into the government fund during all the productive years of his life, so that he will be able to draw social security when he reaches 65. He is forced to do this; he is given no choice in the matter. As a matter of fact, there are countless savings plans, available for example through insurance companies, which would give one a much greater net return by the age of 65. He may subscribe to those now, but if he does so he must pay for these *in addition to* the social security system. And since most persons cannot afford to do both, they stick to the one they are forced to pay into anyway, even though it is the less advantageous alternative. If I were given a choice, I would say, "No thanks" to social security: "I have found much better ways of saving for my old age than by subscribing to the government program"—or I might not want to save at all, or to stake everything on a business enterprise that requires my entire capital outlay *now*. But I am not given this choice: the government says, "You have to pay into this, whether you like it or not."

The system is indeed riddled with disadvantages. Everything that is paid into it is forfeited by the one who pays: he cannot draw a penny of it out for investment, nor can he use any of it to increase his wealth or earning power during his productive years. Perhaps he would feel more secure in a business venture which requires every penny of his capital, than he would depending on the government in his old age. Such a venture isn't absolutely secure, but then neither is the government—countless governments have fallen during the twentieth century and wiped out the people who depended on them. In any case, he is not given the choice: he is taxed to provide for his later years just when he needs the money most to provide for his current needs and to make his current investments. This is surely a loss of liberty, and it may well be a loss in security too, for when he is old the government may be non-existent, or bankrupt, or able to give him back only a small fraction of what he has paid in, or it may repay him in dollars that have become worthless through inflation.

"But it goes into a special fund, waiting for me till I grow old, when I can receive it." This simply is not true. The money taken from millions of people for social security has already been spent. The promise that you will get something later relies entirely on the government's power to tax the next generation.

In the government-oriented plan embodied in Social Security, the Social Security taxes are spent by the Government, an I.O.U. is substituted, and a bookkeeping entry is made as a record of the taking. The money is never repaid; it is gone forever. To add insult to injury, the suckers who "contributed" the Social Security taxes in the first place, must now pay taxes to cover the interest on the I.O.U., besides providing the cash to make good on the future Social Security payments as they become due.[18]

Entire professional groups have been placed by federal

edict on social security, even though scarcely a single member of the group profits by it. When physicians were placed on social security a few years ago, it was a purely political move for taking in extra revenue; for what physician ever really retires? What physician, even if he works only half-time after 65, does not take in more money than the maximum he is permitted to earn while receiving social security payments? In such a case, the system is pure robbery: he has to pay into it knowing full well that he will never receive a penny from it. He knows it, and the politicians know it; but physicians are easily outvoted at the polls by the vast majority who murmur gratefully, "Think what the government is giving us." Yes, the government is "providing for you," if it can be called providing when it takes a dollar from you and, if you are lucky, returns fifty cents.

8. Tariffs

The entrepreneur, we have said, is the risk-taker of society. If his business enterprise fails (in a free economy), he takes the loss. If it succeeds, he has an income, more people are employed, and the consumers have a new product or service (or if it is a kind of product already on the market, more brands from which to choose)—and his income from his new enterprise can come only from consumers who are satisfied enough with his product to buy it in quantity.

The businessman who wants the government to subsidize his product, however, is a robber. The government forces every tax-payer in the nation to pay a higher tax because of the money required to subsidize his product.

A tariff too is a subsidy. It is a subsidy extended to the manufacturers of one nation, by that nation's government, by means of taxing competitive products manufactured by another nation.

Suppose that Japan can sell radios of a certain quality in the United States for $20 each. Suppose also that United States industry cannot produce radios of comparable quality for that amount, but requires $30 to do it. Accordingly, American radios cannot compete with Japanese radios (at least of this size or quality) on the free market, since the Japanese products have underpriced them. Now the American manufacturer sets up a lobby in Congress and asks that Congress enact a tariff on Japanese radios? It's a humanitarian measure, isn't it? After all, he may be wiped out without the tariff, and his employees will be laid off, and we don't want that, do we?

Let us suppose that the tariff is enacted. Then several consequences will occur which the congressmen who voted for the tariff may not have thought of:

1. The American consumer is the loser: he can no longer buy the radio for $20. He must either buy the American-made one for $30 or the Japanese import for $30 (assuming for the sake of convenience that the tariff on it amounts to $10).

2. As a result of this, the $30 he had to spend will now be spent entirely on the purchase of the radio. He won't have $10 left with which to buy *other* products. So the sales of these other products will go down. (Or else he'll buy the other products but not the radio, in which case the sales of American radios will go down in spite of the tariff.) The other merchants will notice that their business has declined, but because the effects of the tariffs are so dispersed they may not be able to identify it. (A tariff on one product would not have that much effect on the economy as a whole, but a host of tariffs certainly will.)

3. And now comes the most important consequence of all: the Japanese will not be very happy about the tariff we slapped on their radios, for the sales of these radios will now decline and the factory will have to lay off workers. And now, almost

as surely as 2 and 2 make 4, the Japanese government will retaliate: it will impose a tariff on some American products—let
us say, computer equipment, which is ordinarily imported
from America. They will stop importing it, or import it in
smaller quantities than before, and perhaps start to manufacture it themselves. As a result, the American computer industry will have to contract because of the decline in exports to
Japan; workers will have to be laid off, and so on.

4. As a result of this mutual raising of tariff barriers, each
nation will be *using its capital in a less efficient way* than it
could have. The United States will be producing some things
that could be best produced in Japan, and Japan will produce
for itself items which on a non-tariff market it would have
found most feasible to buy from the United States. The "tariff
war" in the end hurts them both—not only the producers in
each nation, but the consumers as well.[19]

"But doesn't the tariff at least protect the farmer?" This too
is a popular delusion. First, the tariff raised the price of goods
that the farmer bought:

> Many items protected were such as farmers are most apt to use, e.g.
> crosscut saws, trace chains, hammers, nails, galvanized iron, and so on.
> All mechanical equipment would be affected by tariffs on metals.
> Clothing would be higher, otherwise there would be little justification
> for "protecting" it. Even farm products, which might be effectively
> raised in price, e.g. sugar and wool, would only "protect" some farmers
> at the expense of others, and of consumers in general.[20]

Second, the market for American agricultural products overseas was reduced. The United States exported many farm
products, such as cotton, tobacco, wheat, and beef. But of
course people overseas had to pay for these exports. Foreigners can pay for American goods only if they can also sell goods
in the United States. So the foreign consumers, hit by the tariff, were less able than before to buy American goods. Thus,

exports were less than they would have been without the tariff. And as a result of this decreased purchase of American products overseas, the income from them in the United States declined. When consumers overseas could not buy as many American products as they otherwise would have, the demand for the products was reduced.

Farmers, then, were buffeted by the contrary winds of government intervention. By one policy, they were encouraged to produce as much as possible, to go into farming, to move onto western lands, to settle and bring more land under cultivation. By the tariff policy, what they bought was priced in a protected market while most of what was sold was on the world market. Hence, there was a great expansion of agriculture, followed by declining prices and often accompanied by the heavy indebtedness of farmers. . . . The deflation, or depression, of the mid-1890's finally succeeded in driving out many marginal and submarginal farmers. The innocent word, "adjustment," hides the dashed hopes, the years of struggle amidst dreams turned to nightmares, the bankruptcy, the shattered lives of those who had staked all on a homestead in the west.[21]

The paradox is that high-tariff policies have traditionally been advocated by the Republican party, the alleged party of free enterprise. The libertarian position is at least consistent: liberty includes economic liberty, and government-imposed tariff is an interference with economic liberty.

9. Automation

"But machines put people out of work. Therefore there should be a limit to the amount of machines that are permitted to replace human labor."

The argument is used by countless people; and it is, of course, true that machines sometimes put people out of work —especially when there are minimum-wage laws and it is cheaper in the long run for the employer to buy a machine than to keep the worker on.

But let us look at the *whole* picture. The manufacture of buggies and covered wagons was widespread during the nineteenth century; and if improvements had been outlawed, no cars would ever have come into existence. But today more than a million people in the United States are employed in the automobile industry—and if you consider other industries such as steel which supply the automobile industry the figures would be much higher. Some human dishwashers have been put out of work by automatic dishwashers, and have gone into other lines of employment—including the manufacture of the automatic dishwashers. And there are thousands of people employed in computer work by IBM and other organizations that did not exist several decades ago. Employment *shifts* from one area to another; it decreases in one type of activity, but increases or starts from scratch in another—and since the new industry involves more production per man-hour of work than the old one, it decreases human drudgery besides providing employment.

If *work* were all that was wanted, it could be guaranteed very easily: just destroy the machines. Dismantle the railroads and have people carry the freight in packs on their backs— that would keep thousands busy all the time. In primitive societies there is enough work for everyone—back-breaking work, around the clock, with people still subsisting at starvation level. It is not just work, but the release from drudgery that work provides, that people find desirable, and this is possible only in an industrialized economy.

In the nineteenth century in England, workers destroyed the new machines that would replace the knitting of stockings by hand. But the effect of the machines was to make the mass-production of stockings possible; instead of a rarity it became common for women to wear stockings, because, thanks to the machine, the price of stockings plummeted to a small fraction of what it had been—more were made, and the machine could turn them out not only more numerously but also more cheaply. By the end of the century the stocking industry was employing over a hundred men for every man it had employed at the beginning of the century. Such was the effect of automation in the stocking industry.

Even before that, Adam Smith remarked in the eighteenth century that a worker making pins by hand could hardly make one a day, but that with the new machinery he could make 4,000 a day.[22] Now, if the automation of that time had really thrown the vast majority of pin-makers out of work, one might argue that the new machinery caused 99.98 percent unemployment in the pin industry because the same number of pins could now be made with that much less human labor. But of course it didn't work out that way at all: because of the machinery, more pins were made; and pins became cheaper, ever so much cheaper, than before, with the result that more people could buy them, and because more people could buy them more of them could be made, and more could be employed in the industry than ever before.

Suppose that a clothing manufacturer installs a machine that will make overcoats with half the labor he previously hired. He buys the machine and drops half his labor force. Of course, the machine required labor to make it. But that is only the beginning. The manufacturer has more profits than before because of the economies brought about by the machine. And out of these extra profits financial gains to others will come. This is how:

The manufacturer must use these extra profits in at least one of three ways, and possibly he will use them in all three: (1) he will use the extra profits to expand his operations by buying more machines to make more coats; or (2) he will invest the extra profits in some other industry; or (3) he will spend the extra profits on increasing his own consumption. Whichever of these three courses he takes, he will increase employment.[23]

In other words, the manufacturer, as a result of his economies, has profits that he did not have before. Every dollar of the amount he has saved in direct wages to former coat makers, he now has to pay out in indirect wages to the makers of the new machine, or to the workers in another capital industry, or to the makers of a new house or car for himself, or of jewelry and furs for his wife. He gives indirectly as many jobs as he ceased to give directly.

But that is not the end: as his competitors buy the machines, more work will be given the makers of the machines. And competition will force down the price. In other words, the savings will be passed along to consumers. And since overcoats have now become cheaper, more people will buy them. Finally, with the money these consumers save on a new overcoat they will have that much left to buy other things—which in turn will provide increased employment in other lines.

What one sees, what everyone can easily see, is that some people are forced out of their chosen line of work by new machines. For the workers thus displaced, the situation is indeed an unfortunate one; they will have to train themselves for a new line of endeavor, and some of them are too old to do this without great effort. But that is only a small part of the picture, as has just been explained. Would you wish on account of that part to hold back automation, thus holding back the production per man-hour of work in the future, and holding back the surcease from drudgery which the machine has wrought for the human race? Suppose that when the manufacturer of covered wagons and buggies was decreasing because

of the rise of the automobile, it had been suggested that the
government subsidize the buggy-maker at his old job—that we
turn out buggies year after year for which there is no longer
public demand and store them at government expense in gov-
ernment-constructed garages. How long should this be tolerated? The men continuing to work at their old jobs—this we
would all see; but what most of us would not see would be
the other jobs that *would have* become available through the
new machines, the advantages of the new over the old, the
ball-and-chain that the subsidization of the old would have on
the growth of the new, the creative energy that would be
dammed up by the artificial continuation of the old. And in
the end, it would be throwing away a dollar to save a penny.

The fact is that people would rather ride in cars than in
buggies; it is this overwhelming consumer demand that determines the direction of the economy, as long as it remains free.

10. Monopoly

One of the principal sources of opposition to laissez-faire
capitalism is the fear of monopoly. "Won't the manufacturers
of a product get together, jack up the price and bilk the consumer? Or else won't the most powerful manufacturer buy out
the others and then charge runaway prices? And shouldn't this
be stopped by government?"

The quick and easy answer would be; "Yes, if that's the
way things would go under a system of pure capitalism, then
government should intervene in order to preserve free competition and free choice by the consumer."

But this is a big "if." Is it really true that the freedom of
competition and freedom of consumer choice has to be bought
at the price of less freedom for the manufacturer?

Let us first make a most important distinction. There is *coercive* monopoly, in which government does not *permit* competition in a given area of goods or services. There is also *noncoercive* (or *de facto*) monopoly, in which more than one firm in a given area is legally permitted, but does not in fact exist. Let us examine these in order. Public utilities in most countries are run as government monopolies. No organization other than the one designated by government is legally permitted to supply the utility. As a result, of course, the system is inefficient and unresponsive to public demand, and the utility lacks the competition which would keep it on its toes—all would-be competitors are excluded by law. Characteristically it runs at a deficit, but the deficit is simply made up each year by additional money from the hapless taxpayer.

Sometimes an industry that is privately owned, such as the railroads, succeeds in obtaining a monopoly within a given area because it bribes the appropriate government officials to make a regulation or pass a law that forbids all competition. After the Civil War the officials of four railroads in California (called the "Big Four") bribed the members of the state legislature into granting them a monopoly on rail transport within the state; from then on, no other railroads were permitted to operate in California. The result was predictable: since these railroads needed no longer fear that any competitors would come along and undercut their prices, they charged what they liked. In fact, they gouged the public. The grape-growers who had to get their grapes transported to the markets of the world found that all the profits they might have had were eaten up by prohibitive freight rates. If other railroads had been permitted, they would have rendered the service at a much lower price and still made a profit; but no other railroads were permitted. Whenever such a coercive monopoly exists, a special-interest group can profit hugely from it while it lasts, but the general public is a victim—in this case it was both the grape-growers who couldn't make a profit, and the consuming public which couldn't have the grapes, or could obtain them only at such high prices that they usually bought something else instead.

A coercive monopoly is indeed greatly to be feared, because such a monopoly can be sustained only by force, that is, by the organization of physical force possessed by the government. Yet the public seems to think little about government monopoly: it is always "private monopoly" which is the object of its fear and its hatred.

Now what of non-coercive monopoly? Alcoa is the only producer in the United States of primary aluminum. Other firms are not prohibited by law, but in fact there is only this one; if you want primary aluminum you must deal with Alcoa (unless you want to buy overseas) because there is no other domestic source. Does Alcoa charge prohibitive prices for its product? It does not. It behaves for all the world as if it had many competitors. And indeed this is so: it has many *potential* competitors. Alcoa knows well enough that if it were suddenly to double its prices, it would lose and not gain: other firms that had been waiting in the wings for the right moment would find that they could now undersell Alcoa and still make a profit; and besides, aluminum isn't that indispensable—if it became overpriced, consumers would turn to other metals instead, perhaps to iron pots and pans instead of aluminum ones, or perhaps to stainless steel or plastic or something else. Few, if any, products are so indispensable that people will buy them no matter what the price.

Many people believe that a company can lower its prices below cost, then drive out its competitors, and then raise its prices above the old competitive price to make up its losses—and keep on charging these prices indefinitely. It has never been done. And no company could profit from trying:[24]

A. Suppose a firm cuts its price on a product below what it costs to produce it. It is then, of course, taking a loss. The larger the firm's share of the market, the greater is this loss. Meanwhile, what of the competing firms? The demand for their product will be reduced, lessening their profits; *or* they will shut down, to reopen later; *or* they will "produce for inventory," storing the products for later sale when the first producer has had his fill of losses. They might even buy the cheap product for their own inventory and sell it later. Meanwhile, the consumer is the gainer by all this, as it always is during any price war.

B. The first company cannot continue its policy of producing at a loss indefinitely. Even if it is a wealthy firm, investors will pull out when they know it is taking such losses. When it finally sells again at the market price, it will have grave losses to recoup, which will place it at a disadvantage.

C. If the first firm, to recoup its losses, tried to raise its prices *above* the market level, it would invite competition from numerous other individuals or firms who could produce the same product at a lower price and still make money. And these firms would be at an advantage because they didn't have the previous losses to recoup. Even if the first firm had forced the competing ones to shut down, they would always tend to come back when the first firm tried to raise its prices above a competitive level. Suppose they no longer had the capital to do this: they could go to the first firm's customers—who are now being overcharged—and get a contract to supply their needs at the competitive price. They can protect themselves for the long run by getting contracts even before they open (or reopen).

D. If you want to be the sole producer, the above is clearly no way to do it. There is a much easier way: simply buy out your competitors, or merge with them. But if you do this, and then raise your price above the competitive level, you will again find new competitors appearing—as they will when there is a demand for them.

E. But suppose that a firm were more efficient than its competitors because it could cut production costs more and still come out with just as high-quality a product. (Perhaps the firm has an unusually efficient set of managers; or perhaps it has some patent, or new production gimmick that other firms don't yet have.) It could undersell its competitors, even though not by much, and still make a profit. It would probably capture a larger share of the market. Even if it captured the *whole* market, it would *keep* the whole market only as long as it kept producing *as if* it had a host of competitors; if for a considerable period it overcharged, the competitors, always waiting in the wings, would come in again.

And in fact it *does* have a host of competitors, even when it is the sole producer: the *would-be* competitors who become *actual* competitors the moment they find a chink in the armor: inefficiency in production, managerial incompetence, overgrowth of bureaucracy in the front offices, greed to get more than the market rate for the product, and so on. On the free market, even when for a time there is a *de facto* monopoly, such a monopoly is always in danger: unless it behaves as impeccably as if it were besieged by competitors, it will soon have the competitors.

But perhaps the various producers would cooperate ("go into collusion") with one another to keep the prices high.

If there are only four firms in the pencil industry, it is argued, they can all profit by getting together and restricting their total output so as to raise the price to "monopolistic" levels. But what will happen to their cooperation when a producer who has for years been planning to start up a pencil factory whenever it becomes feasible, sees this price? What will happen when the picture-frame manufacturers start switching their equipment into pencil production? What will happen, when, a

week or a month from now, somebody—either one of the present pencil manufacturers or someone else—invents a machine for producing
pencils more cheaply, a better pencil, or a new device which can write
better than any pencil? What will happen when somebody else thinks
of a better way to advertise pencils? None of these questions are
answered by the adherents of the collusion doctrine.[25]

Besides, if there are five competitors in a given industry,
and four of them agree to "collude," it is not to the interest of
the fifth one to join in. There are many difficulties in getting a
group of sellers together to agree on collusion. Professors
Armen Alchian and William Allen in their classic textbook
University Economics[26] make the following points: (1) How
can one know exactly who one's competitors are (because of
the many substitutes on virtually all products)? (2) It is difficult to get all the sellers to agree on a uniform policy. (3)
Even if they do agree, each stands to gain from secret cheat-
ing. (4) Some competitors will not join anyway: those that do
not, and hence charge less, will be delighted that the colluding
firms are charging more; those charging less will now get more
business. (5) And "if expensive facilities are involved, the
colluders will suffer a loss of their own large investment if new
entrants do appear—an effect that will continue after the effectiveness of the collusion has ended."

The simple fact is that in the entire history of our country
not one monopoly has survived by such practices—eliminating
competition and then gouging the public—*unless it was supported by government*. Without such aid, monopolistic attempts collapse. The Ford Motor Company once possessed
most of the American car market, but only because Henry
Ford mass-produced the Model T and held the price lower
than any competing producer. He was able to do this, however, only by refraining from stylistic variations, and when the
public started to demand such variations and Ford insisted on

sticking to one model and color, while General Motors sold diverse models, General Motors gained the ascendancy over Ford, capturing 50 percent of the American market. But every company, even General Motors, is in constant danger of being outsold by its competition: a few years ago when there was a public demand for compact cars which General Motors didn't anticipate, American Motors, though a small company, made huge gains by correctly guessing what the public would go for. No company can long survive if it does not serve the public at competitive prices.

The Standard Oil Company case is the most constantly cited by critics as the classic one of non-government monopoly. According to one typical account, the Standard Oil Company "established an oil refining monopoly in the United States, in large part through the systematic use of predatory price discrimination. Standard struck down its competitors, in one market at a time, until it enjoyed a monopoly position everywhere. Similarly, it preserved its monopoly by cutting prices selectively wherever competitors dared enter." The main trouble with this "historical account" is that it is not historical. Nothing of the kind happened. The oil business was extremely wasteful and inefficient when John D. Rockefeller appeared on the scene (in 1860, when he was twenty). Rockefeller decided to make it orderly.

What Rockefeller found when he got to the Oil Creek region of Venango was enough to fill his fastidious soul with acute distaste. Oil, in that last pre-Civil War year, was a raffish, up-and-down business, and had been so from the very start. It had had its origins in medical quackery as white men, posing as Indian doctors, put the skimmings from Pennsylvania creeks into eight-ounce bottles and hawked them as a sure cure for "cholera morbus, liver complaint, bronchitis, and consumption." Using by-product oil from salt wells, the greatest of the "Seneca oil" Barnums, Doc Samuel Kier, had made a big enterprise of selling the stuff as "medicine" long before anyone had thought of drilling a well directly to get at it.[27]

Rockefeller dreamed of bringing stability to this chaotic situation. He was a competitor of unusual skill—perhaps the greatest of the nineteenth century—and he hated the unnecessary destruction and waste which abounded in the industry. Rockefeller and two other men formed the Standard Oil Co. of Ohio, which with superior technology and efficient operation in two years had absorbed most of the twenty-five Cleveland refineries. His methods, both of extracting oil from the earth and of refining it, were well thought through and more efficient than those of his competitors, and one by one he bought them out. The invitation he issued them read, in part: "We will take your burdens, we will utilize your ability, we will give you representation; we will all unite together and build a substantial structure on the basis of cooperation."[28] Standard Oil did indeed buy out many competitors, and as the years went by and its financial reserves increased, it was able to buy out many more. But Standard

. . . did not use predatory price discrimination to drive out competing refiners, nor did its pricing practice have that effect. Whereas there may be a very few cases in which retail kerosene peddlers or dealers went out of business after or during price cutting, there is no real proof that Standard's pricing policies were responsible. . . . Standard did not systematically, if ever, use local price cutting in retailing, or anywhere else, to reduce competition. To do so would have been foolish.[29]

Why is it foolish to attempt to engage in such tactics—even if no law prohibits it?

Both the predator and prey lose wealth. The bigger firm with more sales will take a bigger absolute loss. The smaller firms can often shut down production of that item and wait out the return to higher prices, letting the predator take the greater losses. But whether or not the prey can take that action, it still is clear that below-cost selling as a predatory tactic is not as smart as it is alleged to be.

If a firm were to gain by driving a competitor to bankruptcy, the prey's productive assets must be retired from production. Bankruptcy does not *destroy* productive resources; they go to someone else, who

probably acquired them at a sufficiently low cost to make their continued use profitable. The aggressor, who has been suffering losses to impose losses, would have to continue his predatory tactics as long as required to wear out the other resources, and this would mean larger
losses for the predator too. Even if the predator were wealthier, it does
not follow that he would find it sensible to bear greater losses. Careful
study of the Standard Oil example finds no evidence of that kind of
predatory tactic.[30]

There were, indeed, competitors who fought him and remained in business.[31] And with the discovery of oil along the
Gulf Coast, and the rise of the new gasoline market (Standard's technological investment was committed to kerosene),
Standard's share of the market went down. It was the workings
of the market, and not the Supreme Court decision of 1911
that forced Standard to split, which ended the dominance of
Standard Oil.

It is perhaps needless to add that Standard had many thousands of satisfied customers; had this not been so, Rockefeller
would not have been able to make millions selling to them.

Buyers always liked the company's product; they proved it by rushing to substitute petroleum kerosene for the old coal-oil and whale-oil
illuminants. And buyers did not have any particular reason to complain
of Standard's pricing policy; not only did kerosene cost less than the
older fluids, but it had to meet the competition of the Welsbach gas
burner and Mr. Edison's carbon-filament electric-light bulb. Standard
Oil could not have imposed a lighting monopoly even if it had tried.[31]

A very similar story could be told about United States Steel
Corporation, which once dominated the market but which
now holds a smaller percentage of the market than it did fifty
years ago. Smaller companies have kept it on its toes, and they
have accounted for most of the progress in the steel industry in
the last half century.

[It is] absurd to suppose that huge organizations, even those called
"monopolies," can seriously "prey" upon the public—for the obvious

reason that each and all of them is especially interested in producing and in selling at the lowest profitable price. In no other way can they maintain their primacy. Undue profits invite more vigorous competition, and incite the cupidity of other enterprisers, so that no large "monopoly" has ever remained such for any great length of time. Success in any field is the surest stimulus to competition. In the long run the only way that any producer can command a wide market is by making better or cheaper goods, from both of which the public must benefit. It is only when large organizations contribute to further efficiency by utilizing the best talent in every branch of the business that they can compete with the smaller organizations.[32]

Many arguments in this area, however, do not attack the empirical point (a false one, as we have seen) that nongovernment monopolies have occurred; they rather take the form of moral arguments, or pleas to the effect that no company should ever be permitted to become large or to have a predominant share of the market. Here are a few of such objections:

First objection: In many industries, a producer whose facilities are extremely large has a great advantage over others whose facilities are smaller. The larger firm will be able to manufacture the product—say, cars—at a smaller price per unit than the small manufacturer will. No matter how hard the small firm may try, it will be unable to compete with the large firm (such as General Motors) that has a billion-dollar plant ideally set up to manufacture cars in vast numbers at a lower price per car. An established firm has a plant already in operation, whereas a newcomer must build one. Besides, an established firm can get more credit and has easier access to the market than a new one.

Answer: It is true, of course, that in some industries at least, largeness permits cost-cutting. If you manufacture a million cars a year, you can charge less per car than if you manufacture only a thousand or a hundred. (This is not true indefinitely, however. Sometimes a very large organization becomes unwieldy, inefficient, sloppy in its operations, and the left hand doesn't know what the right hand is doing. Presumably this is why General Motors decentralized its operations some years ago, making each of its five brands of cars relatively autonomous manufacturers.)

But the fact that General Motors is now large is not an accident. It *became* large because when it was smaller it satisfied its customers, made money, and was able to plow most of the money back into additional production and plant-expansion. General Motors had to go through that stage—why should the new manufacturer be excused at General Motors' expense from having to go through it too? Or is he supposed to be able to compete with General Motors on an equal basis by tomorrow morning *without* having gone through the years of successful designing and manufacturing that General Motors did? General Motors *earned* its advantage of largeness by efficient production and the ability to satisfy consumer demand. It has proved this—something the new producer has not yet done. He may be able to do so in time, but only by going through the same route that General Motors did. Is this supposed to be unfair?

The firm that is now established once had to build *its* plant too. It was once in the same "disadvantageous position" as the newcomer now is. A newcomer will have to do the same thing. True, an established firm also has easier access to credit; and if you were a lender, would you not more willingly lend to an established firm with a past record for competence and honesty and promptness in repayment than you would to a newcomer whose virtues, if they exist, you cannot yet know? Isn't the latter a greater potential risk? How is this a ground for objection? Rational men judge other people and firms on the basis of their record; what alternative to this would the objector suggest?

Second objection: Sometimes a firm owns or controls a substance used in the production of some consumer goods, and can thus keep potential rival producers out entirely.

Answer: This is a barrier only if there is only *one* substance that can be used. It is doubtful that this ever happens: no one company has ever owned all the oil there is, or all the sulfur, or all the iron. Even if it did, (1) new sources are often discovered, which are not under the firm's control at the time of their discovery, and (2) there are few if any substances for which no substitutes are available: if you can't get copper, use iron, or aluminum, or plastic, etc. Technology has risen to such a point that there is scarcely any indispensable substance in the manufacture of anything.

What does the objector want? How could economic production occur if a person was not permitted to control the resources which he needs to generate his product? And what incentive would there be for people to find a new resource if, the moment they found it, the use of it were taken away from them, or had to be shared by others who had not made the attempt? There is, surely, a difference between the earned and the unearned.

Third objection: The inventor of something may take out a patent on it, thus providing him with a monopoly of its use.

Answer: Of course, and how else would one have it? If you have spent years developing a patentable process, should you then be forced to turn around and share it with those who did *not* invent it? Is not the creator the rightful owner of his own creation? Is there no difference between the earned and the unearned?

The liberals who see red every time they utter the word "monopoly" may perhaps own their own homes. How would one of them respond if trespassers regularly came along, sat in his yard, enjoyed television in his living room, and raided the refrigerator in his kitchen, saying, "We have just as much right to be in this house as you have"? He would probably respond, "See here, I knocked myself out to buy and pay for this house—you didn't. That gives me the right to occupy it and say who else may do so." That prerogative, which he would surely claim (else the house wouldn't be *his* at all), is all that is being claimed for the "established firms" in the situation of economic competition.[33]

11. Union Activities

If workers choose to band together to improve their conditions of work or for any other non-coercive purpose, no libertarian could have any objection. The only reason that union activities might come under the heading of government intervention into the economy is the possibility that government might become involved in union activity. Today, of course, the possibility has become an actuality.

The only proper sphere of government in a strike situation would be, as in every other case, the retaliatory use of force. A worker has a right to strike; in walking off the job he is coercing no one. But if a striker attempts to use force against someone else who accepts his job, the law may use force in retaliation against the person who initiated it. Other than that, the relations between labor and management are none of the government's business.

But the government of the United States in the twentieth century has considered labor relations to be very much its business. The Clayton Antitrust Act of 1914 exempted labor unions from the anti-trust laws: "Nothing contained in the anti-trust laws shall be construed to forbid the existence and operation of labor organization . . . nor shall such organizations, or the members thereof, be held or construed to be illegal combination or conspiracies in restraint of trade, under the antitrust laws. . . . No restraining order or injunction shall be granted by the court of the United States, or a judge or the judges thereof, in any case between an employer and employees. . . ." Then the Norris-LaGuardia Anti-Injunction Act of 1932 ruled that unions were not to be held responsible for acts done by individual members unless it could be shown that union leaders participated in or authorized these acts; and that before an injunction against a union can be given, the court must find that "unlawful acts have been threatened and will be committed unless restrained" (something extremely difficult to do). The National Labor Relations Act of 1935, which gave unions more government-backed power than any other piece of legislation, authorized a National Labor Relations Board, on which was conferred sweeping powers to investigate and settle labor disputes. The company must, by law, bargain with the majority union, whether or not it finds the majority union's demands reasonable. The minority union could then strike if it chose, and if the company committed a single "unfair" act in attempt to operate a struck plant, it had to reinstate all strikers with back pay for the duration of the strike. Armed with these powers, unions grew cocky and bold; and knowing that they had the employers over a barrel, they could force conditions of work upon them that they would otherwise have been unable to do. (In addition, striking employees often receive government relief benefits for the duration of the strike, paid for in part by their own employers.)

Many members of the unions apparently believe that their standard of living is raised by union membership. Other union leaders know better, but their jobs depend on appearing to

believe that they are serving their members and really helping them. What difference have unions actually made in the
economy?

The main effect of unions has been to *create unemployment*. Unions attempt to take the determination of wages and
working conditions out of the market. By forcing the employer
to deal with the unions (by law), and by restricting union
membership in various ways (by race, by ability to pay, by
whether one has a relative already in the union, etc.), they *restrict the supply of workers* that an employer is permitted to
hire. "The unions would raise the wages of those employed by
reducing the number of people employed."[34] Since the union
wage is above the market level, the employer will either lay off
workers or change his plans to hire new workers. Some workers
(the union members who are hired) get more than market
conditions would have given them, with the inevitable result that many other workers in the same profession remain
unemployed. Unions of course do not care how much unemployment there is among non-members (including those who
are qualified to be members but are rejected by the union for
one reason or another)—they care only about retaining the
high wages of their own members.

When a union pushes the wage beyond the competitive level, it is not
the union which suffers the resulting unemployment nor the members
who remain employed at the increased wages. The true sufferers are
the workers who are disemployed as a result of the "false" wage and
the workers who will not be hired because the expansion which would
normally have taken place at a lower level of wages (and prices) does
not take place.[35]

And of course, the higher-than-market wages paid the
members only result in higher prices for the product which the
consumers (including the workers themselves) must pay.
Thus the wage-increases they get are soon reflected in higher

prices which wipe out their gains; and the higher prices hit the unemployed workers still harder. Sometimes it is only the salaried union officials who benefit from these tactics. The higher wages drawn by the workers are always at the expense of the excluded workers (excluded because at the required wage-rates it has become uneconomic for the employer to hire them)—and, in time, at the expense of the industry from which all the workers receive their income. The higher prices which the company must now charge tend to price their product out of the competitive market.

"Hire the handicapped!" we hear on radio and television appeals to employers.

Few stop to ask why it is that the handicapped need such special attention. If there is work that they can do or services which they can perform, we might suppose that this would be well known to employers. Such reckoning ignores, however, the obstacles we have thrown in the way of their employment. Quite often, the handicapped are unable to produce enough to warrant paying them the union wage or minimum wage. They are especially liable to have accidents and thus will drive up insurance rates, which employers take to meet the government requirements of liability for workmen. Their susceptibility to illness may make them a drain on unemployment compensation and company health insurance programs. In short, the scales have been rigged against the handicapped. They become, quite often, the object of charitable appeals when they might be self-sustaining and self-sufficient without the arbitrary obstacles.[36]

But the effects do not end here. Because of the unemployment created by unions,

. . . many sections of cities are today made well-nigh uninhabitable for civilized people by the presence of the idle. Young ruffians, teen-agers with nothing to do, and lounging gangs make the streets unsafe and life for those who live in their midst dangerous and unpleasant. The reason for this phenomenon is not far to seek. The young are supported in their idleness by government doles. The dull are kept in school far beyond the point of usefulness (turning schools in some districts into a

nightmare experience for teachers and less violently inclined students)
by compulsory attendance laws, and induced to stay there by massive
attempts to prevent drop-outs. When they are old enough to be allowed
to work, quite often they cannot find employment. The inexperienced
and the unskilled are not sufficiently productive, at least over a considerable period of time, to warrant paying them the minimum wage or
union wage. Many employers now find it more profitable to pay the
penalty of overtime wages to skilled and dependable employees than to
take on new ones who will have to be trained, be paid minimum wages
during the period of relative unproductiveness, and, above all, for
whom they will have to make additional social security payments and
keep additional records to satisfy government.[37]

There are many other consequences of union activities: for
example,

(1) Work stoppages by strikes reduce production and result in less income for workers. (2) Union dues are a tax in effect, on the income of
workers, and tend to reduce their income to that extent. (3) Individual
workers are kept, in effect, from improving themselves and their wages
by the union's insistence upon equality of pay for a particular job and
resistance to great production by individual workers. (4) Union sen-
iority rules reduce the mobility of workers, reduce competition for
jobs, and tend to fix the worker in his particular factory. (5) Wages
not based on productivity tend to price American goods out of the
world market. . . .[38]

Also, (6) unions often resist technological improvement in
the mistaken belief that it creates unemployment. (7) Workers age 50 or above often cannot find jobs, again because of
obstacles that unions-cum-government place in the way: minimum wage, social security payments, employer's liability for
accidents, and the extra bookkeeping involved. And so on. As
technological improvement continues, as capital accumulation
grows, the real wages of labor increase steadily on the free (uncoerced) market—as they have for the last two hundred years.
The effect of the unions, by short-sightedly *resisting* this tendency, has been to *impede* progress and thus *slow down* the

rise in real wages which would steadily occur on the free market. The union officials either do not see, or choose to hide the fact, that

Wage-rates are prices. Like other prices they are determined by supply and demand. And the demand for labor is determined by the marginal productivity of labor.

If wage-rates go above that level, employers drop their marginal workers because it costs more to employ them than they earn. They cannot long be employed at a loss. If, on the other hand, wage-rates fall below the marginal productivity of workers, employers bid against each other for more workers up to the point where there is no further marginal profit in hiring more or bidding up wages more.

So assuming mobility of both capital and labor, assuming free competition among workers and free competition among employers, there would be full employment of every person wanting and able to work and the wage-rate of each would tend to equal his marginal productivity.[39]

That this desirable state-of-affairs has not been achieved is the fault of both unions and government. Unions have become their own worst enemies: their short-sighted policies, by penalizing productivity, have not increased but rather have lowered the average level of wages and consequently the workers' standard of living. (Not to permit a bricklayer to lay more than a thousand bricks a day when he could have done three thousand is sheer insanity; the time he wastes on the job, while still receiving full pay, cannot help adding to the cost of the house being built—thus lessening the number of houses that will subsequently be built and the number of men employed building them—perhaps extinguishing his job into the bargain.) But union practices and policies, short-sighted though they have been, would not have had such a large effect were it not for the power of union leaders to wangle favors from government, causing Congress and state legislatures to enact coercive legislation that places a ball-and-chain on the company (and thus indirectly on the workers employed by the company). And thus again the heavy hand of government, trying to "manage" businesses when they could much better manage themselves, puts a brake on the creativity and the productivity of both management and labor.

12. Government Medicine

When the average American goes to the prescription counter at a drug store and lays down his money for a medication which his physician has prescribed, he usually curses the pharmacist or the pharmaceutical company as "making profits off of illness," and perhaps expresses the wish that the pharmaceutical business in the United States were handled entirely by the government, "to get rid of the profiteers." Many politicians and career government people encourage such attitudes, and will not be satisfied until the pharmaceutical industry in the United States is as completely socialized as it is in Russia.

Consider first a few facts of which the general public is comparatively ignorant.[40]

1. The average price of a prescription drug in March 1970 was $3.68. Almost 75 percent of prescriptions cost less than $4.50. Only 2 percent cost more than $10. The average cost of a prescription is only 54¢ more than it was in 1960.

2. Average spending per person per year in the United States on alcoholic beverages is $78; on tobacco, $48.60; on radio and television sets, $45.45; on shoes, $36.75; on foreign travel, $20.90; on jewelry and watches, $18.90; and on prescription drugs, $18.

3. After expenses and taxes, the manufacturer's profit on the average prescription price of $3.68 is just twenty cents.

4. There are thirteen thousand companies manufacturing

pharmaceuticals in the United States. No specter of monopoly need be raised here!

5. In 1960, prescription drugs and over-the-counter drugs accounted for 17 percent of the total medical care dollar spent. Today (1970), the percentage is 9.3 percent of each medical care dollar.

6. Pharmaceutical manufacturers spend $600 million a year on research for better products—three times as much as ten years ago.

7. Every year American pharmaceutical companies test approximately 150,000 substances. Out of all these tests, between ten and twenty new marketable medicines result.

8. It costs the industry an average of $37,000 a year to support one research scientist.

9. During the last ten years, the manufacturers' research cost to assure customers a drug that is safe and of high quality has gone up at a rate 50 percent faster than the sales rate.

10. Two percent of the money spent on pharmaceutical research is put up by the government; 98 percent comes out of the companies' own research funds.

11. In the last thirty years, out of 868 major new medicines put on the market, American drug manufacturers produced 536. (Second to the United States was Switzerland, with 57. Great Britain, whose socialized medicine scheme provides little incentive to manufacturers, came up with 40).

12. The drug industry in the United States employs representatives to go to physicians and hospitals and explain new drugs. (Six out of ten drugs prescribed today were not even available ten years ago.) No other country has been as successful in inventing new drugs and getting them to the public so quickly.

13. Mostly because of drugs, the majority of illnesses can now be treated without hospitalization. The patient who used

to develop pneumonia from pleurisy now takes an antibiotic, stays in his own bed, and is up and about within forty-eight hours.

14. The death rate of babies less than a year old has dropped 60 percent since 1940. The average baby born today will live ten years longer than the parents themselves could expect to live thirty years ago.

Nevertheless, it is quite possible that the pharmaceutical industry will be under government control within the next generation, along with medicine in general. Why? Because of the agitation to "get rid of profiteers in disease." These so-called profiteers fully deserve all the profits they get; one could wish that they were more, so that there would be still more research and more available medications. Nevertheless, the general public has been so brainwashed about "profiteers in medicine" that they may well lead Congress toward a nationalization of the drug industry. If this happens, one can expect progress in medications to grind gradually to a halt: there will be a handful of heroic individuals who will lay their professional reputations on the line in arguing for a new drug; but the government bureaucrat, who tends to "play it safe" on innovations lest the man higher up in the bureaucracy remove him from his job, will usually frown on the use of the skill and imagination required for innovations. Government-by-committee will stifle initiative, and the ablest people will tend to leave government "service" and turn to other areas which will still be free. A giraffe has been defined as "a horse designed by a committee"; and an enterprise managed by government will usually turn out to be as ungainly, without being nearly as functional, as a giraffe.

Not long ago a student at the university in which I teach was taken to the hospital, seriously ill. For almost two weeks, the student's condition did not improve and the physicians

were unable to make a diagnosis. Finally it was recognized as
a disease (strongilitis) that rarely occurs in the United States
but sometimes occurs in Mexico from walking barefoot on certain patches of soil (usually around the marijuana plant) con-
taining thousands of microscopic worms, or strongeles. Until a
few years ago the disease was fatal; the worms gradually per-
meated the bloodstream, and the patient died a painful and
protracted death. But now, thanks to research by American
pharmaceutical companies, the patient has only to take three
capsules a day for about ten days and he is usually cured. There
cannot have been much profit in conducting the research leading to this cure—there is not a high incidence of the disease in
this country. Yet as often as not the chief reaction of the patient is the complaint that "the pills are too expensive." In the
case of this particular student, he had for some time agitated
for the socialization of medicine. I knew of this when I visited
him in the hospital. He was grumbling about the fact that he
suffered pain and exhaustion after taking the capsules (the
cost of the capsules themselves had been absorbed by the university). I told him, "If I were you I'd be grateful that our
drug companies have developed a cure for this thing." In response, he muttered something about "the profits the god-
damn drug companies make." "Off of *this*?" I said. "They
used the profits they got from more popular drugs in order to
develop a cure for this disease, which they were pretty sure
would never net them any profits." He looked at me with scorn
and skepticism, remarking that "They made plenty off of it,
don't worry!" "And even if they did," I said, "why should you
complain about it? It saved your life. Up until five years ago
there was no cure for this disease at all—you'd be dead right
now. How much is the saving of your life worth?" He looked
up, a bit startled. I continued relentlessly: "But if you'd had
your way and medical research was socialized, what do you

think the chances are that a cure for this rare disease would have been developed? Would the bureaucrat in charge have been likely to approve expensive research on a disease which hardly anyone in this country ever gets? When you tamper with freedom of research, buddy, you're tampering with your life! Now you'll still have a chance to live and perhaps appreciate the difference between freedom and coercion. But if the policies you advocate had been adopted, you'd never have had that chance. You'd have died, probably still agitating for the nationalization of the drug industry. What will it take for you to wise up?" He did not reply, and to this day I do not know whether my little inquisition had any effect.

What has been said of medical research can also be said of medical practice. Traditionally in the United States, physicians would take a certain percentage of free cases, patients they were fairly sure could not pay for medical attention in the foreseeable future; and often they charged the financially abler patients more because of this—as, of course, they had every right to do. Since they, the physicians, were providing the service, they had a right to set the conditions under which that service would be provided—otherwise they would have been slaves, not free traders on a free market. But increasingly in recent years the citizenry, inflamed largely by the vote-getting tactics of politicians, have come to demand all medical attention as a *right*. "We have a right to free medical attention!" they chant, as if medical attention grew on trees. But medical attention, as well as medical preparations and medical research, are all manifestations of the labor of human beings; and for some human beings to exact non-voluntarily the time and effort of other human beings, is to make them (to that extent) slaves. "We have a right to X" implies "You have an obligation to provide X." And if those being addressed do not provide it voluntarily, they are made to do it by force—by the enslavement of the medical profession. The details vary, of course, from nation to nation; usually the physician is indeed forced to provide the service, but he is compensated for it (even if for no other reason than that his services are needed and he must be paid in order to be kept alive)—compensated not by the patient, but by the taxpayer, who now pays an astronomical price for other people's injuries and diseases, plus the very considerable fee (sometimes half the total amount) charged by the government for handling the transaction. The case of Great Britain seems to be fairly typical:

> British doctors see 700 patients a week to only 170 for U.S. doctors. . . . British doctors can explain the 700 figure: More and more people rush to the doctor because it is "free." They stay in the hospital longer than necessary because it is "free." There is also another reason: Under socialized medicine, the government allots each doctor a minimum fee for each patient seen. To make enough to keep their offices open, doctors step up their schedules to see more patients so they can get more fees. They have to, or close their doors. And more and more of them are closing them and moving to New Zealand, Australia and the United States.
>   . . . If a British doctor works ten hours a day seven days a week—70 hours—then he must see ten patients an hour if he is to take care of 700 a week. That means each patient gets an average of six minutes. What kind of diagnostic examination can be given in six minutes?
>   This time schedule does not include the hours and hours of paper work each doctor must do under government orders. Three forms must be filled out for each patient; this means 2,100 forms a week. . . . [41]

And if a physician prescribes a treatment for a certain patient which in the opinion of the government authorities is too expensive, the patient is denied it and the prescribing physician can be fined for "wasting the people's resources."

The one indispensable ingredient in medical care is, of course, the physician; without the man who can diagnose your

illness and cure you or alleviate your pain, the practice of
medicine would be impossible. It is of first importance, then,
that the physician from whom the care is expected not be
shackled in his attempt to provide it. Yet the attitude of many
citizens, especially those who favor socialized medicine, is that
the physician is their servant, whose services they have a right
to without fee, while yet they may expect him to heal and cure
them, and that he must do this regardless of the conditions imposed upon him; if he does not, they seek to invoke the coercive power of the law against him to force him to do so.

"I quit when medicine was placed under State control, some years
ago," said Dr. Hendricks. "Do you know what it takes to perform a
brain operation? Do you know the kind of skill it demands, and the
years of passionate, merciless, excruciating devotion that go to acquir-
ing that skill? *That* was what I would not place at the disposal of men
whose sole qualification to rule me was their capacity to spout the
fraudulent generalities that got them elected to the privilege of enforc-
ing their wishes at the point of a gun. I would not let them dictate the
purpose for which my years of study had been spent, or the conditions
of my work, or my choice of patients, or the amount of my reward. I
observed that in all the discussions that preceded the enslavement of
medicine, men discussed everything—except the desires of the doctors.
Men considered only the 'welfare' of the patients, with no thought for
those who were to provide it. That a doctor should have any right, desire or choice in the matter, was regarded as irrelevant selfishness; his
is not to choose, they said, only 'to serve.' That a man who's willing to
work under compulsion is too dangerous a brute to entrust with a job
in the stockyards, never occurred to those who proposed to help the
sick by making life impossible for the healthy. I have often wondered
at the smugness with which people assert their right to enslave me, to
control my work, to force my will, to violate my conscience, to stifle
my mind—yet what is it that they expect to depend on, when they lie
on an operating table under my hands? Their moral code has taught
them to believe that it is safe to rely on the virtue of their victims.
Well, that is the virtue I have withdrawn. Let them discover the kind of
doctors that their system will now produce. Let them discover, in their

operating rooms and hospital wards, that it is not safe to place their lives in the hands of a man whose life they have throttled. It is not safe, if he is the sort of man who resents it—and still less safe, if he is the sort who doesn't."[42]

13. Government Impediments to Business

Government is supposed to be the friend of enterprising people, especially workers and small businessmen. Liberals are constantly deploring the cruelty of the American system toward these groups and advocating more government programs to help them. These government programs now exist— and far from helping them, they constitute one barrier after another to the progress and well-being of the very people they ostensibly wish to help.

Suppose that a man wants to start some enterprise on his own. If he wants to manufacture or sell liquor, he will find that there is such a maze of regulations that he must observe before he is permitted to distill alcoholic beverages that only a few large distilleries can do it; and as for selling it, the government requires him to have a license, which is expensive, and to observe numerous petty regulations, and in some states only the government is permitted to own liquor stores. In many industries the government either is in competition with the private enterpriser (conducting the business tax-free, and passing on the losses to the tax-payer) or has a monopoly on the whole type of enterprise—for example, collection and delivery of first-class mail, and the generation and sale of electricity. In many instances the government grants monopolies to single companies, such as the telephone companies, electric companies, urban transit, even the collection of trash—so that the enterprising newcomer is not even permitted to engage legally in these activities. Even in industries where there is private competition, special permits are required, or charters or franchises: so it is with banks, television stations, bars, trucking companies, airlines, taxicabs, and so on. If you want to own a taxicab in New York City, you must buy a permit from someone who already has one and is willing to surrender it—which may cost you more than twenty-five thousand dollars.

Many enterprises require the purchase of land, in which the government also has a large stake: the government is the major buyer of lands (army camps, parks, housing projects, highways, dams, etc.). In fact, the federal government is the biggest landlord in the United States. Moreover, if the government wants a piece of land, it does not have to negotiate the price with the seller: it can simply *take* the land, under the government's power of eminent domain, by condemning the property and recompensing the owner at what the government agent feels is a "fair price." Besides all this, special enterprises must adhere to special government regulations, sometimes very time-consuming, expensive, and cumbersome: becoming a teacher (you have to take a bunch of generally useless education courses for which "schools of education" in our universities have successfully lobbied in the state legislature), or a barber, or a pharmacist, or a beautician (licenses must be obtained, after passing examinations prepared under government auspices).

But these are only the roadblocks in the way of starting an enterprise. Suppose that a man does at least surmount all the initial hurdles and begins a small business.

His troubles have just begun. The man who enters business discovers rather soon, if he did not know it already, that he has a Senior Partner —government. More precisely, he has a committee of Senior Partners, composed of federal, state, county, and (depending on the locale) township and municipal authorities. These Partners may have thrown any number of obstacles in the way of his going into business in the first place; they may be in competition with him; they may have made low interest loans to his competitors or even granted them special privileges which he does not enjoy; they will rarely have invested anything in the business themselves. Yet once he opens his doors those Partners join the firm, so to speak, expecting him to perform special services for them for which they do not pay, having the first go at any profits that he makes, imposing their notions of how the business should be run, what wages he should pay, what prices he should charge, and what conditions should prevail in this place of business. Though they may be in competition with him, they will expect numerous detailed reports about his undertaking.[43]

And now begins the thing that drives as many small businessmen out of work as do the regulations: the ocean of paper work. In most states, the businessman has to collect sales tax on all purchases—which requires considerable bookkeeping and is a nuisance. If he has any employees, he has to deduct income taxes from their checks, as well as pay the social security tax on each individual—more expense and more bookkeeping. The record-keeping he has to do is often quite detailed, and if he isn't already a specialist in bookkeeping he had better become one or else make enough profit to hire one. And of course he has to pay income taxes himself on his business—which is not only a nuisance, but may eat away all his profits or force him to close down (more than half of the small businesses in the United States are forced to close down during the first two years of their existence). And the internal revenue code for business enterprise is so detailed, so chaotic, so hard to understand, that even a Philadelphia lawyer cannot interpret it correctly in many cases ("correctly" means, presumably, the way an internal revenue investigator would interpret it on any given day). One would think that the small businessman who is trying to get ahead was the enemy of government, judging by the regulations and the taxes and the way the government treats him. It is particularly trying that the businessman, after having done the mountain of paperwork and complied with all the regulations, must still pay a prohibitive tax as well—part of that tax supporting his own competitors, the government, which operates its business tax-free and still loses money.

But even this is not the end:

The Senior Partners are not particularly mollified by getting the first fruits from any income and having the businessman collect taxes in general from people. They take an active hand in deciding how the business shall be run. For one thing, some of the Senior Partners exert themselves strenuously on behalf of any workmen he may be able to employ. They will not let him simply take advantage of the labor market. It is not enough for them that the workers be willing to work at the price he offers and under the conditions he provides. In many instances, he must pay a minimum wage prescribed by the federal government, and possibly a higher one dictated by the state. It does not much matter what the exigencies of his business are, he must pay time and a half if they work more than a specified number of hours a day. If a union attempts to organize his employees against him, the Senior Partners will stand by unjudiciously stacking the deck against him. . . . He is subjected to "fair trade laws." These can be particularly burdensome to a trader new in the business. He may want to lure customers by advertising certain bargains for sale, only to find that he is guilty of "price-cutting" and "unfair competition." He may need to reduce prices drastically on some items he has stocked—remembering that he may be inexperienced in establishing an inventory of goods—in order to get them off his shelves. He may find that agreements into which he had to enter to buy goods in the first place prohibit him from doing so.[44]

Besides, the laws of his state or community may prohibit him from keeping his business open during certain hours or certain days. In addition, he is subject to a crazy patchquilt of building codes, fire codes, and other ordinances. If he operates a small shop in which there is a stairway, and the relation between the rise and the tread of the stairs is not what the government says it must be, he must either make the expensive and pointless alteration or close down his shop. In practice, what usually happens is that he bribes the building inspector:

since the regulation would force him to close down his business, he simply pays the inspector $100 or more a month not to report the violation; and then when the inspector comes thereafter on his monthly tour of inspection, he inspects just one thing, the top of the boss's desk, to see if his monthly check is there. Besides all this, he may have to pay hoodlums a certain amount every week *not* to break his windows. And if he finds difficulties in running a shop that is vulnerable because it is at one place and cannot be moved, and goes into something more mobile, such as the trucking business, he finds that . . . "truck operations on the nation's highways are conducted under 49 differing sets of size and weight regulations which act to determine the length, height, and width of trucks as well as the loads they may carry. In addition there is a multitude of tax regulatory features affecting the movement of interstate truck traffic."[45]

And if, after all this, he decides to solve the problems of ownership by selling out to a larger firm, he may find that the larger firm is not permitted to buy him out, lest it would run afoul of the government's anti-merger laws.

Who can say how much financial and emotional grief has been brought to the most enterprising of men, those who only wish to supply consumers with what they want, and whose enterprises should be encouraged, by government regulations and taxes? No one knows exactly how many have ceased operation because of these things, or how much "urban blight" has been caused by government interference.

The empty stores, the abandoned filling stations, the small factory no longer in operation, the fading signs of the premises which tell of the proud aspirations of the man or men who founded a business which once was, tell only part of the story. There are the hundreds of thousands of others who never accumulated enough savings because of inflation and progressive taxation, who backed out when they contemplated the expense of record keeping, who never got franchises, who found their fields preempted by government, whose innovations never got past the government bureaus, and so on. They are not in business, and we do not have their services. The Roadblocks to Enterprise were too much for them.[46]

Though the regulations and taxes are enough to discourage anyone to the point of giving up, the effects have been especially harmful to racial minorities, such as the Negroes. Many blacks have had to leave farms in the South because of government intervention: the government paid large subsidies to the *big* farmers, but the small ones were put out of business by the thousands. They left home in droves for the large industrial cities, only to find that they had been priced out of the labor market by minimum-wage laws and government-created unemployment. For some of them, there was still another possibility: start your own business. But the taxes and regulations described above were enough to prevent that possibility in most cases, or to bring them to financial ruin if they did start.

The liberals pretend to be friends of the Negro; but they have been the advocates of the very restrictions and regulations which stopped the Negro at every turn—as farmer, as worker, as businessman. And so there was no way out but the government dole, year after year, and life in a ghetto which would have been no ghetto if enterprising building constructors had not been shackled by government regulations and taxes. The message to the black race should be clear: the government is not your friend! And those who are responsible for all the government regulations which stop you at every turn are not your friends either, though they may wring their hands for you in their newspaper columns; if they know what their "humanitarian" measures are doing to you and support them anyway, they are hypocritical; and if they do not know, they are hopelessly ignorant of the economic facts of life.

14. Anti-Trust Legislation

Once the bogeyman of monopoly has been dispelled, the need for anti-trust legislation will be dispelled along with it. Businessmen know best how to run their own businesses, and government does not—it withers everything it touches. By what right does government regulate firms and industries that it did nothing to bring about?

First, the anti-trust laws do a great deal of harm. Most of the actual decisions are made not through the court system, by a "rule of law," but by administrative agencies of the federal government such as the F.C.C., the I.C.C. and so on, by a "rule of men": that is to say, the businessman whose whole future may turn on the interpretation of a statute or a regulation has no idea what to expect, for the regulations are often vague and contradictory, and the men in the federal regulatory bureaus make the decisions in such mutually contradictory ways. The businessman may succeed with a merger, or he may be struck down, depending on the whims of the bureaucrat who happens to be deciding his case. He, who may have spent years of his life and millions of dollars getting his plant into operation and functioning, must await the verdict of a man (or a board) incapable of doing any of these things, in order to know whether his business will be permitted to survive. Unpredictability of outcome and irrationality of decision-making are not conditions in which a capable man can continue to operate a business. Yet such are the conditions under which he must now try to continue functioning. Thanks to the anti-trust regulations, a man becomes a criminal the moment he goes into business. "If he charges prices which some bureaucrats judge as too high, he can be prosecuted for monopoly, or rather, for a successful 'intent to monopolize'; if he charges prices lower than those of his competitors, he can be prosecuted for 'unfair competition' or 'restraint of trade'; and if he charges the same prices as his competitors, he can be prosecuted for 'collusion' or 'conspiracy.' "[47]

When one considers that the men who have the guns of government constantly pointing at them are the most productive men in the nation, who annually increase our standard of living by providing us with goods and services unknown even a few decades ago, who deserve our profoundest gratitude as the true benefactors of our country, what conclusion can one draw about the regulations by which they are constantly harassed, and of the people who support such regulations?

It takes extraordinary skill to hold more than fifty per cent of a large industry's market in a free economy. It requires unusual productive ability, unfailing business judgment, unrelenting effort at the continuous improvement of one's product and technique. The rare company which is able to retain its share of the market year after year and decade after decade does so by means of productive efficiency and deserves praise, not condemnation.[48]

Many people would doubtless admit that the anti-trust regulations are vague and contradictory, and therefore demoralizing to any businessman who tries conscientiously to abide by them; but, they would add, aren't they necessary? Don't they do some good in preventing one firm from monopolizing the market? Isn't that why the Sherman Anti-Trust Act of 1890 was enacted into law?

This may have been what led to the enactment of the law; it was indeed thought at the time that if some enterprising companies were not stopped they would become monopolistic. But if there was any reason for thinking this at the time, it has long since ceased to exist. Anti-trust legislation only puts a ball and chain around the producer, and the ills that the ball and chain were supposed to prevent are wholly imaginary. "Texaco and Gulf would have grown into large firms even if the original Standard Oil Trust had not been dissolved. The United States

Steel Corporation's dominance of the steel industry half a century ago would have been eroded with or without the Sherman Act."[49] And so on. No firm can hold a monopoly or a near-monopoly of the market without governmental force to back it, unless it is so efficient and far-sighted in its business operations that no would-be competitor sees a chance of entering the field.

But it was for these very qualities that the leaders of Alcoa were condemned in court on anti-trust action. Judge Learned Hand, who wrote the majority opinion in *U.S. vs. Aluminum Co. of America*, 1945, said,

> It was not inevitable that [Alcoa] should always anticipate increases in the demand for ingot and be prepared to supply them. Nothing compelled it to keep doubling and redoubling its capacity before others entered the field. It insists that it never excluded competitors; but we can think of no more effective exclusion than progressively to embrace each new opportunity as it opened, and to face every newcomer with new capacity already geared into a great organization, having the advantage of experience, trade connection and the elite of personnel.[50]

Was there ever a judicial decision more calculated to discourage productivity, enterprise, the technological creativity of human beings?

In the General Electric case (1961), General Electric, Westinghouse, Allis-Chalmers, and numerous other companies were indicted in one of the most infamous episodes of American history. "The charge against them was that they had made secret agreements to fix the prices of their products and to rig bids. But without such agreements, the larger companies could have set their prices so low that the smaller ones would have been unable to match them and would have gone out of business, whereupon the larger companies would have faced prosecution, under these same anti-trust laws, for 'intent to monopolize.' "[51]

The men who were condemned in decisions such as Alcoa,

and General Electric were condemned *for* the very qualities that made them the great benefactors of the American public. They were the scapegoats, and the government commissions that should never have existed in the first place were the self-styled heroes—and by and large the public went along with it. As long as the public continues to be ignorant, similar things will happen in the future, until, as Benjamin Fairless, president of United States Steel, said, if anti-trust continues as it is now, every business in America will "have to be run from Atlanta, Sing Sing, Leavenworth, or Alcatraz."

When the men in the infamous General Electric case of 1961 were brought to trial, they pleaded *"nolo contendere"* (that is, they refrained from contesting the charge), because had they been convicted they could have been sued for treble damages according to law. When they "threw themselves on the mercy of the court," their lawyers pleaded in their defense that they were good men who had contributed to the welfare of the needy, led Boy Scout troops, and so on. These were supposed to be "mitigating circumstances" in an otherwise black record. The record of these men in producing a vast variety of consumers' goods, which raised the living standards of human beings millions more times than a few paltry gifts to the deprived, was never so much as mentioned. These men were crucified for their virtues, and virtually no one, not the legal profession (which was myopic) or the businessmen's associations (which were scared), nor the American Civil Liberties Union (which is anti-business), raised a finger to help them.

If 1984 comes, and all business is controlled by government, and the entire population is suffering a famine as a result, it would be no more than poetic justice if all those who did not lift their hands, at least to protest and protect their benefactors, were condemned to death by starvation. This, after all, is the vast majority of people who have taken production for granted; they assumed that it would always keep flowing; so confident were they that others would continue to supply their wants that they even sent to prison (or approved sending to prison) the very men on whom the continuation of the chain of production depended. If they were that nonchalant about the continuing sustenance of their own lives, should others be less so? When the Atlases who hold up the world and make it possible for billions to live where only a few millions lived before, under conditions as far removed from a primitive starvation-economy as a mud hut is from a skyscraper, are reviled and stoned for their efforts, who can blame them if they begin to shrug?

15. Inflation

"Why should we mine gold in one part of the world with great expenditure of time and labor, transport it to other countries, and then let it lie in underground vaults at Fort Knox?"

If there is another way to preserve the integrity of currency besides having it backed in gold, it would doubtless be an admissible substitute. But the great advantage of the gold standard, which far outweighs any inconvenience involved in mining and storing the gold, is this: it makes it impossible for a nation to go on a continuous spending binge such as the United States has for the last thirty years, printing paper money at such a rate that the dollar has lost more than half its purchasing power. In short, the gold standard is a guarantee against *inflation*—against the government printing more and more money to "honor" its debts and pay for the extravagant promises the politicians have made in order to get themselves elected.

People are almost inevitably drawn to equate wealth with

money—if they get $20,000 this year and only got $10,000 last year, aren't they twice as rich? That depends on what the money *will buy*. If the money will buy twice as many goods as last year, then they have indeed taken in twice as much wealth. But if the dollar has been debased by inflation, so that it will no longer buy the goods, the person is no richer; if the $20,000 will buy less goods than the $10,000 did before, the person is less wealthy than he was before. Wealth is not money, but the ability to purchase the things that money will buy. And the power to purchase these things is not increased by having more green pieces of paper around; it is increased only by increased production—more milk, more homes, more washing machines.

When money is not backed by anything, there is no limit to the paper money the government may print. And the more dollars it prints, the less each dollar is worth. Suppose that the amount of paper money in circulation is doubled, while the quantity of goods produced remains the same. Then we have more dollars chasing the same amount of goods as before— and each dollar will buy fewer goods. People will have more dollars (or some people will), and they will be willing to pay more for goods, and thus bid up the price of the goods. Everyone will then have to pay a higher amount for these goods, including the people who do not possess any more dollars than before—and these people will be losers. Finally, as inflation permeates the entire economy, even the persons who originally benefited from it will no longer do so, for prices will be so much higher that they can no longer buy for $150 the same amount of goods that they could formerly get for $100.

In the long run, inflation harms almost everyone. But it harms most of all the people on fixed incomes, those living on retirement benefits, etc. These people are caught in the inflationary squeeze brought about by the government's dishonest monetary policy. They could buy $1,000 worth of goods last year, and this year the same amount of dollars will buy only $800 worth of goods—they have been cheated of the $200 as surely as if they had been robbed by a bandit. These are the unsung victims of the government's reckless spending.

In 1933 the United States went off the gold standard; from then to now an increasing percentage of dollars has not been backed by gold. At the present moment less than 15 percent of the paper money is backed by gold, and more such paper money is being printed every day and carried into the currency as "Federal Reserve Notes," as loans to banks, which then treat it as currency and make other loans on the basis of it. People seeing their dollars deteriorate in value, and realizing how impossible it is to accumulate savings for their old age, naturally would wish to trade in their dollars for gold, which at least is not likely to depreciate in value. But the government has blocked this move also: since the inception of the New Deal, American citizens have been prohibited from trading in their paper money for gold. Exchanging paper dollars for gold was every American's time-honored privilege throughout this country's history, but it has now come to an end. Foreign citizens who hold dollars may still trade them for gold, but to U.S. citizens this is prohibited. What has been the effect of this maneuver? To make the individual powerless where his currency is involved. Every American citizen's dollar is decreasing in value every year, and the only way to stop the dollar erosion is one that is legally prohibited. The water is flowing out of the tub and we are not permitted to use the stopper; so all we can do is watch helplessly. Control over a matter vital to the individual's very survival has now been taken out of his hands, and has been put into the hands of government. This is perhaps the most important of the many ways in which, in the last generation of American history, the individual has no longer been able to make his own decisions. He must succumb to whatever decisions are made for him, with the money that he has earned with *his* labor, by the people who have taken this money from him and are now using it to further their purposes. Officially they use it to further "his" purposes, particularly if he votes and if he is poor and is on the receiving end of government welfare checks, the promise of which led to the inflation of the currency in the first place. If he approved of such maneuvers, however, he has sold a pound of security for an ounce of welfare.

But the myths die hard. "It's a shame that the government isn't paying more money for housing, unemployment, and welfare!" exclaimed an acquaintance. "And how is it supposed to be paid for," I said, "seeing that we're already overtaxed?" "Well, let them print up more money!" he said; "then we'd all have more!"

This was a recommendation of inflation in its crudest form, but no different in principle from that advocated by many persons who pretend to greater economic sophistication. If the government could make us rich by increasing the supply of paper money, then it has indeed kept us poor during all the years in which it failed to do so. But this recommendation for increased riches is like trying to increase the size of one's family by multiplying the names of one's children. If everyone received today $100,000 in paper money, it would be virtually worthless. We would be flooded with paper money, but as long as the amount of goods and services remained the same, there would not be the slightest increase in our wealth—we would just have to pay more for whatever we purchased. The moment you telephoned the plumber to fix a leaky pipe, he would either not come at all (having just received $100,000 in paper money and thinking himself wealthy) or would come only for perhaps $50,000 per call (and then only if he thought that the paper was still worth something—that is, that he could buy some goods or services himself with it). Surely it is obvious that your material wealth can be increased only by an increase in the *goods and services you can obtain.* In Germany after World War I, the government printed billions upon billions of marks in paper money to satisfy its debts: finally one had to take a wheelbarrow full of the paper money to the grocery store in order to purchase one small sack of potatoes. People who had borrowed money (e.g. to buy homes) while the mark was still worth something were better off in that they could now wipe out their debts with a day's pay in paper money (since the government called this "legal tender" and forced others to accept it in payment); but those who had lent the money, and indeed virtually the entire middle class in Germany, were wiped out by the inflation.

"But suppose we don't inflate *that* much—just a little." Very well—though it is difficult to see why, if a little inflation makes us a little richer, a lot of inflation wouldn't make us a lot richer. But to the degree that inflation occurs, every dollar you have earned is worth less. If the process is gradual, it is not immediately noticed, and the administration in Washington that does it often finds that the effects are most pronounced a couple of years later when the next administration can take the blame for the rise in prices. It works something like this: the government prints a large amount of paper money, unbacked by gold, calling it "Federal Reserve Notes." These notes, via the Federal Reserve Bank, go to various banks in the country, and are available for making loans. Because of the increase in the money supply, the interest rates on loans goes down, and many enterprises that are fiscally unsound are given loans because "after all, the money is there." The recipients of this money use it for speculative ventures which should never have been undertaken, and which will boomerang in time, since there is not sufficient demand for their goods or services. To the recipients of the money, there is *for the time being* an increased purchasing power.

Or perhaps the government allots the money directly to defense industries, which find themselves happily with an increased supply. Wherever it goes, there is an increase in money to the recipients, and for the time being an increase in their purchasing power. But now there are more dollars chasing the same amount of goods as before: since the merchant can now get more dollars for his merchandise, the price of the items goes up. The new recipient of government money won't mind this, since he has money to spend anyway and is willing to spend it. But the other sectors of the population, who haven't received this money, will find that their goods cost more although their money-income has not increased, and the new inflation will hurt them as much as it helped the ones who were on the receiving end. Finally, if the inflation increases and the paper money percolates through the whole economy, most people will now have more money, but since the price of everything has also gone up (it has to, since the price of labor has gone up too), no one will any longer gain by the inflation. And those people who are on fixed incomes, or have no new money coming in and are living off the savings of pre-inflation days, will be hurt badly. The dollars they have saved through the years are now worth much less than they were when they had to earn them. This of course is what has happened to the United States economy; the dollar is now worth less than 40 percent of what it was in 1939.

Officials of the government know all this, of course, But the temptation to inflation is practically irresistible to them. After all, the government has made extravagant promises of what it will do for numerous special groups who have voted for Candidate X on the basis of that promise. If they make the taxes so high that all the promises are paid for, people will indignantly turn them out of office. But then the delightful idea occurs to them that they can simply keep the promises by inflating the currency, i.e. increasing the amount of paper money in circulation. With this paper money, endless government projects can be "financed," and the promises will have been technically kept. True, the dollars will soon be worth less than before (but by that time perhaps the voters won't notice, or their attention will be directed to something else, perhaps a government-created crisis as a diversionary tactic). True, the people on fixed incomes and savings will find that their real income (i.e. their purchasing power) has gone down—but this effect takes a little time, and the next president will get the blame. Anyway, they are in a bind now and the inflation will get them out of it. This has been the strategy of virtually every government in the Western world, which is why no currency (except perhaps the Swiss franc) is trustworthy any more. And when there is a war, the inflationary tendency skyrockets: how can one pay for a war except through paper money? At such times people will be less critical, thinking of their "patrotic duty," and anyway the real financial crush won't come till after the war is over, when the next generation will have to pay the piper.[52]

16. Business Collusion with Government

The libertarian advocates a complete separation of government from economics, just as he would advocate a complete separation of government from religion. Government should neither support nor suppress any particular faith, this being a purely personal and individual matter in which government has no place. And similarly, government should not attempt to conduct a business enterprise, nor regulate it, nor interfere in any way with its operation. Every time it does so, it casts a blight upon every activity it touches.

But now comes a common objection: "You have been praising the business community, including big business. And yet big business has had a great deal to do with government. Don't businessmen put money (voluntary contributions) into the coffers of political parties, so that these parties if elected can do favors for business? Don't businesses have huge contracts with the government? Don't businessmen often form powerful lobbies in Washington to get preferential treatment, such as the elimination of competition and a tariff on their particular goods? And isn't all this just the opposite of separation between economic matters and government which you advocate?"

Unhappily, all these charges are true. Businessmen, though not all businessmen, have done all of these things.

Some businessmen have simply been short-sighted. They have agitated for special favors from Washington, such as a tariff, often knowing full well that it was bad for the economy as a whole. When Group A got its tariff, then a precedent was set for B, C, D, E, F, etc. to get a tariff placed on *their* products too. Group A knew well enough that a tariff on these *other* products would hurt them. But they were in no position to complain, for they accepted the principle of tariff in the first place. Then, when consumers had less money left to buy their products (because of the high tariffs), and many items formerly flourishing on international trade were languishing because the other country had imposed a retaliatory tariff, the chickens came home to roost. Group A complained that "the government ought to do something to stimulate business"—but government was only being called on to correct a situation that government interference had caused in the first place.

Besides, some businessmen can't make it on their own, and they try to get government to subsidize them to keep them going—that is, to make every taxpayer help pay for their failures. This, of course, is nothing less than legalized plunder of some to pay for the failures of others.

But a large number of businessmen know well enough that government is not their friend. Government imposes on them a very high taxation; it bedevils them with all conceivable kinds of regulations, involving a great expenditure of time and unnecessary paperwork; it makes them do business in ways they would not have to do ordinarily. It snoops into every aspect of their work, and administers and regulates with something less than perfect wisdom. Sometimes the government even sets up a business in competition with one's own. Government imposes licensing laws for most businesses; all businesses selling goods outside a state must conform to interstate commerce laws; and government can close down virtually any business it wants to under anti-trust laws, according to such whims as no business can anticipate. This gives the government officials a life-and-death control over business. There are very few businesses which can even operate today without running afoul of some law or government regulation—and the government could close them down for violating that regulation. Government has business at its mercy.

Under these circumstances, what is business to do? It has to turn a profit or close up shop. It may not like doing business with government, but it often has to, for sheer survival. (1) With high taxes and an infinity of government regulations, there are fewer contracts available to business from private sources than there would be without the government interference—so businessmen go to government to get the contracts which they need to keep going. Besides, (2) with the threat of government controls breathing down their necks, businesses have to prove willing to "cooperate with government"; they know well enough that government could extinguish them at any moment on some legal pretext or other, so it often becomes a matter of "If you promise not to penalize me too heavily, I'll vote for you and even put some money into your pocket." (3) Businessmen cannot perhaps be blamed too much for bribing public officials when this is the only way that they can keep the house from falling down upon them. Vanderbilt was criticized bitterly for bribing the New York state legislators at Albany; but in one session of the legislature the men of Albany had voted over eighty separate taxes on Vanderbilt's railroad (New York Central), which if passed would have bankrupted him—and this in spite of the fact that the railroad was beneficial to New York state and also brought in large tax revenues. Bribing the members of the legislature was the only way he could survive. The blame should be placed not on Vanderbilt but on the legislators.

Government often tries to use one businessman to ruin another. A friend of mine who owns a factory was approached by representatives of the Justice Department who said to him, "Wouldn't you like to ruin your competition, the X Co., by testifying against it in court? I think we can put them out of business." My friend replied that he would gladly testify in court, but it would be *against* the government and *in favor of* his competition. The government agent was visibly shocked, but my friend held his ground. If all businessmen did this, it would help to paralyze the hands of government in trying to regulate, tax, and hold a life-and-death control over the intricate machinery of production. The men in the productive process can create that which is of value to the consuming public; the men of government can only retard and inhibit that process.

17. Taxation

The most obvious interference by government with the supply of money in the country is *taxation*. Government takes by force from every citizen: from every wage-earner in the form of income tax, from every buyer in the form of sales tax and all the other taxes applied in the production of goods that are bought. In general, the most productive people—in producing goods that others are willing to buy—are those who make the most money; and those who make the most money are the most heavily taxed. Never mind that these are the people on whom the welfare of the huge mass of employees depends; never mind that these are the people whose prosperity, if interfered with, will mean a drop in the prosperity of virtually everyone else; never mind that by taxing them most, the government is draining its tax-incomes in future years; the government blindly taxes them the most. It has nothing to do with justice—it is simply that the government, in its unending hunger for revenue, taxes most highly where there is the largest amount of capital available to be taxed. To a productive individual, government is more of a nuisance than a protection. Its police don't really protect him very effectively—in fact he has to hire private policemen on his own to keep his physical plant protected. For every dollar he gives to government in taxes, he may, if he is lucky, get back 2¢ in services. It is the productive individual who is most heavily taxed by government: he is taxed in proportion to his productivity, to pay for all the people who produce nothing. Government systematically drains him, bleeds him in order to give transfusions to others. After all, what can government get out of the nonproductive? There is nothing that government can take from them.

One way of taxing would be to charge a certain fixed

amount of everyone, on the theory that every citizen is getting equal protection from the government. The majority of tax-payers would feel that they were paying far too much, and they would vote against this mode of taxation. A second way of taxing would be to charge a certain *percentage* of a person's income; if it were 10 percent, the man earning $5,000 would pay $500 and the man earning $50,000 would pay $5,000. In some ways this would be considered fairer—everyone would be out by the same percentage of his income. But this tax too is soon voted down by the populace, since they would have to pay less if the richer person were taxed more. This leads to a third type of income taxation, the one employed by virtually all countries today, *graduated* income tax: here the man with a high income is not only taxed a higher *amount* than the lower income man, because 10 percent of $50,000 is more than 10 percent of $5,000, but he is also taxed a higher *percentage* of it: if he earns $100,000 he may be taxed 80 percent of it, or $80,000. The less rich always outnumber the more rich at the polls, and are most likely to vote for a tax scheme which "soaks the rich." Knowing little about econom-ics, they do not see that by taxing so highly the most produc-tive members of society, they are decreasing the wealthy man's incentive to continue to be productive—and thus they are making him indifferent to whether he earns $50,000 or $100,000 the next year, and whether he expands his plant or not or hires those new employees or not; that if it doesn't pay him to take business chances any more, his productivity will decrease (and with it the government's tax revenue), and that he will lay off employees rather than take more business chances—including those employees who voted to tax him to death, but who still don't see the connection between the poli-cies they voted for and the subsequent loss of their jobs.

Now, taxation, to use Morris Tannehill's metaphor, is eco-nomic hemophilia. "It drains the economy of capital which might otherwise be used to increase both consumer satisfaction and the level of production and thus raise the standard of living. Taxing away this money either prevents the standard of living from rising to the heights it normally would or actually causes it to drop. Since productive people are the only ones who make money, they are the only ones from whom government can get money. Taxation must necessarily penalize productivity."[53]

The taxes that go to poor-relief and, in general, to the redistribution of income ("taking from the rich and giving to the poor") are presented to us by government as a way of ameliorating poverty. Thus, we are supposed to have guilt-feelings at earning more than someone else, and be willing to be taxed in order to "help the poor." But the fact is that government more than anything else *creates* the very poverty it pretends to alleviate. High taxes mean that more must be charged for products before the producer can break even; so *higher prices* are an inevitable effect of taxation. Moreover, money that would have been invested in future production is drained off into taxes, meaning that the additional jobs which would have been created by this future production never came into existence—thus creating unemployment. This government-caused unemployment in turn the government tries to correct through welfare benefits to the unemployed, which again must be paid for by taxing the better-off still more, which results in still less productivity, and the cycle continues.

The utterly fatuous schemes by which the government tries to implement welfare decrease prosperity still further: for example, farmers are paid millions of dollars *not* to grow corn and grain; this pushes the price of all such grocery products up, forcing all consumers in the land to pay more for them; with higher prices for groceries, more people are unable to break even and are placed on government relief, which means still more tax money to pay for the relief benefits. Thus the taxpayer pays three times over: he pays (through taxation) the farmer for not growing the crops; he pays higher prices for his groceries; and then he pays again in the form of higher relief benefits for the poor. "Insanity" is a mild word to describe this procedure, though this has not prevented it from continuing to exist for more than thirty years. In fact, the situation is worse than has been described, for the government also supports the *production* of farm commodities above their market price. "This, of course, brought about unsold surpluses of these commodities, surpluses aggravated by the fact that farmers shifted production out of other lines to enter the now guaranteed high-price fields. Thus, the consumer paid four ways: once in taxes to subsidize the farmers; a second time in the higher prices of farm products; a third time in the wasted surpluses; and a fourth time in the deprivation of foregone products in the unsupported lines of production."[54]

But it is so easy, so fatally easy, every time a senator has an idea for "just one more" government project that will redound to his honor, for the tax on everyone to be raised once again, just a little. (And once raised, how often does it come down again?) But the result is cumulative and devastating: every shopkeeper in the nation has to pay just that bit more in taxes to break even, has to work just that bit harder and longer every day, before he can afford an evening out. He has to work that much more just to stay where he was before. And the customers, for their part, will not be likely to increase: on the contrary, their taxes are higher too, and the things that they can't buy now (because the money has to go to pay their taxes) may just include the things they would have bought at his shop. He is the unsung victim of government's interference in a once free economy.

One often encounters persons who are aflame with righteous indignation at some particular act of government—an administrative program, or a bill passed by Congress, or a Presidential order. At the present moment it is most likely to be Vietnam and the draft, but there are other targets as well. Yet these very same persons have for years advocated government intervention in all manner of other things; usually they can roughly be described as "liberal" (twentieth-century sense), "leftist" (though both "left" and "right" favor government intervention, disagreeing only on the kind and extent), "welfare statist," and so on. It is because of the advocacy of thousands of these people that the government has become as far-reaching as it has in the life of every citizen; yet when it comes to a particular measure or program of government, they are enraged. They have advocated endless governmental violations of human rights, yet one or two such violations in a particular area arouse their indignation. One is tempted to say to them, "You made your beds, now you can lie in them. It was thanks to you that government has become near-omnipotent in the lives of our citizens. It was you who fought against economic liberty, individualism, and self-determination when the rest of us were warning you about the consequences of the measures you wanted. It was thanks to you that we now have a prohibitive taxation which enables those in power to do pretty much what they want with the rest of us. Where were you when we fought for freedom from government controls? You were on the other side, loading up the government with one coercive power after another. You didn't mind using government to coerce others when it was for something *you* favored —but you didn't realize that your friendship with government is a two-edged knife. When the measures for which you agitated coerced others more than you, you didn't mind; and now when some of them hit *you,* you cry out in horror. But it is your own chickens coming home to roost. When you have chosen the government as your bedfellow, what other result could you expect?"

5
Profits
and Liberty

A man recently from Argentina, owner of a small shop before he came to the United States, said to me, "When Juan and Evita Perón were the dictators of Argentina, they were very popular with the working people. Evita would talk over the radio very frequently, addressing the 'masses' in honeyed tones. She would invite people to write her letters telling what they most wanted, and she would read some of these letters over the radio and grant the requests. A worker would write in that he needed a whole new living room and kitchen suite, saying just what kind of furniture he wanted and what color combination and so on. Then she'd tell them that he could get it if he went to such-and-such a place, and people would tune in by the millions hoping that they'd be the lucky ones the next time 'round. She wouldn't give the stuff to them herself, of course. She would just tell the owner of some furniture store that he'd better give the man all the stuff he wanted, free. He wouldn't like to do this of course, since it meant quite a loss to him, but he had to—she'd have his shop closed down if he didn't 'cooperate.' She could also have exposed him on the air for not cooperating and the workers would have raided the shop and taken everything in it. So he didn't have much choice, you see. She did this again and again."

"Didn't the people who got all these things free feel guilty, sometimes?" I asked. "After all they were taking it away from the merchant and not repaying him."

"The workers loved it. Things like that made the Peróns very popular with the working people, and the Peróns knew it. They had beat it into the people's heads that the merchants and manufacturers were evil exploiters who were out to bilk the people, and this was one small way of getting even with them. No, there were no guilt feelings about it at all as far as I could see. Evita knew that there were more workers than store-owners, so the workers' votes counted more heavily at the polls. That's all the Peróns cared about—justice was the last thing on their minds. Of course, they didn't see the long-run effects of what they did. Who would want to be a store-owner when he could be wiped out by official decree at any time? The Peróns needed the store-owners too, but as the slaves of the government. So who would want to become an owner any more? Who would want to risk his capital? It was as if you were sitting on a rock fault and you never knew when the next earthquake was coming. The most productive people in the country saw the handwriting on the wall and just got out. Argentina is still suffering from that mistake. But even now the workers don't see the connection. They'd do it all again."

No loss of lives here, no pogroms, no secret police in the night. Just a general insecurity, never knowing when the products of your labor were going to be snatched away from you. Many people in the United States would have approved what the Peróns did as much as the rank and file of Argentinians

appear to have done. But what was done was as clear a violation of rights as the more infamous crimes of the Nazis and the
Soviets. And it is more insidious because it appeals to a widespread human tendency to believe that "if anyone has more
than you do, it should be taken away from him."

But those who advocate such policies seldom see what the
consequences are. The consequences do not stop with the taking away from enterprising individuals the money they have
received for fulfilling the desire of others on the free market
(as if that were a crime); another consequence is that incentive is reduced, and, along with it, production and employment.

It takes profits to build industry. Yet there seems to be a feeling in
this country that making a profit is immoral. . . .

Comments Arthur F. Burns . . . "Perhaps the most serious obstacle
we face to a higher rate of economic growth is the persistent decline in
the rate of profit during the past ten or twelve years. Unless the rate of
profits is increased, I fear that our country will not succeed in attaining
the rate of growth that we would like to have and can have."

Says Roger M. Blough, chairman of U.S. Steel Corporation: "It will
help no one to think of government as a cookie jar out of which everyone can endlessly snatch cookies. Someone must work to put the cookies in the jar."[1]

Only the profits from production can put the cookies into
the jar. Yet it is these very profits that millions of voters, and
the majority of legislators, are doing everything in their power
to curtail, while at the same time grabbing more and more from
the jar.

"He's earning too much—take it away from him!" "A
hundred thousand a year while some people in the world are
hungry? Nobody ought to be allowed to earn that much!"
Such remarks are made, and they have a "humanitarian"
sound. Yet, as I shall try to show, they result from ignorance

of the function of profits in an economy: and to the extent that the suggestion is followed, the result is poverty for everyone.

In a free economy—one in which wages, costs, and prices are left to the competitive market—profits have a very important function: they help to decide what products shall be made, of what kinds, and in what amounts. It is the hope of profits that leads people to make the products (or provide the services): if little or nothing can be made from producing them, or not enough to justify the risk of investing the capital, the product will not be made; but the more one hopes to make from it, the more people will bend over backwards to produce it. The hope of profits channels the factors of production, causing products to be made in whatever quantities the public demands. In a state-controlled economy, controlled by bureaucrats, nothing at all may be made of a certain product much in demand, because the ruling decision-makers have decided simply not to make it; and at the same time, millions of other things that nobody wants may be produced, again because of a bureaucratic decision. And the bureaucracy need not respond to public demand. But in a free-enterprise economy, the producer who does not respond to public demand will soon find his warehouse full of unsalable products and his business bankrupt.

The hope of profits also makes for an enormous increase in the efficiency of production, for, other things being equal, the most efficient producer—the one who can cut out waste and motivate his workers to produce the most and best products—will earn the highest profits. And is there any reason why these profits should not be applauded? To the consumer, these profits mean that the industry producing the goods he wants is healthy and nicely functioning—one that can continue to deliver the goods, and probably for at least as low a price as its competitors, since otherwise more customers would have turned to the competitor. To the workers, profits of their employer mean that the employer is doing a good job for his customers—good enough so that they keep buying his product—and thus that they, the employees, are more secure in their jobs, and are more likely to receive higher wages in the future than are the employees of a company that is just barely making it. And as for the enterprisers, who can honestly say that they do not deserve the profits they received? First, they are risk-takers: they risked their capital to start the business, and had they lost no one would have helped them. Second, they spent not only their money (and borrowed money) on the enterprise, but, in most cases, years of their lives, involving planning, down to the last detail of production, the solution of intractable problems having to do with materials, supplies, and availability of trained help. Third, they anticipated the market, and did so more expertly than their competitors, for in order to make profits they had to have the right amount of merchandise at the right places for sale at the right time. Fourth, they provided the consumer a product or service (they could not *force* the consumer to buy from them; the consumer voluntarily elected to buy), in quantity—for a price, of course (after all his time and effort, should the enterpriser give it away, or sell it without receiving a return on it?), but nevertheless they provided it at a price which the consumer was willing to pay.

But the public, or a large segment of it, becomes envious and bitter, seeing that the man makes a profit. Perhaps the envious man has tried to start a business himself and lost it; or perhaps he just lost his job or can't pay some of his bills, and sees the employer living in a large luxurious house; in any case, he doesn't understand what side his bread is buttered on, for he doesn't realize that if the employer couldn't keep going, he himself would have no job. For whatever reason, he curses the employer because the man has a larger annual income than he does. Never mind that the employer took the risks, made the innumerable decisions (any one of which could have wrecked the business), and made *his* job possible in the first place: he, the employer, must be brought down to the worker's level. So he curses him, envies him, and votes for higher taxes for his employer, which, if passed, will mean that the employer won't expand his business and hire extra employees, and in fact may even have to cut it down some, even including his (the worker's) job. Officially, his line is that the employer's profits are ill-got. And yet when one examines it carefully, the complaint is groundless and absurd.

Suppose that an enterprise can make a thousand dollars in profits by a certain amount of capital investment; let us call this amount of investment C. Suppose also there is a second enterprise, less efficiently run than the first, which can only make that same amount of profit by investing twice the capital —2C. People will then say that the first, the efficient, manager, is reaping an excessive profit. For on the same investment of capital he can make twice the profits as his sloppy competitor; and for this his profits are branded as "excessive." But this is absurd: the efficient producer who gets more profits has more money to convert into plant expansion, more reserve for research so that he can improve his product, more wherewithal to reduce consumer prices and still make a healthy profit, thus benefiting the consumer with lower costs. The consumer ought to be anxious to have the most efficient producer possible; for only in that way can he be sure of getting the best possible product at the lowest possible price. By producing efficiently, the producer can undercut his competitors and thus benefit the consumer, while at the same time earning larger profits by capturing a larger share of the market for himself. We should applaud, not condemn, efficient production.

Add to this the fact that our present insane tax laws penalize the producer for his profits, and thus penalize efficiency. "Taxing profits is tantamount to taxing success in best serving the public. . . . The smaller the input (of money) required for the production of an article becomes, the more of the scarce factors of production is left for the production of other articles. But the better an entrepreneur succeeds in this regard, the more he is vilified, and the more he is soaked by taxation. Increasing costs per unit of output, that is, waste, is praised as a virtue."[2]

There would not be any profits but for the eagerness of the public to acquire the merchandise offered for sale by the successful entrepreneur. But the same people who scramble for these articles vilify the businessman and call his profit ill-got.

One of the main functions of profits is to shift the control of capital to those who know how to employ it in the best possible way for the satisfaction of the public. The more profits a man earns, the greater his wealth consequently becomes, the more influential does he become in the conduct of business affairs. Profit and loss are the instruments by means of which the consumers pass the direction of production activities into the hands of those who are best fit to serve them. Whatever is undertaken to curtail or to confiscate profits, impairs this function. The result of such measures is to loosen the grip the consumers hold over the course of production. The economic machine becomes, from the point of view of the people, less efficient and less responsive.[3]

Many people are so envious of, and bitter against, the man who earns a large salary or makes large profits, that they are unable to stand back impartially and try to understand what the role of profit is in an economy, and how it tends to increase everyone's income, not merely that of the man who receives it.

The man who receives a salary of $100,000 a year from his company—why does he get it? If he rendered no service, or if the company gained $10,000 as a consequence of hiring him, they would never pay him the $100,000. If they did, their

costs of production overhead would be that much higher and
they would have to charge more for their product (thus causing consumers to buy another brand instead) or absorb the
cost somewhere else. Even if the man saved them just
$100,000 a year, it would be no gain to them—they would
just break even with him. But if his services save them
$1,000,000 a year, then paying him the $100,000 is well
worth it—and they would gladly pay him more in order to
keep him. People who begrudge him the salary should ask,
"Am *I* ingenious enough to save the company over $100,000
a year, if it hired me?"

Now the man who does the employing: let us say that his
business is successful and through the years he has become a
millionaire. Special venom is reserved by the populace for
such men, but this is entirely without justification. If he got a
million a year as salary for some tax-supported office, or in
graft from the taxpayers' money, then they would have a right
to complain; for they would have to work that much harder to
make up the difference. But if he gets a profit of a million a
year *on the free market,* there is no cause for complaint. I
may dislike the latest rock-and-roll singer who gets a million a
year, but not one penny of his income comes out of my taxes;
and on a free market I am in no way forced to buy (or listen
to) his product. I can live in serene independence of his millions; I didn't pay a dime non-voluntarily to put this money
into his coffers. I may think the public foolish for buying non-
nutritional cereals, thus making the company receive large
profits, but this only prompts in me a reflection on the foolish-
ness of much public taste: I do not have to buy the cereal nor
contribute to the cereal company in any way. (In fact the shoe
is on the other foot: the company, because of its large profits,
pays extremely high taxes. Could it be that I pay less tax as a
result?) Should I then support a campaign to force people by

law *not* to buy the cereal, and thus decimate the company's profits? If I do this—and thus set a precedent against freedom of choice—the next year or the next decade, by the same token, by the same precedent I have set, someone may mount a successful campaign to force people by law not to buy whatever goods or service *I* produce. And if this happens, I shall deserve my fate, since I approved the principle of coercion in the first place. People should be free to make their own choices—which includes, of course, their own mistakes.

Instead of resenting it when individuals or companies make a million dollars, we should be happy. That million dollars means that there is a prosperous enterpriser who has created many jobs for people and bought equipment and so on (which in turn requires jobs to produce) to keep the product going. A million dollars made on the free market means that a great deal of money has filtered down to a very large number of people in the economy—and that a product is available at a competitive price, else the consumers would not have bought it in sufficient quantity to make our company its million. By contrast, a million dollars earned in government jobs means a million dollars milked from the taxpayer, which he could have spent in other ways.

The future prosperity of everyone—including the needy—depends on *encouraging* persons to become millionaires; to build railroads, houses, and power plants; to develop television, plastics, and new uses for atomic power. The reason is simple: *No man in a free country can make a million dollars through the machinery of production without producing something that we common men want at prices we are willing to pay.* And no man will continue to produce something we want at a price we are willing to pay unless he has the *chance* to make a profit, to become rich—yes, even to become a millionaire.[4]

There is an old saying, "No one should have caviar until everyone has bread." This is, when one examines it, one of the most confused statements ever made, though it is easily mouthed and chanted and is useful for political campaigns. If the enterpriser were not permitted to have his caviar, he would have far less incentive (perhaps no incentive at all) to produce anything, with the result that in the end fewer people would have even bread. The correct slogan would be, "If no one were permitted to have caviar, finally not many people would have bread."

One of the prevailing impressions, which underlies many arguments in this area but seldom itself surfaces to the level of explicit argument, is that the riches of the rich are the cause of the poverty of the poor. The impression is one of a certain fixed quantity of wealth, and that if some persons have more, this must inevitably mean that others have less.

A little reflection is enough to refute this assertion. If there were only a fixed quantity of wealth, how is it that we have many hundreds of millionaires now, hundreds and even thousands of men with elaborate houses, cars, lands, and other possessions, whereas only a few kings and noblemen had anything like this in bygone ages? Where long ago only a comparative handful of people could live, at the borderline between existence and extinction, in a given area of land, today a thousand times that number live, and live so well that they need spend only 10 to 15 percent of their income on food and all the rest goes for other things, most of which were inconceivable to the population of centuries past.

What people do not comprehend is that wealth is not static, but *grows* as long as people are free to use their ingenuity to improve the quality of their life. Here are deposits of iron, lying in the ground century after century; they do no good to anyone as long as they are just lying there. Now someone devises an economical process for removing the iron from the ground; another devises a means for smelting it, and another for combining it with manganese and other metals to produce steel that can be used in buildings, railroad tracks, and countless other things, When all these factors of production are functioning and the steel is produced, the world's wealth has been increased. Consumers have something to use that they didn't have before, and workers have jobs that didn't exist before. Every party to the transaction is a gainer.

When ten men are adrift on a lifeboat and there is only a certain quantity of provisions, if one person takes more than his share it necessarily follows that others must have less. The example of the lifeboat, or something like it, seems to be the dominating image of those who think in this primitive way about wealth. They apparently believe that because some men are rich, others must therefore be poor, since the rich have taken it away from the poor. Now this *is* the case when a bandit takes away some of your possessions—he has more, and as a consequence you have less. Bandits do not create wealth, they only cause the same amount to change hands. The same happens when the tax-collector takes away by force some of what you have earned; the government too is not creative—it takes away from you to give to others. But the capitalist in a free society is *not* like that: he cannot force the money of you, the consumer, out of your hands; you pay him for a product or a service that did not exist, or did not exist as efficiently or in the same form, prior to his creative endeavor; his product (e.g., a car) or service (e.g., railroad transportation) is good enough in your eyes so that you voluntarily pay some of the money you have earned in exchange for it. The entrepreneur has brought something into being and offered it on the open market in exchange. He has created something new under the sun, which people may buy or not buy as they prefer.

No, the world is not like a lifeboat. Wealth does increase, and it increases for all as a result of the efforts of a few creative men. The riches of the rich are not the cause of the poverty of the poor: the rich in a free enterprise society can become rich only (1) by hiring workers to produce something and (2) because these consumers on a free market choose to buy what the entrepreneur has offered. They are rich precisely *because* innumerable consumers have, through their purchases, voted for whatever product or service they have to offer. Not one penny of their income on the free market came from the taxed income of anyone else.

One would think that entrepreneurs were armed bandits robbing them by force, to hear the complainers talk, instead of the risk-takers who had the ideas, and, if things went right, benefited the public. But the fallacy persists; many well-meaning people, ignorant of how an economy functions, are trying their best to do them in. In a South American factory, workers agitated, demanded a larger share of the profits, held meetings and finally burned down the factory. "That'll show the filthy profiteer!" they cried. And it is true that they had indeed done him in: his entire life's work and capital were burned to the ground in one night. But they too had lost: they were out of jobs—the jobs that the factory had provided no longer existed. Neither did the products that the factory had made, and consumers had that much less choice in deciding what to buy at the store.

A millionaire industrialist, Aristotle Onassis, has created millions of dollars' worth of wealth for the Greek nation by starting shipbuilding plants and many other enterprises, thus increasing production and making possible thousands of jobs for people who would otherwise be unemployed.[5] Yet the average Greek worker does not see this; he hates Onassis because Onassis is rich and he, the worker, is not. He hates Onassis furthermore because Onassis invests most of his profits outside of Greece. What he does not see is that his own materi-

al well-being is tied up with those of Onassis and other enterprisers like him. Apparently Onassis does not consider Greek
investments the safest ones under present conditions; when he
does, he, himself a Greek, will doubtless start investing in
Greece. But the fact that he does not do so now should not be
a source of anger to the Greek workers; indeed, it should be a
source of gratification. For it is the very safety of Onassis' investments which makes the security of the Greek workers' jobs
possible. The unions cannot make it possible; *they* cannot
guarantee that Onassis will be able to continue in business; and
indeed, if their demands become exorbitant, it will *not* be possible; and then they themselves will be out of jobs, for their jobs
will collapse along with his enterprise. It is to *their* interest as
well as his that Onassis make the safest investments possible, so
that he will have more wherewithal with which to expand his
plant operations and thus hire more and more Greek workers.
But most of them do not see this; all they see is that he is rich
and they are not. What workers all over the world need more
than anything else is a little elementary knowledge of
economics.

Ever since 1945, Great Britain has had some form of socialism or other. The greedy capitalist monster was to be destroyed forever. More and more industries were to belong to
"the people"—that is, run by the government. Thus no more
"exploitation" was to be possible. Socialist prophets had declared that workers would have a new energy when they
worked for the socialist state instead of the capitalist masters.
"But in fact the worker has now merely exchanged the old
boss for a new bureaucrat. The old boss might have been a
tough fellow, but he might also have been a fairly decent
human being and most of them were. The boss now is a cold,
impersonal being, full of theoretical humanity, far away in
London, and no decision can be made by any small foreman

on the job without an immense amount of paper work that begins at the local office and moves snail-like through various local boards, sub-councils, regional boards and other bureaucratic nests up to London and finally back through the same succession of petty bureaus. Decisions are made by inflexible rule, with the human element extracted as, for instance, the laying off of a coal miner just a month before his pension would accrue and the bald refusal to reinstate him for the extra month to hold on to the benefit he had put in twenty years accumulating. . . . The workers are not producing as much for the State they supposedly love as they did for the boss they were supposed to hate."[6]

With the gradual erosion of private industry, private profits also melted away. Why knock oneself out running business efficiently or expanding it when the government took most of the proceeds anyway? The Labor Party propagandists had fed the workers the delusion that they could get more income without increased production. Who would make up the difference? The rich, of course; the rich would be soaked to pay for the workingman's benefits. This policy found great favor with the workingman of Britain. But of course there was a catch in it: in a couple of years there were practically no rich left in Great Britain. The rich had been rendered extinct through heavy taxation. And now the common man himself would have to assume the heavy burden of the benefits he was receiving.

Yet the common man of Great Britain, while agitating for ever more free benefits from the government, agitated also for a lessening of taxation. But how else could these increased social services be paid for except by increasing taxes? Sir Stafford Cripps announced this fact to the British public: "When I hear people speak of reducing taxes," he said, "and at the same time see the cost of social services rising rapidly, very often in response to the demand of the same people, I wonder if they appreciate to the full the old adage: We cannot eat our cake and have it."[7]

Well then, why not charge more for British exports and get the added income that way? But of course Britain must compete for export trade in an international market. Britain's economic survival depends on being able to produce manufactured goods cheaply for an export trade. But this is precisely what socialist Britain is unable to do. Numerous strikes paralyze British industry from time to time; orders for goods cannot then be delivered abroad on schedule—thus making overseas buyers beware, and leading them to order their goods elsewhere next time; finally the strike is settled, only by large wage-increases; these increases force the employer to charge more for the finished product, which is already overpriced in the competition of the international market. Worst of all, in Britain, cheap production is simply no longer possible, for every industry must include, in its cost of production, the killing taxes which the government exacts from it. The manufacturer of goods for export, already heavily strapped and bedeviled by inefficient labor, must now operate with a heavy ball and chain around his feet in the form of the prohibitive taxation. And so more and more overseas buyers purchase Volkswagens and fewer purchase MGs. This of course leads to more taxes to support the unemployed workers who become unemployed because the contracts are going to overseas producers: when the voters killed off the profits, the activities performed from the profit motive ground to a halt. The voters had killed the goose that laid the golden egg.

Winston Churchill once observed that the real crime against society is not profit but loss. "Private industry runs at a profit and uses the profit to expand producing capacity. Government industry runs at a loss and taxes the substance of the people to pay for its inefficiencies. Which is the greater crime against society?"[8]

But perhaps the most telling argument for profits is that the hope of profit is the surest way to get increased production. Whenever the chance of profit is removed, production lags or ceases. And production is a basic human need: man must produce in order to live—that is an inescapable fact of man's situation on this planet. If some men do not produce, others must produce that much more if they are all to remain alive. A considerable amount of productive labor is required for the bare necessities of life; and if one desires more of life's goods than those required for subsistence, still more production is required.

When, in a free-enterprise economy, many thousands of kinds of items are produced, consumers scramble to buy them —if they didn't buy them, of course, they would not long continue to be produced. In practice, then, people do value the fruits of the productive process. But the moral code to which they give allegiance in their day-to-day talk puts no premium on production at all. According to popular morality, it is charity that is the supreme virtue. Presumably the production of the goods needed to sustain life is not considered virtuous because people produce to enhance their own lives and to make profits—all of which is selfish. And what is selfish, according to the popular morality, cannot be virtuous.

Yet charity is possible only from the surplus of production. Without production, there would be nothing for anyone to be charitable with. In a society on a bare subsistence level, charity would be near zero, for one could give food to another only by consigning oneself to starvation.

I shall not attempt to consider to what extent charity is a virtue. Let us say that charity to the right person and at the

right time is a virtue—typically as a temporary measure to
help put a person on his feet again. But charity is not virtuous
no-matter-what: to work to support someone who could just as
easily support himself is not even helping him—it is getting
him habituated to a life of dependency and parasitism. Before a person gives of his hard-earned money he would do well
to be sure what the effect of it will be on the recipient.

But however virtuous charity may be, it is a dependent virtue: it rides piggy-back on the primary virtue, namely production. The greater the surplus of production, the greater the
amount of charity that is possible.

The producer, however, produces primarily for himself,
and for his profit. Because of this fact, his activity—the supreme virtue of productivity—is not included on the popular
list of virtues at all. Whatever his motives are, however, let us
consider his deeds. His deeds, surely, are quite clear.

The man who perfects a method for taking materials out of
the earth, and starts a factory to produce them, spends years
of his time and thousands or millions in money, hoping quite
properly to have a financial reward for his pains; and in the
process he provides work for large numbers of people. Nevertheless, popular morality considers him an evil exploiter who
deserves only to be taxed out of existence for the sake of the
rest of us. And yet this man has, in all candor, probably done
more good than any other kind of person in our society. The
entrepreneur may not *want* to pay out money to get a product or
hire workers; he would rather get the income without any effort, let us say: but he cannot get a product mass-produced
without doing these things, so perforce he does them. And
when he is left free to do these things, the economy of the nation flourishes; the system of free enterprise, that is economic
freedom, has provided the highest standard of living ever
known in the world to the degree to which nations have per-

mitted economic freedom. In the nations which do not permit economic freedom, production stagnates, constant shortages appear, and the majority of the population fall well below the poverty level. Economic freedom, and the fruits of it, are perhaps the principal positive *moral* force in the history of America; to take just one example, the American supermarket, selling thousands of items at marginal profits per item, and making available thousands of items to thousands of people otherwise unable to buy them, has probably done more good than all the charitable schemes of the last two thousand years put together. And yet the professional do-gooders castigate and condemn the producer on whom they are dependent for the handouts they wish to give, and they praise their fellow do-gooder who, having taken it away from the producer, then undertakes to distribute these bounties to the needy—and what he is distributing isn't even his own money, but money taken by force from the men who produced the goods. Was there ever such a total inversion of moral values?

Government vs. Profit-Makers

In their eagerness to prohibit profits, the Soviets paid an enormous price. They did away with the entire managerial class—the men who could conceive a productive enterprise, raise the money, plan it to the last detail, and put it into practice, all without spending the tax-payers' money and bearing the entire risk of the venture themselves. "Profiteering" was what they called this activity, and they drummed the "evils of profiteering" into the minds of workers to get them to approve the new regime. It was not to their interest to have the people think otherwise, for else they could not have got into power with a wide base of popular support. Nor was it to their interest to teach people that on a free market the riches of the rich are not the cause of the poverty of the poor; on the contrary, it was to their interest to make the people think precisely that, so that the people themselves would rise up to rid the society of the "profiteers." The so-called profiteers knew better, but they were vastly outnumbered, and when the revolution came, not only were the fruits of their labors taken away from them by force (and given to "the people"—that is, taken over by the government), but most of them did not even escape with their lives. If they had owned so much as a corner grocery store, they were considered suspect and relegated to the lowest and most menial jobs in the new "workers' paradise"; if they had employed even a small number of people in a shop or a mill, they were taken out and shot.

Who filled the breach? Who took over these positions? The government—which performed it with only a few percentage-points of the efficiency, the know-how, and the expertise of the men who had done it themselves and invested their own time and money in it. And the government, with unlimited police powers, and powers to send workers anywhere for whatever reason, soon proved to be a far harsher taskmaster than any private employer had been: the most an employer could do to a worker was to fire him, and leave him free to seek employment elsewhere; but the government could find other work for him in Siberia, or starve him to death, or put a bullet between his eyes. And the government was omnipotent, involved in every aspect of a citizen's life—and one could disagree with its policies only at the price of one's head.

According to his biographers, Lenin himself had only the vaguest idea of how a complex operation like a factory would be run after the revolution. He apparently possessed the naive idea that the workers would band together and work for the glory of the state, toiling side by side, their sickles waving together in the sunlight. But every enterprise involving human labor must have an organization: there must be a *managerial hierarchy,* to decide what enterprise should be entered upon, what physical plant and machinery it would take to do it, how many should be employed in this department and how many in that, and countless decisions from day to day and hour to hour. Only the people who know the business from the inside, who have worked their way to the top at it, are competent to handle such a complex, delicate mechanism. But the Atlases of the nation upon whom the nation's wealth and welfare depended were rewarded by being riddled with bullets by the very workers who would starve without their efforts. With the end of the "profiteers" went the end of any hope for freedom and prosperity in Soviet Russia.

"No one should have caviar," they said, "until everyone has bread." But unless a man has at least a chance to work for caviar, soon no one will even have bread. And so a minimum degree of profit motive had to be admitted, even in Soviet Russia, in order to stave off mass starvation and make possible just enough of life's necessities to keep body and soul together.

"Exploitation"

Among the clichés constantly mouthed by people who are ignorant of the economic facts of life, none is more often encountered than the charge of exploitation. "The employer exploits the employee," is the usual refrain.

Now there is a great deal of exploitation going on in the world, almost all of it in totalitarian nations with centrally controlled economies. In Soviet Russia the state is the sole employer, and it decides what work you are to do and how much you are to receive in wages for your work. It can, and often does, exploit workers, for if they are dissatisfied with the wage they are receiving there is nothing they can do about it. Soviet citizens who arouse the disfavor of the rulers are even more exploited in the slave labor camps, where they work for no wage at all under impossible conditions, beaten by guards, starved, or frozen by cold, with the result that large numbers of them die every year. Human beings are the cheapest of commodities in that totalitarian state, and when the state is the master and you are its vassal, there is nothing to stop the exploitation—the state needs your labor, and it doesn't much care what happens to you.

But in a free economy you are not forced to take and stay with a certain job. The greater the diversification of jobs the greater your opportunities for changing jobs. And in the United States throughout its history, it has been comparatively easy to change jobs. If you don't like the wages one employer is giving you, you change jobs and get a higher wage; this happens thousands of times every day throughout America. The cure for any attempts at exploitation is to have great diversity of employment, so that a worker can be more and more independent of any specific employer.

"But the employer will give as low a wage as he can get by with, won't he?" Yes, usually he will, because the higher the wages he must pay, the higher the cost of his product must be, and the more likely he is to be outpriced in the open market. The employee too, for his part, normally does as little work as he can get by with and still keep his job, and the employee who does more than this is likely to be rewarded with a higher wage. But every firm must compete for good workers; if it pays too little, the workers will desert the firm and go and work elsewhere. And as virtually every employer knows, it doesn't pay to hire underpriced workers—they will stay only until they can get a better job elsewhere, and while on the job they will not work well—the employer gets his money's worth much better by paying his workers well than by paying them little (if indeed he can keep employees at all by doing the latter). But if he suddenly decided to become philanthropic and double or treble wages, unless he suddenly got *much* more value out of each worker he would soon have to close down—and his philanthropic experiment would end with his factory closed and his workers unemployed. And if he suddenly decided to turn Scrooge and cut the wages in half, he would soon have no employees left, or at best a few bottom-of-the-barrel workers who would deliver such bad service that he would do better to close the plant and have no workers at all. There is, in fact, not very much latitude open to the employer in the wages he pays his employees.

Given the conditions which the employer faces, he must pay workers pretty much the values that consumers place on their contributions. If the employer pays a higher wage, he suffers a loss. If he does not then reduce his wage rate, his number of employees, and his production to what he can sell at a price that covers his costs, he will eventually be forced out of business. No businessman can long pay costs which he cannot get back from consumers.

In the long run it is the consumer who pays the wages. The businessman is merely a middleman.[9]

The best and only cure for the danger of exploitation is the free market:

No businessman in a free market society can long pay a worker a dollar an hour and sell his product for five dollars an hour. Why not? Because you and I and thousands of others like us would be very happy to go into that business, pay those men two dollars and sell their product for five dollars if we could. Others would soon offer them three dollars, four dollars, or even four-fifty. In fact, large corporations would be very happy to make profits of just two cents an hour for every worker they employ. They are just not able to pay them much less than the market value of their product.[10]

But didn't Henry Ford in the midst of the depression suddenly start to pay his workers $5 a day (a very high wage for that time)? Indeed he did, and by doing so he got some of the best workers from all over the country. But that added wage —double what many had been receiving—might have added so much to his overhead that he would have had to charge more for his cars than the competition would bear, had it not been for another factor:

Just at that time the motor car business was having a tremendous boom. Orders were piling up that could not be filled. It was impossible at the time to expand the plant quickly. Someone hit upon the idea that to boost the wage rate sharply would draw the best workmen from the other motor car factories, and increase the output. This it did, according to the account, by something like 20%. And 20% was about the average rate of increase in Ford's wages. In this instance, the higher wages paid for themselves in increased "efficiency" and in increased product per worker.[11]

Wages have, of course, gone up considerably throughout the years—not merely in money, but in the goods the money would buy. In each generation of American history, wages have been higher (real wages, not only money wages) than in the generation before. "Real wages are determined by the product per worker, and are a fairly fixed share of the value of the product. Unless the product can be increased, the level of real wages cannot."[12]

But what makes it possible for the product per worker to increase? The product per worker is determined, in the long run, by the *capital investment per worker* (in the American steel companies, for example, this is an investment of about $20,000 per worker). And the higher capital investment per worker, the greater his productivity and the greater the savings that can be invested in new processes and machines.

The real secret of higher wages is increased savings per capita. Increased savings are a result of producing more than is consumed. If more goods and services are produced than consumed, then these unconsumed goods and services are available for making tools, factories, and other things needed to help increase production. American living standards have gone up over the years because generation after generation our parents have provided their children with a better start in life than their parents had.[13]

The term "exploitation" is commonly used, as we have used it here, to refer to underpayment for work done. But in a somewhat different sense, exploitation occurs when someone takes from you by force the things you have previously worked to own. In this sense, the bandit exploits you when he takes your valuables at gun-point; and the tax-collector exploits you when he takes from you a portion of what you have earned. The Vikings raided numerous towns and looted the fruits of people's labor. Chinese warlords for generations exploited the people by taking their produce from them and using them for their own purposes. But if this is exploitation, then what the employer does in relation to an employee on the free market is emphatically *not* exploitation. When the manager of a department store or office offers you lower wages than you will accept, he is not exploiting you: he cannot force you to work for him, and you will probably laugh at him and turn around and go elsewhere. The more developed an economy is, the greater the diversity of employment, and the more independent a worker can be of any one employer. To use the same word, "exploitation," to cover robbery by marauding gangs (or by the government) on the one hand, and conditions of employment on a free market on the other, is more than to be guilty of semantic sloppiness—it is to use words deliberately to mislead people into a false picture of the facts.

But weren't the workers exploited during the early days of capitalism? And aren't some workers exploited still, even on the free market?

There are, and were, always workers getting less than their talents could capture on the free market. Sometimes the worker in question is ignorant of what wages he could command elsewhere. Sometimes he knows he could get more in another area, but is unwilling or unable to move. Sometimes he simply prefers his job where he is at lower pay to the one for which he could get higher pay. And, in many contemporary cases, he would have to pay so much more income tax by taking the higher paying job that it isn't worth it to him to get the added pay—it would merely kick him into a higher income bracket, with his net income being no greater than before. Sometimes the plumber who gets $12 an hour for his daytime services attends meetings at night to protest the condition of the "poor exploited workers of America."

It is quite true, of course, that conditions in the early days of the Industrial Revolution were horrible by today's standards. As we have already observed, the rise in wages had to wait upon the gradual growth of capital accumulation, thus making possible labor-saving machinery which meant a larger investment in machinery per worker—which multiplied production, increased consumer consumption at a lower price per item, and by turning the item from a luxury into a necessity led the manufacturer to expand his plant and take on new workers. This process was gradual and slow. Still, it is worth observing that in the early days of the Industrial Revolution those workers who came from the farms to the factories did so voluntarily, because of the higher wages they received in the factories—low though they were by our standards, they were higher than the income possible to the same workers before, else they would not have changed jobs. In many cases, the presence of factory work meant the difference between life and death, for a non-industrialized small farm could often not support the large families, where many died of starvation. It was capitalism that enabled the population of Europe to double within a century. Capitalism has been given such a bad press often by historians themselves, that the facts of the situation have not become generally known to the public. Anyone who does not know about the genuine rise in the standard of living resulting from the Industrial Revolution should read Professor F. A. Hayek's book, *Capitalism and the Historians.*

The actual history of the connection between capitalism and the rise of the proletariat is almost the opposite of that which theories of the "expropriation of the masses" suggest. The truth is that, for the greater part of history, for most men, the possession of the tools for their work was an essential condition for survival, or at least for being able to rear a family. The number of those who could maintain themselves by working for others, although they did not themselves possess the necessary equipment, was limited to a small proportion of the population. The amount of arable land and of tools handed down from one generation to the next limited the total number who could survive. To be left without them meant in most instances death by starvation, or at least the impossibility of procreation. There was little incentive and little possibility for one generation to accumulate the additional tools which could have made possible the survival of a larger number of the next, so long as the advantage of employing additional hands was limited mainly to the instances where the division of the tasks increased the efficiency of the work of the owner of the tools. It was only when the larger gains from the employment of machinery provided both the means and the opportunity for their investment that what in the past had been a recurring surplus of population doomed to early death was in an increasing measure given the possibility of survival. Numbers which had been practically stationary for many centuries began to increase rapidly. The proletariat which capitalism can be said to have "created" was thus not a proportion of the population which could have existed without it and which it had degraded to a lower level; it was an additional population which was enabled to grow up by the new opportunities for employment which capitalism provided. . . . It raised the productivity of labor so that much larger numbers of those who had not been equipped by their parents with the necessary tools were enabled to maintain themselves by their labor alone; but the capital had to be supplied first before those were enabled to survive who afterward claimed as a right a share in its ownership. Although it was certainly not from charitable motives, it still was the first time in history that one group of people found it in their interest to use their earnings on a large scale to provide new instruments of production to be operated by those who without them could not have produced their own sustenance.[14]

It is sometimes alleged that an employer is exploiting a worker when he fires him from a job. "Isn't having the power to hire and fire just another form of exploitation?" some have asked.

Now if an employee has a contract with an employer, agreeing to keep him on for a specified period (such as a year's teaching job), then the employer who fires him is guilty of breach of contract and can be sued. But if there is no such contract, as there typically isn't in seasonal trades, the employer is free to fire the worker at any time, just as the employee on his part is free to leave the firm at any time and obtain employment elsewhere. Here the situation is the same on both sides: either party is free to terminate the exchange at any time.

And this of course is just what it is: an *exchange*—the exchange of wages for labor: money (from the employer) for work done (by the employee), no different in principle from the exchange of money for goods when you buy something at the store. When the employee decides to quit or go elsewhere, he is freely terminating the exchange; and when the employer decides that it's slack season and he should lay off the worker, *he* is freely terminating the exchange. " 'Economic power' is simply the right under freedom to refuse to make an exchange. Every man has this power. Every man has the same right to refuse to make a proffered exchange."[15]

Though the point is a simple one, many are misled by it. When an employer lays off an employee, they call it "coercion by economic power" (though they say nothing of the kind when the employee quits). The employer and employee have previously made an exchange; now the employer, for one reason or another, prefers not to continue (or believes it impossible to continue) that exchange. No one is coercing anyone else. If, now, someone says, "The employer is coercing the employee! Make him keep the worker on! Pass a law!" he is not only recommending a measure that (if generalized) would bankrupt the employer; he is advocating the use of force against one of the parties to a previously voluntary exchange. The employer has refused an exchange; now the social do-gooder wants to *impose* one on him by force (via government). And by doing so, he will have set a precedent in the advocacy of force which will go far beyond the single situation confronting him—though usually he does not realize this. Let us suppose, with Rothbard, that the employee had a job with Ford Motor Co. He condemns the employer who lays him off as exercising "economic coercion." Now, the robber and the thief are quite literally exercising coercion. But the employer is not—he is, as we saw, simply *deciding against continuing a voluntary exchange*. But if the do-gooder has his way, the employee will assert a claim (and if he has his way, the law will uphold it) on the employer's property. And in this case the employee is plundering the employer, not the other way around.

Those who lament the plight of the automobile worker who cannot obtain a job with Ford do not seem to realize that before Ford and without Ford there would be no such job to be obtained at all. No one, therefore, can have any sort of "natural right" to a Ford job, where it IS meaningful to assert a natural right to liberty, a right which each person may have without depending on the existence of others (such as Ford). In short, the libertarian doctrine, which proclaims a natural right of defense against *political* power, is coherent and meaningful, but any proclaimed right of defense against "economic power" makes no sense at all. Here, indeed, are enormous differences between the two concepts of power.[16]

Those who talk loosely about the workers being exploited should consider the important way in which *all* taxpayers are being exploited. According to Albert Jay Nock, the entire producing class (those who work, and pay taxes out of the proceeds of their labor) are the exploited class; the exploiting class, by contrast, is those who live off of the first class at the taxpayers' expense: this includes all persons on welfare, all employees of the government (except for that portion of their income which is deducted from their wages in taxes), and in general all those who are on the receiving end of the benefits handed out non-voluntarily by the working taxpayer. The government, according to Nock, is a device for maintaining the stratification of society permanently into these two classes. Surely, if the word "exploiter" is to be used at all, it should refer to those who do not work but who live at the expense of those who do work.[17]

There are those who might agree with this, and yet insist that within the productive class the employers are exploiting the "real" workers, those who work primarily with their hands rather than with their heads. But what are a worker's unaided muscles worth? To see how much, look at the standard of living that they produced in times of ancient slavery; the standard of living of medieval blacksmiths—just enough to keep body and soul together if one toils from dawn to dusk and never becomes ill. All the rest—all the difference in the standard of living of the ordinary worker between that day and this—is a gift from the Thomas Edisons, the Andrew Carnegies, the James Hills of this world. Because they lived and accomplished what they did, our standard of living today is higher—just as, because Bach and Beethoven lived, our musical standard of living today is higher. These men, often hated and maligned, were the real benefactors of mankind—more than all the givers of charity put together; they are the ones who created the improvements that made charity on a large scale possible. The rewards that we—each one of us—owe these men is so great that it could not be repaid in a hundred lifetimes.

Creative men in science, technology, and medicine have reduced the amount of work required of every worker in America to a fraction of what it would otherwise have been—besides providing such benefits as heated homes, electricity, and modern medical discoveries. Even if there had been just *one* benefit—the discovery of anesthetics for use in surgery, or the discovery of the processes that made iron usable in steel rail and steel cars—could we safely set a limit to our indebtedness to its creator? Can you estimate the worth to you of having a house that is heated by something more than a fireplace? Or of being able to go into surgery anesthetized instead of being tied to a bed and cut open while fully conscious?

But since we cannot create or carry out ideas on a par with theirs, and thus repay them in that way, the least that we can do on their behalf (those that are still alive to be repaid) is not to interfere with their lives by maligning them, harassing them, calling them public enemies, and then taxing them to death. The man near the bottom of the economic ladder, the humble worker with no particular creativity of his own but able in his own way to carry out the plans of others, would be near to starvation, or dead, today, as he has been throughout history, if it were not for these maligned benefactors. Owing to the science and technology which they perfected, he now has as a gift *the inestimable bonus of their brains*.

"Stand on an empty stretch of soil in a wilderness unexplored by men and ask yourself what manner of survival you would achieve and how long you would last if you refused to think, with no one around to teach you the motions, or, if you chose to think, how much your mind would be able to discover—ask yourself how many independent conclusions you have reached in the course of your life and how much of

your time was spent on performing the actions you learned from others
—ask yourself whether you would be able to discover how to till the
soil and grow your food, whether you would be able to invent a wheel,
a lever, an induction coil, a generator, an electronic tube—and then decide whether men of ability are exploiters who live by the fruit of *your*
labor and rob you of the wealth that *you* produce, and whether you
dare to believe that you possess the power to enslave them. . . .

"When you work in a modern factory, you are paid, not only for
your labor, but for all the productive genius which has made that factory possible: for the work of the industrialist who built it, for the work
of the investor who saved the money to risk on the untried and the
new, for the work of the engineer who designed the machines of which
you are pushing the levers, for the work of the inventor who created
the product which you spend your time on making, for the work of the
scientist who discovered the laws that went into the making of that
product, for the work of the philosopher who taught men how to
think. . . .

"In proportion to the mental energy he spent, the man who creates a
new invention receives but a small percentage of his value in terms of
material payment, no matter what fortune he makes, no matter what
millions he earns. But the man who works as a janitor in the factory
producing that invention, receives an enormous payment in proportion
to the mental effort that his job requires of *him*. And the same is true
of all men between, on all levels of ambition and ability. The man at
the top of the intellectual pyramid contributes the most to all those
below him, but gets nothing except his material payment, receiving no
intellectual bonus from others to add to the value of his time. The man
at the bottom who, left to himself, would starve in his hopeless ineptitude, contributes nothing to those above him, but receives the bonus of
all of their brains. Such is the nature of the 'competition' between the
strong and the weak of the intellect. Such is the pattern of 'exploitation'
for which you have damned the strong.

"Such was the service we had given you and were glad and willing to
give. What did we ask in return? Nothing but freedom. We required
that you leave us free to function—free to think and to work as we
chose—free to take our own risks and to bear our own losses—free to
earn our own profits and to make our own fortunes—free to gamble
on *your* rationality, to submit our products to your judgment for the
purpose of a voluntary trade, to rely on the objective value of our work
and on your mind's ability to see it—free to count on your intelligence

and honesty, and to deal with nothing but your mind. Such was the price we asked, which you chose to reject as too high. You decided to call it unfair that we, who had dragged you out of your hovels and provided you with modern apartments, with radios, movies and cars, should own our palaces and yachts—you decided that *you* had a right to your wages, but *we* had no right to our profits, that you did not want us to deal with your mind, but to deal, instead, with your gun."[18]

When I see the ruined palaces and monuments of ancient emperors, and read of their profligate spending and festive balls, I cannot help thinking of the money and labor, the sweat and tears, that have been the price of these things, expropriated from the poor, with nothing given in return, taken by force from the last of what the worker could save, often resulting in his starvation or death from overwork. But when I read of a lavish party given by an American industrialist—provided always that he has earned the money on a free market, from consumers who bought his product voluntarily, and not by robbery via government subsidy and the taxation of others—I think of what he has *achieved* to make it possible for him to possess this wealth—not by diminishing the wealth of others as taxation does, but by increasing it through increased production and employment; not by forced expropriation through taxes, but by voluntary trade of value for value. But the majority of people, even of Americans, who ought to know better, do not recognize this difference. All they see is "he has more than we have," and they are envious and bitter. Yet when the industrialist takes a vacation on his yacht, the taxpayer has not paid a penny toward that yacht; and when a king or a president takes a vacation on his, the taxpayer has paid for it down to the last bolt and screw—and is that much poorer for the king's enjoyment. Such is the difference between the economic realm, where wealth is created, and the political realm, where wealth is seized from those who created it in order to be enjoyed by those who have not.

6
Socialism and Liberty

"Socialism," says Webster, "is any of various economic and political theories advocating collective or governmental ownership and administration of the means of production and distribution of goods." In socialism's purest form, as in the Soviet Union, the government owns not only the means of production but the real estate—the individual is a perpetual renter. In a less extreme form, as in Great Britain and Sweden, the individual may own real estate, and only some of the industries and other means of production are owned by the government, but every individual in the nation is subjected to a central economic plan, to which each must conform; and in addition, heavy taxes are levied to pay for the benefits of unemployment, medical care, etc., provided in the central economic plan.

With increasing degrees of socialism, the control of the government over the lives of individuals tends to become complete. The state (that is, the bureaucrats who administer the functions of government) decides who is to be educated—in

government schools of course—and who is not; how many
doctors there shall be, how many teachers, and so on, and who
these shall be; how many theaters, how many parks and play-
grounds, etc. If a foreigner asks a Russian, "Have you decided on a profession?" the Russian citizen will typically answer,
"The state has not yet decided where it can best use me." In
America such a reply would be greeted with, "The state?
What's the state got to do with it? Why don't *you* decide?"
Since it decides what profession you will pursue, it also decides where you shall go to pursue it—if there is a shortage in
town X, you will be sent to town X, and you will have nothing
to say about it; one cannot after all control the work without
controlling the worker. You live in a house owned by the government; your medical care is arranged by the government,
and if it is inadequate you can turn nowhere else; you cannot
buy food without a card issued by government (which can be
withdrawn the moment you disagree with the government or
for any reason become "an enemy of the people"). The government has power of life and death over you, in virtually
every aspect of your life.

Suppose, for example, that a planning bureau regulates the
entire economy, as in Soviet Russia. The state then becomes
the sole employer. "If the worker fails to please the powers
that be in the State, or if he arouses their active animosity,
there is no one else to whom he can turn. A far greater tyranny
may be exercised over him under socialism than . . . was ever
possible under capitalism. For if a worker failed to please a
particular employer under capitalism . . . he was free to go to
another. . . . But under socialism, if a worker falls out of favor
with the powers that constitute the State he can be forced to
starve; there is no one else to whom he can turn."[1] Trotsky
himself once said, "The old maxim, 'He that does not work
shall not eat,' has been replaced by the maxim, 'He that does
not obey shall not eat.' "

Every part of our lives, every decision we make, is dependent on and affects someone's "economic activities." If you decide to go to the movies, the planner must agree. He must determine how many movie theaters there will be, how many ushers, how many movies. Your decision to go on a picnic depends on prior decisions of (for example) the Department of Parks. If you decide to read a book, it will affect either the economic activities of the Department of Publishing and Distribution of Literature or the economic activities of the Department of Libraries. All of these decisions by you must be planned by the government. It is no accident that in Russia the question of how to organize the people's leisure is a problem of planning—of the leisure being planned for them, not by them. The State will handle every major decision from the cradle to the grave. The type of planning and control involved is often not obvious to superficial inspection. If the planner does not want people to read books, all he has to do is make the price of a book very high. If books were $100 a piece, not many people could buy them. In a free market the fact that the books are not selling would force the publisher to lower his price. But not so in a planned economy.

But can there not be "democratic socialism," socialism without dictatorship? Such a state is likely to be an unstable one, and lead back to free enterprise without centralized planning or to centralized planning imposed by dictatorship. There will always be disagreement on what plans should be adopted, and here the advocate of "democratic socialism" is faced with a difficult choice: either he must forget about planning (give up socialism) or forget about reaching agreement on a common plan (give up parliamentary government). Unless he hopes for the miracle of a majority agreement on a particular plan for the organization of all society, the democratic statesman who sets out to plan economic life will soon be confronted with the alternative of either assuming dictatorial powers or abandoning his plans; for how else but by force will he impose his plans on others who want no part of them? Planning will lead to dictatorship because dictatorship is the most efficient instrument of coercion, and coercion will have to be employed if central planning on a large scale is going to work.

Many socialists are aware of this and do not shrink from the dictatorship which their view leads to. Harold Laski, the most eminent contemporary advocate of socialism,[2] writes,

> I believe that the attainment of power by the Labor Party in the normal election fashion must result in a radical transformation of parliamentary government. Such an administration could not, if it sought to be effective, accept the present form of its procedure. It would have to take vast powers, and legislate under them by ordinance and decree; it would have to suspend the classic formulae of normal opposition. . . . A labor government may take office and embark on its policy; but it may be met with resistance, either tacit or overt, which strikes at the root of its purposes; under such conditions the suspension of the Constitution is inevitable.

And according to Sidney and Beatrice Webb, well-known British socialist writers,[3]

> In any corporate action a loyal unity of thought is so important that, if anything is to be achieved, public discussion must be suspended between the promulgation of the decision and the accomplishment of the task. Whilst the work is in progress, any public expression of doubt, or even fear that the plan will not be successful, is an act of disloyalty and even of treachery because of its possible effects on the will and on the efforts of the rest of the staff.

What has happened now to freedom of the speech and of the press? The entire socialist society would be an army, for a military-type organization would be the only one which could possibly carry out what the socialists are advocating. The individual will be relieved of the responsibility of making his own decisions; they will be made for him. The delegation of authority to a central commission must be employed because matters could not be settled by general rules which a majority of the people could act on. What should be the price of milk in New York? What should be the train rates from Los Angeles to Chicago? What type of car shall we produce next year? All these decisions must be made by government officials, rather than being left to the operation of the free market. It wouldn't be practicable to vote on all of them. And so they must be left to the decisions of a central planning bureau, which forces them upon each individual by means of the enormous coercive powers of the state.

In a free-enterprise society, people who disagree with the government, even those who disagree with the whole system, can still find employment. They can in fact usually earn their living by attacking the existing state of affairs. In a socialist society, people who disagree with the government can easily be disposed of. In both systems there will always be people who disagree; but with socialism the political leader has the power to shut up the opposition. In Russia what happens is that an economic demand is "created" for a worker in the salt-mines of Siberia. Only in a free-enterprise economy can the individual be in a position where his income is *independent* of the government. In a centrally planned economy, the worker must ultimately lose his freedom to choose his own line of work. For, if no one wants to go to a certain area for a certain type of job and the government determines the wages, the government must force him to go there. It must control the worker along with the work.

When we discuss "freedom to choose one's job" we mean freedom in its primary sense, as absence of coercion, not as the power to do something. Someone who wants to be a college professor and isn't, is not necessarily unfree. If nobody is willing to buy his services because he is ignorant, he may call himself "not free to become a professor" but the fact is simply that others choose not to avail themselves of his services. He may not get the job he wants, but he is still free because he is uncoerced.

But in a socialist system all such choices *would* be coerced, because of the power of unlimited government. Perhaps the most foolish thing that Marx ever said was that under socialism the state would eventually wither away. For ". . . it is above all under socialism, where the state owns all the means of production, does all the planning and assigns and controls all the jobs, that the state is and must be closest to omnipotence. . . . It is precisely under a socialist state that the least liberty can exist. Under complete socialism, in fact, liberty for the individual is simply impossible."[4]

In a free-enterprise economy, of course, all this is different. There, if someone plans to start a business, and his plan is unwise or short-sighted, he goes bankrupt. No one forces him to start the business, and no one will stop him. Nor can he coerce employees into working for him: he cannot command their services by edict, but only by paying them at least as much as the going wage for the type of work in question. The worker voluntarily chooses to work for him, and consumers voluntarily choose to buy his product (if they don't, he goes broke). The manufacturer of the product cannot coerce the consumer. In a free economy, the consumer determines the economic fate of the manufacturer (and with him, his employees). This provides the manufacturer, of course, with a natural motive for providing the best possible product at the lowest possible price, so that his product will outvote that of his competitors in the economic plebiscite of the consumers.

It should be clear by now how closely freedom of speech is based upon economic freedom. Many intellectuals in America, including, it would seem, the majority of college professors, are deeply concerned about freedom of speech—and quite rightly so, of course—but they couldn't care less about economic freedom. Indeed, many of them are socialists, and some of those who aren't or haven't thought about the matter very much retain in their minds a collection of tired clichés about the greedy capitalist who exploits his workers and ought to be controlled, and that "redistribution of wealth" is required for humanitarian reasons. But the fact is that without economic freedom, the continuation of freedom of speech is extremely precarious. One example will suffice:

Imagine a socialist society that has a sincere desire to preserve the freedom of the press. The first problem would be that there would be no private capital—no private fortunes that could be used to subsidize an anti-socialist, pro-capitalist press. So the socialist state would have to do it. But now the men and women undertaking this task would have to be released from the socialist labor pool and would have to be assured that they would never be discriminated against in employment opportunities if they were to wish to change occupations later. Then these pro-capitalist members of the socialist society would have to go to other functionaries of the state to secure the buildings, the presses, the paper, the skilled and unskilled workmen, and all the other components of a working newspaper. Then they would face the problem of finding distribution outlets, either creating their own—a frightening task—or using the same ones used by the official socialist propaganda organs. Finally, where would they find readers? How many men and women would risk showing up at their government-controlled jobs carrying copies of the *Daily Capitalist*?[5]

If a government has control over your economic life, it has control over your very means of survival. The government can cut you off from food by refusing to employ you, or by taking away your ration card, and it can deprive you of a physician's care by taking away your state-controlled medical benefits. One can be safe only if one's livelihood is *independent of* government by having the government divorced from economic affairs. But give a government control over a man's economic actions, and it controls his very means of survival.

Since the government subsidizes research in the socialist state—no private sources being available—people will perforce undertake only such projects as the government bureaucrats are willing to have them pursue. And candidates for research grants, knowing where their hoped-for money is coming from, will fall over each other trying to get their projects approved by the bureaucrats who hold the purse-strings and accepting any kind of party line that will permit them to do so. And the psychologists who must depend on government to get any of their projects through, will gladly do what the government asks of them in return: they will devise methods of thought-control, and the technicians will devise methods of wiretapping and other more subtle invasions of privacy. To the extent that the economy of a nation is centrally controlled, as with Soviet Russia and its satellites, the educated elite of these countries, who depend for their future on favors from the government, will be forced to fawn on every local bureaucrat who has it in his power to dispense these favors, and give them whatever devices the government requests in return for the favors, including finally the noose that will hang the researchers themselves. Can anyone doubt that the other freedoms are dependent on the preservation of economic freedom? When economic freedom goes, the other freedoms will soon follow, to be replaced by centralized control over the economy, over workers, over speech, and finally over thought.

Planning

"But," it is objected, "socialism is at least a *planned* economy, and don't we need planning? Isn't something planned better than something unplanned?"

The question is who is to do whatever planning there is to be. Are we to have one plan imposed on all of us from the outside, or is each of us to be free to make and execute *his own* plans? The difference between a free-enterprise economy and a centrally planned one is that in a free-enterprise economy every individual is free to construct and implement his own plans to the best of his ability, and as far as his initiative will carry him; whereas in a centrally planned economy the planner *eliminates everyone's plan except his own.* A socialist scheme can be made to work only by imposing one central plan on everyone in the nation, whether they like it or not. It is amazing how many people delight to indulge in armchair planning, fitting everybody into the plan like pawns on their own private chessboard. They never think of themselves as victims of other people's plans; no, as they imagine it everyone is to be subjected to *their* plan. But of course, different people will have different plans. And if one central plan does become adopted, what are the chances that it will be *your* plan, or your neighbor's plan? The chances are millions to one that instead of being able to impose your plan on other people, you will become the victim of someone else's plan, the pawn on someone else's chessboard.[6]

And by what right does some other person or group force me to conform against my will to *his* plan? If A has a right to impose his plan on B, C, and D, then doesn't B have a right to impose his very different plan on A, C, and D—and so on? Does any human being have a right to plan other people's lives against the will of those whose lives are being planned?

"But," it will be said, "aren't you doing the same as they are? Aren't you setting forth your plan, your political ideal or utopia, to which you would like everyone else to conform?" The answer is no, and we should be quite clear why. The political philosophy of libertarianism is one which leaves everyone free to implement his own plans, to do his own thing, compatible with the equal right of everyone else to do the same.

In a free-enterprise society, a group of people who wanted

to get together and form a communist colony somewhere would have a perfect right to do so. They would have to buy the land, of course—if they took it by force they would be violating the rights of the people who owned it. But with some expenditure of time and labor they could do it, as they often have in the past in the United States, and they could then go into the hills and do their thing with perfect legality and without encroaching on anyone else's rights. They can form a commune in which the policy is share-and-share-alike, if this is how they prefer to live; this would be *voluntary* collectivism, in which each person freely enters upon the scheme and leaves it again if he elects to do so. It is a far cry from the *enforced* collectivism to which everyone is subjected in the Soviet Union and other countries.

Contrast this situation with one in a socialist country where a group of people want to form a free-enterprise enclave. This is the very thing they would not be permitted to do. At once the government officials would descend upon them, forcing them to contribute to the National Health Plan and every other government scheme even if they preferred not to and desired no benefits from it.

The truth is of course that *every* plan that involves the forced submission of other people means a considerable loss of liberty. Under capitalism, however, there is no such loss of liberty. If a man plans to start a clothing store in a town and is not foresighted enough to realize that there are already more clothing stores in the community than the traffic will bear, he will lose his investment, and the consequences of his bad planning will be on his own head. On the other hand, if a Central Planning Board makes an unwise decision, the ill consequences are borne by every taxpayer; they must pay for the incompetence of another person. And under those conditions, such incompetence is far more likely to occur.

Consider a specific example, the publishing business. Authors and would-be authors are constantly complaining that publishers don't accept manuscripts which are not going to make money. On the whole this is true enough: the publisher can, and occasionally does, publish a book that is pretty sure to lose money, either for the sake of prestige or because he considers it of unusual worth; but he can do this only with the surplus from other books which do make money. He cannot make this a constant policy without going bankrupt himself, after which he is of course unable to publish any books at all, good *or* bad.

Now at this point our objector will say, "That's just the trouble; there should be a Central Planning Commission which decides which books should be published. These men should be devoted to quality, and should publish only the best books, whether they will make money or not." Very well—and who pays for the books that don't make money? It has to come from somewhere—and it comes, of course, from the taxpayer —who is forced to subsidize the book, whether he approves it or not. His liberty is interfered with every time he is forced to pay in taxes for a project of which he disapproves.

And is there any guarantee that books of higher quality will now be published? On the contrary. A central committee will make the decisions, and they are not likely to be any more far-sighted than the private publisher. Besides, they are employees of the government, and the end-result will usually be that only those books get published which are in accord with the opinions of those persons who are in political power. Dissenters will not be able to get their books published at all—whereas under capitalism, a book that is turned down by one publisher has a chance of being accepted by one of a hundred *other* publishers. Where there are competitors in the market, the author has at least a chance; but when the government owns all the printing-presses, there is no appeal from the Planning Board's decision. If your book disagrees with the views of the government or if you are disliked by some bureaucrat in power, it is most unlikely that what you write will ever see the light of day. The government will squelch your ideas, and perhaps you along with it.

Of course, planning may not go as far as this. The government may not own all the printing presses, but one might say, it should still own all the means of production. But are advocates of this policy aware of its implications? Even if we do not consider human rights or liberty, the practical task of economic planning is so bewilderingly complex as to be impossible. A socialist state could not do it were there not free economies whose prices on the open market could be used as guidelines for what price to charge for what product.

No better illustration of these points could be given than is contained in Henry Hazlitt's novel, *Time Will Run Back* (from which a passage was quoted in Chapter 1). In the passage quoted here, the main character, Peter, is about to become dictator of Wonworld (centered at Moscow), since his father Stalenin has just had a stroke. Nothing is known about capitalism, since all records of it have been destroyed and nothing except Marxist literature is permitted in Wonworld. Step by step Peter rediscovers capitalism entirely on his own, as the only feasible economic system for Wonworld. But at the early stage of the book in which this quotation occurs, Peter has not yet discovered capitalism, but is only speculating about the ills of the socialist regime which he is about to inherit. He is discussing the issues with his second in command, Adams.

"But of course people ought to consider it a privilege to work for the State, because when they work for the State they are working for themselves; they are working for each other. . . ."

Peter stopped. He found that he was mechanically repeating the arguments of Bolshekov.

"I agree that people ought to feel this way," said Adams, "but our experience shows that they just don't. The hard fact is that some people simply have to do more unpleasant chores than others, and the only way we can get the unpleasant chores done is by compulsion. Not everybody can be a manager, or an actor or an artist or a violin player. Somebody has to dig the coal, collect the garbage, repair the sewers. Nobody will deliberately *choose* these smelly jobs. People will have to be assigned to them, forced to do them."

"Well, perhaps we could compensate them in some way, Adams— say by letting them work shorter hours than the others."

"We thought of that long ago, chief. It didn't work. It unluckily turned out that it was only the pleasant jobs, like acting or violin playing, that could be reduced to short hours. But we simply can't afford to have people work only a few hours on the nasty jobs. These are precisely the jobs that have to be done. We couldn't afford to cut our coal production in half by cutting the hours in half, for example; and we just haven't got the spare manpower to rotate. Besides, we found that on most such jobs a considerable loss of time and production was involved in merely changing shifts."

"All right," agreed Peter; "so under our socialist system we can't have freedom in choice of work or occupation. But couldn't we provide some freedom of initiative—at least for those who direct production? Our propaganda is always urging more initiative on the part of commissars or individual plant managers. Why don't we get it?"

"Because a commissar or plant manager, chief, is invariably shot if his initiative goes wrong. The very fact that he was using his own initiative means that he was not following orders. How can you reconcile individual initiative with planning from the centre? When we draw up our Five Year Plans, we allocate the production of hundreds of different commodities and services in accordance with what we assume to be the needs of the people. Now if every plant manager decided for himself what things his plant should produce or how much it should produce of them, our production would turn out to be completely unbalanced and chaotic."

"Very well," Peter said; "so we can't permit the individual plant manager to decide what to produce or how much to produce of it. But this is certainly a big disadvantage. For if someone on the Central

Planning Board doesn't think of some new need to be satisfied, or some new way of satisfying an old need, then nobody thinks of it and nobody dares to supply it. And . . . how can we encourage individual plant managers to devise more efficient ways of producing the things they are ordered to produce? If these plant managers can't be encouraged to invent new or better consumption goods, at least they can be encouraged to invent new methods or machines to produce more economically the consumption goods they are ordered to produce, or to produce a higher quality of those consumption goods."

"You're just back to the same problem," Adams said. "If I'm a plant manager, and I invent a new machine, I'll have to ask the Central Planning Board to get somebody to build it, or to allocate the materials to me so that I can build it. In either case I'll upset the preordained central plan. I'll have a hard job convincing the Central Planning Board that my invention or experiment won't fail. If my invention does fail, and it turns out that I have wasted scarce labour and materials, I will be removed and probably shot. The member of the Central Planning Board who approved my project will be lucky if he isn't shot himself. Therefore, unless the success of my invention or experiment seems absolutely certain in advance, I will be well advised to do what everybody else does. Then if I fail, I can prove that I failed strictly according to the rules. . . . Suppose I devise a more economical method of making the product assigned to my factory. I will probably need different proportion of labour and materials, or different kinds of labour and materials, than I would with the old method. And in that case I will again be upsetting the central plan."

Peter sighed. "That doesn't seem to leave much room under our system for initiative, improvement and progress."

Adams shrugged his shoulders.

"Very well then, Adams. So under our socialist system we can't have freedom of choice of work or occupation; we can't have freedom of initiative. But can't we at least give people more freedom in the choice of what they consume?"

"How are you going to do that?" Adams asked. "We issue ration tickets for everything we produce, and we try to distribute them evenly —at least within each of the Four Functional Groups. We can't let people have ration tickets for more than we produce. They complain about that already."

"No, Adams; but some people like cigarettes and others don't; some like beer and others don't; some prefer spinach to potatoes, and some like it the other way round. Why not permit everyone his choice?"

"Well, maybe we could work out something better than the present rationing system, chief, but the fundamental problem remains. People can consume only what is produced. We must draw up our production plans in advance, on the basis of the known needs and assumed wants of consumers. And then . . . well, I repeat: people can consume only what is produced. So how can they have freedom of choice?"

"I think there are two answers to that," said Peter, after blowing a few more smoke rings. "We could still give consumers considerable freedom of choice *individually*, even if they did not have much when considered *collectively*. In other words, out of the stock of goods already produced, we could devise some method under which one person could get more spinach if he preferred, and the other more potatoes, instead of each having to take the exact proportion in which the total supplies of spinach and potatoes were raised."

"Well—maybe, chief. But I still insist that the fundamental problem would remain unsolved. Considered collectively, how can consumers have any freedom of choice? They have to take what there is."

"But can't we find out in advance what it is they really want, and then make that? In other words, can't we guide production to anticipate the wants of consumers, instead of merely obliging consumers to take what we have produced?"

"We are always trying, chief; but it isn't so simple. Suppose, for example, that in relation to the wants of consumers we turn out too many peanuts as compared with pins? Then we will run out of pins sooner than we run out of peanuts. In other words, people will use up their ration tickets for pins before they use them up for peanuts. They will then start taking peanuts because they can't get any more pins—"

"Oh, come!"

"Well, change the illustration— They will start taking more spinach, for example, because they can't get any more potatoes. But because they are entitled by their ration tickets to the entire supply of *both*, and because their need for goods exceeds the entire supply of goods, they will end by consuming the entire supply of spinach as well as of potatoes."

"But if people consume all of one product before they turn to another," asked Peter, "don't we know that we are producing too little of the first or too much of the second?"

"Usually we do, chief. But we can't know from that just how *much more* of the first we should have produced and *how much* less of the second."

"Can't we tell from the preceding *rate* at which the two products have been consumed?"

"No. Because if people begin to think that soap is going to run short before salt, they will all scramble for soap. Therefore soap will run short in the state commissaries sooner than otherwise. The relative rate at which soap is taken by consumers while it lasts will be faster than if people thought that both soap and salt were going to last them throughout the consuming year."

"But can't we keep making readjustments in the relative amounts produced, Adams, based on this experience, until we get consumption of soap and salt and everything else to come out even?"

"That's what we are always trying to do, chief. But I still haven't got to some of the real problems. The trouble is that very few things are consumed evenly throughout the year even if we should get the relative production of each thing exactly right. People can't burn coal evenly throughout the year, but only in winter. And if they have the storage room, they ask for the entire supply the are entitled to as soon as the ration ticket permits it. Yet the fact that three-quarters of the whole supply of coal is asked for in the first week of the consuming year doesn't necessarily mean that the coal supply is short or is going to run short. Again, ice is consumed mainly during the summer, and all sorts of other things are wanted only seasonally. The only reason people turn in their coupons for new clothes evenly each month throughout the year is that we stagger the validity dates on the clothes coupons in the first place so only one-twelfth become due each month. . . . And still again, some things, like vegetables and fruit, are consumed entirely within a few months of the year for the simple reason that that's when they come on the market, and they won't keep. In short, trying to figure relative shortages and surplusses by relative rates of consumption throughout the year is a tough problem, In most cases we who direct the economy have to solve it by pure guesswork."

"Couldn't we figure it out by mathematics?" asked Peter.

Adams grinned and shrugged his shoulders. "How are you going to find the mathematical formula for somebody's wayward desires? How are you going to find the equation for when I want a cocktail—or whether I want a Marxattan or a Stalini? . . . And I haven't even memtioned one problem. Suppose there is some product, or some potential product, which is not produced but which, if it were invented or discovered or produced, people would want in great quantities? How are you going to find by mathematics that people would want such a product *if* it existed? Or even that such a product is missing?"

Peter sighed. "It's all pretty discouraging. We seem to be reduced to the conclusion that under our socialist system we can't have freedom of choice of work or occupation and we can't permit freedom of choice for consumers. Is that right?"

"People are free to use or not to use their ration tickets," answered Adams.

"In other words," said Peter, "they are free to consume what we tell them they can consume. They are free to consume what we, the rulers, have decided to produce."

"Right, chief."

There was a long pause . . .

"What did Engels mean when he said that socialism was 'a leap from the kingdom of necessity to the kingdom of freedom?' "

. . . "He meant, I take it," answered Adams, "that under capitalism the individual was not free but enslaved, because one class was dominated and exploited by another; . . . the worker had to obey the orders of his employer or starve. And socialism means freedom from all this."

"I don't quite see it," Peter said. "Under any system of production whatever, there has to be social organization. There have to be those who direct the work and those who are directed; those who give orders and those who follow them; those who boss and those who are bossed. There has to be, in other words, a managerial hierarchy. If it is merely a question of building a single house, there has to be someone to decide that the house has to be put up, and what kind and where. There has to be an architect to design it, a builder to interpret the plans and to decide what workers to use and what to tell them to do—"

"But under socialism, chief, unlike capitalism, there is no exploitation of the workers for the profit of the employer."

"Under socialism," retorted Peter, "the State is the sole employer. If the worker fails to please the powers that be in the State, or if he arouses their active animosity, there is no one else to whom he can turn. A far greater tyranny may be exercised over him under socialism than I imagine was even possible under capitalism. For if a worker failed to please a particular employer under capitalism, I imagine he was free to go to another. And the fear of losing his exploited workers to some other employer must have mitigated the exploitation practiced by each employer. . . . But under socialism, if a worker falls out of favour with the powers that constitute the State, he can be forced to starve; there is no one else to whom he can turn."

"What I think Engels meant, chief, is that under capitalism the workers were exploited by the capitalist class, and crises and depressions seemed to come like visitations apart from anybody's wishes; while under socialism, society takes its destiny into its own hands and is in that sense free."

"I see," said Peter sarcastically. "And in practice, who constitutes 'society'? Who *is* 'society'?"

"Society is everyone."

"Oh, come now! *Everyone* can't make the decisions. No two persons' decisions would ever agree."

"Well, by society I mean the State."

"And by the State—?"

Adams grinned. "I mean us."

"Exactly. The hierarchy momentarily headed by me," said Peter. He had a sick feeling as he thought once more of his appalling responsibility. "What it comes down to is this, Adams. Society consists, and consists necessarily, of a small body of rulers and a large body of ruled. And this body of rulers itself consists of a hierarchy, finally topped by one man with the power to resolve disputes and make final decisions. So when we say that 'society' does this or that, we mean that the State does this or that. And when we say State, we mean the ruling hierarchy. We mean the Protectors; we mean the Party; we mean the Central Committee; we mean the Politburo; we mean merely the Dictator himself—or," Peter grinned, "the Dictator's Deputy."

"But under socialism," protested Adams, "the State reflects not the will of the exploiters against the proletariat, but, the will of the proletariat themselves. The State is just the mechanism by which the people express their will. It is a dictatorship of the proletariat—"

"Or a dictatorship *over* the proletariat? Let's face the real facts. Under our socialist system a few people—say the Central Planning Board—make the economic plan, and the rest of the people are ordered to carry out the plan. All initiative must come from the centre, and none can come from the periphery."

"It *has* to be that way, chief. There would be no point in having a master overall plan, deciding just what goods should be produced, and just how much of each, and by just whom, if anybody anywhere were free to decide to make or do something else. That would be chaos."

"But isn't there any productive system that would allow more liberty, Adams? Isn't there any system that would allow more centres of initiative? What actually happened under capitalism? Were workers free to change from one job to another that they liked better? Was the individual capitalist free to decide to make what he pleased, and in the way he pleased? Was the consumer free to consume what he preferred, and to reject what he didn't like?"

"I don't know what happened under capitalism, chief. Nobody knows. And we destroyed the capitalist literature so completely that I don't see how we are going to find out. But surely we are not going to turn back to that discredited and vicious system—which the world got rid of at the cost of so much blood and sacrifice—to take lessons in how to improve socialism!"

"All right," agreed Peter, "let's forget about capitalism. But I still don't understand what Engels meant when he called socialism 'the kingdom of freedom.' I still don't know what Marx meant when he said that under socialism the State would 'wither away.' For it seems to me that it is above all under socialism, where the State owns all the means of production, does all the planning and assigns and controls all the jobs, that the State is and must be closest to omnipotence. . . ."

He gazed unseeingly out of the window.

"Adams, you have convinced me. It is precisely under a socialist State that the least liberty can exist. Under complete socialism, in fact, liberty for the individual is simply impossible."[7]

The socialist planner is caught in a dilemma from which he cannot escape: if people are sufficiently rational and farsighted, they can be trusted to carry out *their own* plans. (If their plans include using force against someone else, the law is there for the purpose of stopping them, to protect the liberty of others. And if their plans, though not violating others' rights, are unwise or scatterbrained or just plain crazy, they will have to find this out in the course of *their own* experience: the consequences of their own actions will come down on their own heads, and hopefully cause them to be a bit saner next time.)

But if people are *not* sufficiently rational and farsighted to be trusted to carry out their own plans, then what superior endowment of wisdom entitles the politicians to make these plans for them? Are not the politicians human beings too? If they want to be shepherds and consider the rest of mankind to be sheep, what evidence can they give of their ability to manage by force the lives of others? And by what right do they do it even if they do have the ability? If history teaches us any one thing, is it not the very opposite—that men placed in a position of power over other people will be not better but worse?

Power does corrupt, and absolute power does corrupt absolutely, and a man who may be a saint in his relations with his own family may be a power-hungry manipulator when he is given a chance to govern other human beings. The socialist state puts such enormous power into the hands of politicians that the thought of using it is frightening; who among all of mankind can be trusted with that much power? Will he not abuse it? and even if he exercises it conscientiously, how can he, or any small group of individuals at the helm of such a government, exercise it wisely and well, considering the thousands of decisions they would have to make daily affecting the entire population? If you have a hard enough time making decisions for yourself—or yourself and your family—in your own life, consider the difficulties in the case of a government executive who has to make every day countless decisions that affect the lives and welfare of individuals whose unique personalities, situations, and problems he knows nothing about.

There once was a traveler who arrived in the midst of a tribe of savages when a child had just been born. A crowd of soothsayers and magicians and quacks surrounded the child. One said, "This child will never smell the perfume of a peacepipe unless I stretch his nostrils." Another said, "He will never be able to hear unless I draw his earlobes down to his shoulders." A third said, "He will never see the sunshine unless I slant his eyes." Another said, "He will never stand upright unless I bend his legs." A fifth said, "He will never learn to think unless I flatten his skull." "Stop," cried the traveler; "God has given organs to this frail creature; let them develop and grow strong by exercise, use, experience, and liberty."[8]

The socialists among us are the magicians and quacks in Bastiat's example who would force everyone else into conformity with *their* ideals. But over all social philosophy rules the principle of human rights: the lives (and the livelihood) of others are not theirs (or yours, or mine) to dispose of. The socialist, who wants to build society by forcing others to conform to his plan, is the most flagrant violator of the rights of man.

When one considers the mistakes he has made in regulating his own life, what temerity is involved in the attempt to regulate the lives of others!

If in these personal affairs, where all the conditions of the case were known to me, I have so often miscalculated, how much oftener shall I miscalculate in political affairs, where the conditions are too numerous, too widespread, too complex, too obscure to be understood. Here, doubtless, is a social evil and there a desideratum; and were I sure of doing no mischief I would forthwith try to cure the one and achieve the other. But when I remember how many of my private schemes have miscarried; how speculations have failed, agents proved dishonest, marriage been a disappointment; how I did but pauperize the relative I sought to help; how my carefully-governed son has turned out worse than most children; how the thing I desperately strove against as a misfortune did me immense good; how while the objects I ardently pursued brought me little happiness when gained, most of my pleasures have come from unexpected sources; when I recall these and hosts of like facts, I am struck with the incompetence of my intellect to prescribe for society. And as the evil is one under which society has not only lived but grown, while the desideratum is one it may be spontaneously obtain, as it has most others, in some unforeseen way, I question the propriety of meddling.[9]

But the socialist state is simply meddlesomeness exhibited on a large scale, extended to virtually every aspect of human life; its keynote is the regulation of human lives through the coercive force of the political power. On this point no one has spoken more eloquently than Herbert Spencer almost a century ago:

A cardinal trait in all advancing organization is the development of the regulative apparatus. If the parts of a whole are to act together, there must be appliances by which their actions are directed; and in proportion as the whole is large and complex, and has many requirements to be met by many agencies, the directive apparatus must be extensive, elaborate, and powerful. That it is thus with individual organisms needs no saying; and that it must be thus with social organisms is obvious. Beyond the regulative apparatus such as in our own society is required for carrying on national defense and maintaining public order and personal safety, there must, under the regime of socialism, be a regulative apparatus everywhere controlling all kinds of production and distribution, and everywhere apportioning the shares of products of each kind required for each locality, each working establishment, each individual. Under our existing voluntary cooperation, with its free contracts and its competition, production and distribution need no official oversight. Demand and supply, and the desire of each man to gain a living by supplying the needs of his fellows, spontaneously evolve that wonderful system whereby a great city has its food daily brought round to all doors or stored at adjacent shops; has clothing for its citizens everywhere at hand in multitudinous varieties; has its houses and furniture and fuel ready made or stocked in each locality; and has mental pabulum, from halfpenny papers hourly hawked round to weekly shoals of novels and less abundant books of instruction, furnished without stint for small payments. And throughout the kingdom, production as well as distribution is similarly carried on with the smallest amount of superintendence which proves efficient; while the quantities of the numerous commodities required daily in each locality are adjusted without any other agency than the pursuit of profit.

Suppose now that this industrial regime of willinghood, acting spontaneously, is replaced by a regime of industrial obedience, enforced by public officials. Imagine the vast administration required for that distribution of all commodities to all people in every city, town and village, which is now effected by traders! Imagine, again, the still more vast administration required for doing all that farmers, manufacturers, and merchants do; having not only its various orders of local superintendents, but its sub-centres and chief centres needed for apportioning the quantities of each thing everywhere needed, and the adjustment of them to the requisite times. Then add the staffs wanted for working mines, railways, roads, canals; the staffs required for conducting the importing and exporting businesses and the administration of mercantile shipping, the staffs required for supplying towns not only with water and gas but with locomotion by tramways, omnibuses, and other vehicles, and for the distribution of power, electric and other. Join with these the existing postal, telegraphic, and telephonic administrations; and finally those of the police and army, by which the dictates of this immense consolidated regulative system are to be everywhere enforced. Imagine all this, and then ask what will be the position of the actual workers! Already on the Continent, where governmental organizations are more elaborate and coercive than here, there are chronic complaints of the tyranny of bureaucracies, the *hauteur* and brutality of their members. What will these become when not only the more public actions of citizens are controlled, but there is added this far more extensive control of all their respective daily duties? What will happen when the various divisions of this vast army of officials, united by interests common to officialism—the interests of the regulators *versus* those of the regulated—have at their command whatever force is needful to suppress insubordination and act as "saviors of society"? Where will be the actual diggers and miners and smelters and weavers, when those who order and superintend, everywhere arranged class above class, have come, after some generations, to inter-marry with those of kindred grades, under feelings such as are operative in the existing classes; and when there have been so produced a series of castes rising in superiority; and when all those having everything in their own power, have arranged modes of living for their own advantage: eventually forming a new aristocracy far more elaborate and better organized than the old? How will the individual worker fare if he is dissatisfied with his treatment, thinks that he has not an adequate share of the products, or has more to do than can rightly be demanded, or wishes to undertake a function for which he feels himself fitted but which is not thought proper for him by his superiors, or desires to make an independent career for himself? This dissatisfied unit in the immense machine will be told he must submit or go.[10]

Such a worker has become a slave—a slave to the coercive regulations of government. Indeed, as Herbert Spencer pointed out,

All socialism is slavery.

What is essential to the idea of a slave? We primarily think of him as one who is owned by another. To be more than nominal, however, the ownership must be shown by control of the slave's actions—a control which is habitually for the benefit of the controller. That which fundamentally distinguishes the slave is that *he labors under coercion to satisfy another's desires.*

The relation admits of sundry gradations. Remembering that originally the slave is a prisoner whose life is at the mercy of his captor, it suffices here to note that there is a harsh form of slavery in which, treated as an animal, he has to expend his entire effort for his owner's advantage. Under a system less harsh, though occupied chiefly in working for his owner, he is allowed a short time in which to work for himself, and some ground on which to grow extra food. A further amelioration gives him power to sell the produce of his plot and keep the proceeds. Then we come to the still more moderated form which commonly arises where, having been a free man working on his own land, conquest turns him into what we distinguish as a serf; and he has to give his owner each year a fixed amount of labor or produce, or both, retaining the rest himself. Finally, in some cases, as in Russia before serfdom was abolished, he is allowed to leave his owner's estate and work or trade for himself elsewhere, under the condition that he shall pay an annual sum. What is it which, in these cases, leads us to qualify our conception of the slavery as more or less severe? Evidently the greater or smaller extent to which *effort is compulsorily expended for the benefit of another instead of for self-benefit.* If all the slave's labor is for his owner the slavery is heavy, and if but little it is light.

Take now a further step. Suppose an owner dies, and his estate with its slaves comes into the hands of trustees; or suppose the estate and everything on it be bought by a company; is the condition of the slave any the better if the amount of his compulsory labor remains the same? Suppose that for a company we substitute the community; does it make any difference to the slave if the time he has to work for others is as great, and the time left for himself is as small, as before? The essential question is: how much is he compelled to labor for other benefit than his own, and how much can he labor for his own benefit? The degree of his slavery varies according to the ratio between that which he is forced to yield up and that which he is allowed to retain; and *it matters not whether his master is a single person or a society.* If, without option, he has to labor for the society, and receives from the general stock such portion as the society awards him, he becomes a slave to the society. Socialistic arrangements necessitate an enslavement of this kind; and towards such an enslavement many recent measures, and still more the measures advocated, are carrying us.[11]

Such measures were characterized as enslavement by Spencer when he wrote these lines in 1884. Yet they are liberty itself compared with what they are today, and they are likely to be still worse on the arrival of Orwell's prophetic year, 1984.

Equality of Opportunity

"But even if all men shouldn't be forced to be equal in income, because of their differing efforts and achievements, still shouldn't they all have equality of opportunity? Isn't it unfair that some young people, born let us say to poverty-stricken parents, start on life's journey with an enormous handicap as compared with others who are born with a silver spoon in their mouths?"

First let us consider: how would you enforce equality of opportunity if you decided to make it a national policy? Clearly, the son of a man who earns three thousand dollars a year has a great disadvantage compared with the son of a man who earns thirty thousand dollars a year. (At least, he has a financial disadvantage—he may have other compensating advantages, such as parental love which is not forthcoming from the father who is too busy earning money to pay much attention to his growing son. But of course it may go the other way also: the son of the wealthier man may be more favored in parental confidence and affection than the poor man's son.) Now, how could one change this advantage? Obviously one could do it by taking income away from the rich man and putting it into the hands of the poor man; and this, as a regular policy, could be done only by the government. And what would happen as a result? The story is predictable: perhaps for a while the rich man would work that much harder to recoup his losses, while the poor man took an extended vacation on his sudden unearned income. Within a year the first man would have a much higher income than the second—there would be inequality again, which the state would equalize once more. It wouldn't take long before the rich man got the idea: "If I work it will only be taken away from me—so why work?" So he closes down his plant, and lets his employees go. The employer waits to receive his handout from the state, and the employees, now discharged, do the same—and who will now support them both? Compulsory equalization of income will kill incentives and close down the business which made the rich man rich, thus making the poor man poorer.

It is surely plain that the cure is worse than the disease: not only because of the poverty that would result from everyone trying to live off of everybody else, but because it would take a police state with a huge and expensive bureaucracy to sustain it.

A man, even after he has earned enough to keep him going for the rest of his life, may still be motivated to keep producing, hiring new personnel, etc., in the hope that he may pass it on to his son. And when this hope is justified, productive industries will be kept functioning. Besides, if the man earned the money, he has the right to pass it on to his son if he so chooses. Who has the right to dispose of the money he has earned if he himself doesn't?

How great an advantage does the son of a rich man have? Some—for a time. If he is able and industrious, the industry he has inherited will prosper and he can make money more quickly than if he had had to start from scratch. If he is idle and wasteful, the money will pass through his fingers soon enough. And much depends on what it is that he has inherited: more often than not he does not inherit cash as much as a going industry, which will see deficits very quickly unless he is able to make the right decisions. (The Ford Company almost went under after Henry Ford died.) Those who inherited railroad companies were often worse off than those who started the airline companies from nothing. Besides, the great achievers in industry (just as much as in the arts and sciences) owed very little to their immediate ancestors:

When he began, Ford knew nothing of gasoline engines; Rockefeller knew nothing about oil refining; Carnegie knew nothing about steel making; Vanderbilt did not go into railroading until he was 68 years old, and 90 of the 100 millions he died with were gained in the fifteen remaining years of his life. The almost invariable record [is] that the richest men have started as poor boys, as a rule devoid of any special opportunity. . . .[12]

The important thing is not for everyone to have equal opportunity in the sense of equal income available from his parents; the important thing is *leave the lines open* from poverty to affluence, so that anyone has a *chance* to rise, as high as his ability can carry him. A man may grow up poor, but if he has ability and ingenuity and industry, he may end up a millionaire if that is what he wants to be. *That* is the condition that must be preserved—and it is precisely this condition that is threatened by socialism. With its emphasis on enforced equality, it makes it infinitely more difficult for people of ability to rise, for they are blocked at all turns by an entrenched and inefficient bureaucracy, and a crippling income tax which they have to pay from the inception of their labors, making any rise from a state of poverty enormously more difficult.

The Springs of Socialism

Why do people come to believe in such socialistic schemes?

One reason is the belief that they will get *something for nothing*. It is the allure of the magic word "Free!" in advertisements. They have been treated by government propagandists and liberal commentators (is there a difference?) to vilifications of the rich exploiters, greedy capitalists, and the like, and this provides, in their minds, a moral justification for fleecing them—which they can do via taxation with "soak the rich" policies. They do not, of course, see the end-results of these policies—the loss of incentive, the decline of industry, the rise of unemployment, the decline of consumer goods. But as a way of "getting even" with their supposed enemies, the appeal to "something for nothing" may often succeed. The price paid, however, will be enormous: the people will think they are getting more out of the government than they pay in taxes because the rich are paying more and getting less—and for the moment this may be true. But because of it, in the long run the most productive and successful people will reduce their efforts or throw in the towel entirely—and then the same people who voted these schemes in will experience a lower standard of living, unemployment, an industrial blight settling over the land like a miasma. They will wonder why. They will know that something has gone wrong, but they will not usually see that the cause lies in the very policies they voted for. Their shortsighted greed has boomeranged. This chapter of their endeavors might well be called "the case of the cheated cheaters."

There are, as Albert Jay Nock pointed out in the 1920s, two ways by which human beings can satisfy their needs and desires.

One is by work—i.e., by applying labor and capital to natural resources for the production of wealth, or to facilitating the exchange of labor-products. This is called the *economic* means. The other is by robbery—i.e., the appropriation of the labor-products of others without compensation. This is called the *political* means. The State, considered functionally, may be described as *the organization of the political means, enabling* a comparatively small class of beneficiaries to satisfy their needs and desires through various delegations of the taxing power, which have no vestige of support in natural right. . . .

It is the primary instinct of human nature to satisfy one's needs and desires with the least possible exertion; everyone tends by instinctive preference to use the political means rather than the economic means, if he can do so. . . . This instinct—and this alone—is what gives the State its almost impregnable strength. The moment one discerns this, one understands the almost universal disposition to glorify and magnify the State, and to insist upon the pretense that it is something which it is not —something, in fact, the direct opposite of what it is. One understands the complacent acceptance of one set of standards for the State's conduct, and another for private organizations; of one set for officials, and another for private persons. One understands at once the attitude of the press, the Church and educational institutions, their careful inculcations of a specious patriotism, their nervous and vindictive proscriptions of opinion, doubt, or even of question. One sees why purely fictitious theories of the State and its activities are strongly, often fiercely and violently, insisted on; why the simple fundamentals of the very simple science of economics are shirked or veiled; and why, finally, those who really know what kind of thing they are promulgating, are loath to say so.[13]

It is the nature of man's situation on this planet that he must work to make provision for himself and his future; but if a person thinks he can get the rewards without the effort, he usually submits to the temptation to do so—particularly when he can do it by means of government, so that he himself need not use a gun to hold anyone up, and the people from whom he takes are an anonymous mass who cannot easily be identified individually, and who therefore cannot rise to accuse him of any crime.

Many people, of course, do know the economic facts of life —that man must produce to live, that you can't get something for nothing, that all production is the outcome of man's work, and that interfering with the source of production will cause it to falter—but the number of people who are aware of this is so small in comparison to the total population, that there is little they can do: when they try to point out the economic facts of life, they are condemned by an irate populace as selfish exploiters of the poor. And then, of course, they are outvoted at the polls. And so the morally brainwashed majority carries us all forward on the road to ruin.

Another reason for the voting in of socialistic schemes is a shortsighted and misplaced humanitarianism. Welfare to the poor—"they need it so much"—but the causes for their being poor are seldom investigated, but taken as a given, a simple fact of life. Government ownership of railroads, of steel, of utilities, and countless other things—true, it may be less efficient but "at least other people won't be making profits off of us." Minimum-wage laws—"otherwise the employer will never pay the poor man enough." Subsidies for various industries to lower prices—again, "to lower prices for us and keep the rich bastards from making so much profit." And so on, and so on—we have considered many too many examples in the preceding pages to need to recite them again. Every bit of reasoning, of course, tragically mistaken; but all of it justified in the minds of the unthinking proponents of these government schemes under the general banner of humanitarianism. If this be humanitarianism, then by all means give us selfishness and the profit motive—that way the goods will be produced, profits will be made, prosperity will permeate the economy, and the poor will find, again without knowing why, that their standard of living has risen and they can now look out for themselves.

The professional humanitarian, the philanthropist who would be the benefactor, with large masses of the population grateful for his beneficence, often sees this and tries to avoid it. As Isabel Paterson says in her chapter "The Humanitarian with the Guillotine":

> If the primary objective of the philanthropist, his jusitfication for living, is to help others, his ultimate good *requires that others shall be in*

want. His happiness is the obverse of their misery. If he wishes to help "humanity," the whole of humanity must be in need. The humanitarian wishes to be a prime mover in the lives of others. . . .

But he is confronted by two awkward facts; first, that the competent do not need his assistance; and second, that the majority of people, if unperverted, positively do not want to be "done good" by the humanitarian. When it is said that everyone should live primarily for others, what is the specific course to be pursued? is each person to do exactly what any other person wants him to do, without limits or reservations? and only what others want him to do? What if various persons make conflicting demands? The scheme is impracticable. Perhaps then he is to do only what is actually "good" for others. But will those others know what is good for them? No, that is ruled out by the same difficulty. Then shall A do what he thinks is good for B, and B do what he thinks is good for A? Or shall A accept only what he thinks is good for B, and vice versa? But that is absurd. Of course what the humanitarian actually proposes is that *he* shall do what he thinks is good for everybody. It is at this point that the humanitarian sets up the guillotine.

What kind of world does the humanitarian contemplate as affording him full scope? It could only be a world filled with breadlines and hospitals, in which nobody retained the natural power of a human being to help himself or to resist having things done to him. And that is precisely the world that the humanitarian arranges when he gets his way. When a humanitarian wishes to see to it that everyone has a quart of milk, it is evident that he hasn't got the milk, and cannot produce it himself, or why should he be merely wishing? Further, if he did have a sufficient quantity of milk to bestow a quart on everyone, as long as his proposed beneficiaries can and do produce milk for themselves, they would say no, thank you. Then how is the humanitarian to contrive that he shall have all the milk to distribute, and that everyone else shall be in want of milk?

There is only one way, and that is by the use of *the political power in its fullest extension.* Hence the humanitarian feels the utmost gratification when he visits or hears of a country in which everyone is restricted to ration cards. Where subsistence is doled out, the desideratum has been achieved, of general want and a superior power to "relieve" it. The humanitarian in theory is the terrorist in action.[14]

The socialist dreamer with "humanitarian" ideals, and the

tough, no-nonsense government planner, hungry for power in planning other people's lives—these two strike up a natural alliance. The second's power-lust only implements the "idealistic" dreams of the first, and provides him with a moral alibi. The rationale is left to the humanitarian, who tries not to notice while the power-luster moves others about on his chessboard, causes the poverty, sees the blood flow from his victims —all in implementation of the humanitarian's plan. The productive people, both managers and workers, are the ones who have to pay the costs and take the blame.

Power: Nature vs. Man

Many people are strongly opposed to any exercise of power. They consider power itself to be an evil. But there is power and power: they do not draw the distinction between *power over nature* and *power over men.*

Power over nature is the touchstone of human progress; on it civilizations are built. The record of man's climb from savagery is the record of the advance of that power: power to invent, to build, to produce, to use nature for man's benefit. But power over men does not raise mankind's standard of living or improve the quality of his life: for clearly, only *some* men can wield power over other men. And the remainder must be the *victims* of that power.

Governmental power is the faculty to beat into submission all those who would dare to disobey the orders issued by the authorities. Nobody would call government an entity that lacks this faculty. Every governmental action is backed by constables, prison guards, and executioners. However beneficial a governmental action may appear, it is ultimately made possible only by the government's power to compel its subjects to do what many of them would not do if they were not threatened by the police and the penal courts. A government-supported hospital serves charitable purposes. But the taxes collected that enable the authorities to spend money for the upkeep of the hospital are not paid voluntarily. The citizens pay taxes because not to pay them would bring them into prison and physical resistance to the revenue agents to the gallows. . . . Governmental power means the exclusive faculty to frustrate any disobedience by the recourse to violence. . . .

. . . Economic power . . . is the capacity to influence other people's behavior by offering them something the acquisition of which they consider as more desirable than the avoidance of the sacrifice they have to make for it. In plain words: it means the invitation to enter into a bargain, an act of exchange. I will give you *a* if you give me *b*. There is no question of any compulsion nor of any threats. The buyer does not "rule" the seller and the seller does not "rule" the buyer.[15]

Every human being does to varying extents achieve power over nature, even if he is a simple peasant growing crops and extracting his foodstuffs from the soil. The only way that man can advance himself is to conquer nature—"to transform the face of the earth to satisfy his wants."

Only such a conquest is productive and life-sustaining. Power of one man over another cannot contribute to the advance of mankind; it can only bring about a society in which plunder has replaced production, hegemony has supplanted contract. Violence and conflict have taken the place of the peaceful order and harmony of the market. Power of one man over another is *parasitic* rather than creative, for it means that *the nature-conquerors are subjected to the dictation of those who conquer their fellow men instead.* [16]

Productive men have always tried to advance man's conquest of nature. And always other men have tried to widen the scope of political power in order to seize for themselves the fruits of that conquest. Political power is the power of man over man—that is why we should minimize it and reduce it to nothing if possible; economic power is the power of man over nature. History is a race between the two kinds of power. The power of capitalism and the free market lies in an ever-increasing standard of living resulting from the conquest of nature. The reascendance of power over man, the political power, is what reduces us again to the level of savages.[17]

The three billion people that the earth now holds—and the larger number presumably still in store—can, as we have seen, be kept alive in comparative safety, and with some reserve for emergencies, only on a free-market economy. The further they move toward a non-market (coercive) economy, the smaller the incentive to production, the greater the shortages, the greater the chance of something going wrong in a critical place at a critical time, and the more frequently mass starvation and famine will occur. The British scientist-novelist C. P. Snow has predicted that before the end of this century "many millions of people in poor countries are going to starve to death before our eyes. We shall see them doing so upon our television sets."[18] The countries most affected, of course, will be those which either have a primitive barter economy and already live on the edge of starvation (as in the jungle or the Arctic), and those with a centrally controlled economy—that is, the socialist countries of the world, whose economic systems cannot solve the huge problems of production, supply, and distribution to an ever-increasing population.

If this happens, many among us will tell us that *we* are guilty, that we should try to equalize incomes all over the world, that the others are starving because we are too stingy. And if we act on their advice, we will finally starve ourselves in a vain attempt to keep them from starving. The whole thing would be fruitless unless we can come to grips with the *cause* of their starvation—the coercive statist economies under which these populations live, the forced collectivism by which a man who would gladly work hard to support his wife and family becomes discouraged at having to share the benefits with 200 million others, in which matters of life and death are left to bureaucrats as incapable of handling them as a child would be in calculating the trajectories of spaceships as now done by computer. The fate of these people could be avoided if they could have free-market economies; but most of the victims of the suffering and death will not even know that their fates are avoidable. Only a capitalistic economy could solve their problems, and many of them have never been permitted to learn about capitalism.

Just as a capitalist economy is "an incredible bread machine,"[19] providing amply for the needs of millions, so the socialist economy, in the face of a burgeoning population, is a guaranteed starvation machine which needs only time to perfect its deadly work. Why do you suppose that Soviet Russia permits the 3 percent of its land area to remain privately owned? Because the garden and agricultural plots of this 3 percent produce 48 percent of Russia's foodstuffs, and its leaders well know that without it Russia would starve.

But the danger does not end there: the danger is that by the end of the century we ourselves may have fallen victim to the same kind of starvation machine that is already afflicting them. Once our citizens no longer question the policies of centralized control, deficit spending, inflation, and social insecurity which they now appear to favor, even the strong economic reserve generated by a century and a half of economic freedom will at last break down. And if this happens, it is we who will turn on our television sets and watch the starvation of our own people. Our own formulas for disaster will have come back to haunt us, but by that time it will be too late. By the time catastrophe strikes, a military dictator will probably take over the country, with "sweeping emergency powers," and for those of us who remain alive, our heritage of liberty will have vanished.

In the face of all this, student groups in the United States are almost all fiercely opposed to capitalism. Of the dozens of confusions and fallacies about the nature and functioning of a free market, they fall victim to one after another; no slogan is too false for them to repeat as if it were an obvious truth. What account will they give of their present views if mass starvation stalks the world?

Perhaps, one suspects, it was what some of them wanted all along: the poverty of millions means little to those with an insatiable appetite for power. The vast majority of them, of course, desire no such terrifying outcome; they are simply misguided idealists who know nothing about how production can be generated to fulfill human needs. Totally ignorant of the role of liberty in economic matters, they chant any slogans they hear as long as they have a humanitarian ring. But in the end they will be simply cannon-fodder, to be used by their leaders as long as they are useful, and then thrown on the trash-heap when the time for power comes.

7
Welfare and Government

The question of federal relief projects arose in the very first Congress, in 1789, when a bill was introduced to pay a bounty to fishermen at Cape Cod, as well as a subsidy to farmers. James Madison spoke in debate on this bill:

If Congress can employ money indefinitely to the general welfare, and are the sole judges of the general welfare, they may take the care of religion in to their own hands; they may appoint teachers in every State, county, and parish and pay them out of the public treasury; they may take into their own hands the education of children, establishing in like manner schools throughout the Union; they may assume the provision of the poor . . . Were the power of Congress to be established in the latitude contended for, it would subvert the very foundations, and transmute the very nature of the limited government established by the people of America.[1]

Congress rejected the Cape Cod fishery bill, and with relief Thomas Jefferson said: "This will settle forever the meaning of the phrase ["promote the general welfare"], which, by a mere grammatical quibble, has countenanced the general government in a claim of universal power."[2]

Jefferson's belief that the matter had been settled forever was, of course, one of the cruelest delusions of history. If it had been settled, the United States would not today be riding the rapids that end in unlimited government.

When a government ceases to be limited, it tends to become unlimited principally in the direction of welfare: "the poor must be taken care of" is the refrain, and billions are spent on it, in ever-increasing amounts, to keep up with the increased demand for handouts. It is done officially in the name of humanitarianism: if one does not approve welfare one is accused of "not caring for his fellow men." (Actually, it is often done by politicians for the sake of political *power*: "I voted your scheme in, didn't I? Aren't you getting $500 a month from the government? So vote for me the next time, so I can get you some more.") But of course welfare must be paid for in ever-increasing taxes, and it is questionable whether the humanitarian feelings of its proponents extend to the workers and shopkeepers who often are forced to sacrifice all their own savings or profits in order to help pay for the program. And of course the money doesn't all go to the poor: a considerable percentage of it—sometimes most of it—goes to the huge government bureaucracy that administers the program.

According to *U.S. News and World Report* (February 8, 1971), "Social-welfare spending of all kinds by all levels of government this year is likely to top 160 billion dollars—and by 1972 more than half of all the money American taxpayers contribute will be going for such purposes."[3] This figure includes not only direct welfare payments to the needy, but public housing, rent supplements, food stamps, "model cities," community-action projects, legal services for the poor, neighborhood health centers, and other items in the "war on poverty."

And "in New York City, the number of welfare recipients has tripled in ten years. The cost of welfare and social services has gone up 700 percent. The total of persons on welfare is 1.4 million. The number of AFDC recipients (Aid to Families with Dependent Children) has quadrupled. Costs are going up at the rate of 20 percent a year."[4] Meanwhile, "The recession is dragging ever more clients onto the welfare rolls while inflation magnifies the costs to government and diminishes the value of the dole for the recipient."[5]

Consider another of the welfare programs, devoted to providing medical assistance for the poor. Medicare is a federal medical program; but in addition to it, various states have their own tax-supported medical programs, called Medicaid, in which federal and state funds are combined. In California, the Medicaid program is called "Medi-Cal". According to the *San Francisco Examiner*,

Medi-Cal's costs have doubled in four years and are still climbing. The system could bankrupt the state government of California. . . . It has become a monster devouring the state's dollar resources. Currently it is consuming an amount equal to the total sum raised by the state income tax.

In 1967, the first full year of Medi-Cal, it had 1.1 million on its rolls. Today the number has more than doubled to 2.4 million. In 1967 it cost $600 million. This year it is costing $1.2 billion. In 1967 it provided free health care to one of every 15 Californians. Today one of every eight is on its rolls.

Medi-Cal gives to the poor broader health care—free—than the average working man can afford to pay for. And the cost is greater. It was $517 per person for Medi-Cal in 1970. It was only $312 per person for the entire American population in the same year.

Among the Medi-Cal services that the private paying customer doesn't get at all or gets in minimum degree under his Blue Cross or other private plans, are: nursing home care, home health agency help, drugs, dental care, optometrics, chiropractic, special duty nursing, psychology, occupational therapy, physical therapy, speech therapy and hearing aids. Under Medi-Cal most of these services are provided on a

100 per cent basis. That is to say, no limit is placed on the patient's hospital stay, physician's fees, lab and X-ray costs, etc. Such limits are common in private health insurance plans. Nor is there a requirement for patients to make a partial payment of any bills, although experience has shown that even a nominal co-payment serves as an effective check on extravagance.

. . . The individual on welfare is now getting, free, better health care than the average working man can afford to buy. And the working man's taxes, which support Medi-Cal, are one reason he can't afford more health care.[6]

Imagine two elderly ladies; I have actual ones in mind, but since there are thousands like them, let us simply call them Mrs. Smith and Mrs. Jones. Mrs. Smith has saved for years, kept a bank account, denied herself travel and other luxuries, and carefully taken out hospitalization insurance policies. But today, with inflation and medical expenses (paid for by herself), she can barely make ends meet; she gets no welfare aid because she owns her own house. Mrs. Jones, by contrast, has never taken out insurance, saved a dime, or given any thought to the future. Now she is old and needs expensive medication. Both Medicare and Medicaid are taking care of these expenses, including hospital, X-rays, false teeth and eyeglasses, and so on. She goes to the hospital in taxis which Mrs. Smith can't afford (but Mrs. Smith has to help pay, in taxes, for the taxis that Mrs. Jones takes). What qualities in human beings are encouraged by a system which condones such practices? What will happen as more people come to follow the practice of Mrs. Jones, and decide that "it's not worthwhile to save anything anyway, since if you earn it they take most of it away from you, and if you don't earn any you get taken care of by welfare"?

Recently a colleague of mine was involved in an automobile collision; the driver of the other car, who was intoxicated, was a 22-year-old father of three, perfectly able-bodied but living entirely on welfare payments. Although he was to blame for the accident, there was no chance of collecting from him: he was not insured, and any money received in the form of welfare checks cannot be taken away from the recipient—not for taxation or garnishee or any other purpose. (However, my colleague's monthly paycheck, a return for work performed, could be garnisheed any time that someone sued him or claimed a debt from him. Earned money can be legally taken; unearned money cannot.) The welfare father added, moreover, that he had not the slightest intention of ever going off welfare; he and work didn't get along too well, he said, and he would just as soon leave work to the suckers. What would happen if everyone took the same attitude was a thought that apparently did not occur to him, or if it did, the thought did not disturb him.

In California recently, the same person in the same welfare office applied for, and received, welfare funds under five different names in one day. Apparently very little was done to determine identity; nor is much checking done to determine need. (It is considered "demeaning" for a welfare recipient to prove his need, or to open up his home for inspection to determine the conditions in which he lives; however, it is not considered demeaning for a wage-earner to be taxed all his spending money for the week to support these same welfare payments.) Hundreds of cases of the same kind have been reported. In one case, a woman had left the state and been in Soviet Russia for half a year, but her welfare checks were being forwarded to her address in Russia.

Every time a woman on welfare has another child, legitimate or illegitimate, she receives an increased allowance under A.F.D.C. The welfare laws in fact encourage her to have more children, since five can live almost as cheaply as four, but the payments to her increase in proportion to the

number of children she has. These same laws encourage the
husband to leave his wife, for if he does she can get higher welfare payments because of his non-support. (In some cases the
husband is there all the time and hides under the bed when the
welfare worker comes.) Would you willingly use your money
to encourage the breakup of families? But your money is being
used for that purpose now, whether you approve it or not.

When the Supreme Court struck down state residence requirements for welfare, thousands of people had to be added
to the already overburdened state welfare lists. Formerly they
had had to wait a year (different states had varying residence
requirements) before being able to collect welfare checks, but
now they could spend the summer in New York or Pennsylvania and the winter in sunny California (all of these states
have relatively high welfare payments), being assured that
their welfare checks would be forthcoming within a week after
their arrival. This decision alone has almost bankrupted some
state treasuries.

And then there are many cases such as that of

. . . a Negro woman with eleven children. She had a job from late af-
ternoon until about 11 o'clock at night. And she liked it. She liked
working. She'd go to work and leave the oldest child in charge of the
others.

Then she came home one night, and there was her welfare worker
sitting in her living room with her oldest child waiting for her. And the
welfare worker said: "Welfare is going to take these children away
from you." The woman said: "Why?"

And the caseworker said: "Because we don't think that this child
that you're leaving in charge is capable and old enough to supervise the
other children. Therefore, we're going to take them away from you."

The mother said, "What can I do?" And the welfare worker said:
"Well, you can quit your job and go on welfare, and then you can stay
home and take care of the children, and that'll take care of everything
and we won't take the children away from you."

So the woman said: "Here I am on welfare. I've never been on welfare before. I don't want to be on welfare. But I have been ordered on welfare if I want to keep my family."[7]

And then there are those who feel no qualms about accepting welfare at all; not only do they embrace it as a way of life, they demand it as a right and spurn all offers of jobs that do not "suit" them.

You go out and check in any community on the jobs that are going begging, and you'll find that for some time past they have not been the jobs for highly skilled people. They are such jobs as waitresses, domestic help, department-store clerks and those in service trades.

I remember a statement in one hearing where one of these women from the Welfare Rights Organization got fired up and screamed out: "And don't talk to us about any of those menial jobs."

. . . Here's a woman who is demanding her right to be supported by the working people, and she's saying to millions of other people who are chambermaids in a hotel or maids in homes—she is insulting them and saying that somehow they're beneath her and that she will work only if you can guarantee that the job will be at an executive level.[8]

Besides direct aid to the poor in the form of welfare checks, there are numerous government bureaus—most of them lodged in the Department of Health, Education, and Welfare —whose tasks consist in "helping the poor" by paying them, housing them, educating them, diverting them, and so on. One of these, the Office of Economic Opportunity, a few years ago spawned the Job Corps, an attempt to equip uneducated and "deprived" young men and women with a trade at government (for "government" always read "taxpayer") expense. Now many firms and corporations, from General Electric to Eastman Kodak, have long paid for the training of their own chosen candidates for jobs; and many private charitable institutions and individuals have helped to support similar enterprises for youngsters from poor families. But the federal government decided to get into the act also, "to increase the employability of youngsters [and] to prepare them for the responsibilities of citizenship."[9] A director was appointed "to make any arrangements he desired regarding selection of enrollees, discipline, removal quarters, equipment, services, transportation, and other expenses as the Director may deem necessary or appropriate for their needs."[10] Since O.E.O. paid $80 a head for screening applicants, there was an avalanche of applications, and the information contained in the applications was scarcely checked. Boys with criminal records were knowingly accepted. At the same time the various centers scattered throughout the country were not permitted to expel any enrollee for any reason without specific permission from Washington—which of course was ponderously slow in coming and resulted in a complete breakdown of discipline in the centers. Many of the applicants went to the centers, were accepted, and enrolled with high hopes, only to find that nothing was ready for them—no courses, no teachers, no equipment; they waited in idleness until these things were slowly and gradually supplied. In the resulting chaos, a policy of "everything goes" prevailed; as one corpsman who left in disgust reported, "Liquor, narcotics, sex—all these things were normal. It was a madhouse."[11] Robberies and stabbings took place under the noses of the administrative officials, but without resulting in expulsions.

The director of the Job Corps Conservation Centers "made it clear that violating the law did not bar service in the Job Corps. Enrollees who got into misdemeanor trouble could expect to have their fines paid by O.E.O., provided they later reimbursed it from their Job Corps pay, he declared."[12] . . . When two corpsmen were arrested on charges of robbery, "O.E.O. hired a separate lawyer for each and posted bonds and accepted them back at camp."[13] Senator Mansfield reported after an investigation that "A boy from Billings,

Montana, had enrolled in the Job Corps. Before leaving for camp in Kentucky, however, he was involved in a barroom brawl and shot a patron. Job Corps officials, rather than reject him on such grounds, took over his defense and paid for his plane transportation back to Billings, when required by the court. Later he escaped from the camp, stole a car and was involved in an auto accident that took the lives of two people and hospitalized others in critical conditions, including himself. . . . [It was later] disclosed that the Job Corps had posted $2,500 bond for the boy in the shooting."[14] These examples could be multiplied indefinitely.

Nor was there any attempt to economize in planning and executing the program. Buildings were rented and renovated at twice the usual cost (for the sake of speed, it was said). The renovation of some camps cost a million dollars or more although they usually housed no more than a hundred boys. When it came to paying for the boys' transportation to and from home on leaves, the government was prodigality itself: in the case of one enrollee from Rhinelander, Wisconsin, the trip from his Job Corps Center at Clam Lake (90 miles away) was handled as follows: "Before reaching his destination, the enrollee's travels spanned two days and more than 400 miles. He had to be put up for the night and fed two meals, changed planes three times, took a bus ride, and ultimately a car ride; all paid for with federal funds. The trip could have been much quicker and cheaper ($35) by taxicab. . . . The final touch of irony was that a free ride could have been secured with a Forest Service Radio Operator who travels daily from Rhinelander to Park Falls, Wisconsin, which is very near Clam Lake."[15] And so on, and so on.

What of the training these youngsters received after this monumental expense? Very few of the "graduates" were sufficiently skilled to get even the lowest jobs in the trades for which they had ostensibly been trained. Here is one example of many:

The Capital Job Corps Center tried at every hospital in greater Washington to arrange for on-the-job training for girls who had graduated from Job Corps courses as practical nurses and nurses' aides. There would have been no cost to the hospitals; the pay would have come from the Job Corps. Yet a center official told me, "We have been unable to persuade a single hospital here or in nearby Virginia and Maryland to accept a single graduate as anything higher than a bedpan emptier, and our graduates won't do that."

Amazed and shocked, I replied, "I can't understand it. There is a severe shortage of help in Washington hospitals, and many of them are strapped for funds. Why won't they accept your graduates at no cost?"

"There is not a nursing or nurses' aide course taught in any Job Corps center anywhere in the entire country which meets the minimum requirements of any hospital in the whole Washington area."[16]

And what was the cost to the taxpayers of the United States for the training just described?

"The combination of high property rentals, excessive salaries, and underestimated site rehabilitation costs has resulted in a cost per enrollee that has been variously estimated as $9,210 to $13,000 per year. . . . When costs are evaluated on the basis of cost per graduate, the results are even more astounding." . . . They came to $22,000 [per enrollee, not per graduate] at Camp Atterbury, and . . . $39,205 at St. Petersburg, Florida.[17]

When some of these facts came to light in a Congressional investigation, Representative Edith Green of Oregon (who had previously supported the Job Corps) said to the House of Representatives: "I had a letter the other day from a woman in my district who said, 'How can I possibly pay taxes to support people in the Job Corps centers at $13,000 a year?' She said, 'Our total income is $4,000 a year, and we have three children. We had hoped that we would be able to send our three children to college. Instead of that you are passing a program in the Congress of the United States which says that I am to pay taxes to support one person at $13,000 a year.' "[18]

The question to be repeatedly asked is: Would you voluntarily take part of your paycheck and use it for such purposes? But you are non-voluntarily doing it all the time. Can you still countenance such programs, or vote for the congressmen who vote them in? How much of the paycheck that you wanted to spend on your own needs—or for that matter on your own charities—were you prevented from spending because it was withheld at the source to pay for such programs as these, operated by the government?

Volumes could be (and have been) written on the monumental waste, inefficiency, and corruption which always attends such programs when they are operated by government. But we should not feel that this is a mere accident, that "if only we had more responsible men running the programs, they would be all right." It is true that having more responsible administrators in key places would probably prevent some of the more scandalous wastes. But overspending, waste, and inefficiency would occur always, when government is at the helm.

It is not, however, these abuses of the welfare system that constitute the principal objection to it. If this were so, one could say that it would work all right if only the abuses were weeded out. But it will not work, no matter how efficient and above bribery the administering officials are. Any intervention by government will only have the effect of putting a monkey-wrench in the economic machinery—it will not increase wealth and productivity, but act as a damper on it; it will discourage productivity, never stimulate it. The effect of the government welfare system is that increasing millions of people are dependent on government, reduced to lifelong unproductiveness. And to do this the productive people who have to pay

the bill for the whole proceedings have themselves been made
dependent on government through crippling taxation, through
endless red tape and regulations, and have been treated as if
they were public enemies—thus discouraging more people
from trying to make an economic go of things through the
exertion of their own efforts.

And who is there in the world who is as careful of other
people's money, if it is entrusted to him to spend, as he is of his
own? His own money he has worked to obtain; if he spends it
carelessly he is frittering away years of his life's effort. But
when he has millions of other people's money in his hands, and
his task is only to spend it, and he knows in advance that the
losses won't come out of his own pocket but out of the pocket
of every taxpayer in the nation, well, he just won't be as careful. Indeed, his worst impulses will probably come out: he will
go hog-wild on a spending spree, or give it to his friends and
cronies, or use its blackmail power over people whom he
doesn't like: "You don't do it my way, you don't make a deal
with me, and I'll cut off your funds!" The welfare state puts
into a position of power the people who are least worthy to
exert it; it penalizes the productive people on whom the entire
economy depends, and it places above them, managing them,
people who probably couldn't produce a thing themselves and
who, at the very least, are being generous with other people's
money, not with their own.

Even if there were no corruption or mismanagement of the
programs, they would fail in their professed goals.

The programs have failed because they misconstrue the nature of
government and economy. They have attempted to employ force to
produce economic results. Men cannot be forced to be economical; yet
when left to their own devices, men *will* be economical. Economy
results from *willing* efforts, from *willing* innovation, from *willing* exchange, from *free* decisions, and from *voluntary* combinations. Gov-

ernment action tends to produce rigidity, to keep things the way they are, to make it much more difficult for the poor to improve their lot. It raises costs, raises prices, produces surpluses (goods that will not be bought at the prices it decrees), causes unemployment, reduces competition, removes opportunities, and results in shortages, depending upon how it is employed. The poor cannot benefit from all this because they need economy.

The war upon the poor will be ended when the numerous interventions are ended. . . . The hope of the poor lies with freedom.[19]

Sometimes those who cry for help could easily help themselves, if they would discipline themselves a little to do without something today in order to have something left to save or invest tomorrow—as virtually all self-made men have had to do. Many of today's youth refuse to work at all unless they can start at the top, and lay down their own conditions of work. If they cannot receive the wage of experienced workers while they are themselves still inexperienced, they cry that they have been abused and exploited.

But there are others who, even with the best will in the world, cannot make it because of the government harassment and regulations and taxes on enterprise. For this, it is only necessary that the government remove itself from interference in the economy.

No one should have to struggle against such odds as the government programs put in the way of material success. Surely, the poor should not. Their hope lies in lower prices, in higher *real* wages, in freedom of enterprise to innovate and build, in loosing the ingenuity of private enterprise (so much of which is now devoted to circumventing government programs) to meet their needs and wants. In short, if the government were to get off the backs of the poor, there would be every reason to suppose that many, or most, of those who desire to improve their lot could and would do so. Millions of jobs would open up; thousands of companies of all sizes would come into being, bringing new products and services for the benfit of all; "pockets of poverty" would be apt to get so much new industry that before long real wages there would ap-

proximate those elsewhere; juvenile delinquents would, in many instances, become productive workers; and tasks of law enforcement
would be greatly diminished; an integrated society would emerge, integrated because its members would be serving one another, not organized against one another.[20]

Let us consider now some other points about government
programs for the poor:

1. When payments are made in the form of cash, as they
ordinarily are in welfare to the needy, an additional evil occurs. "Payments should be in cash, so that the people can determine for themselves what it is to be used for," runs the
humanitarians' argument. But then no one has any control over
what it *is* used for.

You would never willingly spend *your* hard-earned money
to promote gambling or heroin addiction. But you would be
forced by law to give up your money so that other people
could spend it on that if they chose to.

Cash is the very last thing to be given to a compulsive gambler, a
drunkard, or a drug addict. As soon as he has gambled the money
away, or spent it on whiskey or heroin, is the government to telegraph
him more? But if it doesn't, how is it to see that he and his family get
proper nourishment, or that he has enough left over for the rent, or
that his family are decently dressed, or that his children are properly
educated?

It overlooks the liberties of the industrious and prudent people from
whom money is being either withheld or seized, in order to pay the
cash handouts. It makes no sense to preserve the "liberty" of the irresponsible at the expense of the liberty of the responsible.[21]

2. Another effect of the welfare programs, which may not
be intended by its proponents but invariably occurs once the
programs have gone very far, is the *stratification of society*.
Those who speak in the most heartfelt manner about equality
of opportunity, are by the very policies they advocate freezing
the mobility of workers in such a way as to frustrate them at

every turn and forever prevent their rising to the level of their abilities. Government tends to put them on a treadmill from which they cannot escape. It is not merely that the programs tend to perpetuate people in welfare down to the third and fourth generation; this is true, and tragic enough. But one effect of the monumental taxes required to sustain the program is to keep working people, even those with imagination and ability and ambition, frozen into their present stratum of society, without a chance to improve themselves. One example will illustrate the point: I have an uncle in Holland—which is as "advanced" a welfare state as Great Britain—who, being enterprising, hardworking, and full of ideas, hoped to rise from his job as employee of a cleaning establishment to the position of owning a shop of his own. But after much effort in this direction he gave up: he figured out that at the rate of taxation imposed by the Dutch government, and considering the inflationary cycle that always goes with welfare states, and knowing what he would have to spend on his wife and child, it could take him between thirty and forty years to be able to own his own cleaning establishment. He would have to be given it, or inherit it, but otherwise the thing was hopeless. So he left the country that he loved, and came with his family to the United States—where, in spite of increasing socialization and ever-higher taxes imposed by government, it took him five years to own his own place complete and clear. He still is nostalgic about his life in Holland, but, as he said to me many times, "It's no place for anybody who *wants to get anywhere.*" How many times has not the same thing been said by victims of every welfare state known to man in history! And *this* is presented to us as a humanitarian ideal! In a free economy can the lines remain fluid, can the able man go from rags to riches, can Horatio Alger stories still come true. It is not important that he start with a silver spoon in his mouth; it is important

that he be able through his own efforts to get to the top, or as
high as his ability will carry him. But this is possible only in a
free economy.

3. Once relief benefits are known to be available from government, a kind of chain reaction occurs. If Mr. A and Mr. B
have got money out of the government (that is, out of your
and my taxes) for doing nothing, then Mr. C might as well
start doing the same thing. "I don't want to be left out while
the public pie is being distributed, especially when I have contributed to the making of the pie myself! If favors are to be
got, I might as well get some too." People who wouldn't think
of doing it if others weren't doing it, climb over each other to
get it if they know someone else is getting it too.

And once the spigot of public funds begins to run, more
and more people rush to get water from it. Some people, of
course, know that at this rate the spigot will soon run dry and
there won't be any more water to be had. But the comparatively few people who think this far are usually outvoted at the
polls by those who think only of what they can grab next. And
so the amount extorted from the productive people becomes
more and more, and the purposes for which it is used become
more and more outlandish; the power of the bureaucracy increases, the waste becomes so colossal that many people are
sobered by it, but in the end it doesn't make any difference—
as long as the fountain works we might as well all drink from
it and *après moi le déluge*—or should one say, *après moi le
drought*?

4. The net effect of the humanitarian's effort is to underwrite the ethics of parasitism and to condemn or demean the
ethics of work. Yet it is, of course, on work that handouts
depend.

Here is a man who is down and out. Who, in the end, has
helped him more, the philanthropist who gives him a handout

or the businessman who gives him a job? The philanthropist is the one who gets praised. "How generous," we say; "what an example of Christian charity." But the businessman who gives him a job gets no praise because, after all, he did it for profit.

So much for the motive; but now what about the deed? There is surely no doubt that the businessman has helped him much more. He has made the man self-sufficient; he has put him back on the production line, that vital line of energy in the nation's economy; he has given the man back his self-respect, by making him no longer dependent on handouts—he can carry the load now for himself.

But the more we expand welfare legislation, the more we increase the producer's tax burdens, and the more we keep his business from expanding, and thus keep our man from being employed. By putting a ball and chain on the producer we increase the need for handouts—and, incidentally we have less wherewithal for handouts because there is that much less of the producer's profits to tax. Surely when this is seen, any sane man will want the business to flourish, so that more men can get jobs, and fewer of them will need handouts.

Often, however, the professional humanitarian sees the job as a *threat*. He wants to "help" as many people as possible—with other people's money of course—and in order to help them they must first be in *need*. If they weren't in need, they might well say "No thanks" to his offer of charity. The humanitarian's ideal is then of a society in which vast numbers of people are perpetually in need—and thus they can be dependent on his charity and must remain grateful to him or lose it. The humanitarian's ideal is often that of a vast needy population which can be rescued from starvation only by his beneficence. The prospect of long headlines with him as the savior is what gives him an inner glow. Deep down, he doesn't really want an economy to flourish or businesses to expand or millions to be gainfully employed, because this would interfere with his self-styled ideal of humanitarianism. It is no coincidence that there is a natural historical alliance between the humanitarian, who needs more poverty to inflate his ailing ego, and the dictator (or Central Committee), who needs more poverty to keep his subjects passive. The humanitarian needs the government to make his welfare scheme compulsory and the dictator needs the humanitarian as a moral alibi that the people will accept. They are natural allies, fellow vultures preying on the production of others. Between them they carve up the corpse of economic freedom.

But the "liberals" today are almost always on the side of the professional humanitarian and against the producer. Whenever the chips are down, they favor taking away from the people who produced the items in order to give to those who did not. The liberals are in no way believers in economic freedom; they, along with most university professors, couldn't care less how much the producer is shackled. They favor every possible interference of government in the economy of a nation; they are quite indifferent to the fate of the people who provide the goods, from whose surplus they must draw in order to promote their various schemes of charity and welfare. One would think that out of sheer expediency they would give some thought to the origin of all their intended beneficences, that they would at least not jeopardize the source of all this bounty, that they would take measures to insure that the flow of money and supplies would continue uninterrupted. After all, you don't beat to death the cow who is supposed to provide the milk. But the vast majority of liberals are not that farsighted. In their blind hatred of the entrepreneurial class, they claim as a right the receiving of goods in whose production they have had no share. For the most part, these people are economic dropouts who could not produce anything of value if they tried; but being unable or unwilling to produce, they would like nothing better than to *control* the producer and take his products away from him once he has produced them. Since they can't do this by holding him at gunpoint themselves, they do it another way: they lobby for legislation which would take away by force (or threat of force) the income the producer has earned, and use it for the purposes which *they* have designated themselves. If they did a holdup job on him in person, at least this would be more honest.

"But it's charity," they say, "and charity is good." No, it is not charity, it is robbery. Charity is a voluntary act of giving from his own surplus to what one believes is a worthy person or cause. If you think the cause is worthy, by all means give to it yourself, encourage others to do so, and form charitable organizations whose task it is to do so. But charity does not consist in forcing every taxpayer at gunpoint to give to X, Y, and Z because *you* think the cause is worthy. You can make the decision for yourself; you have no right to impose it on others.

"But isn't it moral to give?" To give voluntarily, sometimes; that depends on the situation. It is foolish to give to someone who could earn it for himself, and by starting him in habits of dependency one would be doing him more harm than good. But the giving to the government is not voluntary but forced—and that is an entirely different matter. To be forced to give to causes we would never give to voluntarily—to causes we regard as immoral—is this a virtue?

If it is, and if it is immoral of everyone not to give, give, and give, then what of the takers? There can be no givers without takers—and is it virtuous of them to take, take, and take? The legislation in a welfare state is designed to create a class of professional takers. But what of the morality of the takers?

Why is it immoral to produce a value and keep it, but moral to give it away? And if it is not moral for you to keep a value, when you give it, are they not selfish and vicious when they take it? Does virtue consist of serving vice? Is the moral purpose of those who are good, self-immolation for the sake of those who are evil?[22]

"Higher taxes? That's good! I don't like it, but we need them! I'm a registered Democrat and I believe in these social services!" The libertarian would say to him, "The social services you speak of may or may not be fine—we would have to analyze them separately. But they should not be handled by the coercive activity of government. Whether you or I or Jones want to support them should be up to us. If we don't believe in one, we shouldn't have to support it. If you do believe in it, nothing prevents you from paying toward its support yourself, and banding together with other individuals who will do the same. But by voting to make *everybody* help pay for your pet cause, you are voting for *coercing* them into spending their money for something they may not believe in, need, or want."

"But shouldn't some income be guaranteed?" How can it be? The manufacturer's income and the businessman's income are not guaranteed; indeed, nothing is guaranteed on the free market. If he does not anticipate next year's market, and allocate his materials and employment accordingly, he won't have any income at all next year, or he may lose the whole company. His income depends on a thousand factors which he will have to predict and control with success; otherwise, disaster faces him, and the loss of years of time and effort and money. How, then, if the income of the maker and supplier of the goods is not guaranteed, can the income of the man who lives off of him be guaranteed? If he and his lose their income, there is nothing left to supply the incomes of those who live off of his earnings. You cannot distribute when the barrel is empty. And the more of his income you distribute now, the nearer to empty the barrel will become. The history of every welfare state is a living example of this.[23]

5. But those who approve such measures are forgetful of

one important fact: that such a process cannot go on indefinitely without the collapse of the entire economy. Sooner or later the producer rebels, or is simply unable to obey the laws passed against him and still survive; at the very least, his motivation declines as every risk he takes, every bit of time and effort and money that he puts into his enterprises, has a more uncertain payoff because of higher taxes, more government red tape, and other modes of government interference. Finally his attitude becomes: "What's the use? I have taken the risks; I have given them jobs; I have put my time and money into the enterprise; and so, if the only thing that they can give me in return for all this, namely profits, is going to be taken away from me to be thrown into the bottomless pit of government spending, I might as well quit. Let them see how they can get along without me. Let them support *me* for a while." And when nobody finds it worth his while to produce any longer, but everyone is clamoring for a free bite of the fruits of production, we have a state of affairs that can be called "splendidly equalized destitution"—with everyone trying to live off everyone else, and nothing left any longer to live off of.

The fact is that the great mass of people depend for things worth having in their lives on a comparative handful of people with genius, courage, and imagination; the very least the rest of us can do with regard to the productive enterprises of these men is to *leave them alone.* Do not put a ball and chain around them, for not only they, but we also, will be gradually destroyed as a result. Yet that is what every demonstrator does who echoes the popular cries, "Down with the exploiter!" "Kill the filthy capitalist!" "They have too much—let's take it away from them!" What the masses who chant these phrases don't know is that by slow degrees—and not so slow at that—they are cutting off the very source of the affluence they expect to enjoy.

6. The cruelest hoax of all is that the welfare schemes are

passed off as providing *security,* whereas the fact is that in the long run they take away security. Let us see why this is so.

If the enormous costs of the welfare state had to be paid out of current taxes, those taxes would be so high that people would rebel, and would probably scuttle the whole scheme. The politician's trick is to tell people all the wonderful things he will do for them (with other people's money of course), re-assure them that it will mean no increase in taxes, and then, instead of paying for it, go into debt: deficit spending. That's the only way you can give the benefit while not increasing taxes at the time. But as the deficits accumulate and you see that you can't possibly pay them, and the welfare schemes keep on increasing instead of subsiding, the next trick is to inflate the currency—to increase the quantity of money by keeping the printing-presses rolling overtime. This, of course, decreases the value of the dollar, and everything you buy now costs more money, and the government pays off its bonds in currency which is worth a fraction of what it was initially. Those on pensions of fixed incomes who are caught in the squeeze, or those who have saved for their old age carefully year after year, find that the money they have saved no longer buys what they need to live. These are the ones who have been really cheated—they are the victims of theft as surely as if 50 percent of their income had been taken away from them by bandits. The end-result of the liberals' dream is that people get repaid in worthless currency—and *that* is supposed to be moral?

"Oh, the people must have security," say the "liberals." But to take away from the workingman is to take away *his* security —and by creating debt and inflation it takes away from *every-one* just that much chance of security. Even at this very mo-ment, in the U.S.A., who is really able, with confidence, to save money for later years, in view of the probability that the money he has saved will be a small fraction of its present value by the time he needs to use it?

An elderly man just recovered from a somewhat lengthy illness recently said to me, "My, I wouldn't have known what to do without my Medicare payments—they took care of everything! I'll never say a word against Medicare again."

I replied: "Now suppose you hadn't had to pay, during all those earning years, a portion of your salary to pay for our government relief projects—which last year came to 75 million dollars. Wouldn't that have been an enormous saving? What could you have done with all that money? With the saved money you would have been able to buy three or four or five medical insurance policies, and been able to take a few trips to Europe besides on the savings. What government has done, to get hold of your money, is to take a dollar away from you and years later return you twenty-five cents—in inflated currency at that—and then it asks you to be grateful for the 'favor!' "

I stopped there, but thought of the further things I could have asked him: whether he approved of all the things done with his money by the government, and whether he could do anything about this fact; whether he had thought about all the medical improvements, insurance offers and other advantages that did *not* come into existence because the government took this money at the source from the pharmaceutical houses, the insurance companies, and all other producing organizations, thus making it impossible for the pharmaceutical house to put the money into research, for the insurance company to offer a better deal to its clients—and so on.

But in the end I refrained: it is so easy to take cognizance of that which is seen, and it takes such a leap of the imagination to grasp what is not seen—that which cannot be seen because it never came into existence, and never came into existence because it was never given a chance to come into existence, and was never given a chance to exist because the government forced out of the hands of potential innovators the money that they might have used for these purposes. How many patients have died because of research that didn't get done, which would have been done if the government hadn't taken the money first? But the people that died thus didn't know this was why they died; they may well have died with praise on their lips for the socialized medicine that killed them.

A cousin of mine is president of a company that makes window sashes, screens, Venetian blinds, and other furniture. He started from scratch with borrowed money in the 1920s, and after a long struggle, with ingenuity and hard work and careful planning, he finally made a go of it. At first he employed only a dozen people; now he employs more than six hundred, and many workers from outlying towns come to work at his factory, whose good reputation has been untarnished through the years. In the last few years the company has been providing scholarships for needy students, as well as summer camps for underprivileged youths, gifts with no strings attached, simply a humanitarian measure. Then the latest tax-increase came, making it harder than ever to turn a profit and riskier than ever to expand capital to expand his business. The scholarships continued nonetheless. It was the facts about the Job Corps which finally broke him, the cost to the taxpayer of an average of $13,000 per year per pupil. "I see the government is going into the humanitarian business," he said. "I could train ten kids for what it costs the government to train one—and I'd do a better job of it. But they're doing it, and I don't even have anything to say about it. Well, let them do it then. I quit!" That was the end of the voluntary charity. And now the government "trains" the "students," and my friend's margin of profit has increased a bit (it would have increased more but for the

heavier taxation to support these government programs)—
and the really deserving children have no more privately spon-
sored summer programs.

Obviously, the government has taken unto itself the function of "promoting the general welfare." This may, to some
people, have a pleasant enough sound—even after they know
that to the extent that government takes over this function (inefficiently, as always) individuals are prevented from carrying
out this same function (often very well). But this thought, at
least, should be alarming—that if the government has absolute
power to promote the general welfare, it also has absolute
power *to decide what the general welfare is.* And is this a matter which it is safe to leave in government hands? Thoughtful
people should be shaking in their boots at the thought that
they have delivered this enormous power, the proud preserve
of individuals, into the hands of an impersonal devouring
monster.

John Stuart Mill was aware of this danger when he wrote,
more than a century ago: "That a handful of human beings
should weigh everybody in balance, and give more to one and
less to another at their sole pleasure and judgment, would not
be borne unless from persons believed to be more than men,
and backed by supernatural terrors."[24]

And in the end, of course, it is the needy—the very people
who most vociferously advocate these schemes of legalized
plunder—who will be the chief sufferers from it. They do not
see this, of course, and when in the course of time their standard of living goes down and they can't squeeze any more from
the milk-cow because they have beaten it to death, they will
wonder why—still ignorant of what it was that hit them.

It is because the movement for sharing the wealth and redistributing
the income of the country endangers progress that it is so important to
understand its implications. *The capital supply upon which the wealth*

and well-being of the people of the United States depends was
accumulated out of the profits by the owners and managers of business
enterprises. Every diminution in their income must diminish the capital
supply of the future. And it is these incomes—those of the owners and
managers of business enterprises—that will be most sharply reduced if
the various proposals for sharing the wealth are put into effect. The
immediate loss will fall on this comparatively small group of capable
and successful men. But the ultimate loss, and this is the tragedy, will
fall on the very group that the equalitarian schemes are designed to
benefit—the working class.[25]

Government vs. the Poor

The final irony is that these government-financed and
government-sustained programs, which politicians attempt to
justify as a way to *help* the poor, are actually a *war on* the
poor. Though welfare costs double every few years, the position of the poor has not been improved by the millions of dollars that have gone down the government sinkhole to "help"
them; on the contrary, their condition appears to have deterio-
rated. Why? Chiefly because government intervention
throughout the economy has blocked at every turn the efforts
of the poor to improve their own lot, leaving them no choice
but to be the victims of handouts. Without this vast interlocking network of government interventions, the vast majority of
them could have helped themselves.

There are millions of urban poor who populate the "inner
cities"—the central areas of the cities, the first to be built,
locked inside the more affluent suburbs. They are poor, partly
because of government-created unemployment (such as the
minimum wage law); partly because of the tax structure,
which does not provide an incentive for owners and landlords
to own or improve the property they own; partly because of

government subsidies to farmers, which increase the city-dwellers' price for groceries (as well as increasing his tax burden); partly because of government tariffs, which increase the domestic prices on countless products, and also keep cheaper products of all kinds from entering the country; and most of all because of the interstate highway program, which typically routes the highways through the inner city. Every one of these programs, and countless others, increases the tax burden on everyone, including the poor in the inner cities.

The Urban Renewal Program has razed thousands of acres of land in the inner cities, tearing down houses and apartment buildings occupied by the poor, presumably with the idea of replacing them (at the taxpayers' expense) with new buildings for these same poor.

To date, the program has thrown out of their homes more people than it has put into them. Those who are relocated elsewhere find their rents increased, their neighborhoods different, and owing to the kind of high-rise-with-grass apartment buildings favored by the federal planners (where neighbors cannot see who enters and leaves the area as they could in the old apartment-above-the-store-directly-on-the-street neighborhoods), the incidence of crime goes up by several hundred percent. Those who are thrown out of their stores are not reimbursed for their property according to its value, particularly the value of being in that neighborhood and known to many people: many have not been reimbursed enough to start a business elsewhere, or, if they did, have found it a losing proposition outside the old neighborhood. Almost all the people who have been relocated by the urban development program have disliked the change, and much preferred things the way they were before, slums and all. In addition, zoning regulations hurt the poor, for the man who had a store next door to or downstairs from his house is no longer permitted to have this

—stores have to be all together, away from the houses. The result is that (1) the only strategic advance the corner store-owner had against the supermarket, namely that the store was right near home, is now gone; (2) people have to go much further to shop, which means that one practically has to have a car—with all that implies as to parking problems, smog, and pollution.[26]

The effects of the urban renewal programs have gone hand in hand with the effects of the construction of the interstate highway system. Again and again, the new interstate highways —subsidized of course by the federal government—have been routed directly through the inner cities, which involves the tearing down of the inner city to make room for the new highways. Even apart from the merits of having a federally subsidized highway system (pp. 354-60), it is pointless to route the highway through the inner city, where traffic problems are already acute, thereby forcing the interstate traffic into the same areas which are already glutted with local traffic; besides, it is very expensive to build eight-lane limited-access highways through the cities. Many areas of cities have been razed to make room for the interstate highways that should never have been there in the first place—and there have been more people forced to move from their homes than have had housing built for them to replace what they had. As a final irony, much of the new housing that has gone up to replace the old is in the form of one-family dwellings clearly designed for people with much higher incomes than the ones who were forced out of their homes when the areas were razed to make room for the highways. The urban poor are indeed the *victims* of government:

Those in the government have for years conspired to raise prices. They have inflated the currency, mainly by way of the Federal Reserve system. They have restricted agricultural production, used price supports, established minimum wages, supported union monopolies, established prices as in transportation—all of which have had the impact of raising prices or, on occasion, maintaining them at artificially high levels. Those policies weigh particularly heavy on the poor who have the most limited assets and may be expected to suffer the most from any rise in prices. With such friends in high places, the poor could hardly endure enemies![27]

Many individuals must have passed through block after block of slum tenements in large cities, cursed by "urban blight," and asked themselves, Why? Why? The question is indeed appropriate, but most people have no clues to an answer. There are plenty of people in the building trades who would gladly build low-cost urban housing; there are plenty of architects who would be happy to design such housing; there are men ready and waiting *now* to take on such employment. There are also many who have the money to invest in such ventures; but as things are now they won't touch it. Why not? Is it cruelty, greed, insensitivity to the plight of the poor, as the liberals say? No—it is the heavy hand of *government* which stops them, in a thousand different ways permeating the whole economy: there are the artificially high prices of materials, the result of subsidies and taxes and other government interventions in the economy; there are the ruinously high property taxes, which make any new enterprise chancy, taking years to break even if it ever does at all—taxes which mount dizzily whenever one wants to improve the condition of his property; there are, further, the taxes on income, which eat away one's profits if one has profits at all; there is tax-free competition from the government, which is itself in the building business; there is constant harassment from government officials in the form of impossibly idealistic building and housing codes, as a result of which one ends up bribing the officials (an additional cost); there is the fact that many tenants who could otherwise afford to live in the new buildings cannot do so because of *their* high taxation; and so on. Without these interventions, cities would never have become rows of slums. If the interventions ceased tomorrow, the cities could begin to be habitable again.

The War on Poverty is a war on the poor especially. Government intervention in the economy produces distorted signs from the market. Any attempt to eliminate poverty by government action interferes with the signaling devices by which men calculate where to invest their time and money. If government subsidizes this, makes grants for that, offers a bounty for one thing, ameliorates the consequences of effort for another, all sorts of false signs abound to lead the unwary astray. The rich man may hire a clutch of experts to help him wind his way successfully through the maze of government programs. The poor do not have the resources to do this, plus the fact that they are likely to be the most unsophisticated and ignorant portion of the population. They are easily victimized in an increasingly complex situation.[28]

If the government programs do not benefit the poor, whom then *do* they benefit?

The most obvious beneficiaries of the government programs are the politicians who advance them. They have acquired a vested interest in moving the United States toward socialism. Not only does it provide them with prestige and power, but it helps them get elected to office. Politicians run for office on the basis of benefits, favors, subsidies, exemptions, grants, and so forth which they did or will provide for the electorate. Notice how this impels us toward more and more governmental activity, for the man who would continue to be elected should promise ever greater benefits to his constituency.[29]

Thus, when government has intervened in one sphere, intervention becomes a habit: even when government has been responsible for a catastrophic situation, the majority of people do not know this and call upon government to intervene to correct the very situation it has caused. And the paid interveners (paid through taxation) favor more intervention in order to protect their government jobs and increase their importance by increasing the number of jobs under their control. As Herbert Spencer clearly saw almost a century ago, there comes to exist

... the tacit assumption that Government should step in whenever anything is not going right. "Surely you would not have this misery continue!" exclaims some one, if you hint at demurrer to much that is now being said and done. Observe what is implied by this exclamation.

It takes for granted, first, that all suffering ought to be prevented, which is not true; much of the suffering is curative, and prevention of it is prevention of a remedy.

In the second place, it takes for granted that every evil can be removed: the truth being that, with the existing defects of human nature, many evils can only be thrust out of one place or form into another place or form—often being increased by the change.

The exclamation also implies the unhesitating belief ... that evils of all kinds should be dealt with by the State. There does not occur the inquiry whether there are at work other agencies capable of dealing with evils, and whether the evils in question may not be among those which are best dealt with by these other agencies. And obviously, the more numerous governmental interventions become, the more confirmed does this habit of thought grow, and the more loud and perpetual the demands for intervention.

Every extension of the regulative policy involves an addition to the regulative agents—a further growth of officialism and an increasing power of the organization formed of officials. . . .

Indeed the more numerous public instrumentalities become, the more is there generated in citizens the notion that everything is to be done for them, and nothing by them. Each generation is made less familiar with the attainment of desired ends by individual actions or private combinations, and more familiar with the attainment of them by governmental agencies, until, eventually, governmental agencies come to be thought of as the only available agencies.[30]

The facts of the case are dismal enough to throw anyone who clearly perceives them into a state of depression. And yet they are so plain, so obvious once pointed out, that one is tempted to believe that if only everyone were educated, there would be a quick end to all support for such political programs. On this point, once again Herbert Spencer has spoken more wisely perhaps than anyone else:

Yes, if the education were worthy to be so called, and were relevant to the political enlightenment needed, much might be hoped from it. But knowing the rules of syntax, being able to add up correctly, having geographical information, and a memory stocked with the dates of kings' accessions and generals' victories, no more implies fitness to form political conclusions than acquirement of skill in drawing implies expertness in telegraphing, or than ability to play cricket implies proficiency on the violin.

"Surely," rejoins some one, "facility in reading opens the way to political knowledge." Doubtless; but will the way be followed? Table-talk proves that nine out of ten people read what amuses them rather than what instructs them; and proves, also, that the last thing they read is something which tells them disagreeable truths or dispels groundless hopes. That popular education results in an extensive reading of publications which offer pleasant illusions rather than of those which insist on hard realities, is beyond question. . . .

Being possessed of electoral power, as are now the mass of those who are thus led to nurture sanguine anticipations of benefits to be obtained by social reorganization, it results that whoever seeks their votes must at least refrain from exposing their mistaken beliefs; even if he does not yield to the temptation to express agreement with them. Every candidate for Parliament is prompted to propose or support some new piece of *ad captandum* legislation. Nay, even the chiefs of parties— these anxious to retain office and those to wrest it from them—severally aim to get adherents by outbidding one another. Each seeks popularity by promising more than his opponent has promised, as we have lately seen. And then, as divisions in Parliament show us, the traditional loyalty to leaders overrides questions concerning the intrinsic propriety of proposed measures. Representatives are unconscientious enough to vote for bills which they believe to be wrong in principle, because party-needs and regard for the next election demand it. And thus a vicious policy is strengthened even by those who see its viciousness.[31]

Care of the Needy

Are the above remarks anti-humanitarian? By no means: none of them is intended to exhibit any indifference to the well-being of human beings, if one means *all* human beings, both the recipients of government welfare, who are often reduced to accepting it by the constant tampering of government with the intricate machinery of a free economy, *and* the providers of it, for whom the added burden of taxation often spells the difference between solvency and bankruptcy, or between being able and not being able to save and plan ahead with some reasonable prospect that one will be able to dine out once a week or send his son or daughter to college. Among the consequences of government welfare, some consideration should be given to the welfare of the people who are called upon to provide it.

Nor are any of the above remarks intended to discourage giving, even to the limit of one's ability, to worthy recipients who are in need. But government-administered charity programs are not only inefficient (because the money spent does not belong to the people who administer the programs) and wasteful (with much of the money going to the government administrators of the programs); they are also immoral: humanitarianism does not consist of a gun directed at the pocketbooks of productive men, to enforce their compliance in programs of which, for very excellent reasons, they may disapprove.

Did [our concern for others] prompt personal effort to relieve the suffering, it would rightly receive approving recognition. Were the many who express this cheap pity like the few who devote large parts of their time to aiding and encouraging, and occasionally amusing, those who, by ill-fortune or incapacity, are brought to lives of hardship, they would be worthy of unqualified admiration. . . . But the immense majority of the persons who wish to mitigate by law the miseries of the unsuccessful and the reckless, propose to do this in small measure at their own cost and mainly at the cost of others—sometimes with their assent but mostly without.[32]

Incorporated humanity is very commonly thought of as though it were like so much dough which the cook can mould as she pleases into pie-crust, or puff, or tartlet. . . . [But] facts forced on his attention hour by hour should make everyone skeptical as to the success of this or that proposed way of changing people's actions. Alike to the citizen and to the legislator, home-experiences daily supply proofs that the conduct of human beings baulks calculation. He has given up the thought of managing his wife and lets her manage him. Children on whom he has tried now reprimand, now punishment, now suasion, now reward, do not respond satisfactorily to any method; and no expostulation prevents their mother from treating them in ways which he thinks mischievous. . . . Yet, difficult as he finds it to deal with humanity in detail, he is confident of his ability to deal with embodied humanity. Citizens, not one-thousandth of whom he knows, not one-hundredth of whom he ever saw, and the great mass of whom belong to classes having habits and modes of thought of which he has but dim notions, he feels sure will act in ways he foresees, and fulfill ends he wishes. Is there not a marvellous incongruity between premises and conclusion? . . .[33]

Though we no longer presume to coerce men for their *spiritual good*, we still think ourselves called upon to coerce them for their *material good*; not seeing that the one is as useless and as unwarrantable as the other. Innumerable failures seem, so far, powerless to teach this. Take up a daily paper and you will probably find a leader exposing the corruption, negligence, or mismanagement of some State-department. Case your eye down the next column, and it is not unlikely that you will read proposals for an extension of State-supervision.[34]

Ill as government discharges its true duties, any other duties committed to it are likely to be still worse discharged. To guard its subjects against aggression, either individual or national, is a straightforward and tolerably simple matter; to regulate, directly or indirectly, the personal actions of those subjects is an infinitely complicated matter. It is one thing to secure to each man the unhindered power to pursue his own good; it is a widely different thing *to pursue the good for him*. To do the first efficiently, the State has merely to look on while its citizens act; to forbid unfairness; to adjudicate when called on; and to enforce restitution for injuries. To do the last efficiently, it must become an ubiquitous worker—must know each man's needs better than he knows them himself—must, in short, possess superhuman power and intelligence. Even, therefore, had the State done well in its proper sphere, no sufficient warrant would have existed for extending that sphere; but seeing how ill it has discharged those simple offices which we cannot help consigning to it, small indeed is the probability that it will discharge well offices of a more complicated nature.[35]

"But if the government doesn't take care of the needy, who will? Or doesn't the libertarian want them to be cared for at all?"

The libertarian's answer is very simple: Care for the needy should come from private charity, through voluntary gifts from those more able to give than the recipients.

"But we can't afford it!" Again, who is the "we"? The we's are nothing but you's and I's, every individual in the country; and every individual in the country has the right to determine by his own choice to what uses to put his income. Moreover, it is not possible, without bringing on economic catastrophe, for the "we"—all the taxpayers in the nation—to underwrite such programs indefinitely. On this point Isabel Paterson has spoken with eloquence and conviction in what must surely be one of the four or five greatest books on political philosophy written thus far in the twentieth century:[36]

Very well; take a specific case. In the hard times of the Nineties, a young journalist in Chicago was troubled by the appalling hardships of the unemployed. He tried to believe that any man honestly willing to work could find employment; but to make sure, he investigated a few cases. Here was one, a youth from a farm, where the family maybe got enough to eat but was short of everything else; the farm boy had come to Chicago looking for a job, and would certainly have taken any kind of work, but there was none. Let it be supposed he might have begged his way home; there were others who were half a continent and an ocean from their homes. They couldn't get back, by any possible effort of their own; and there is no quibbling about that. They couldn't. They slept in alleyways, waited for meager rations at soup kitchens; and suffered bitterly. There is another thing; among these unemployed were some persons, it is impossible to say how many, who were exceptionally enterprising, gifted, or competent; and that is what got them into their immediate plight. They had cut loose from dependence at a peculiarly hazardous time; they had taken a long chance. Extremes met among the unemployed; the extremes of courageous enterprise, of sheer ill-luck, and of downright improvidence and incompetence. A blacksmith working near Brooklyn Bridge who gave a penniless wanderer ten cents to pay the bridge toll couldn't know he was making that advance to immortality in the person of a future Poet Laureate of England. But John Masefield was the wanderer. So it is not implied that the needy are necessarily "undeserving." There were also people in the country, in drought or insect-plagued areas, who were in dire want and must have literally starved if relief had not been sent them. They didn't get much either, and that in haphazard, ragbag sort. But everyone struggled through to an amazing recovery of the whole country.

Incidentally, there would have been much more severe distress instead of simple poverty at the subsistence line, but for neighborly giving which was not called charity. People always give away a good deal, if they have it; it is a human impulse, which the humanitarian plays on for his own purpose. What is wrong with institutionalizing that natural impulse in a political agency?

Very well again; had the farm boy done anything wrong in leaving the farm, where he did have enough to eat, and going to Chicago on the chance of getting a job?

If the answer is yes, then there must be a rightful power which shall prevent him leaving the farm *without permission*. The feudal power did that. It couldn't prevent people from starving; it merely compelled them to starve right where they were born.

But if the answer is no, the farm boy didn't do wrong, he had a right to take that chance, then exactly what is to be done to make certain he will not be in hard luck when he gets to his chosen destination? Must a job be provided for any person at any place he chooses to go? That is absurd. It can't be done. Is he entitled to relief anyhow, when he gets there, as long as he chooses to stay; or at least to a return ticket home? That is equally absurd. The demand would be unlimited; no abundance of production would meet it.

Then what of the people who were impoverished by drought; could they not be given political relief? But there must be conditions. Are they to receive it just as long as they are in need, while they stay where they are? (They cannot be financed for indefinite travel.) That is just what has been done in recent years; and it kept relief recipients for seven years together in squalid surroundings, wasting time, work, and seed-grain in the desert.

The truth is that any proposed method of caring for the marginal want and distress incident to human life by establishing a permanent fixed charge upon production would be adopted most gladly by those who now oppose it, *if it were practicable*. They oppose it because it is impracticable in the nature of things. They are the people who have already devised all the partial expedients possible, in the way of private insurance; and they know exactly what the catch is, because they come up against it when they try to make secure provision for their own dependents.

The insuperable obstacle is that it is absolutely impossible to get anything out of production ahead of maintenance.

If it were a fact that the producers generally, the industrial managers and others, had hearts of chilled steel, and cared nothing whatever about human suffering, still it would be most convenient for them if the question of relief for all kinds of distress, whether unemployment, illness or old age, could be settled once for all, so they need hear no more of it. They are always under attack on this point; and it doubles their trouble whenever industry hits a depression. The politicians can get votes out of distress; the humanitarians land lucrative white-collar jobs for themselves distributing relief funds; only the producers, both capitalists and workingmen, have to take the abuse and pay the shot. . . .

The proposal to care for the needy by the political means gives the power to the politicians to tax without limit; and there is absolutely no way to ensure that the money shall go where it was intended to go. In any case, the business will not stand any such *unlimited* drain.

Why do kind-hearted persons call in the political power? They cannot deny that the means for relief must come from production. But they say there is enough and to spare. Then they must assume that the producers are not willing to give what is "right." Further they assume that there is a collective right to impose taxes, for any purpose the collective shall determine. They localize that right in "the government." . . . But if taxes are to be imposed for relief, who is the judge of what is possible or beneficial? It must be either the producers, the needy, or some third group. To say it shall be all three together is no answer; the

verdict must swing upon majority or plurality drawn from one or other
group. Are the needy to vote themselves whatever they want? Are the
humanitarians, the third group, to vote themselves control of both the
producers and the needy? (That is what they have done.) The government is thus supposed to be empowered to give "security" to the needy.
It *cannot*. What it does is to seize the provision made by private persons for their own security, thus depriving everyone of every hope or
chance of security. It can do nothing else, if its acts at all. Those who do
not understand the nature of the action are like savages who might cut
down a tree to get the fruit; they do not think over time and space, as
civilized men must think.

The people of the United States have always been generous
to those in need. Their generosity is very considerable even
today, when the Red Cross, the Salvation Army, and thousands of charitable enterprises receive billions of dollars per
year from American citizens. But this amount is small compared with what it could be: for *nothing inhibits voluntary
charity as much as forced charity in the form of taxation.*
When you have paid all your spare money to the Internal Revenue Department on April 15, and perhaps borrowed money
to meet the payment, you may feel less than charitable when
the Red Cross representative calls at your door for a donation
on April 20. The vast enterprise of government relief leaves
you no choice as to where it shall be spent, or whether the recipients are worthy or unworthy; much of this money would
do as much good being thrown down a sewer; but you have no
control over it in any case. Quite naturally, with the government playing fast and loose with your money, you may feel
that you have already paid your debt to charity by contributing
your part to the billions that the American people currently pay annually for government welfare purposes. If this enormous load were lifted from people's backs, it is difficult to
imagine how much real generosity would be manifested,
which now finds expression in vague resentment and impotent

fury, combined often with a feeling of guilt that one finds one-self having these feelings.

When I say that all relief should come from private funds, I do not mean *as things are now*. That is a crucial difference that is often forgotten. For how many people are on government relief because government taxation has deprived them of jobs, or raised the price of everything they buy? How many firms are there in the land that haven't gone ahead with that planned expansion because the outcome was uncertain and if it succeeded the gains wouldn't be worth the effort, since most of the profit would be gobbled up in taxes anyway? And how many people are there who are now out of work because this planned expansion, which would have given them jobs, didn't take place? How many people have been laid off, and how many firms have gone out of business, because they couldn't break even after the crushing load of high prices and taxation? Perhaps no one will ever know precisely; but the number must be very large indeed. Without having tried very hard I know in my own experience a good many of them, and doubtless there are thousands more. If one thinks of what a shot-in-the-arm these expansions would give the economy, and how many people then would be gainfully employed who are now kept going at government expense, one cannot help be appalled at the enormous *waste* of creative energy that is constantly taking place—a waste that is caused by government and growing at an ever greater rate.

How long can an economy withstand such a drain? How many wrenches can be thrown into the intricate machinery of the free market before it grinds slowly to a halt, taking the sources of future production along with it? Yes, if you ask them, people want the country to be prosperous and produc-tive; they want the water-level above the dam to remain high, to provide more electrical power from the waterfalls—and yet they approve now this scheme and now that, and hundreds of schemes that will pipe and divert the water away before it has a chance to fall over the dam—and then, later, when the flow is reduced to a mere trickle, they wonder what could have happened to the supply of water on which their lives depended.

When a child burns his finger on a hot stove, the relation of cause and effect is immediately obvious to him, and he does not repeat his mistake; would that the relation of cause and effect in economic matters were as instantaneous, that mistakes would as quickly and easily be brought back on the head of the doer, as they are in simpler matters! Then no one could get by with suggesting hairbrained schemes "in the name of the people" that will in the end mean poverty for virtually everyone.

The poor always will be able to obtain in the open competition of the market more of the life-sustaining and life-enriching goods and services they want than can be had through political warfare against successful private enterprise. The market leaves the planning and managing to those who continuously prove their ability, whereas political class warfare tends to redistribute resources among those most likely to waste them.

When government becomes the guarantor of "freedom from want," this means that the poorest managers within the society have been put in charge of human affairs; for they always do and always will outnumber those of superior talent. What is now advertised as a war on poverty is really a confiscation of the fruits of production; and the consequence has to be disastrous for everyone, especially for the poor.[37]

8
Taxation
and
Civilization

The British historian W. E. H. Lecky wrote in 1899: "Highly graduated taxation realizes most completely the supreme danger of democracy, creating a state of things in which one class imposes on another burdens which it is not asked to share, and impels the State into vast schemes of extravagance, under the belief that the whole cost will be thrown upon others."

Fifteen years prior to this, Herbert Spencer had written:

Partly for defraying the costs of carrying out these ever-multiplying sets of regulations, each of which requires an additional staff of officers, and partly to meet the outlay for new public institutions, such as board-schools, free libraries, public museums, baths and washhouses, recreation grounds, etc., etc., local rates are year after year increased; as the general taxation is increased by grants for education and to the departments of science and art, etc. Every one of these involves further coercion—restricts still more the freedom of the citizen. For the implied address accompanying every additional exaction is: "Hitherto you have been free to spend this portion of your earnings in any way which pleased you; hereafter you shall not be free so to spend it, but we will spend it for the general benefit." Thus, either directly or indirectly, and in most cases both at once, the citizen is at each further stage in the growth of this compulsory legislation, deprived of some liberty which he previously had.[1]

There is nothing as sure as death and taxes; but this is no reason why we should be taxed to death. There are taxes on sales, taxes on services, taxes on income (federal, state, and sometimes municipal)—these are known and obvious to everyone. There are also "hidden" taxes, such as the taxes on every product we buy, imposed on it at every stage of its production: there are now more than 150 taxes on every loaf of bread, and 100 taxes on every egg. But of all the devices of government to increase its power over the individual, perhaps the most dangerous is the income tax. Begun at the turn of the century in the United States when the maximum tax (for a few of the rich) was in the neighborhood of 5 percent, it has grown to such proportions that today, a generation after World War II, the government takes away in the neighborhood of 70 percent of the income of an affluent man, 40 percent of the income of a man of average means, and 20 percent from the poorest individual who draws a paycheck. This is surely going some distance toward taking away by force the means by which you live! There is no legal limit on it, and the increases are slow and gradual so that one gets used to the next increase before still another one follows it. If it had all happened suddenly, there would have been such an outcry that the thing would have been stopped. The trick is to tighten the rise so gradually that the victim becomes gradually desensitized to pain.

For every dollar you pay in taxes, there is a dollar you cannot spend according to your own judgment. Every dollar taken away from you means a dollar more that people in government spend, withdrawn from your control. Every dollar paid into it gives you less power and the government bureaucracy more power. Every dollar you pay into it takes that much liberty away from you, and puts the decisions that could have been yours into the hands of people who, to put it mildly, do not inspire infinite trust.

Bureaucrats are always crying for more funds; not only to make their jobs seem more important and to create other jobs for their friends, but because it is always pleasant and easy to spend other people's money. Besides, there comes to be a kind of cynicism about individual liberty among government spenders; the formula seems to be something like this: "*You* don't know how your own income ought to be spent. But we politicians do know, being wiser than you. And so we'll just take it away from you, so that we can spend it on what we know is best—best for you, of course."

There is a popular delusion about taxation: "Taxes really don't hurt the producer. The amount of the tax is simply added to the cost of the product, and everything is the same as before." Nothing could be more mistaken. If a product is taxed at various places along the process of its production (as every product now is), and the producer doesn't want to raise the cost of the product to the consumer, he must absorb the amount of tax himself, decreasing his profits by that amount. The tax has to be paid somewhere along the line, and he pays it. In some cases this would mean that the producer, who is already producing at marginal profits, has his profits wiped out entirely, and has to go out of business. In other cases, his profits will simply be decreased, meaning that he has less leeway for other things, such as research projects, expansion of his business, new employees, and so on. But in the long run, he cannot remain in business simply by continuing to absorb losses in the form of tax-increases.

The other alternative is for him to increase the cost of his product by the amount of the tax. If all the other producers do the same, all the prices to the consumer will be increased, but no producer will lose out in relation to the other ones because they will all have increased their prices. But this, of course, is not the end of the matter. Because of the price-increase, fewer consumers can afford to buy the product: instead of selling a hundred coats, the clothier may now sell seventy-five. Moreover, if a consumer does buy a coat for the present $50 instead of the former $40, he now has $10 less to spend on other things—and the sales of the other products will go down because the consumer could not afford them. Before the tax, he could afford to buy a coat, a shirt, and a pair of pants; after the tax, he must choose two of the three but cannot buy all three—with resulting loss of sales to one of the three producers. The tax, then, dries up the sources of income. The clothier may notice that his sales for the month have gone down, and not know why. He is aware of what he sees, but he does not stop to think through what he does not see.

The unrestricted power to tax is a powerful weapon for the destruction of liberty—more powerful, because more slowly encroaching, than the guns of a dictator's firing squads. A United States senator said in a recent broadcast, "Your government has the power to take from you everything that you earn, and return to you only as much as it thinks that you need or deserve." He did not say that the government should have this power—indeed he seemed to deplore it; but he was simply stating as a fact that it has this power. In the light of this remark, who can say that the government is not encroaching, and encroaching dangerously, upon your right to the use and disposal of what you yourself have worked to earn? When the fascist state comes to America, it will most probably come through the gradual encroachment of government upon the individual via the income tax. The individual will have less and less to say about how his earnings are to be spent, and the government will have more and more; it already has a first crack at all the income of every citizen in the land, and gradually it will seize a higher percentage of one's earnings, and at last it will have control over the nation's production and trade. And then 1984 will have arrived. It may be that things have gone so far even now that something like Orwell's vision of 1984 can no longer be prevented. In 1884, Herbert Spencer wrote in *The Man vs. the State*:

Regulations have been made in yearly growing numbers, restraining the citizen in directions where his actions were previously unchecked, and compelling actions which previously he might perform or not as he liked; and at the same time heavier public burdens . . . have further restricted his freedom, by lessening that portion of his earnings which he can spend as he pleases, and augmenting the portion taken from him to be spent as public agents please.

In 1840 Alexis De Toqueville, in his great book *Democracy in America*, wrote that the government was becoming for its citizens

. . . an immense and tutelary power, which takes upon itself alone to secure their gratification, and to watch over their fate . . . For their happiness such a government willingly labors, but it chooses to be the sole agent and the only arbiter of that happiness; it provides for their security, foresees and supplies their necessities, facilitates their pleasures, manages their principal concerns, directs their industry, regulates the descent of property, and subdivides their inheritances—what remains, but to spare them all the care of thinking and the trouble of living? . . . The will of man is not shattered, but softened, bent, and guided; men are seldom forced to act, but they are constantly restrained from acting; such a power does not destroy, but it prevents existence; it does not tyrannize, but it compresses, enervates, extinguishes, and stupefies a people, till each nation is reduced to be nothing better than a flock of timid and industrious animals, of which the government is the shepherd.[2]

I sustain my life by my work, and try to save from what I have earned as a bulwark against the future. But if others can come in and simply take it, then of course this bulwark is gone, and the means of sustenance is outside my control. I grant to no burglar the right to one dish on my shelf—nor to any bureaucrat. Antecedent to my sanction he has no claim. If I give it, today he claims three dishes, I claim one, and he takes two. Tomorrow he returns and claims five, and takes four. Before the compromise is granted the only issue is whether it should be granted at all. After it is granted, the only issue is how much. Once I have started on the slippery slope, a series of compromises finally exacts the price of my life.

Let us suppose you have a wife or husband or fiancé whom you trust completely—so completely that you give that person access to your checking account and all your worldly goods, for whatever purposes she wishes to use it: "Here, any time you need it, here are the papers that give you control over it." Would you be quite sure that the person you know and trust most would not think of new things she wanted, for which she could use this open account? Are you quite sure that your own bank account would not be overdrawn just when you needed it most for some emergency in your life or work?

But this is the way we all stand in relation to government. Government has an open claim on the earning power of every citizen; it can take what it wants and impoverish any group of citizens any time it so decides. And the government isn't even a trusted friend—indeed, judging by the record of governments in the history of the world, we have much less reason to trust it than we do most enemies.

Yet if you would not willingly give a wife or a trusted friend such power, would anyone in his right mind willingly give it to government? If one could not entrust a beloved and doting parent with such power, why grant it to an indifferent mass?

Why grant to millions of people the power to take from you a few coins only, when without ill-will or malice, they will drift like a ship without anchor, taking the slack from its hawser to cinch the rope around your neck? Why, when there is no chance of rescinding, altering, or retracting the present demand, or possibility of appeal, expose yourself to such overwhelming, brute force?

Yes, help your fellow man as you choose. When you choose, when you consider the cause a just one, surrender your last coin to help him. But do not hook a siphon into your veins while he holds the spigot which controls the exodus of your life's blood. The world abounds with people who would gladly drain you of all of it, and demand it as their right. And once they have tasted of these unearned riches, they will vote into power governments which use the enormous coercive power of the state to force the spigot into your veins, to empty you of blood in order to fill the bottomless well of their desires.

A Historical Parallel: Caesar and Caesarism

In the centuries of the existence of the Roman republic, Rome had a political system of great stability and strength. There was government by law, not by men. The succession of power, the makeup of the Roman Senate, and a host of other political processes were determined by law and steadfastly adhered to. Though it was admittedly a society in which slavery existed, it was not a society of status; men of talent could rise from the lower ranks and make a name for themselves. Civilian authority over the military was constantly emphasized: the Romans forbade a victorious commander to enter Rome without permission from the Senate, in order to prevent seizure of the government by the military. (No other nation in ancient

times maintained civil control of the military for centuries.)
Contracts were scrupulously observed and protected by law.
Perhaps most important of all, each citizen's life and property
were inviolable: a man was secure from the state in the possession of his life and his property—which, of course, was an incentive to work; and Rome became about as prosperous as any
pre-industrial society could become.

Then came the era of the emperors, from the first of the
Caesars to the fall of Rome five centuries later—and all this
was changed. The transition figure was that of Julius Caesar;
and although he was a hero compared with most of the emperors who followed him, he was the initiator in Rome of the era
of government by men, gradually eroding government by law.

In his earlier years Caesar employed the tactics of manchine politics
with which Americans are so well acquainted. His machine operated
through bribery, daring usurpations, and public benefactions with
money provided by callous and ambitious rich Romans. His henchmen
won support by public handouts when expedient and occasionally by
planned violence and disorder. As he rose to supreme power, Caesar
secured for himself election to one republican office after another,
even attaining the sacred office of pontiff to clothe himself with religious authority. Later his well-advertised military expeditions yielded
personal glamor and spoils for the Roman mobs. In the aftermath of
the Cleopatra affair he beguiled Romans with the absurd image of
himself as a peer of the gods.

Caesar substituted a new mystical basis of authority for the traditional sanctions of the old Republic. At the moment of his death he
had built nothing, founded nothing, except a psychological acceptance
for his rule. Into this vacuum moved the emperors and the praetorian
guard.[3]

Many great men in Rome saw what was happening and tried
to prevent it. Cicero, the famous orator, in his writings and in
his speeches before the Senate, constantly urged a return to the
supremacy of law as the source of justice rather than the

whims of individual men; to limitation of state power rather than the magnification of state power under Caesar; to government of checks and balances rather than the one-man performance by which Caesar was mesmerizing the populace. Cicero held government to be an agency for the protection of individual citizens, above the caprice of individual men. He knew what was coming if his warnings were ignored, and he labored to his death for the restoration of the limited government Rome had had under the republic. But he failed—and the result is history.

With Caesar, vanity fed on itself. He instituted public works projects which employed thousands of men. He claimed divine descent from Venus, and wore every day the toga reserved for triumphs. He had statues of himself built in temples. When important cases came before the court, he judged them alone. His was to dispose, through the length and breadth of the territories under the control of Rome.

Gradually, through the ensuing centuries, Rome became a welfare state. The number of people supported by government increased until the population could no longer bear the heavy load of taxation brought on by extravagant government spending and the large number of parasites on the government payroll. Life could be taken and property confiscated at the twist of an Emperor's finger, until no one was secure. Finally,

. . . The exactions of the bureaucracy increased, and the number of officials multiplied. More and more of the flow was diverted from production into the political mechanism. Whatever elements in motion compose a stream of energy, enough must go through to complete the circuit and renew production. Water running in an aqueduct to turn a millwheel is a stream of energy; or electricity going through insulated wires; or goods in process from raw materials to finished product and conveyed by a stream of transport. If the water channel is pierced with many small openings en route; or electricity taken off by more and more outlets; or the goods expropriated piecemeal at each stage of the process, finally not enough will go through for maintenance of the system. In the energy system comprised in an exchange of goods, the producers and processors have to get back enough to enable them to keep on producing and working up the raw materials and to provide transport. In the later Roman empire, the bureaucrats took such a large cut, that at length scarcely anything went through the complete circuit.

Meanwhile the producers, receiving less and less in exchange for their products, were impoverished and discouraged. Naturally they tended to produce less, since they would get no fair return; in fact, effort from which there is no net return automatically must cease. They consumed their own products instead of putting them into exchange. With that the taxes began to dry up. Taxes must come from surplus. The bureaucrats (inevitably) come down on the producers, with the object of sequestrating the energy directly at the source, by a planned economy. Farmers were bound to the soil, craftsmen to their workbenches; tradesmen were ordered to continue in business although the taxes and regulations did not permit them to make a living. No one could change his residence or occupation without permission. The currency was debased. Prices and wages were fixed until there was nothing to sell and no work to be had.

Men who had formerly been productive escaped to the woods and mountains as outlaws, because they must starve if they went on working. Sealed at the source, the level of energy sank until it was no longer sufficient to operate the mechanism. The Roman Wall in Britain marked high tide. When the Legions were withdrawn from the wall, they had not been defeated by the barbarians; they were pulled back by the ebb of energy, the impossibility of maintaining supplies and reinforcements. The barbarians were not a rising force; they floated in on the ebb. They had no objective, and no ability to take over or set up any system; they came in as wild animals will graze across once-cultivated fields when the cultivator cannot muster sufficient strength to keep his fences in repair. The tax-eaters had absorbed the energy. A map of the Roman Empire in the fourth and fifth centuries traced with the route of the barbarian migrations is a network of wandering lines showing where the East Goths and the West Goths, the Huns and the Vandals, simply followed the main trade routes. There was nothing to stop them. The producers were already beaten by the bureaucracy.[4]

Caesarism in America

The above is a horror story—all the more horrible for being true. Here is another horror story, a more recent one, and one whose ending has yet to be written.

In 1929 there began in the United States the Great Depression, by far the most serious of all the economic depressions in our history. It not only was the most severe, but it lasted the longest: it did not cease until World War II broke out in 1939. And its effects are not yet over, as we shall see. So much are its effects still with us, that as a result of the ineffectual attempts by government to get out of it, the history of the United States may yet parallel the later history of Rome.

The initial act in the chain reaction of events that led to the Great Depression occurred in 1913 with the creation of the Federal Reserve Bank. Throughout the history of privately owned banks, bank officials had been willing to lend money for enterprises they considered sound—with interest, of course, to make it worth their while. The rate of interest charged on loans would naturally vary somewhat: when economic and political conditions are stable, many people are willing to lend money—that is, they are willing to forego consumption now in favor of more income later on. And when many people are willing to lend money, the interest rate at which they are willing to lend it, being competitive, goes down. And when it goes down, many more people will be able and willing to borrow money to start new enterprises and expand old ones. When large amounts of money are deposited in banks, it becomes available to others for such loans. The bank, of course, wants the return of its money plus interest, so it is careful to whom it lends and for what purpose.

When political conditions are unstable (decreasing the likelihood of the money's return), or when many loans have al-

ready been made so that less money is available to float new
ones, interest rates tend to be high. A higher rate of interest
means, of course, that fewer people will borrow money, and
certain enterprises that would have expanded had the money
been available at low interest will now not do so. The high interest rate at such times acts as a check on the economy; if
interest rates were low at such a time, many economic enterprises would be encouraged which should not be encouraged,
given the context of the time and place.

The interest rate acts as a road sign indicating to the businessman the
direction his investment should take: If rates are low, investment in
long-term capital goods is encouraged; if rates are high, investment in
long-term capital goods is discouraged. But suppose the rates would
have been high but are *held at artificially low levels* by some kind of
government intervention, such as artificial credit expansion? The road
signs have been switched. As a result, excessive investment will occur,
particularly in the capital goods area. This is not, then, "over-invest-
ment," but rather "mal-investment"—investment in the wrong things.
An example of mal-investment might be the construction of a railroad
to an area not yet sufficiently populated to provide a market for the
railroad's service. Another example of mal-investment might be the
construction of a steel mill before the complementary factors of production such as power and transportation have been developed. Or it
might involve excessive speculation in land or heavy industry or in any
such long-term capital goods area. In any case the businessman has
been misled by the artificially low rates. Sooner or later he will be
forced to realize that he has on his hands an expensive "white ele-
phant." The day of reckoning can be postponed by further credit expansion, but it cannot be evaded permanently, for businessmen have
invested in things that simply cannot be successfully integrated with the
rest of the economy. Accordingly, these ventures must finally cease
operation. Workers will be laid off, and the effects will quickly percolate down to the consumer goods industries as well. The depression has
begun.[5]

When the roadsign—free-market interest rate—has been
tampered with by government, the businessman is in the posi-

tion of the driver on the highway at night who cannot trust the roadsigns because they have been switched. When the Federal Reserve Bank was created, it artificially held down the interest rates below the free-market level, "in order to promote business expansion"—but what it encouraged was the wrong kind of expansion. Many businessmen knew of course what the interest rates should be for the investments being proposed to them—but with the Federal Reserve Bank itself offering the money at the low rates, what could these businessmen do? A few of them foresaw the results of the policy, but by refraining from the unwise lending policies they would not be staving off the catastrophe to come, so they went along with it in the hope of wresting at least a temporary gain.

All through the 1920s the Federal Reserve, by keeping interest rates artificially low, encouraged a wild orgy of speculation in enterprises that were economically unsound and should never have been undertaken in the first place. That is, the government enforced on the banks a "cheap money" policy. The stock market soared wildly, and then came the bust and the depression.

There had been depressions in the United States before. After the War of 1812, there was rapid economic development. Prices of land began to rise sharply. People borrowed money from banks to buy land, secure in the belief that even if they paid a high price it would be worth it in the end. By 1837, these prices had been bid up to irrationally high levels, without a clear view of the risks and expenses in developing the land. Because of the large demand for loans, the bank reserves were stripped; and as a result, interest rates rose sharply. The speculative boom came to an end with the Panic of 1837, the first American depression.

But the crisis did not last long. Economic activity was normal again within a year. Why? The banking system had put it to an end before it could lead to a major disaster. The banks, whose every piece of paper currency had to be backed by gold, could only say to more would-be borrowers, "We have no more money to lend." If they could have printed paper money and used it as a basis for loans, loans would have multiplied and interest rates gone down still further. But the private banking system, together with the gold standard, put an end to the wild speculation before a major depression could occur. Nevertheless, the public considered the banks not as heroes but as villains. "They wouldn't lend me the money!" was the response, rather than "Both the interest rates and the price demanded for the land to be bought, have become too high."

With the extensive development of the railroads in the succeeding decades, there was again great expansion of economic activity. Bank reserves were again inadequate to the tremendous tendency toward expansion, and interest rates rose. Again the private banking system, backed by the gold standard, checked the boom. There was no government intervention, as there is today; the government allowed the economy to correct itself. But the role of the banking system was still not understood; it was looked upon as a malefactor, rather than as a benefactor.

The National Banking Act of 1863, during the Civil War, was the first major intervention of the government into the economy. It enabled the government to issue bank notes against government bonds. The Civil War was financed largely by the printing press, and this paper was not redeemable in gold. As a result, there was a severe inflation. However, fortunately for the economy, the war greenbacks were withdrawn from circulation in 1879 and *redeemed in gold*. Again, the money supply was stable. A panic had meanwhile occurred, in 1873, partly because of lack of faith in the dollar and partly because of the government intervention in the railroad business: with the government handing out money to speculators for the building of tracks, millions of dollars had been spent on comparatively few miles of track (often separated), and the market for railroad bonds had become worse. But with the expectation of restored full gold convertibility, there was again confidence in the dollar, a stoppage of inflation, and a decline in the previously inflated prices. With the restoration of gold convertibility, the government accepted (as it does not today) the full consequences of its previous errors.

But more trouble was on the way. Farmers wanted to increase the money supply so that they could pay their debts with cheap money, and with the influx of silver in the 1880s and 1890s they looked upon silver as a magic solution. There was a great temptation to go off the gold standard. The Sherman Silver Purchase Act became law in 1890, but was repealed in 1893—President Cleveland was determined to keep the U.S. on the gold standard. A victory for Bryan in 1896 would have taken the United States off the gold standard. But Cleveland's determination stopped the gold exports. And the victory of McKinley in 1896 and 1900 helped the cause of economic stability and the gold standard. The gold standard was still working. Banking remained closely tied to the amount of gold in the country.

But again the banks were blamed: "There's a shortage of bank reserves!" and "Not enough money in the banks!" were the complaints. The goal envisioned by many people was to fix things so that the banking system would not run out of reserves.

And at last this was done, with the creation of the Federal Reserve Bank in 1913. This was the initial act in the chain reaction that led to the Great Depression of 1929.

The stock market soared, triggered by the speculation which was in turn triggered by the inflation and the low interest rates. A few far-seeing persons warned of the inevitable consequences, but most people were wildly speculating, caught in the orgy. But then the chain reaction started. As one stock after another plummeted on the Exchange, payment was demanded of speculators for one credit purchase after another, and when the money could not be paid, the items on the Exchange fell to a fraction of their former value. Black Tuesday in October 1929 was the turning point—a day that will never be forgotten by those Americans who lived through it.

What had happened? Prior to the Federal Reserve system, the banking system was like a safety fuse in the electrical system. When it was heated, the fuse always blew and the situation corrected itself again. But the government didn't like for the fuses to blow—so it put a penny into the fuse box, and the house burned down.[6]

The government, however, did not take the blame. Blamed instead were capitalism, the businessman's greed, the gold standard. The solution adopted was: shackle the businessman, make him pay for his greed. It was, of course, no solution at all; it only diverted attention from the real culprit; but the people by and large accepted it, thus opening the way for socialism-fascism in America. The "solution" has not been repudiated to this day.

The President of the United States at that time, Herbert Hoover, was no believer in laissez faire, though most people now seem to believe that he was. He believed that government was called upon to try to correct the evils of the depression which (apparently, in his opinion) private businesses had brought about. He believed firmly that high wages cause prosperity, and the way to bring back prosperity was to force business to guarantee continued high wages. (In fact, of course, it is prosperity that brings about high wages.) Every leader of big business was asked to promise in November 1929 that he would not reduce wages. The result was predictable: if you keep wages high while profits are low or nonexistent, many businesses will fail, and tremendous unemployment will result: those who can't afford to pay the high wages will have to lay off the workers, or close the shop entirely. Bankruptcies multiplied throughout the country, and unemployment soared. By 1931 there were eight million unemployed in the United States.

Hoover did other things as well which prolonged the depression. He established the Federal Farm Board, which enabled government money to be used to subsidize farmers—their grain prices were too low, weren't they, so the obvious move seemed to be to give federal guarantees of minimum prices per bushel for grain. The farmers grew more grain than ever, with their prices guaranteed, with the result that there was more of a surplus of grain than ever before—which forced down the market price of grain still further, and led the Federal Farm Board to subsidize grain prices to the tune of another hundred million dollars of the taxpayers' money.

When the grain surpluses had mounted alarmingly, the Board decided to pay farmers, not for growing grain, but for plowing it under; not only grain but figs, grapes, potatoes, apples, nuts, etc., etc. By the end of 1932 the wheat and cotton programs alone had cost the taxpayers three hundred million dollars, besides increasing the cost of their groceries because of the lessened supply.

This was not the end of Hoover's maneuvers. Hoover supported and signed the Smoot-Hawley Tariff Act, which provided for the highest tariffs in United States history. "To protect our own industries" was the official reason; but as we have already observed, "protectionist" measures against other countries never go unanswered: the country against which the

tariff is levied, levies higher tariffs against us, thus causing
many American businesses, which depend on export for a living, to shut down entirely. When tariff is raised by nation A
against nation B, nation B always retaliates—and both are the
losers. Hoover was apparently not aware of this elementary
economic fact.

Equally disastrous, in 1930 Hoover called for lower rates
of interest as well as public works "to get the economy moving
again" (he had never read Bastiat). He signed a billion-dollar
public works bill (the Wagner Wage Stabilization Act), to be
paid, of course, out of taxes—which higher taxes hit the public
at a most inopportune time. Even more important, he created the Reconstruction Finance Corporation to make government loans to businesses which were in danger of going under.
(The reason why so many businesses were going under, of
course, was the government policies themselves. Government
was being called in to cure a disease which government itself
had caused.)

The depression was caused by malinvestment (investment
in capital goods for which no real demand exists); it could
have been lifted only by investment being placed instead in
economically useful things. But the Reconstruction Finance
Corporation, at the taxpayers' expense, provided artificial res-
piration for countless malinvestments—thus intensifying the
disease. R.F.C. loans were constantly increased, and taxes increased throughout the nation to make up for the losses. But
the project was unsuccessful. By the end of 1932 there were
twelve million unemployed in the United States.

In the wake of Hoover's failures—failures which any free-
enterprise economist could have predicted even with half his
faculties about him—Roosevelt was elected in 1932, on a
platform of balancing the budget, adhering to the gold standard, and cutting government spending by 25 percent. (Every

one of these promises was broken within a year.) Many businessmen, who were quite properly disenchanted with Hoover's constant recourse to government intervention to cure the economic ills of the nation, voted for Roosevelt.

Roosevelt was the first American Caesar:

His leadership was not collective but intensely personal. He consulted many men but always made his decisions alone. Nothing could have been further removed from a parliamentary type of government. The New Deal "brain trusts" were unique in their conception, a typical American creation attempting to mechanize and mass-produce ideas by pooling human minds. But they had nothing in common with parliamentary debates. They operated like the general staffs under military discipline. Only the Commander in Chief was entitled to make decisions and he did not have to give any explanations. He was like another typical American creation, the master-mind sports coach who bosses his team, devises its tactics and strategy, switches players and substitutes at will. However, endowed with true political genius like all Caesarian figures, Roosevelt always knew how to give to the American people the feeling that his power and his decisions were theirs.

. . . A new device, the radio, had prevailed over the older printed word; and when his magnetic voice purred its way into the ears of millions of his compatriots, he managed to cast an unbreakable spell on America. Logical argumentation could no longer prevail, as it had in the days of the Founding Fathers. Political speeches had already long ago become what rhetoric and diatribe had become in the Classical world when they displaced eloquence: they were used for effect, not for content. They conjured emotions but did not appeal to the intellect; and at this game, Franklin Roosevelt was unrivaled.

This leadership was closer to that of popular pre-Caesarian Rome than it was to the Wagnerian tyranny of Germany's Nazism with its terrifying *Götterdämmerung* atmosphere. But its humane and humorous aspect was only a mask, a psychological compensation for the almost absolute power behind it. . . . The lengthening shadow of growing Caesarism was unmistakably there.[7]

Roosevelt, when he assumed office in March of 1933, had an unparalleled opportunity. The key to lifting the pall of de-

pression was the restoration of business confidence. Only by
leaving the entrepreneur free to plan could he have restored
that confidence; by constantly tampering with the economy,
piling government agency upon government agency and debt
upon debt, he clearly did *not* restore it. Indeed, Roosevelt's
use of government intervention was so enormous and so para-
lyzing that it made Hoover, with all his interventionism, seem
like a laissez-faire economist by comparison. Businesses did
not dare to spend any money or invest in anything, not knowing how the winds from Washington would blow the next day
or the next week. If they took on new employees, they would
only be cut down by federal regulations requiring economically impossible conditions which would have bankrupted
them, or they would have been ruined by heavy taxation in a
time that was economically hard to bear at best. Roosevelt
could have caused the depression to lift within half a year by
simply putting into practice these three words: De-control,
de-control, de-control! But instead he followed exactly the opposite course: he initiated policies which left business, the key-
stone to recovery, so demoralized that the business world, now
utterly terrified of government, was reduced to inaction—and
the promised recovery did not arrive.

Roosevelt was an astute politician, a powerful manipulator
of men, who knew nothing whatever of economics, and even
boasted that he had never read a book on the subject. When
he went into office he had not the slightest idea how to cure
the depression, nor did he have any insight into the causes and
cures of depression or any other economic maladies. He used
political blackmail to achieve his ends: if a senator from South
Carolina didn't agree with his policies, well, South Carolina
would receive no federal funds next year. (South Carolina fell
into line.) He gathered around himself, increasingly through
the years, an unsavory group of spenders and planners who

couldn't run their own lives, much less those of 150 million other people, but who flattered Roosevelt's ego and encouraged him to use the enormous "emergency funds" at his disposal in the interests of their pet projects. They spent the taxpayers' hard-earned money on countless crackpot schemes; the more hairbrained they were, the more acceptable they seemed to be to the new emperor. The least of the concerns of these men was the only thing that was needed to bring America back to prosperity—bringing the American system of private enterprise back into operation.

He had promised a reduction in government spending—but under his leadership government spending ran amok as never before in the nation's history. During his administration the annual *deficits*—the red ink on the government books—were as follows:

1933	$2,245,542,000
1934	3,255,393,000
1935	3,782,966,000
1936	4,952,928,000
1937	2,777,421,000
1938	1,176,617,000
1939	3,862,158,000
1940	3,918,019,000
1941	6,159,272,000
1942	21,490,243,000
1943	57,420,430,000
1944	51,423,393,000
1945	53,940,916,000

Each of these innumerable alphabetized spending projects which took money from the taxpayer and placed it in the irresponsible hands of the government spenders had the excuse that it would "prime the pump" or "get the country moving again"—but the one thing, known to every reflective banker and businessman in Midtown, U.S.A., that *would* have got the country economy moving again, was never even considered by the Roosevelt administration. After all the pump-priming and the orgy of drunken relief projects and public-works programs and spending, at the end of 1937 there were still twelve million unemployed in the United States. Roosevelt himself appears at last to have seen that it had all been a gigantic failure, and begged his advisers to tell him what to do. But they had no advice more useful than the old blueprints for catastrophe.

When World War II broke out in 1939, and overseas sales multiplied, the depression lifted—but only to be followed by America's involvement in the conflict and a far greater national debt even than before. Meanwhile the endless schemes whereby government had taken money out of the hands of the taxpayers and placed it into the hands of government, had put this country well on the way to socialism—government control of the economy—even before the war began; and war, as always, accelerated this trend by placing ever greater emergency powers into the hands of government. The trend toward the fascist state in America received under Rooosevelt its most powerful shot in the arm—and by putting the American people into the habit of depending on government, and rendering them complacent about this dependency, the Roosevelt administration planted a time-bomb in American history which may well, within our lifetime, spell the end of the American republic as it was during the first century and a half of its existence.

"But Roosevelt got us out of the depression!" No greater falsehood could be uttered. He kept us in depression and debt for six years of his administration, and the war over which he presided called for still greater debts, which have never been paid.

All the prosperity which the nation has "enjoyed"—created by the mountainous sums paid for war, militarism and foreign and domestic handouts—remains unpaid for. Does anyone suppose that it will ever be paid? It consists of a numerous collection of separate bond issues. These continue to fall due. When each one falls due it must be paid. And some person or interest must be found willing to advance the money to pay it and accept a new bond. It was possible to force these bonds on the investing public during the war and under the influence of the unending succession of "crises." But this obviously cannot last forever. The day will come when this staggering load of debt must be faced.

In appraising the career of this shallow but bold man, it must be kept in mind that all the gaudy performances, all the handouts to the unemployed, all the billions paid to farmers to destroy food or to store it, all the extravaganza of "saving the free world," have yet to be paid for. And the nation draws closer and closer to that inevitable "pay-day." After all the heroics are silenced and all the captains and orators are retired or dead, a generation will appear that must face the bills—bills to be paid by the innocent victims of this costly and tragic circus. The depression which Mr. Roosevelt was to conquer has been hiding behind the immense curtain of the war and its gaudy post-war boom on the cuff. It will one day come peeping over the horizon for a return engagement. This was his first complete failure—his utter ignorance of the nature and the genius of the system of private enterprise.[8]

"But he provided security." This too is cruelly false; you don't provide security for B by taking it away from A. The Social Security Bill was supposed to provide for a "reserve fund" which the workers could count on when they retired. But

In [its first] twenty years of operation, the government [took] from workers and their employers nearly 25 billion dollars which it has spent on everything under the sun *except* social security. Then it taxes the same workers and employees *again* to pay the benefits. And while the benefits themselves have increased over the years, under the pressure of the Roosevelt inflation, so have the taxes, and the inequalities and injustice in the whole fake "insurance" scheme cry aloud for complete revision and correction.

But what of the millions of people who through long years of thrift and saving have been providing *their own* security? What of the millions who have been scratching for years to pay for their life insurance and annuities, putting money in savings banks, commercial banks, buying government and corporation bonds to protect themselves in their old age? What of the millions of teachers, police, firemen, civil employees of states and cities and the government, of the armed services and the army of men and women entitled to retirement funds from private corporations—railroads, industrial and commercial? These thrifty people have seen one-half their retirement benefits wiped out by the Roosevelt inflation that has cut the purchasing power of the dollar in two. Roosevelt struck the most terrible blow at the security of the masses of the people while posing as the generous donor of "security for all." During the war boom and in the post-war boom created by spending forty billion dollars a year, the illusion of security is sustained. The full measure of Roosevelt's hopeless misunderstanding of this subject will come when security will be most needed—and most absent.[9]

The history of the post-Rooseveltian era is too familiar to need recounting. The freedom of the individual to make his own decisions has not been restored; it was taken away from him by the collectivist projects of the Roosevelt administration, and has never to any substantial degree been returned to him. People have exchanged liberty for security—or the illusion of security; the young who now constitute the majority of the United States population can remember no time at which their lives were not heavily restricted by government, and subject to large government taxation. With an increasing percentage of voters, the primary, or the only, criterion by which to judge a candidate for office is "Will he increase our welfare and social security benefits?" A politician who came along and exposed the whole stinking fraud, and tried to imbue the voters with a few economic facts of life, would be driven out of office, or never achieve it in the first place. And the debt? Even in peacetime it has only increased: for only by deficit spending can the promises to the voters be fulfilled, and the burdens placed on the next generation of taxpayers. Indeed, the day seems to have come when " . . . to get elected, a politician has to promise higher pay, lower costs and more leisure than his opponent. Then the next time, the challenger raises the ante. Result: a constantly expanding pressure for inflation."[10]

Under such circumstances, the debt will only continue to mount: in lean times "government must spend more to meet the emergency," and in prosperous times the politicians will be unable to resist the demands for increasing the "security payments." In either case, the debt will continue. It will never be paid; or if it is, in part, it will be repaid in currency which is by that time practically worthless—perhaps with a note attached saying, "Here you are, sucker! Much good may it do you!" Meanwhile, government now has such a stranglehold on the life of the individual, taking away more and more of his free decisions from the cradle to the grave, that the very feeling for freedom has gradually oozed out of him: he doesn't know what it's like any more to make his own decisions, and perhaps before long, like a child, he would just as soon leave all personal responsibilities to others, let government make his decisions for him, and be inert and passive in the great womb of government care.

Who is there in America today who can plan with any assurance for his own future? The dollars he saves will be near to worthless by the time he needs them. And such a high percentage of his income is taken from him in taxes that it is very difficult for workers to save for the time when they cannot work any more. Since the tax has prevented them from saving enough to meet their future needs, those future needs must be

taken care of by government, through social security, Medicare, and so on—all of them compulsory, at least in that he is
forced to pay for these things now, whether or not he ever in-
tends to use them. Rational planning has been taken out of the
individual's hands, and has been placed instead—in the form
of *ir*rational planning—in the hands of government, whose
whims are unpredictable. Even the stability of money supply,
the rock on which American savings and incentive have rest-
ed, is in such jeopardy that few people any longer trust it, and
with good reason. Governments who have taken to the habit of
spending the taxpayers' money have seldom decreased their
appetite for looting once it was aroused.

Is it possible any longer to reverse the trend? Possible, yes;
likely, no. Once set in motion, the trend never seems to be reversed. Once the government got to the position of power over
the individual's *economic* life that it achieved in the Roosevelt
era, and has increased ever since, it has never voluntarily gone
back to an era of individual liberty. It goes like the era of the
Roman emperors, with the statist takeover of the whole economy, and the public going along in the name of security, and
the far-seeing objectors being persecuted or exterminated as
being "against the wishes of the people" or "opposing the public interest," and finally, the collapse of the economy that can
no longer maintain itself or even feed itself. Then the barbarians come in and roam where once was the abode of free and
productive men.

9
Social Functions in a Free Society

But aren't there many functions which are of value to everyone which can be instituted and sustained only, or best, by government?

Let us consider some of the principal functions which traditionally have been regarded as necessarily the problems of government and examine whether this is in fact the case.

1. Public Utilities

"Such items as water supply, telephone, electricity are necessities in urban living. This being the case, they should be in the hands of government, so that private exploiters cannot deprive us of them or raise their prices so as to make it impossible for us to have them."

Food is a necessity of life, and it has been privately produced in this country throughout its history. It is precisely because it has been thus produced, on a free (non-coercive)

347

market, that it has been available in abundance, with many
competing farmers, competing distributors, competing grocery
stores, dealing in the growth, preparation, and sale of food. If
anyone suggested that government should be involved in the
growth and distribution of food, one could point to those nations in which this has been the case: the Soviet Union, for example, which still does not grow enough food for its own
people.

Water is admittedly somewhat different; one does not grow
it, but since it is a need in everyone's life it is unbelievable that
no individual or company would come into existence to supply
this need, for a price. But how is this need in fact supplied? In
most communities in the United States, the government holds
a monopoly of this function: there is a city water pump or fil-
tering plant, city employees lay the pipes to one's home, and
one pays his water bills to the city (only if something goes
wrong with it on your property does a "private" plumber come
to repair the damage). The city handles it—with the usual inefficiency that goes with government handling of anything. It
is not a coincidence that when private corporations handle
something, they compete with one another for your services,
and shortages seldom occur: we are never told that there is a
shortage of radios or automobiles (barring long strikes) and
that we must all be patient and cooperative and buy fewer of
these things until the shortage is over. All such articles are
produced in as great a quantity as the market demands. But
New York City, which is certainly not located in an area lack-
ing in rainfall, is perpetually on the brink of (if not in the
midst of) a water shortage—a shortage that can be produced
and sustained only by the heavy hand of government.

But how could different companies compete with each
other to pipe water to people's homes in the same area?
Wouldn't there be a needless duplication, or triplication, of

pipes in the ground, some leading to your house and a different company's to your neighbor's house? Doesn't this show that the city should own it all, as the sole source of supply?

Some such duplication might occur at first, as companies vied with one another for the customers' business. But it would soon be evident to the companies that they were all losing money by not cooperating; soon enough an agreement would be reached: "You can use my lines in area A to supply these customers if we can use your lines in area B to supply those customers." It is rather ridiculous to think that they would sit it out indefinitely, slitting their own throats rather than engage in any such cooperation. They would tend to do whatever was required for efficient transmission of the commodity to the customer, for only by satisfying their customer could they keep his business.

Huge dams have been built entirely at government expense (that is, at the expense of every taxpayer in America); sometimes these have been frankly political projects, so wasteful and pointless that any engineer could see that they were not feasible projects (such as the recent dam on the Arkansas River); others do have some utility, but not enough to have led private enterprise to initiate the project. Still other dams have been built by private corporations, when the building of them appeared to the investors to be economically feasible. Hell's Canyon Dam (actually a series of three dams on the Snake River), built through the deepest gorge in the entire continent, was built for $230 million; it supplies power, water for downstream navigation, facilities for migrant fish, and scenic areas. The cost was less than half that of *one* proposed *federal* dam for the same area.[1] By contrast, consider the Tennessee Valley Authority (TVA), a much-touted federal project and great "humanitarian" measure, "to provide power to thousands of Americans in the Tennessee Valley." TVA has

cost American taxpayers over two billion dollars in subsidies
—and of course TVA pays no taxes. "Power from TVA is
more expensive than that available from any private company
in America."[2] It is true, of course, that many residents of the
Tennessee Valley have comparatively inexpensive electric
power; but that is only because the rest of us help to pay for
the services which the residents receive but pay only part of.
You are helping to pay part of their expenses; are they helping
to pay part of yours? And how much of a cut is the government taking on the deal? By what right does the government
take money from residents of Maine and Oregon and use it to
pay part of the expenses of the residents of Tennessee?

Unlike most water supplies, the telephone system is privately owned in the United States—well, not entirely, for it is
heavily regulated by government, which sets the telephone
rates and operates the franchise by which the telephone
company is legally permitted to operate. Indeed, a description
of the government regulations under which the telephone companies must operate would take many pages.[3] Still, the telephone companies in the United States are permitted to make a
modest profit (6 percent to 8 percent annually), whereas the
post office, for example, being owned and operated by the
government outright, never makes any profit at all. The post
office continues its antediluvian system of collecting and deliv-
ering mail, inefficiently and at a loss, stagnated by the heavy
hand of government, whereas the telephone companies, de-
spite the crippling regulations, are constantly making improvements. When one thinks of all the thousands of technological
improvements year after year, in laboratories all over the country, which were required from the time of Alexander Graham
Bell to the present, in order to make it possible for one to dial
a few digits and talk to anyone on the continent in less time
than it takes to walk next door, of the patience and skill and

technical know-how required, and of the tremendous convenience and comfort of talking directly with friends and relatives, and the thousands of lives that have been saved because one could make instant contact with a physician or a policeman by telephone, one wonders why such a complex organization, such a boon to the human race, such a testimonial to the power of human ingenuity working for human well-being, should be placed in the hands of government, instead of the men who devised and developed it.

One objection often made to private ownership of telephone companies is that there would be a useless multiplication of companies, so that in a single city block there would be telephone lines from perhaps half a dozen different companies, whereas having only one line would be more feasible. Worse still, it is argued that with so many different telephone companies one would be able to call only a limited number of subscribers on each—so that one would have to have half a dozen or more different telephones in one's home (each from a different company) in order to call up all the people one might wish to. And wouldn't this be a useless duplication of telephones and telephone lines, as well as needlessly expensive?

It would indeed—so much so that no private telephone company that wanted to deliver the best service at the lowest price compatible with making a profit would dream of having such an utterly crazy system. The picture presented is of poor stupid private enterprise, utterly unimaginative and helpless until big helpful intelligent government comes along to rescue it from this horrible mess. Since it is people that operate the government too, one is tempted to wonder how people that are as stupid as this in their private dealings with one another can suddenly become intelligent and farsighted when they become employed by the government.

The fact is, of course, that just as in the case of water supply, private companies would deal with one another for their mutual benefit and profit. Company A would make it easy for its subscribers to call up the subscribers of Company B, and Company B would do the same for the subscribers to Company A—not particularly because each wanted to confer profits on the other one, but because they would want increased profits themselves and this would be the only way to get them. If there was a telephone company that refused to co-operate with the other ones, it would get only a small number of subscribers, for one would be less likely to subscribe to a company that could reach only 5 percent of the population than to one that could reach most or all of them. Free men, with foresight and imagination and their own money at stake, would hardly be too stupid to arrive at this conclusion within ten minutes.

Similar remarks could be made about fire departments, which in most towns and all large cities in the United States are owned and operated by the city government. Could they be owned and operated privately? Of course they could, and in many smaller communities they are. In a community of any size, there would be various competing fire departments vying with one another to offer you service for a fee—just as is now the case with insurance companies. And as always, competition would tend to keep the service high and the fees down. A house-owner would sign a contract with the fire protection company of his choice, and if a fire broke out and the company did not provide service, it would be sued in court for breach of contract. It would certainly be worth most home-owners' while to subscribe, in order to be protected from fire (and to keep one's insurance rates low).

But what of those families that are too poor to pay for fire protection—particularly if their house is adjacent to other houses which would be threatened if theirs were to catch on fire? Let us see how this would operate:

The Nebish family is out of town on a vacation. Suddenly a neighbor notices a fire developing in their house. The neighbor calls the nearest fire department. Upon receipt of the call, the fire department immediately dispatches the needed vehicles to put out the fire. Then they check the records. If the Nebish family is a subscriber, there is no problem; they have already paid for this service. However, if they are not a subscriber and had not specifically requested fire services, they then would be under no contractual obligation to pay any bill. In this case, the fire department would typically send them a bill which the Nebishes would be requested, but not legally required, to pay. Since their home had just been saved by the fire department, it is quite probable that they would be willing to pay at least something. However, if for some reason they decided not to pay, the fire department would simply have to absorb the cost. But this is not all. Since the Nebish family had not paid the fire department's bill willingly, if their house should catch on fire in the future and they did not again request fire protection or had not in the interim contracted for such protection, then the fire department might well let it burn to the ground. A few practical lessons like this of the possible consequences of not paying for fire protection would eliminate most such free-loaders.

Now what if the Nebishes' home is a row house, so that if a fire breaks out there, it also threatens the Ibexes and the Hosenpfeffers who are good paying customers of the fire department? Naturally, in this case, the fire department would put out the fire which was threatening their clients, and the Nebishes would have then received "free" fire protection at the expense of their paying neighbors. However, there are several non-coercive ways in which the neighbors can retaliate. First, they could socially ostracize the Nebishes for not paying. Second, if they had some reason for suspecting criminal negligence, they could then be billed for the cost of the fire-combating services which they necessitated. In any event, the action of the Nebishes is not really economically significant, although it may offend our sense of justice.[4]

Who, after all, can claim as a free gift the effort and services of another? Is a part of the income—that is, of the life-work—

of the other townspeople to be extracted from them without
their consent in order to pay for something that the Nebishes
either don't want to pay for or cannot afford? If the Nebishes
can own a house, why should they expect others to pay for
their fire protection? Must the lives of others be a permanent
non-voluntary mortgage on theirs?

It should be added that in a laissez-faire society, released
from the debilitating effects of government intervention, prosperity would abound and poverty would be virtually nonexistent
as long as the individual was willing to work. Mass-production
of items with constant technological innovations would make
the prices of products go down and down, and there would
be no government-induced inflation to make them go up again.
There would be few if any poverty-stricken Nebishes in a
laissez-faire libertarian society.

2. Roads

"Buildings and lots should be privately owned, but surely
the roads connecting them should be public—that is, owned
and operated by the government!" To most Americans, accustomed as they are to government ownership and management
of the road system, this seems so obvious that no alternative
has ever presented itself to their minds. Yet it is not at all difficult to describe such an alternative system.

The railroads, after all, are privately owned in the United
States. True, they are hedged about with so many government
restrictions and regulations that they are virtually dying today
in spite of the fact that there is need and demand for them.
True, transcontinental rail traffic in the United States began as
a result of government land grants—outright gifts to the
railroads of millions of acres of land, some of it owned by the

government and some of it by farmers and ranchers who had to give strips of their land to the railroads whether they wanted to or not. But these are defects in what would otherwise have been a flourishing railroad system.

Defects? Weren't the land grants an advantage to the railroads, one might ask? Would it have been financially possible for railroads to span the continent without the free territory on which to construct the rails? Yes, the railroads did get to the West Coast faster because of the land grants. But a high price, as always, was paid for the involvement of government. Railroads got to the West Coast sooner than they (economically) should have, and on roadbeds laid through territories so foolishly mapped out that private enterprise would never have touched them under those conditions. Some men who received government money to lay the tracks simply disappeared without a trace into the tropical night and were never heard from again. Others left their tracks uncompleted, or laid them so badly that they had to be relaid later. In many cases they were laid without any consideration of mineral resources, rivers, or cities and towns where future developments might occur; they were simply laid at the easiest places and that was that. It was not so in every case. James J. Hill, founder of the Great Northern Railroad (St. Paul to Seattle), cannot be exonerated from using some government money; for example, he did not reject the land grants. But the railroads themselves he built with private capital; and since he invested all his own capital in the project, he made sure, as a government would not have done, that he built well and in the right place; on the whole his railroad pursued such a course as to be contiguous to the mineral wealth and other natural resources of the Great Northwest, and through the natural sites for future cities. It is no accident that this is one of the few railroads so soundly conceived and financed that it survived the Great Depression of

1929–33 without bankruptcy, whereas other railroads such as the Union Pacific were in receivers' hands several times over.

The moral is clear: if private capital can't finance it, it. shouldn't be financed at all. If you haven't the money yourself, you can usually band together with others and together finance something if it shows a considerable promise of success: investors are always looking for good places to invest their money, where it will reap good returns. The prospect of transcontinental railroads in 1840 was not yet a sure enough bet to justify the enormous expenditure of money and effort; but by 1860 it was, and the railroads would have been built, better than they actually were, by private capital, without the expropriative land grants, and without spending a penny of the taxpayers' money.

The roads could have been built in the same way. No transcontinental network of highways would have been useful prior to the mass-production of automobiles. But after this production, roads—as opposed to horse-and-buggy trails—became a necessity. It would be ridiculous to have millions of cars without any way to get anywhere through using them. And just as private enterprise built the cars, so private enterprise would gladly have built the roads—and offered to do so on some occasions, *without* the use of eminent domain (confiscation of private property without the owner's consent). But the roads were already owned and operated by government: city, county, state, and federal. And the pattern that had already been established was simply continued. In spite of the enormous inefficiency and graft that always characterizes government operations, with expenditure of perhaps twice the amount that private enterprise would have required (and doing a less efficient job), the construction and maintenance of roads continued to be, as it is to this day, an operation of government.

People often tend to assume that "the roads are free": but of course nothing that is the product of human effort is free. The roads, indeed, are far from free: state and federal gasoline taxes average 12¢ on every gallon sold; license plates are fairly costly, depending on the state in which one resides; and tax-payers who do not own cars also pay for the roads via numerous "hidden" taxes, regardless of whether they use the roads, often not knowing that part of their income goes to pay for road construction and maintenance. If every road in America were a toll road, and one paid for its use at the rate one does on the Pennsylvania Turnpike and the New York State Thruway today, one would be paying far less for the maintenance of the roads than one now does in the form of hidden (and not-so-hidden) taxes.

How, then, would privately owned roads function? Would all roads be toll roads like the New Jersey Turnpike? Certainly not, but some of them would be—the major transcontinental arteries. Nor need there be great delays from cars getting on and off these roads:

> The present toll-gate system could be further improved by the provision of special decals to be displayed on the cars of regular road users, who would pay a fixed monthly rate for unlimited use. Such identifying marks would eliminate the necessity for regular road users to stop when entering or leaving toll roads at all. [Furthermore], it should be possible soon . . . to equip cars with electronic identification signals— uniquely identifying each vehicle. A special computer-linked radio receiver could record the entrance of cars so equipped onto a highway, assess appropriate charges, and send a monthly bill to the car's owner —all virtually without human intervention. . . .[5]

So much for the turnpikes and expressways. At the other extreme, there are the streets of a town or city, connecting residences and stores and warehouses. Such roads would be constructed by private developers, and maintained by them entirely as private enterprise. But why, one might ask, should the private developer spend any money on the construction and maintenance of such streets, seeing that he collects rents only from the houses and apartment building he constructs? For the very excellent and obvious reason that without interconnecting streets, people won't be able to get to and from their homes. Developers who build good streets and maintain them well through ice and snow will attain a better reputation, and will be more able to attract buyers and renters, than those who do not maintain their streets or leave them shabby. Indeed, developers would outdo one another in making their streets attractive and usable, so as to gain the largest number of buyers and tenants. Nor would the initial developers have to remain on the scene to maintain the streets if they didn't want to: a community corporation could easily be formed—an association of owners and renters who shared an interest in the maintenance of the adjacent streets—to look after the condition of the streets in their area. Indeed, membership in such an organization might be a precondition for signing a contract for buying a house or renting an apartment.

What of roads intermediate between these two extremes—roads that are now state highways, or links between local residential roads and wide turnpikes? A number of ways could be worked out, and granted human freedom and a willingness to solve mutual problems to mutual satisfaction, would be worked out, which would be more efficient and less expensive than the government-owned roads of today. A number of community corporations could join together to construct and maintain these roads through membership dues.[6] Or an independent corporation could build such roads, and solicit funds from the community corporations; organizations are usually willing to vote funds (collected on a voluntary basis) if they can see the value of the service rendered—and the value of good roads to an automobile-oriented society is surely obvious. There is no limit to the arrangements that could be made, other than the creative ingenuity of free men acting together voluntarily.

At one time, before extensive urban developments, it would have been comparatively easy to buy the land for roads and streets without violating eminent domain. Today it would be much more difficult and infinitely more expensive. If a James Hill could have bought the land for highways using the wisdom he did in building his railroad, the roads could have been built at a cost that is minuscule compared with today's, and the users of the roads could have avoided a large percentage of the costs that now appear in hidden taxes. Doubtless, however, new roads could still be built by private developers, or groups of private developers. They would presumably curve a road around an already existing and expensive apartment or business development, just as they would ordinarily go between mountains rather than across them (with exceptions made for scenic drives, which could be toll roads); but for the most part they would tend to build their roads comparatively straight, at least between cities. Sometimes they would have to offer an extraordinarily high price for a piece of land—which nevertheless it would sometimes be worth their while to pay because of the resultant straightness or other desirable characteristic of the road; sometimes, on the other hand, they would find it not worth their while, and sometimes they would come across a landowner who would refuse to sell his land at any price, and they would have to "build around" his property (occasionally leaving him living in splendid isolation between the two halves of a divided highway!).

One feature of a privately owned and privately paid-for road system, aside from the greater efficiency and responsiveness to the market which always goes with private enterprise, is that the payment for the upkeep of the roads would be made by the actual *users* of these roads, and in proportion to such use. And every individual would know just how much it costs him to use the roads: there would be no "hidden taxes." And if one road from town A to town B were not properly kept up, or became unsafe, there would be increased agitation for a competing road between these towns to be built; the same would occur if a private owner suddenly decided to charge double for the cost of transporting cars over the first road. And then the builder of the first road would find himself without any paying users.

Again, a toll road could increase its rates for use during rush hours, when roads are jammed with bumper-to-bumper traffic. This would create an incentive for the use of roads (and consequently for the work days) to be "staggered," so that not all the cars would pile up on the roads at a few selected hours of the day. At present, of course, it costs no more to use the (government-owned) roads at peak hours than at any other time—with consequent loss of efficiency, and increasing irritation to everyone concerned. Either the motorist would use the road at a higher rate, or he would travel at non-peak hours, or he would get together with others to form car pools during such hours.

There would also be more incentive to have a viable bus and/or streetcar (and sometimes, subway) system in large cities—privately owned, of course, though these are now called "public transportation." Where there is a central city into which most workers go during working hours, it is certainly far more efficient in use of space to transport fifty people in a bus than in fifty individual cars—not to mention the creation of smog by the thousands of car-users. It would also be far less costly: for it is also cheaper to transport many people in one vehicle, or a series of vehicles leaving a point at ten-minute intervals, than by the present motley collection of cars going in crowded streets and freeways and facing almost insurmountable parking problems when they get to their destinations. And in a private system operating for profit (that is, a system which does not force a resident to pay for all those facilities he does not use), the differential costs would be immediately obvious: buses would be cheaper and more convenient than driving your own car. The reason that this fact is not easily perceived under present conditions is that one has a car anyway (because the government-owned transport system is so inefficient) and "the road is free," so why not risk the added inconvenience and drive the car to work? But the road is *not* free; and if the cost of using the road were direct rather than hidden—if one had to pay for every car trip to the central city instead of, as now, paying for the road whether one used it on any given day or not—then the convenience and comparative inexpensiveness of using "public transportation" would be immediately obvious, as it is not now. Buses, streetcars, subways, and monorails (whatever was most appropriate to the size of the city and its geography in the given case), even if they did not exist before because of the *seeming* cheapness of car transportation, would immediately spring up, operate efficiently (it would be to their interest to do so, particularly in view of probable competition), pay for themselves, and *not* have to be subsidized by every taxpayer in order to keep it going. Where there is a need, private enterprise—people acting individually or in concert—will rise to meet it, and meet it far more efficiently, and far more responsively to the demands of the populace, than the present system of coercive domination of transportation by government.

It should be added that if all roads had been privately owned, there would probably not be as many as there are now. Not as many would be needed, because other forms of transportation would have had more of a chance than they have under the present system of state ownership of roads.

By intervening in the transportation market on the side of the automobile and truck, the state has caused an unnatural shift of demand away from other modes of transportation. Dollars which would have been spent on or invested in trains, inland shipping or newer alternative modes of transportation, such as monorails, were diverted to servicing the automobile industry. Dollars which railroad companies could have reinvested to improve service were instead spent by companies making automobile-related products; this, in turn, further fueled the automobile industry. The interstate highway program has therefore seriously damaged if not destroyed the American mixed transport system, and the collapse of the Penn Central Transportation Company is only the most recent and most spectacular proof of this fact.[7]

And as a result of the emphasis on roads and automobile transportation, more air-pollution has occurred than otherwise would have (most smog is still the result of cars); streets are congested to the point of impossibility during rush hours: noise and air pollution are so prevalent in cities that people who could afford it have moved to the suburbs, where as a rule the only present feasible mode of transportation is the automobile—thus worsening the problem once again.

The effects of the distortion of the economy by government lead to still further interventions by government and still further effects, until at last it seems impossible ever to get back on the track again. It would have been so much easier if the government had never started interfering in these enterprises in the first place, and left them to the ingenuity of free men on a free market.

3. Licensing and Inspection

"But surely government is necessary in order to insure that people will not be victimized by false claimants: physicians who aren't physicians, lawyers who aren't lawyers, and so on. Isn't government necessary to police these activities, and see to it that the public isn't swindled?"

Perhaps. If one conceives the role of government as protection, then, by a not too far-fetched analogy, the protection could be extended to these things. Still, libertarians believe that government licensing is a source of more harm than good, for the following reasons:

A. What gives the government any special right, or any special ability, to separate the wheat from the chaff in such matters? In some states the government permits M.D.'s, osteopaths, and chiropractors to practice medicine; in some states only the first two; and in other states only the first. By what right does the government forbid osteopaths to practice in some states? They help some people; at any rate the people, who are spending their own money, voluntarily consult osteopaths and feel that they are helped; who then is the government to tell them that they may not consult osteopaths?

"Because some people are quacks, and these must be rooted out." But it is a matter of opinion who is a quack and who is not. The very same practitioner may be a charlatan according to Jones and according to Smith the world's greatest physician. Why may not the individual decide who has helped him in the individual case? Why must the politician of the licensing board be the one to tell him whom he may and whom he may not consult?

Of course, if a practitioner guarantees a cure and the cure is not forthcoming, or he makes any other claim which is shown by the facts to be false, then the victim can take him to court and sue him. But if the practitioner has not misled the patient or made a demonstrably false claim, should not the individual be the judge of who has helped him and who promises to be most helpful in his own case? It is after all *his* life that is at stake; shouldn't he have the ultimate authority to determine in what manner he shall maintain it?

Certain so-called cures for cancer have been declared illegal, and may not be prescribed under penalty of fine and imprisonment. But some of these very same "cures" have helped many patients, or so the patients themselves believe. In some cases physicians have given the patient up for lost and admitted that no other cure was available; yet they were prohibited from prescribing this medication, which the patients said at least alleviated their pain more than anything else they had encountered could do. And now these patients faced death in the knowledge that the cure (or alleviation) was there but unavailable to them because the physician was not permitted to prescribe it. If you were such a patient, what would be your attitude toward the government prohibition of the medication?

B. When business houses, such as department stores compete with one another, their *good name* is their best guarantee of future business. They must be deemed trustworthy in the eyes of thousands of customers, else the customers will not come back to them. Even when the customer is wrong, the store must satisfy him in order to retain his business. Now a similar phenomenon occurs among universities that turn out doctors, dentists, lawyers, engineers, etc. The university's good name is at stake: when Dr. X, a graduate of (let us say) Harvard Medical School, sits at his desk with his diploma hanging on the wall above it, Harvard's good name is at stake: Harvard hereby certifies that Dr. X has attained enough competence in his designated area to have merited the awarding of a degree from Harvard University. If Dr. X turns out to be a bungler, it will reflect on Harvard's good name, and Harvard, which wants to maintain public confidence, will think twice before turning out a similar man again. The best guarantee of a good physician is that he has been graduated in his profession by a university which has a good past record for turning out able physicians. The physician himself, of course, also has a good name to preserve; if his "cures" do not work, word will get around and he will soon lose business. It is, among other things, good business to be able, conscientious, sensitive and thoughtful in the practice of one's profession. And again, cases of outright fraud can be prosecuted in the courts.

C. When the government controls entry into a profession, it is extraordinarily subject (through the politically appointed board) to bribery and corruption. "We won't vote for your policies if you don't pass our school"—this and a hundred other threats or inducements can be brought to bear upon the political appointee to get him to approve the school or type of professional practice in question. Political licensing is subject to all these infirmities; but the good name developed generated on the basis of past experience, and made a matter of public record, cannot be thus disguised. In a free society, more magazines of the *Consumer Reports* variety would arise, evaluating not only types of products (as now) but types of practice and even individual practitioners.

4. Consumer Protection

The punishment of fraud, already considered, goes a considerable way toward solving the problem of consumer protection.

In a free economy, there would be ample means to obtain redress for direct injuries or fraudulent "adulteration." No system of government "standards" or army of administrative inspectors is necessary. If a man is sold adulterated food, then clearly the seller has committed fraud, violating his contract to sell the food. Thus, if A sells B breakfast food, and it turns out to be straw, A has committed an illegal act of fraud by telling B he is selling him food, while actually selling straw. This is punishable in the courts under "libertarian law," i.e., the legal code of the free society which would prohibit all invasions of persons and property. The loss of the product and the price, plus suitable damages (paid to the *victim,* not to the State), would be included in the punishment of fraud. No administrator is needed to prevent non-fraudulent sales; if a man simply sells what he calls "bread," it must meet the *common definition* of bread held by consumers, and not some arbitrary specification. However, if he *specifies* the composition on the loaf, he is liable for prosecution if he is lying. It must be emphasized that the crime is not lying *per se,* which is a moral problem not under the province of a free-market defense agency, but *breaching a contract*—taking someone else's property under false pretenses, and therefore being guilty of fraud.[8]

It is often held that government is required to prepare and enforce safety codes, for example with regard to buildings. At present, building codes are, as anything regulated by government tends to be, havens of political bribery. The city fathers pass building codes which no one could really live up to, or which could be observed only at so great an expense in building or building-alteration as to make the construction not worth the cost and drive many owners of buildings out of business entirely. So the owner of the building simply gives the inspector "hush-money" under the table, and the violations are never reported. This is the only way in which the owners of buildings can now survive in the face of the laws that exist in many cities.

What is the alternative? It is sometimes said that without such regulations builders would be constantly putting up structures that would collapse. But, first, on a free market there would not be a housing shortage; people could afford to be much more choosy about the buildings they chose to inhabit. Second, every accident would give the builder bad publicity and a bad name, which would make increasing numbers of people boycott his buildings thereafter—hardly an inducement to profitable future rentals. It is to people's interest to live in safe and pleasant apartments; and so it is to the builder's interest to construct such apartments—his income after all comes from renters, and a group of satisfied renters is his best assurance of future business. And third, any injured victims (or their families) could sue in the courts.

The free-market method of dealing, say, with the collapse of a building killing several persons, is to send the owner of the building to jail for manslaughter. But the free market can countenance no arbitrary "safety" code promulgated in advance of any crime. The current system does *not* treat the building owner as a virtual murderer should the collapse occur; instead, he merely pays a sum of monetary damages. In that way, invasion of person goes relatively unpunished and undeterred. On the other hand, administrative codes proliferate, and their general effect is to prevent major improvements in the building industry and thus to confer monopolistic privileges on existing builders, as contrasted with potentially innovating competitors. Evasion of safety codes through bribery then permits the actual aggressor (the builder whose property injures someone) to continue unpunished and go scot free.

It might be objected that free-market defense agencies must wait until *after* people are injured to *punish,* rather than *prevent,* crime. It is true that on the free market only overt acts can be punished. There is no attempt by anyone to tyrannize over anyone else on the ground that some future crime might possibly be prevented thereby. On the "prevention" theory, any sort of invasion of personal freedom can be, and in fact must be, justified. It is certainly a ludicrous procedure to attempt to "prevent" a few future invasions by committing permanent invasions against everyone.[9]

5. Conservation of Resources

The idea of conservationists is that, if the forests and animals and natural resources were left to private ownership, they would all be destroyed within a decade or a generation—and that there we need the government to protect us from this encroachment.

Continued use of forest lands is an economic necessity. The wood is for furniture, for paper, and many other products.

Now, say the government-oriented conservationists, if the government didn't own the forest-land, the private owners would use all this up at once—leaving us as a nation without wood and paper products!

Surely this is foolish. Just as a private owner of his own property will take care of his house and lawn, and not cover it with oil or let it go to rack and ruin, so a large forest preserve owned by a private owner (with a profit motive) would look ahead to tomorrow and try to keep his lands forested, so that he'd have income in the future as well as today. Indeed, where forests are privately owned, this has been the case: "Private timberland owners—at least five thousand of them—are on a *sustained yield* basis, that is, they are planting and growing more than is being harvested. The first tree farm was established in 1941. At that time 20 percent more trees were being harvested than grown. Today, 61 percent more wood is being grown than is harvested and lost to fire, insects, and disease."[10]

Of course, we can't leave every forest there just as it was thousands of years ago: if we are to have them all as they were at the time of the Indians, we could never use wood and wood products commercially, and we'd have no paper to write on.

Apparently the preservationists would have all of us in our present state of affluence being able to tour the forests in their pristine glory. What they fail to realize is that a strict preservationist policy applied to all natural resources would reduce "all of us" to the population of a foraging economy. How many would that be? The number of Indians who lived in this land—less than one-half of one percent of today's population! A conservation policy, on the other hand, counsels the use of trees for homes; indeed, timber now has not less than 5,000 uses. "Retention undisturbed" would hold our numbers at a few hundred thousand and condemn us to huts and tepees.[11]

It is true that if the American continent had never been settled, many millions of square miles of forest would have remained intact.

But so what? Which are more important, people or trees? For if a flourishing conservationist lobby in 1600 had insisted that the existing wilderness remain intact, the American continent would not have had room for more than a handful of fur trappers. If man had not been allowed to use these forests, then these resources would have been *truly wasted,* because they could not be used. What good are resources if man is barred from using them to achieve his ends? . . .

Then there is the common argument that any time a tree is chopped down, we are depriving future generations of its use. And yet this argument proves far too much. For if *we* are to be prohibited from felling a tree because some future generation is deprived of doing so, then this future generation, when *it* becomes "present," also cannot use the tree for fear of *its* future generations, and so on to prove that the resource can never be used by man at all—surely a profoundly "anti-human" thesis, since man in general is kept in subservience to a resource which he can never use. Furthermore, even if the future is allowed to use the resources, if we consider that living standards usually rise from one generation to the next, this means that we must hobble ourselves for the sake of a future which will be richer than we are. But surely the idea that the relatively poorer must sacrifice themselves for the benefit of the richer is a peculiar kind of ethic by anyone's ethical standard.[12]

What of other resources, which cannot (unlike forests) be grown again? Let us consider first the metal and mineral resources of the earth, and then the resources of the oceans. In each case, we shall see that the institution of private property, far from being an enemy of conservation, is its principal savior.

Let us consider, for example, a typical copper mine. We do not find copper miners, once they have found and opened a vein of ore, rushing to mine all the copper immediately; instead, the copper mine is conserved and used, gradually, from year to year. Why is that? Because the mine-owners realize that if they, for example, triple this year's production of copper, they will indeed triple this year's revenue, *but* they will also deplete the mine and therefore lower the monetary value of the mine as a whole. The monetary value of the mine is based on the expected future income to be earned from the production of copper, and if the mine is unduly depleted, the value of the mine, and therefore the selling-price of the shares of stock in the mine, will fall. Every mine-owner, then, has to weigh the advantages of immediate income from copper production as against the loss in capital value of the mine as a whole. Their decision is determined by their expectation of future yields and demands for their product, the prevailing and expected rates of interest, etc. If, for example, copper is expected to be rendered obsolete in a few years by a new synthetic metal, they will rush to produce more copper now when it is more highly valued, and save far less for the future when it will have little value—thus benefiting the consumers and the economy as a whole. If, on the other hand, various veins of copper are expected to run out soon in the world as a whole, and copper is therefore expected to have a higher value in the future, less will be produced now and more withheld for future mining—again benefiting the consumers and the overall economy. Thus, we see that the market economy contains a marvelous built-in mechanism whereby the resource owner's decision on present as against future production will benefit not only their own income and wealth, but also that of the mass of consumers and of the national and world economy.[13]

Now consider a case in which private property rights do not exist: rivers and oceans. When man left the hunting-and-fishing stage, in which he roamed from place to place, and developed agriculture, which required him to stay in one place while the crops were growing, the concept of private property developed as a result of this need. But there is to this day no ownership of bodies of water. With what result?

Since no one can own any part of the ocean, no one will have the incentive to conserve it; furthermore, there is now no economic incentive to develop the great untapped resource of *aquaculture*. If private property rights existed in the ocean, there would be a fantastic flowering of aquaculture, a flowering which would not only use the enormous untapped resources of the ocean, but would enormously *increase* these resources through such techniques as fertilizing, "fencing" of parts of the ocean, etc. Thus, the supply of fish could be increased enormously by simple fertilizing techniques (just as fertilizers led to an incredible increase in the supply of agricultural food). But no one person or firm is going to fertilize a part of the ocean when the fruits of this investment can be captured by some competing fisherman who does not have to respect the first man's property rights. Even now, in our present primitive stage of aquacultural technique, electronic fencing of parts of the ocean which segregated fish by size could greatly increase the supply of fish simply by preventing big fish from eating little ones. And if private property in the ocean were permitted, an advanced technology of aquaculture would soon develop which could increase the long-range as well as immediate productivity of the sea in numerous ways which we cannot now even foresee.[14]

6. Coinage

"But shouldn't the government at least retain control over the monetary system? Surely only the government should be permitted to issue currency, saying 'This coin (or bill) is legal tender of the United States.' If anyone who wanted to were permitted to issue coins or paper and call it legal tender of the United States, wouldn't the result be chaos? And which persons or groups could you trust?"

But there is no reason why the government should have a monopoly on the money supply, or on the minting of precious metals. Throughout history, such a monopoly has always had catastrophic effects. Since paper money is easier to carry around than metal coins, governments have issued paper money—and when they became financially pressed, as a result of military expenditures or welfare or sundry promises of income from the government (promises made in order to win votes), they issued more and more paper money, until it became virtually worthless. Inflation is the perennial curse of monetary systems in the hands of government; and the citizen is forced to accept this debased paper currency in trading and the collection of debts. Today a United States citizen is not permitted to possess gold coins, and he is not permitted to turn in his increasingly worthless paper money in exchange for them.

How would a privately operated system of coinage work? Minters would issue gold coins (and perhaps other metals as well), certifying that they were pure (unalloyed) and of a certain weight. If a minter fraudulently certified these things, he could be prosecuted in the courts for fraud. It would be to the self-interest of minters not to do this, however, because if they did, they would not only take huge losses as a result of court actions against them, but they would no longer be trusted by the populace: the business would go to other minters who had a reputation for honesty and reliability—just as business organizations who deal fairly with their customers are the ones who tend to get the most business as the result of their good name. In response to public demand, there would arise many publications of the *Consumer Reports* variety, which would evaluate the minted products, just as they now evaluate other consumer products from automobiles to can-openers, thus relieving the consumer of the tiring responsibility of testing all of these products himself.

These minters will place *their* stamps on the coins, and the best minters will soon come into prominence as coiners and as assayers of previously minted coins. Thus, ordinary prudence, the development of good will toward honest and efficient business firms, and legal prosecutions against fraud and counterfeiting, would suffice to establish an orderly monetary system. There are numerous industries where the use of instruments of precise weight and fineness are essential and where a mistake would be of greater import than an error involving coins. Yet prudence and the process of market selection of the best firms, coupled with legal prosecution against fraud, have facilitated the purchase and use of the most delicate machine-tools, for example, without any suggestion that the government must nationalize the machine-tool industry in order to insure the quality of the products.[15]

But wouldn't the presence of a multiplicity of private

minters lead to chaos in the money system? Wouldn't there be so many denominations of coins, and so many minters issuing them, that the public would have a hard time keeping track of all the denominations and companies issuing the coins?

The answer is that if the market finds standardization more convenient, private mints will be led by consumer demand to confine their minting to certain standard denominations. On the other hand, if greater variety is preferred, consumers will demand and obtain a more diverse range of coins. Under the government mintage monopoly, the desires of consumers for various denominations are ignored, and the standardization is compulsory rather than in accord with public demand.[16]

But need there be coins only? Since it's clearly easier to carry paper around than coins, particularly in larger denominations, shouldn't there be paper money as well? Of course; if the public demanded it, then on a free market they would get it. A company that issued coins would also issue paper, and on each piece of paper would be a guarantee that the paper could be exchanged for coins on demand in any of the company's banks. If a company refused to effect such an exchange, it could be sued in court; and in fact it would not often be attempted, because the public would no longer choose to avail itself of the company's services, and the company would soon be out of business.

Any person or organization that wished to could of course print pieces of paper that looked like money; but if such an organization printed on it a promise to redeem it for gold upon demand, and then refused to redeem it, it would be sued for fraud—and if it printed no such guarantee, no person in his right mind would accept such a piece of paper in payment for anything.

7. Education

Higher education today is in a state bordering on chaos. Everyone seems to be unhappy with it, but everyone seems to disagree on what changes are required to improve it. Black students complain that most of the courses are "irrelevant," and they demand the offering for credit of more "black studies" courses and "soul" courses. Many parents of the "white majority," on the other hand, complain bitterly that the state universities and state colleges are populated with "leftist liberal" and even Communist faculty members who are undermining the foundations of society and misleading the youth by teaching them false doctrines cleverly packaged so as to appear plausible. There are many reasons for this almost universal discontent; but one of the principal reasons is that every taxpayer is forced by law to contribute to the state-controlled educational system. They may disapprove some or most of the ways in which their money is being spent, but aside from making some (usually fruitless) complaints and writing irate letters to their congressmen and "letters to the editor" in newspapers and magazines, there seems to be little that they can do about it. They are forced to pay for the educational system no matter how strongly they may disapprove of it; even if the students wreck the university buildings in a campus "demonstration," they (the taxpayers) are made to pay to replace the destroyed property, and then to pay again for the continued education of these same students.

"Why should I pay for it?" they ask. The question is a good one; why indeed should they? And of course they shouldn't; why, for example, should the businessman be forced to pay a portion of his income to finance the teaching of social and political theories which, if put into effect, would eliminate the businessman from society and substitute a commissar? Why should he have to commit slow suicide and have to pay for it in the bargain? His indignation at having to pay for his own destruction is not only understandable but entirely justified.

In the State of California, for example, one reason for the high state income tax is the enforced support of the nine universities and twenty-odd state colleges—not to mention the numerous state junior colleges and the city and municipal colleges scattered through the state. Everyone has to pay to support these, regardless of their merits. Nor should it be thought that by this means the poorer students are supported by the wealthier taxpayers. Most of the students in state universities and colleges are from upper- or middle-class parents. The situation is rather that of the taxpayers of Watts supporting the students from Beverly Hills.

Meanwhile the private colleges and universities, not having access to the taxpayers' funds, find it harder and harder to survive: they must charge more and more tuition in order to keep operating, and many students who would ordinarily go there attend the tuition-free state universities and colleges instead in order to avoid the high tuition. Even so, the private colleges and universities are increasingly strapped for money: so no matter how independent they wish to be, they are forced to accept government grants, knowing full well that their increasing dependence on government may lead to educational disaster: when they have become dependent on government funds, and the government decides to lay down unwelcome conditions for its continued support, they must comply with the conditions or go out of existence. It has become a matter of sheer survival for them, because they are forced to subsidize their own competition.

One suggestion that has been made, and that has won a fairly wide acceptance among the citizenry, is the "voucher system": according to this view, the state (i.e., the taxpayers)

should support education, but it should give each student a
voucher covering the costs of his tuition and other expenses,
and permit him to use this at the college or university of his
choice (provided of course that he has a good enough scholastic record to be admitted): thus he can go to a private university as well as a state-supported one if he chooses, and he is not
locked into a system which would require him to go to a state-
supported college or university when he prefers to go to another one. As a stopgap measure, this would surely be an
improvement: it would discriminate less against the private institutions, which may well be forced to close their doors in the
near future or become controlled by the state. But even the
merits of the proposed voucher system are gradually being
eroded by the stipulations attached to it by those who support
it: so many impossible conditions are being attached to the
proposed system—the college must be approved by a state ex-
amining board, the curriculum must be fairly set, the tuition
low, etc.—that it would amount, once again, to government
control.

In any case, no libertarian would find the voucher system
acceptable (except perhaps as a temporary measure) any
more than the present system of state control which forces the
parents of students in private universities to pay for the support of the state universities at the same time. Both would take
from the taxpayer part of his income to subsidize an enterprise
of which he might disapprove; both constitute the legalized
plunder of his income for purposes to which he would not contribute voluntarily. What solution, then, would the libertarian
suggest? Nothing less than the complete separation of education from government—entirely analogous to the complete
separation of religion from government and of economic activity from government.

But how would this work? Limiting ourselves for the moment to higher education, there would *be* no state-supported (taxpayer-supported) colleges and universities at all. Education would be an entirely private affair. There is a market for education, as there is for any other needed commodity, and private institutions would supply it. They would supply it—for a price, of course, since no man is a slave, and teachers and buildings and equipment cannot be had for nothing. The institution would charge tuition in order to receive payment for its services. At its own discretion, it could offer scholarships and fellowships to needy students, and voluntary gifts to the university would make this possible to an increasing degree—far greater than it is now, since so many people who today would gladly be donors are prevented from giving by the enormous taxes they already pay to support the state-controlled education system. The university could also agree to pay the student's expenses with a contract specifying that the money would be returned at a low rate of interest when the student has finished college and has a job. All this of course would be up to the college or university itself, but a college that refused to do these things would be at a competitive disadvantage with those that did.

Extending our discussion now to include primary and secondary school education, exactly the same principles would apply. There would be no "public" schools, no "public" (taxpayer-supported) education. No bachelor or childless couple could be taxed to pay for the education of the family next door with sixteen children. By what right, in any case, is money extracted from the childless couple without their consent to pay for the education of the children of the couple who chose to dispense with all methods of birth control?

"But don't those children have a *right* to an education?" As we have already seen, no one has the right to the free services or free products of another human being; no human being is a

non-voluntary mortgage on the life of another, and if A had a
right to the free services of B, then B would be to that extent
A's slave. It was the free decision of the couple next door to
have all these children (or to do without birth control), and
the consequences of that action should be on *them,* not on
their neighbors or their neighbors' neighbors. Perhaps if they
knew this, they would even decide to have something less than
sixteen children.

As things are now, many parents are so dissatisfied with the
public education system that they send their children to private or parochial schools, which in thousands of cases provide
the child with a far better education in "reading, writing, and
arithmetic" than the public schools do. But the parents are
forced to pay a high price for this act: while paying tuition to
send their children to the private schools, they must also pay
taxes to support the public schools which they do not use; thus
they are doubly penalized. If there ever was an obvious case of
injustice, this is it. Their indignation is, again, understandable
and entirely justified. Why should they be forced to support
something they want no part of and of which they disapprove?
(And if they did approve it, they could support it voluntarily,
not by force.)

If all elementary and high schools (as well as colleges and
universities) were private, many if not most of the current
complaints about education could be wiped out at one stroke.
In the South before the Supreme Court action of 1954, public
schools were segregated by law ("separate but equal"—
though the schools for blacks were seldom the equal in quality
of schools for whites). Today, public schools are integrated by
law: pupils are even bused from one district to another, often
miles away from their homes, in order to achieve a "racial
mix" sufficient to satisfy the bureaucrats in charge of the program and thus keep the federal funds coming in. The result

here is just as disastrous: formerly peaceful schools now are scenes of racial warfare and knife fights, with no pupil of either race being safe for a moment; schools that formerly had a high scholastic record now have two teachers in each classroom, one to try to teach something in the midst of the pandemonium and the other to keep the pupils from killing each other. Outside the classroom, neither the halls nor the rest rooms nor the streets and alleyways nearby are safe, and every parent knows that his child's safety is in jeopardy every moment he is off at school, yet the parent is forced by law to send the child to such a school or else (if he can afford it) send the child to a private school while still paying his tax dollars for the support of the public school. Rather than be required to send their children to such a school, many parents have sold their houses at a loss and moved to other communities where the racial problem is less urgent or where the enforcement of the law is more lax. *Forced* integration is as bad as *forced* segregation; just as the latter has become illegal, so should the former be, and for the same reason.

What, then, is the solution? To have no public schools at all; to leave the parents free to send their children to whatever private schools they like—and on the free market a competition among private schools would spring up, just as competition exists among grocery stores and drug stores and other enterprises. If no schools existed nearby which satisfied the parents, they could band together and start one of their own, also appointing or electing a school board to screen candidates for teaching positions, as was done in the United States during the first century of its existence as a nation.

But might not some parents choose not to send their children to school at all? It is possible, in isolated cases, that this might happen; but as the system of voluntary education progressed, such cases would become rarer and rarer. In contemporary life, education is a virtual necessity: no one can get a well-paying job without a modicum of education. Most parents, realizing this, would be willing to pay and even to sacrifice to make their children's education possible. And if, in a given community, the parents decided against having a school, that generation of children would grow up so disadvantaged—or with so much to make up later in adult-education courses if they wanted good jobs—that they would probably make sure that this would never happen to *their* children. Besides, commodities on a free (uncoerced) market are always more efficiently produced than when interfered with by government; the present unwieldy bureaucracy would not exist, and what the parents would pay for their children's education would be much less than they now pay in taxes for the support of public schools. Again, many schools would offer education free of charge, or with only a minimal charge compatible with the parents' ability to pay, in cases of real financial need—remembering once again that in a free economy the cases of real financial need would be much rarer than now. Besides, it would become a matter of pride among parents to have their children educated well, and with the best-quality teachers—it would be pride in *"our* school" rather than enforced conformity to the public schools now regulated by the government, and ridden by rules handed down from the state or national capital, with no comprehension of local problems, and disapproved by the majority of the parents themselves. (One might even sacrifice a libertarian point and have a law requiring students to attend *some* school or other for a given number of years, but *never* have the government regulate or control such education.)

Bertrand Russell once said, "The government distorts the minds of the young and calls it education." When the government—that is, the officials in the employ of the government—make and enforce the rules and regulations governing schools and teaching, there is not only waste and inefficiency and an unbelievably unresilient bureaucracy (as in the public schools of any large American city), there is a pattern of uniformity imposed on every school and every pupil. In former years, history was taught from the point of view of "my country right or wrong," which, repeated in the education of every nation, led to international tensions and conflicts. More recently, since the elementary and high school textbooks were written by men who grew up during the New Deal era, children have been taught that Soviet Russia is just as good as the United States, that a world government is needed to save the world, and that Roosevelt saved the country from depression in 1933. Parents who know well enough that all these teachings are false are nevertheless required to send their children to schools which impress these doctrines on their children's impressionable minds—unless, once more, they pay double taxation and can send their children to a parochial school which does not teach these things. And even here, the parochial school must be accredited by the state, else the children are legally truants and the parents can be taken to court for not sending their children to a state-accredited school.

Would not the education offered in a free-market system be sheer chaos? At the beginning, it might be; but it would not stay that way for long.

At the beginning, anyone who wanted to set himself up as a teacher could do so, simply by hanging out a shingle, or taking out an ad in the paper. He could teach the subjects he chose, at any level, or at any pace, to whomever he chose, for whatever fees he could get people to pay of their own free will. If he wishes, he could restrict his clientele to any ethnic, religious, or cultural group he chose—or he could accept all comers, if he preferred. He could vary his fees in accordance with ability to pay (or ability to learn, or any other factor), or he could charge all students equally. He could specialize in teaching youngsters, or adults, bright or dull, or anyone else. He could set his own hours, and open his classes with prayers, yoga exercises, or whatever he pleased.

Anyone who wished to learn any subject could apply to any teacher of that subject, and contract with him for whatever degree of education in that subject he desired. Contracts could be set up so that pupils (or their parents) would pay only for the actual amount of education they actually received. And, of course, under this system, people would pay only for those courses they wished to take—be they courses in physics, history of the Catholic Church, or African culture. Students could select their teachers on any basis they chose, just as teachers could choose their students according to *their* standards.

At first, such a system may seem utopian or anarchistic in its concept—but, in reality, it would be kept from becoming a chaotic, impractical mess by the mechanisms of the market. People will not voluntarily pay for a bunch of kooky or badly-run courses; teachers will have to be good to prosper, especially if they get paid only for what they deliver.[17]

Private organizations would arise whose function was, for a fee, to provide achievement examinations for students in all schools who wished this service. Indeed, a private organization, the Educational Testing Service of Princeton, New Jersey, already exists, which issues comprehensive examinations in virtually every subject to test the student's achievement in these subjects. In a free-market educational system, other similar organizations would probably arise, administering tests through the various school systems so that they could evaluate their achievements as compared with others. Moreover, employers in various firms (as well as graduate schools) would want to know the student's performance on such tests in order to get the best qualified employees. And it would be to the interest of school administrators to have their students do well on such tests, so that their school would acquire a good reputation and be able to attract the most (or the best) students in the future. "In order to get a job as an engineer at General Electric, for instance, one might have to have passed a Level

16 test in math, a Level 10 test in English, a Level 8 test in American history, and a Level 18 test in electrical engineering."[18] And if a given high school or college did not provide good training, most of its students would not be able to pass the tests. As with a department store, the greatest asset of an educational institution would be its good name, its reputation for turning out well-trained and well-balanced students. (Scholastic achievement of course would not be the *only* index of potential as an employee; personality characteristics would also count heavily.) The state would not license teachers any more than it would physicians or lawyers (pp. 362-5); anyone would be free to hire the student for whatever reasons he wished—the results of the examination would give him an index of the student's ability and achievements, but would not be binding on the employer; but the employer would ignore them at his peril if he wished to have a well-qualified employee.

Teachers, to prove their qualifications, would be certified by a testing bureau or other professional organization. Such qualifications would not be compulsory, but any would-be teacher who lacked such certification from a reliable organization would be at a competitive disadvantage in seeking employment. And school boards would want to know whether the man or woman had been certified by such an organization before hiring him as a teacher, otherwise the risks of hiring incompetents would be too great.

In higher education, in a free market system, there would be a great deal of incentive for companies that are not now in the education business to make loans and give scholarships. Why? Because,

. . . contrary to the situation today, they could be sure they would get what they paid for. General Motors, for instance, might offer to pay a student's "tuition" if he would then come to work for GM for five years after reaching certain required proficiency levels. GM would then contract with the teachers who were instructing that student on a "C.O.D." basis—or, in other words, that they (GM) would pay the fees when the student passed the required tests, just as the student himself or his parents would do under a conditional contract arrangement. All things considered, there would be little difficulty for poor families to get a good education for their children—or, at least, their bright children.[19]

Meanwhile, many young people who are not really material for higher education would not pursue it, as they do now. Often they do it now because the state offers them a free college education (free to them, not to taxpayers) anyway, and the work required of them (thanks to the cumbersome educational bureaucracy) is minimal, and they simply become "perennial students" or educational freeloaders; besides, they can get draft deferment by pretending they are interested in going to college, and exerting a token amount of effort. Many of these students would go to trade schools, where they belong, instead of to colleges as they do now because the state subsidizes college education far more than it does trade schools.

Education freed from government interference and regulation would become more efficient, more responsive to the requirements of industry and of the student himself who wants or needs the training. In a complex industrial society, desirous not only of higher technological standards but higher standards of medicine, dentistry, and other professions, the output would be responsive to the demand, when it was no longer bedeviled by state licensing boards, state educational requirements (lobbied for by schools of education at our universities), and the vast sprawling bureaucracy spawned by these requirements wishing to perpetuate itself in existence by always increasing the requirements at the next session of the state legislature. Teachers who were unable to teach would be more quickly eliminated, instead of (as now) being kept secure in tenure and refusing to improve themselves or keep up to date in their field because of the knowledge that they have tenure anyway, and in some cases, that their annual pay-increase is automatic regardless of any continuing achievements on their part. A free-market system of education would tend to eliminate this dead wood. In education as elsewhere,

> Free enterprise acts like an ever-rising elevator; it has both a ceiling and a floor, but both are constantly moving upward. Government enterprise acts like a great press: extremes are equalized at the price of variety and innovation.[20]

A Taxless Society

"But as long as there is government at all, surely there have to be taxes to support it. And what does the libertarian say of taxation? Surely he must reject it. Taxation is forced, non-voluntary payment; and isn't the libertarian ideal that of an entirely 'voluntaristic' society, in which no one is forced to do anything unless he has first used force against another?"

One answer that has been given to this question runs as follows: Since the libertarian government consists only of protection of the rights of each individual, the only proper functions of a government are to maintain the police (protection from within), the armed forces (protection from without), and the courts (for arbitration of disputes). The cost of this would be minuscule compared to the cost of today's government, which consists chiefly in legalized plunder (robbing Peter to pay Paul). Not only would its cost be comparatively small, except perhaps in a time of extreme international emergency, but a government so restricted in its function would be limited to operations which are for the benefit of everyone: if everyone's rights are protected, no one is harmed except those who would violate these rights. And since everyone is equally protected in such a government, it would not be unreasonable for everyone to pay a fair share of taxes to support it.

The libertarian, however, is usually more inclined to the position that there is still too much coercion involved here. Taxes are non-voluntary payments to a government, and what is non-voluntary is coercive—surely taxes always are. Even taxes for a good purpose are still coercive; and coercion to a good end is still coercion. What if the end is good but an individual does not see or believe it to be so? Is he still to be forced to pay? Perhaps it is to his interest to do so, but what if he does not see that it is? Must he then be forced at gunpoint to do what he does not believe to be to his interest? But to admit this is to go contrary to the dominant thrust of libertarianism, which is totally anti-coercive.

A different suggestion, which would eliminate taxation as compulsory payment to government, is the following: To the extent that a service is desired by a given individual, he must pay for it if he wishes to avail himself of it—but he is not required to avail himself of it. For example, you can sign a contract with another individual or company if you wish to do so, without charge; but if you wish to have the use of the courts in case there is ever a dispute about the contract, you will have to make a payment (on each contract to which you are a party) to insure this result; after all, you can't expect others to spend time as judge and jury etc. and not repay them for their efforts —they are not your slaves—so if you want to make sure that your contract has the backing of the law in case of need, you must pay for it as you would for any other service. This payment could be called a "contract tax." But the term is unfortunate because a tax is a non-voluntary payment, whereas this would be strictly voluntary: it is up to you whether you prefer to take the risk and pay nothing or avoid the risk by paying the fee. To the extent, then, that the court-system would be likely to be needed for such matters, it would be paid for by the contract fees. Most people would surely find it to their interest to pay the fee.

Men would pay voluntarily for insurance protecting their contracts. But they would not pay voluntarily for insurance against the danger of aggression by Cambodia. . . .

A program of voluntary government financing would be amply sufficient to pay for the legitimate functions of a proper government. It would not be sufficient to provide unearned support for the entire globe. But no type of taxation is sufficient for that—only the suicide of a great country might be, and then only temporarily. [21]

What about police protection? The same kind of arrangement could be suggested here: if you want police protection, you will have to pay a fee to obtain it, but of course you are free not to want it or pay for it, in which case you will not have the protection even if you need it. Again, most people would find it to their interest to pay the fee, for most people do desire to have police protection when their house is burgled or their car stolen, and so on. But the decision would be up to the individual; he is not required to pay for the service if he doesn't want it.

On this second solution, there are no taxes at all; only fees to be paid for special services, which the individual may choose to avail himself of or not, as he wishes.

Still another suggestion is that the services of protection (police, armed forces, courts) are so vital to everyone's interests that everyone should have them available, whether or not he wants to use them and whether or not he elects to pay for them. People will usually be willing to pay for a service when they see its value; and most people would surely be willing to pay for protection of their rights even if they were not coerced into doing so. It is true that there would be some freeloaders, who were able to pay but decided not to because "we've got the protection anyway"; but hopefully their number would be small, and the donations of the vast majority who appreciate and value the service would be quite sufficient to sustain the system. This solution would have the advantage that if the police force and the court system ceased to be efficient arbiters of justice, the donations would decline. It would have still another advantage, that people too poor to pay (though these would not be many in a truly free economy) would still be protected, via the payment of others who were better able to do so.

Either of these last two solutions would provide the essential function of protection of individual rights, while yet retaining the typically libertarian feature of non-coercion. The society would remain a "voluntaristic" society, with no individual being coerced by another individual or group of individuals, no, not even to pay taxes to support a system designed for his own protection.

It is argued that taxes are necessary to support services of government. It is claimed that garbage would lie knee deep in the streets if trash removal wasn't provided by government; that muggers and rapists would roam at will without government police on hand; that the commuter train and bus lines would cease to exist if turned back to private enterprise. Why, we might ask, would men be so foolish as to allow such services to cease without the government's intervention? Do men go barefoot because the shoe industry is still a private operation? Do men forget to report to their jobs every morning because the government does not yet provide them with alarm clocks? Of course not. It is ridiculous to assert that rational men would fail to voluntarily support services they need if they were not forced to do so. And it is ridiculous, as well as immoral, to force men to support services they do not use and do not value, just because one man or group of men think they know what is best for everybody else.[22]

Could such a plan be implemented at once, with the functions that were formerly governmental becoming voluntary tomorrow morning and compulsory taxation simultaneously abolished? Not without very great economic dislocation and hardship. It would have to be a gradual process. All government regulation of business, labor, and agriculture would be among the first to go, and along with it such governmental units as the Department of Agriculture, the Department of Health, Education, and Welfare, and others that had no excuse for coming into existence in the first place. Promises that had already been made would be kept: for example, farmers who had already planted a certain crop on the basis of a promise of government subsidy would be told that the price support would not be eliminated for this year's harvest, but that this would be the last year for such handouts. Those on relief would either be given a cutoff date or told that their government handouts would gradually decrease until they found employment; and of course—here is the important point—such employment would not be long in coming: with the abolition of the income tax, the capital gains tax, and the huge assortment of other taxes that bedevil industry, there would be a tremendous increase in business activity, with new research, new expansion, new employment which would not have been feasible before owing to the crushing load of taxes; and with the abolition of the regulation boards and the repeal of the National Labor Relations Act and other legislation that for a generation has placed a ball-and-chain on industry, businessmen would be able to plan again. It would not be long before the effects of this enormous release of energy would percolate through the economy: production would boom, new inventions would abound, new kinds of jobs would become available and the old kinds would be available in increasing numbers, and people with energy and enterprise would be at a premium instead of (as now) threats to the government's "management of the affairs of the nation." It is true that most people who had government jobs would now be out of work, but this would be only temporary—they would have to adjust to productive work instead of work parasitic on the taxpayer's energies; but even here the readjustment would often be painless—a person who had previously administered a government relief project might now administer funds to the needy and disabled in a private charitable organization(such organizations which would also receive a shot in the arm when taxation, the great enemy of charity, ceased to exist).

There would remain one intractable problem: the national debt. It now exceeds 400 billion dollars—that is, over two thousand dollars for every man, woman, and child in the United States. This debt represents the unpaid bills of the generation past—the generous promises politicians made in order to get elected, which could not be kept without foisting part of the bill on the next generation of Americans. Without continued taxation—taxation for the express purpose of paying them off, not for financing new government expenditures—it is doubtful that they will ever be paid. They could of course be repudiated outright; but this would mean that every American in the last generation who trusted his government to the extent of a $25 savings bond would in effect be told, "We're sorry for you, sucker! Better luck next time round!" Or they could be paid in devalued currency, with tons of unbacked paper money, which would mean of course that each investor would get back only a small fraction (in real value, not in paper dollars) of his original investment.

One possible solution would be to sell, at government auction to the highest bidder, the post office department, as well as all government-owned roads, all government-owned schools, and all government property and enterprises not having to do directly with defense (police, armed forces) and arbitration (courts). The sale of all these items would net the government many billions of dollars. That it would be sufficient to liquidate the staggering national debt, however, is probably an overoptimistic expectation. And that the balance would gradually be paid off by voluntary subscription is also perhaps too much to hope for. How to eliminate the national debt, then, is a problem that, in the language of the entertainment industry, is a "show-stopper." The consequences of more than a generation of profligacy cannot be canceled out in a year or a decade.

10
Liberty and International Relations

The domestic policies of the United States in the last forty years—to go no further back—have been an almost unmitigated catastrophe, and it will be a long time before any citizen can escape their consequences. But bad as these policies have been, the foreign policy of the United States during the same period has been appallingly worse—and its consequences have been so catastrophic that it may never be possible to escape them at all; nuclear war may yet be the price to be paid. And in both cases the reasons have been the same: these policies have been conducted in utter disregard of the rights of individuals.

If one is a libertarian and believes that no one should initiate force against other human beings, one could hardly be confronted with a more gruesome horror story than the history of international relations in the twentieth century. The tale is so long that it would take volumes to recount it; but a few examples may suffice to illustrate the point.

Soon after the Bolsheviks took over Russia in 1918, it was clear enough that the regime was even more totalitarian than the czarist regime had been, and more careless of the rights of individuals. But in the extreme economic dislocation of those early years the Russian population was starving, and was kept alive partly by huge gifts of food and supplies from the United States. It would be interesting to speculate whether the Bolshevik government would have survived those years without the gifts, presented as a gesture of American humanitarianism.

When prisoners were taken by the thousands in the holds of ships to the Kolyma region of eastern Siberia, to build a port and roads to the gold mines, they died by the thousands of malnutrition, overwork, starvation, cold, and torture by the sadistic guards. Aiding these enterprises in mass slavery, American gifts of mining and gold-refining equipment were sent to "our Soviet brothers" as a token of international goodwill. Sent into temperatures as low as 90° below zero without extra clothing or even tents in which to sleep at night, the prisoners died like flies; in the first year of the "Dalstroy experiment," during which the Soviet government sent thousands of prisoners into the area, fewer than one out of fifty came back alive. The enormous casualties were always replaced by new shiploads of prisoners, who in turn worked till they died and were replaced. One such sailing became indirectly involved with attempts at American aid. The matter is described dramatically in a book that should be required reading for every American citizen, David Dallin's *Forced Labor in Soviet Russia*:

One of the early—and the most tragic—of the sailings to the Kolyma estuary was that of the steamer *Dzhurma*. The *Dzhurma*, a large ocean liner especially equipped for shipment of Dalstroy prisoners, sailed from Vladivostok in the summer of 1933 on its maiden voyage to Ambarchik (a distance of over 4,000 miles) carrying a capacity cargo of about 12,000 prisoners. The time of sailing was not carefully calculated, the ship reached the Arctic Ocean too late in the season, and was caught in pack ice in the western part of the Sea of Chukotsk, near Wrangel Island. We are not likely ever to learn what went on in the ship during that terrible Arctic winter, how the doomed prisoners in its holds struggled for life, and how they died. The fully authenticated fact is that the *Dzhurma,* when it finally arrived at Ambarchik in the summer of 1934, did not land a single prisoner. It is also further reported that on their return to Vladivostok nearly half the crew of the *Dzhurma* had to be treated for mental disorders. However, what mattered for the government was not the loss of prisoners and the sufferings of the crew but the fact that the valuable ship was saved.

In the same winter of 1933–34 and in the eastern part of the same sea, another ship became locked in the ice. That was the famous *Chelyushkin* which had been sent from Leningrad to Vladivostok to prove that the Great Northern Sea route could be navigated without "wintering" in the ocean. Crushed by the ice, the *Chelyushkin* sank on February 13, 1934, but the members of the expedition, numbering 104 persons, set up a camp on the ice. The entire world became concerned for their safety. There was only one way to rescue them—by air—and many persons in the United States were anxious to undertake the task. All such efforts of help were declined by the Soviet Union, whose representatives declared that it was a matter of national honor for Russia to organize for the "saving of her sons." She accepted only technical aid, and only the Soviet fliers made trips to the Sea of Chukotsk, in spite of the fact that this meant great delay in the salvaging operations. The evidence that has since come through suggests that national honor was merely a screen to hide quite different motives of the Soviet Government. The place where the 104 members of the *Chelyushkin* party were waiting for deliverance was not far (no more than 200 miles) from the wintering place of the *Dzhurma* and its 12,000 prisoners doomed to death from cold and starvation. Moscow feared that in the course of saving the heroes of the *Chelyushkin,* American fliers might by accident uncover the terrible secret of the *Dzhurma* martyrs.[1]

Even after the United States joined the war against Germany and Japan and became an ally of the Soviet Union, the Soviet policy did not change. When American fliers were forced down in Russia, they were interned by the Soviet government until the war was over, as if they had been enemy prisoners—and this in spite of the fact that the United States gave Russia more than eleven billion dollars worth of aid, much of it shipped over the hazardous sea route to Murmansk, with tremendous casualties from German U-boats.

Franklin Roosevelt, until very shortly before his death, was on friendly terms with Stalin, looked upon him as a friend, and expressed confidence that the Soviet Union would be a worthy ally after the war was over. Perhaps he thought he had "won over" Stalin, but the shoe appears to have been on the other foot: Stalin had figured out just how he could appeal to Roosevelt's enormous vanity and every conference between them resulted in Roosevelt making one concession after another while Stalin, on the whole, got what he wanted. Churchill knew better, but since America held the purse-strings he was outvoted and usually reduced to silence. Casablanca, Teheran, and most of all Yalta are examples of the United States in a position of great strength giving in to one Russian demand after another. In the end, the Russians took East Germany, half of Poland, the Baltic nations, and all the Balkans—thereby placing several hundred million people under the heel of the Stalinist terror. Roosevelt even acceded to Stalin's infamous demand that all persons displaced by the war be forced to be "repatriated" to their home countries—which for thousand of Russians meant death camps and the firing squad. But it was Roosevelt's order and his generals carried it out.

Many individuals in and out of government in the United States were well aware of the true nature and intentions of Soviet Russia, but one after another they were silenced by Roosevelt and his alter ego, Harry Hopkins. Roosevelt refused to hear anything said against his Russian ally, and if any official did so he was silenced or dismissed. Russian agents were performing acts of espionage all over America and by Roosevelt's own order nothing was done to stop them or their access to military secrets. Russian agents even obtained American uranium (when the United States was first experimenting with it in preparation for the first atomic bomb) and took large quantities out of the country in sealed diplomatic pouches from the airfield in Great Falls, Montana, whence it was flown to Siberia. The American commander in charge of the Great Falls airport sent a plea to Roosevelt, revealing his suspicions, as well as his discovery of uranium when he had some of the "diplomatic pouches" unsealed. But Roosevelt refused to hear of it and ordered that the Russian packages not be tampered with in the future. Again, it is interesting to speculate how much progress the Soviets would have made with the atomic bomb had it not been for materials and technological secrets stolen from the United States, under the noses of people who knew what was happening but were prevented by executive order from doing anything about it.

The story of the Great Falls incident, as well as of Soviet espionage in America, is told (among other places) in another "required" book, Werner Keller's *East Minus West Equals Zero*.[2] And the full story of Roosevelt's dealings with Stalin during the war, and their consequences for world history, is told in George Crocker's *Roosevelt's Road to Russia*.[3] These books rival in excitement any spy drama ever written, but one can only read them with horror, since the recital of betrayals is all true, and the present generation of Americans (and the world) are the victims of the acts described.

The betrayals, of course, did not end with Russian-American relations. An equally hair-raising horror story is to be found in the series of steps by which the United States helped to unseat Chiang Kai-Shek and place Mao Tse Tung at the head of the government of China. (The fully documented story of this shoddy chapter in American history is told in An-

thony Kubek's book *How the Far East Was Lost.*[4]) Stalin
oversaw the starvation of six to eight million peasants who resisted giving up their farmlands in the forced collectivization
policy of the late '20s and early '30s, besides being responsible
for the death of millions of others at the hands of firing squads
and in slave labor camps scattered all through the Soviet empire; but in mass murder Stalin was outdone by the Maoist regime. Was it fifty million, or only twenty million, Chinese
landowners who were shot by the peasant armies under Mao's
command in order to "give the land to the people"? Most
Americans seem neither to know nor to care. At any rate, it
was probably the greatest mass murder in all history. From
then until now, many Chinese have tried, usually in vain, to
escape via Hong Kong or the sea the tyranny of their viciously
totalitarian regime.

And then, of course, there was a little incident known as the
"rape of Tibet"—the invasion of the mountain nation of
Tibet, followed by the decimation and enslavement of the
proud Tibetan people. It is this added bit of mass slaughter
that American liberals have justified by saying, "After all, historically Tibet was a part of China." And so the story goes on.
Are we to conclude that the American student groups that
label themselves as "Maoist" would, if they had the power,
deal with American dissenters from their policies in the same
way in which the Maoist regime deals with dissenters in
China?

The attitude of libertarians to the history of American
foreign policy since World War II is surely plain. Libertarians
take human rights seriously, and the doctrine of individual
rights is the cornerstone of their political philosophy. When
rights are violated in other nations, especially as flagrantly as
they have in recent world history, the facts are not ignored or

forgotten; and the libertarian would not consent to having *relations of any kind* with such nations—not diplomatic and, more important, no trade: without gifts and trade many such regimes, with their cumbersome economies, would long since have collapsed without the loss of a single American life. If one does not sit at his dining room table with a murderer, by what kind of double standard should he sit at an international conference table with the murderers of millions? Can one have sympathy for the *victims* of torture and slavery if one sits at council tables and elaborate state dinners with the torturers? What must the victims of their aggression think when they see the representatives of the "free" world doing these things? And had we not dealt with them at all, would they now be in a position to threaten the world with nuclear extinction?

"That is all very well," one may say. "But the world does not consist of free nations *now*. And in our present situation, what are we to do about war and threats of war?"

Unfortunately, the catastrophic effects of the insane policies of the United States in World War II cannot be canceled out by the stroke of the pen. Actions have consequences, and acts of international import have consequences of international import. These consequences are still with us and will be in the foreseeable future. The pattern of World War III was already taking shape before World War II was over, thanks to Allied stupidity in giving to a ruthless totalitarian regime, Soviet Russia, a huge empire constituting almost one-fourth of the world's land mass and a billion people (as opposed to the 200 million it had before), while the United States and Britain got nothing out of the war except mountainous debts.

The chief victims of this momentous giveaway, of course, have been the captive nations. The Balkan nations, which were swallowed up into the Soviet tyranny, and the Baltic nations, which were plundered and enslaved, and remain so in varying degrees to this day, can thank (to a large degree) American policies for the omnipresence of their Soviet aggressors. They deserve our help, and restitution for the slavery into which Roosevelt sold them in return for nonexistent favors from Stalin. But the time has passed in which anything could be done for them without endangering civilization itself in a nuclear war. Soviet Russia has now reached nuclear parity with the United States; so the evils have been done to these masses of people and can no longer be corrected, any more than the millions now dead at the hands of Soviet firing squads and masters of slave labor can be resurrected to live their lives out in the peace and happiness which they deserved.

War in any form must now be opposed, even though it means that the peoples who were enslaved must remain slaves. The damage can no longer be undone. In order to rescue innocent people, who were sold down the river by American policies, millions of other innocent people would be killed, and possibly the entire human race would be annihilated. To make restitution to innocent people, one cannot let millions of other innocent people die. Those are the international facts of life in 1971.

To see what the rationale is of the libertarian position toward war, let us return to the level of single individuals:

If Smith and a group of his henchmen aggress against Jones, and Jones and his bodyguards pursue the Smith gang to their lair, we may cheer Jones on in his endeavor, and we and others in society interested in repelling aggression may contribute financially or personally to Jones' cause. But Jones has *no* right, any more than does Smith, to aggress against anyone else in the course of his "just war": to steal others' property in order to finance his pursuit, to conscript others into his possible use of violence, or to kill others in the course of his struggle to capture the Smith forces. If Jones should do any of these things, he becomes a criminal as *fully* as Smith, and he too becomes subject to whatever sanctions are meted out against criminality. . . .

Suppose that Jones, in the course of his "just war" against the ravages of Smith, should kill a few innocent people, and suppose that he should declaim, in defense of this murder, that he was simply acting on the slogan, "Give me liberty or give me death." The absurdity of this "defense" should be evident at once; for the issue is *not* whether Jones was willing to risk death personally in his defensive struggle against Smith; the issue is whether he was willing to kill other people in pursuit of his legitimate end. For Jones was in truth acting on the completely indefensible slogan: "Give me liberty or give *them* death"—surely a far less noble battle cry.

The libertarian's basic attitude toward war must then be: it is legitimate to use violence against criminals in defense of one man's rights of person and property; it is completely impermissible to violate the rights of *other* innocent people. War, then, is only proper when the exercise of violence is rigorously limited to the individual criminals. We may judge for ourselves how many wars or conflicts in history have met this criterion.[5]

There is no way to rescue the peoples that U.S. policies have sold into enslavement, which would not risk our lives, their lives, and the lives of the Soviet people themselves, who also are victims of their government. If there was any measure we could take which would exterminate the leaders of that government while not killing innocent people, we would be justified in taking it: we may quite properly kill the slavemaster as long as we do not thereby also kill the slaves. But in the present state of the world, there is simply no military means of doing so. It might have been done in 1945 by an ultimatum to Russia, when the United States still possessed a monopoly of nuclear weapons; it could probably have been done in years immediately thereafter by cutting off *all* trade relations with the slave-countries—this would, however, have involved starvation for many people before the government that was tyrannizing them was brought down, but it seems very likely that it would have happened. Perhaps it could still be done today, but with far more difficulty: when we ourselves have nurtured the newly-hatched serpent into a king cobra with fangs, who can kill many creatures before we can even get at him, the case is more complex and difficult. At the moment we can only work toward nuclear disarmament among nations, making quite sure that the United States does not disarm while other nations continue to arm in violation of the agreement.

It may yet come to pass that the Soviet government, and perhaps its Chinese counterpart as well, will be overthrown by its own people, who, having tasted a few liberties since Stalin, may work revolutionary changes in order to obtain the other liberties which are their right. Though the chances of this happening seem dim at the moment, because the government has all the guns, there are writers within the Soviet Union who predict that some revolutionary changes in the direction of liberty will occur, though at the price of much bloodshed.

It is at least as likely, however, that Soviet Russia (perhaps in combination with China) will unleash an aggressive war against the United States: its growing missile system is (unlike that of the United States) geared less for defense than for an aggressive first strike. As its nuclear weaponry increases and that of the United States decreases relative to it, as is now happening month by month, there is a strong possibility that once the Soviet Union has attained a clear nuclear superiority over the United States, its leaders will issue an ultimatum to the United States government, presenting it with a choice of nuclear annihilation or military takeover and enslavement.

There is also a strong possibility that instead of such direct shoot-it-out methods, the Soviet Union may play a waiting game: its leaders, seeing how much of the world has already fallen to them with American help, and seeing how successfully they have mesmerized and deluded American liberals for fifty years, and aware that the United States is become gradually collectivized in any case, have only to continue their present policies and the entire world may yet drop into their lap like a ripe plum. With American policy as it has been since World War II, there is a considerable likelihood that things will happen exactly in accordance with such anticipations.

Government-to-Government Aid

Since World War II, countless billions of dollars have gone out of the American taxpayer's pocket into "foreign aid." Has the foreign aid helped Americans? Only occasionally and incidentally, perhaps; but for the most part it has been a total waste—the money might as well have been thrown down a sewer. It has not made foreign nations friendlier to America; as always, beneficence given one year is claimed as a right the next year, with threats and imprecations when the amount to a given country was stopped or reduced. It has not made the United States a single ally that it otherwise wouldn't have had (with a few possible exceptions such as Greece; Marshall Plan aid in 1949 may have kept Greece from being sucked into the Soviet orbit). It has not even helped the poor of those countries, for the money seldom reached them: when money goes from government to government rather than from individuals to individuals, it is generally used to line the pockets of politicians who administer the program—and the program seldom gets realized.

Even if the poor had been helped by these programs, this would be no justification for them. By what right is money taken non-voluntarily from the citizens of one nation and placed into the pockets of citizens of another? If individual Americans, or groups of them, wish to help this or that person or group in another country, they are free to do so—and they will usually do so once the need is made clear to them. But when it is done by government, every taxpayer is forced to contribute even if he recognizes the whole program for the fraud that it is. The very fact that it is done by government makes it coercive, and at the same time inefficient: what program of government-to-government gifts (euphemistically called loans) has ever achieved its desired goal, or placed the money in the hands of the people who most needed assistance?

Colonialism

In discussions of colonialism, the lifeboat fallacy is used with a vengeance. "The people of Africa are poor," chants the liberal press, "because we are rich"—and we are expected to feel guilt, to such a degree that the United States and other countries are supposed to give aid to them in the form of government-to-government loans. "We have more and they have less, therefore they have less *because* we have more." But of course it is not so. Had Americans not become prosperous, the unfree economies of the world would still be living at starvation level. (Recall the lifeboat fallacy, pp. 222-4.)

Africans are human beings with the same innate capacities as others, and the natural resources of their countries are tremendous. *We* are not preventing *them* from developing those resources for human use, in order to improve the quality of their life. But when Western nations do go to Africa, and take some of the mineral or metal resources from the earth and use them, they are accused of exploitation, imperialism, and colonialism. Indeed, Barbara Ward has suggested in her book *The Angry Seventies* that the hungry overseas will wreak vengeance on us if we do not take a certain percentage of the U.S. Gross National Product and give it to them as an outright gift.

There is of course colonialism and colonialism. Some of it was so bad that no excuses for it could be given, involving as it did human slavery and the unpaid expropriation of human resources and labor. But it is also true that colonialism at its best made possible for the first time the safety of the individual against the tribe, and the respect of his rights before the law. In addition, the colonial powers provided the colonies with roads, railroads, hospitals, health services, schools, and military and naval installations. Perhaps most important of all, the colonizers represented the "Protestant work ethic," without which these changes could not have been imposed upon a native population—indeed, they could not have been made *by* a native population. "Industrializing a happy-go-lucky, dreamy, agrarian nation without strong material ambitions can be done only with a great deal of training, education, motivation."[6] All these are expenditures of tremendous time, patience, and money by the so-called imperialists.

What did they get out of it? Sometimes, to be sure, they got the mineral resources of the colonized land, after going to the labor of mining them and making them commercially viable. But what, one might ask, is so bad about that? Did the resources really belong to "the people" of a jungle society that never even began to use them? Did they not belong rather to those who mixed their labor with them, and provided the ideas, the technology, for their use? And what is so objectionable about one nation owning property in another land? Also, the colonists made homes for themselves in the new land, and cleared the forests and created farms and factories—from which they were usually expelled when the "release from colonialism" came about.

The colonies, most of the time, were a losing proposition.

Colonies, contrary to a generally accepted myth, were profitable only in a very few cases. Of Germany's colonies before 1914, only little Togo was in the black. The Belgian Congo was a sound financial proposition only in the 1940–1957 period. Between 1908 and 1960 Belgium invested no less than 260 million gold francs and earned 25 million. The profits France derived from its colonies in this century was about one-fourth of the original investments. Disraeli thundered against the "miserable colonies" and Richard Cobden inquired: "Where is the enemy who would do us the favor to steal them from us?" . . . Colonies might be a matter of national pride or of military interest, but if inhabited by a "backward" population, they seldom are a paying proposition.[7]

When one observes the mass butchery going on in some of the "newly developing" nations of the world (for example, Nigerians against Biafrans), one may well wonder whether an Ibo tribesman had his right to life and liberty (not to mention property) respected more by Nigerians than by his former colonial "masters."

The United Nations

Let us consider, now, the libertarian position on the United Nations.

There are now some 130 nations which are members of the U.N. The vast majority of them are dictatorships, ruled not by the best but the worst of the people whom they claim to represent—the men who seek power desperately over other human beings that they do not mind taking great risks to attain it. These men, or their hired stooges, sit together and discuss the fate of nations over the U.N. council table. If the people of these nations had any voice in the matter, they would cry out: "Who are these anthropoids who have taken to themselves the right to tell the world what our country wants? *We* are our country, and we don't approve their policies!"

But even if these nations were represented by their best men instead of their worst, what right would their representatives have to vote on any matter affecting the rights of individuals in their country or any other? Can the rights of individuals be bargained away by majority vote? No, not by the majority vote of the citizens of their own nation—and not a whit more by the majority vote of a United Nations organization.

Though the Bill of Rights of the American Constitution has been increasingly violated during the past century, via legislation and Supreme Court decisions, it is still the bulwark of American constitutional government. It protects citizens against the violation of their rights by other individuals and by government, and by doing so it limits the authority of that government over their lives. True, legislation and Supreme Court decisions have increasingly dampened its role as a protector of rights, by interpreting such phrases as "the general welfare" in a way that would appall the Founding Fathers or any other person really interested in protecting these rights. But even in its present damaged condition it still protects the citizen against a great deal of encroachment by government. What would be likely to occur if Americans were subject not to the laws of the United States but to those of a United World Government under the United Nations, or even a confederation of independent nations with the United Nations in control of a Unified World Army? Considering the present membership of the United Nations, what chance is there that the rights of individuals would be protected? The prospect of such an occurrence is one that can only be contemplated with horror. Considering that totalitarian nations of one kind or another comprise a U.N. majority, what chance is there that the rights to life, to freedom of speech and assembly, of the press, and so on (not to mention the economic freedoms), would be respected? On the contrary, a world under the U.N. would make short shrift of such rights. And what redress would an American citizen then have, seeing that there was no longer an American Army but only a World Army and a World Police Force under "World Law"?

It is true that there is a Universal Declaration of Human

Rights in the U.N. Charter. Much of it reads like the Bill of Rights of the American Constitution. Not all of it is equally unobjectionable—for example, Article 25 states that everyone has a right to an adequate standard of living, food, clothing, housing, and medical care, without stating who is to provide these things or under what conditions. As we have seen, all these things do not exist in nature and can be provided only by the labor of other men; and the question then becomes how can some persons receive such services from others without the providers of the services being deprived of their right to the fruits of their labor. Much of the U.N. Declaration of Human Rights has a fine sound—on paper. But it is shot through with internal contradictions, making any parts which seem valid spurious and transparently insincere, since the other provisions entirely nullify that which would be desirable. What chance is there that even the desirable portions would be implemented in practice? And what would force the U.N. to abide by it, once it had a monopoly on the armed forces of the world? Considering that most of the governments in the world have no respect for human rights, the outcome is predictable. The U.N. Declaration of Human Rights is only a scrap of paper even now: the member nations have affixed their signatures to it, and yet they ignore it constantly. Everyone has the right to life, liberty, and the security of his person, says Article 3; no one shall be held in slavery or servitude, says Article 4; no one shall be subjected to torture or to cruel, inhuman or degrading treatment or punishment, says Article 5; no one shall be subjected to arbitrary arrest, detention, or exile, says Article 9; everyone is entitled to a fair and public hearing by an independent and impartial tribunal, says Article 10; everyone has the right to freedom of movement and residence, as well as the right to leave any country, says Article 13; everyone has a right to own property, and no one shall be arbitrarily deprived of his property, says Article 14—and so the list goes on. Now consider just one member nation, the Soviet Union, and run through the list again, and you will see that there is not one item on the list that has not been flagrantly disregarded by the Soviet government again and again, not as exceptions to the rule but as standard procedure. Is there any more reason to believe that a United Nations, composed chiefly of totalitarian nations, with a monopoly of the armed forces of the world to back it up, would respect the rights listed any more than the Soviet Union does now?

In a recent novel by Daniel McMichael, *The Journal of David Q. Little*, the future of the United States under such a world government is vividly and horrifyingly depicted. After a confrontation between Russia and the United States nearly resulting in war, a Treaty of Friendship is signed and the entire world becomes one governmental unit, with a single world army. Since the Soviet Union and its satellite nations are in the majority (as a result of policies that started with World War II), its rulers are successful in forcing its policies on all the rest. Gradually the United States becomes Sovietized; American-manufactured goods are sent to Russia for Russian use; government controls the economy, and private entrepreneurs are taken from their jobs and disappear one by one. The main character, David Little, can keep his job only if he says nothing against the new regime.

"Has the full impact reached you yet?" [his boss asks him]. "Have I made myself clear? For all practical purposes—and I suggest you get used to this—you no longer are a citizen of the United States in the same way you once were. You are a subject of the World Order of Nations." He spoke in open triumph, as if he could no longer contain within him the *good news*. But that was not what brought the chills and a whole new set of fears. We had long anticipated the day of world government. Rather, what left me frozen in my chair was the dawning realization of the *kind* of world government this was.

"And the Soviet Union? They are also subjects of the World Order of Nations?" He read it in my eyes. He saw what I feared to say. I wanted to scream and throw myself at him. I wanted out. I wanted to go home and be a little boy again. I wanted to hide my head in my mother's lap and have it all go away—like after a bad dream. Only Mr. Tidings would not go away. The small desk and the small chairs and the small room—they did not go away either. The voice cut through, cold, sharp and vicious. It sang of power supreme and vengeance completed.

"Not quite," the unmasked face pronounced. "You see, the Soviet Empire *is* the World Order of Nations, and the whole world *is* the Soviet Empire."[8]

Being too intelligent and honest, he loses his job. His children are taken away from him to go to government indoctrination school. When they come back, their words are the slogans of the Party and their attitude toward him is one of contempt and hatred. He sees that they will turn him in for saying even a casual word against the Party. Yet he has no choice but to send them back to school again. What happens to him, and what happens to what once was the United States, is described in the novel, which one should read for himself.

Today the delegates of the Soviet Union and other terror-states, their hands dripping with the blood of their nations' victims, sit on the General Assembly and the Security Council of the United Nations, uttering sanctimonious phrases about peace, while presuming to judge whether or not *other* nations (which are pure as snow beside them) should be expelled—and all the while, their international policies and their day-to-day relations with other nations perpetuate the very concept of omnipotent government and violation of human rights, which they eschew in the U.N. Charter which they signed. Can an organization thus constituted receive the moral sanction of a person who takes the rights of man seriously?

War and Economic Liberty

The nineteenth century has been called the century of individualism—and in the Western world there were no major wars for an entire century, from the defeat of Napoleon in 1815 to the outbreak of World War I in 1914. The twentieth century has been called the century of collectivism, and it has already been ravaged by two world wars of a scope unparalleled in all the world's history, with a rash of other bloody wars thrown in.

The twentieth century has also witnessed the rise of the Total State—of governments more powerful, more nearly omnipotent, than in any previous era of the world's history. There have always been dictatorships, but some of those that have arisen in the twentieth century have strangled the liberty of their citizens better than any that the most despotic ancient emperor was able to do. With government managing the economy, the fate of all production, of all work, and with it of all workers, lay in the hands of the government, which could now enforce its decrees more efficiently than ever before by means of the "new technology"—brainwashing, wiretapping, computerized information-banks providing data on every individual in the nation, all of which were gladly supplied by the rulers' psychologists in return for the privilege of continued research. Government now has the power to dominate the life of every individual and squelch incipient rebellion as never before in history.

The greater incidence of totalitarian governments and of war, is no sheer coincidence. Anyone who has not pondered the correlation would do well to read Ludwig von Mises' epoch-making book, *Omnipotent Government: the Rise of the Total State and Total War.*[9] The greater the hold of government upon the life of the individual citizen, the greater the risk of war. If a dictator already has control of the printing presses, so that he can turn out nationalist propaganda without fear of opposition, and of the secret police, so that any dissenters can immediately be consigned to secret cellars or firing squads, and the ordinary citizen trembles with fear even when speaking on the street to another ordinary citizen (or even in his home, lest the room contain electronic devices planted by the government), he can be quite sure that only his propaganda and not the truth will sink into the minds of most people—and that if there are exceptions they won't dare to do anything about it. If on top of this the government owns the means of production (as in Soviet Russia) or controls it from top to bottom (as in Nazi Germany), then the entire economy of the nation is a pawn in its hands: the people, employers and workers alike, are in bondage to the state as much as any serf. Governments of this kind are gangsters: instead of protecting the rights of their citizens, they hold the power of life and death over the citizens; the representatives of government can send them to concentration camps, torture them, kill them, or move them about to do forced labor at gunpoint.

But slave labor will not yield as much production as voluntary labor; free men will produce on an open market for their own self-interest much more efficiently than slaves will work for masters. Production will falter (except sometimes in a few sectors such as military research and production, where the government gives the researchers considerable freedom in return for developing new weapons); bottlenecks develop; shortages are perennial. There is never enough agricultural produce, never enough shoes and clothes to wear, the quality is bad, and no one is motivated to do better, because the economic system is so devised that there is no personal reward for doing so. When this happens, the rulers of state will not of course blame their insane system of centralized economic planning; they will look about for a scapegoat (the Jews, the "profiteers," or other "enemies of the people") and train all their propaganda-organs incessantly on these scapegoats in order to whip up public opinion against them. The propaganda often is directed against other countries as well—and when the citizenry (or at least the army) is even half-convinced that the trumped-up charges are true, and inflamed to hatred against the scapegoats domestic or foreign, the ruler plans war. The war is an economic measure to loot the produce of countries more productive than his own: it is also a diversionary tactic to turn people's minds from his failures at home.

War is typically started by totalitarian (statist) nations against free (or at least freer) nations. World War I was started by Germany (then a monarchy) and czarist Russia, with freer countries being dragged in by previous treaty-commitments. World War II began with the natural alliance of two totalitarian nations, Nazi Germany and Soviet Russia (though the one later turned on the other). The United States, though it became involved in both, did not want war, did not need war, and did not profit from it; World War II not only left the United States with a staggering national debt (still unpaid), but ushered in an era of government-to-governemnt aid from the American taxpayer to every government that might thereby become an ally, a policy that has proved worse than futile.

A laissez-faire capitalist nation—which of course the United States in the twentieth century is far from being—would have no use for war. A capitalist society is a society of free traders on a free (uncoerced) market; and war is the enemy of trade. Wars are expensive, and the most productive people in the nation are the ones most heavily taxed to support it (from unproductive citizens there is nothing for governments to take). When a citizen's home or factory is destroyed in war, his losses are not recovered, even if his nation wins the war. The trader in search of profit desires peace.

The trader and the warrior have been fundamental antagonists throughout history. Trade does not flourish on the battlefields, factories do not produce under bombardments, profits do not grow on rubble. Capitalism is a society of *traders*—for which it has been denounced by every would-be gunman who regards trade as "selfish" and conquest as "noble."[10]

Besides, people who believe in individual rights do not believe in violating them by aggressive acts against others, whereas citizens of a dictatorship do not have such a concept. Being sacrificial animals for the government themselves, they see no harm in making sacrificial animals of others. In addition, they receive glowing promises about the fruits of conquest, and they have much less to lose.

Private citizens—whether rich or poor, whether businessmen or workers—have no power to start a war. That power is the exclusive prerogative of a government. Which type of government is more likely to plunge a country into war: a government of limited powers, bound by constitutional restrictions—or an unlimited government, open to the pressure of any group with warlike interests or ideologies, a government able to command armies to march at the whim of a single chief executive?[11]

What would the world be like if it were composed only of free nations—leaving people free not only in life and limb, but in their economic activities as well, in other words capitalistic nations? Such nations would of course be producing nations, nations with a high standard of living because of the free exchange of the fruits of production: a standard of living ever so much higher than that of the United States in 1971, where production has been constantly impeded and harassed by government. Every citizen would have a great deal to protect, and a great deal to lose by war. There would be free trade not only within each nation but between one nation and another, with no tariff barriers and with high mobility so that a person in one country could visit or emigrate to another (without even a passport, as was the case before World War I). There would be no need, and no motivation, for citizens of one nation to plunder the goods of another. It wouldn't even matter much on which side of a national boundary a person lived; every citizen of every country would enjoy his rights, no matter where he lived, he would have no reason to be envious of the citizens of other nations, except for such matters of taste as climate and topography, in which case he could buy or rent property in the nation of his choice and reside there. The propulsive forces that generate wars would be absent; and a world of free societies (which includes, of course, a free economy as an essential part) would be a world most likely to enjoy perpetual peace.

11

Is Government Necessary?

Libertarianism is first and foremost a view about liberty and human rights. Since economic liberty is a part of liberty, the economic consequences we have traced in Chapters 3–8 follow: a libertarian who did not believe in economic liberty would be no libertarian at all, and no believer in liberty. But on the topic of the present chapter there is a legitimate disagreement among libertarians—it has to do with the implementation of the libertarian view in regard to the question of the existence of government as a protective agency. And although my own option is for limited government, many libertarians who agree with everything that has been said up to this point would disagree about this one matter: they view government, all government, as an unnecessary evil, and argue that society would be much better off without it. This issue will be considered in the present chapter.

There are many advantages that can accrue to human beings only by living in society: human companionship, the exchange of knowledge, the enjoyment of works of art created by others, the cumulative benefits of cultural and technological improvements which can be transmitted from one generation to another, with the result that we have at our disposal today such a variety of improvements and inventions that if we had to start all over, it would take thousands of generations to come up to the present level. In economic matters, the principal advantage of living in society is the vastly greater efficiency brought about by the specialization of labor—whereby each individual produces the kind of product or service that his skill and talents make possible, and each individual exchanges his goods or services on the open market with other individuals; this makes possible a variety and sophistication of products and services that would be quite impossible if each man had to make his own shoes, his own clothing, his own shelter, his own food.

In spite of all this, there is a great potential disadvantage in social existence: the possibility of having one's rights violated by the aggressive actions of others. In order to forestall this possibility, a social agency is needed whose purpose it is to protect each man's rights against infringement by others. This, according to the libertarian, is the justification—and the only justification—for the institution of government.

It was Ayn Rand who first formulated the libertarian principle that no man, or group of men, may seek to gain values from others by the imposition of physical force upon them. But of course there are always some men who are willing to gain their values from others by force (or its derivative, fraud), and it is to protect citizens against such people that government is needed.

Without a legal structure to protect him from the use of force by others, a man cannot engage in his chosen activities—farming, teaching, studying, managing a factory or a

store or working in it, or any other non-coercive endeavor—
with any degree of security. He needs the protection of a legal
system if he is safely to continue in his chosen activities without having to worry constantly about protection against possible violators of his rights.

Besides the need for protection against criminals and
foreign invaders, men need a system of laws and courts to deal
with disputes. Disputes are not always the result of aggressive
intent or malice; there may be legitimate disagreements among
well-intentioned human beings over matters of fact that have
to be determined, over property rights, over the interpretation
of contracts, and so on. An objective, impersonal umpire is
needed, so that people are not obliged to settle disputes by
resorting to personal feuds, vendettas, or gang wars.

A government possesses exclusive jurisdiction over a certain
geographical territory, and it exercises a monopoly on the use
of force within that geographical area. This does not mean that
a man attacked on the street has no right to defend himself
personally against the attacker; it means that if he uses force to
answer force, he must be prepared to justify his action before
the law. In a libertarian society, men would be free to engage
the services of protective agencies; but when such agencies re-
sorted to the use of force against those who initiated force,
*they would have to be prepared to justify their actions before
the law*. The matter would not be left to their personal discretion. Force is too dangerous a thing, even in its retaliatory use,
to be left to the whims of individuals. A system of laws, published in advance and knowable to all, is required to regulate
the use of force, if men are to enjoy any sort of security in their
social existence.

A limited government supplies an indispensable need of
men living in a society: the *rule of law*. A constitution, supple-
mented by laws, specifies the principles pertaining to what

men may and may not do in relation to other men, and what others may and may not do in relation to them. And under a system of limited government such as libertarians advocate, government is confined in its function to the protection of individual rights.

The constitution protects individual citizens against the power of government by specifying what the government is permitted to do and what boundaries it must *not* cross. A government may do only that which the constitution permits; that which is not explicitly permitted is forbidden. On the other hand, private citizens under such a political system have unlimited freedom, within the sphere of their own personal rights.

In a libertarian constitution, the guiding principle is the prohibition of initiatory force by one human being against another and by a government against any of its citizens. The specific laws which implement the constitution spell out in detail the ways in which this principle is to be actualized: laws concerning murder and manslaughter, attempted murder, assault, robbery, invasion of privacy, trespass, negligence (and the penalties for each); laws protecting property and specifying the conditions of contracts, patents, copyrights, and other products of man's labor; procedures for the enforcement of these laws by the police; and procedures for arbitration in the courts in case of disagreement in the application or interpretation of these laws. In a limited government, men who have violated no one else's rights lose nothing in empowering the government to use force in retaliation against the violators of rights; indeed, they have everything to gain.

In a society where men's rights are protected by objective law, where the government has no other function or power, men are free to choose the work they desire to do, to trade their effort for the effort of other men, to offer ideas, products and services on a market from which force and fraud are barred, and to rise as high as their ability will take them. Because they deal with one another as producers, not as masters or slaves, they are able to achieve the full advantages of social existence: the advantages made possible by the human capacity to transmit knowledge, and by specialization and exchange under a division of labor. Among men who do not seek the unearned, who do not long for contradictions or wish facts out of existence, who do not regard sacrifice and destruction as a valid means to gain their ends—there is no conflict of interest. Such men deal with one another by voluntary consent to mutual benefit. They do not reach for a gun—or a legislator—to procure for them that which they cannot obtain through voluntary exchange.[1]

No-Government Libertarianism

Recently another group of libertarians has arisen who agree with the advocates of limited government about the use of force and the nature of rights, but who disagree about the function of government; they contend that government should be not merely limited, but nonexistent. The very reasons which we have given in Chapters 3-8 for government keeping hands off economic matters are given by them as reasons why government should stay out of even the area of personal safety, as well. Just as there should be no government intervention in the economy, so there should be no government intervention in the protection of individual rights. But this is the only area allotted to government by the limited-government libertarian. The conclusion is obvious: these libertarians would do away with government entirely.

The no-government libertarian—or anarcho-capitalist, as he is sometimes called—contends that government, all government, is an unnecessary evil. All the supposed services of government, he holds, are better supplied via the free market, and without doing violation (as government so often does) to human rights. There are several arguments which the no-government libertarian uses to support his view of a no-government society:

1. *The argument from consent.* In any association of human beings, each individual must have consented to belong to the association; the alternative to voluntary consent is that coercion be used upon him. You voluntarily decide to belong to a church or a club or a fraternity; you voluntarily choose to become a stockholder in a corporation, and so on. But did you ever consent to be under the dominion of the government whose laws you are forced to obey under penalty of punishment if you do not? Clearly, none of us made this choice; we were simply born in a nation with an already existing government and an already operating system of law and judicature. But then there is no justification which the government has for coercing you or in any way holding sway over your life.

Economic activities, the libertarian has argued all along, are not matters for government but for the free market: the voluntary exchange of goods and services by individuals. In all such activities, there is no problem about consent when one has a genuinely free market: you freely choose the kind of economic activity you wish to undertake, and you exchange values with others on an uncoerced market. Now why, the no-government libertarian asks, should economic activities be left to the voluntary choices of individuals, while police protection is a function of government, whether you want the protection or not and whether you wish to pay for it or not? If the individual should be free in the first category, why not in the second? And if not the second, why the first? Why draw the line at just this place? If economic activities belong to the category of "voluntary contract," why should not police protection and court arbitration belong there also? And if the principle of "total voluntarism" must be sacrificed in the case of police and courts, if one can compromise the consent principle thus

far, why not further? After all, *I* never appointed the police to
protect me, nor did I consent to their doing so, nor to the laws
which they enforce. By what right does the government take
over this protective function for my life without my consent?
This last consideration leads us directly into the argument
from rights.

2. *The argument from rights.* If an individual has a right
to his life, doesn't he also have, concomitant with it, the right
to defend that life if it is threatened—the "inalienable right of
self-defense"? If he chooses to hire someone to protect him, he
has the right; and if he prefers to have no protection at all, isn't
this his right too?

Suppose the police force is not all that it might be—as is indeed often the case. Suppose you are not getting the protection
you believe you deserve—either the police force is corrupt
(perhaps it is in collusion with the very criminals it is supposed to protect you against); or perhaps it is just inefficient,
or so thinly strung out that it doesn't answer your emergency
call for hours; or for any reason you are dissatisfied with its
services. Why then should you have anything to do with its alleged services at all? Perhaps, if you can afford it, you will
hire a bodyguard to protect you, or belong to a private protection agency that can do the job better than the police are
doing. Don't you have that right? If it's moral for governments
to protect your rights, isn't it moral for individuals to do like-
wise?

Thus far, every libertarian will agree, the limited-government advocates no less than with the no-government ones.
Many individuals do hire bodyguards; many hotel owners and
owners of industrial plants, as well as universities and colleges, hire men (often off-duty policemen or men retired from
the force) to guard their physical plant and the safety of their
patrons, at their own expense. All this is not only morally per-

missible, but perfectly legal. These men supplement the regular police force, which is presumably still "on top"; but of course they are supplementary only: they have to enforce the law of the state and nation (or campus regulations, provided these do not conflict with those of the state and nation). They cannot in any way act contrary to the laws of the state and nation.

And there's the rub. Suppose that the campus police or the factory police did, in the course of apprehending a suspect, something in violation of state or federal law. Then these policemen would themselves be in violation of the law, because the state and federal laws *take precedence* over the campus or factory regulations, and over the desires of the individual who gave instructions to his bodyguard. When the chips are down, it is the law of the land which is decisive, and determines in what situations force can be used against individuals or groups. But then our question again arises: by what right does it do this? Not only did I not consent, but may not my rights be violated in submitting to whatever laws there may be, and to whatever policemen there may be to enforce those laws?

To compound the matter further, suppose that I pay taxes to support the police force. And suppose that they are doing virtually nothing, and I feel that as they are constituted at present I can be as well off or better off without them—so I withhold my taxes. The government would still force me to pay, wouldn't it? Surely they would force me to pay. They would not force me to use their services, but they would force me to pay for them whether I used them or not.

Under either of the plans described in Chapter 9 (pp. 385-387) for social services without taxation, advocated by libertarians, this situation would not arise, since there would be no forced payment of taxes. Under any system involving taxation, however, the problem would be an acute one.

But let us assume that there are no compulsory taxes. There is still a problem. What if not only colleges and factories, but individuals by the thousands start hiring their own guards and bodyguards, and subscribing to private protection agencies in preference to using the police force? What would be the attitude of the government "protectors" toward this situation?

If the government says no, this is not all right, it will then have to *initiate* the use of force to stop the private agencies from doing their job. And the moment this happens, it is the government, not the individual, that will be initiating the use of force against those who have used none against it. It will now be government that is violating the rights of individuals.

If the government says yes, it's all right, then, as one private agency after another takes over its function, it may gradually slip out of business entirely. In fact, it probably *will* do so, since private organizations can usually do a job with greater efficiency, and with less waste and expense, than the government can. Soon the private agencies would dominate the field of protection, and the government's "protection service" would be without any customers. When this happened, would the governmental organization be content simply to close up shop, to offer no resistance in the process of its own annihilation?

If all police became "private police" in the manner suggested, this would still be no threat to the limited-government libertarian as long *as they all enforced the law of the land*, the scope of these laws being limited of course to the protection of the individual against the use of force.

Even if all police protection came to be by voluntary subscription, the police would still have to obey the law of the land and not simply their private whims or the whims of the people who hired them—so says the limited-government libertarian. Law, he says, is a necessity for any form of social organization. And if the no-government libertarian says that most of the laws that the police are required to enforce now shouldn't be on the books at all, the limited-government libertarian can only agree; but, he would add, in a proper government, the only laws there would be would be laws prohibiting people from violating other people's rights. Thus, if you have violated no one's rights, you would have nothing to fear from government: your life could proceed as if government did not exist. Laws penalizing interference with others' rights are the only laws which it is right that you should be made to obey, the only liberty you would not have is the liberty to deprive others of their liberty.

The no-government libertarian, for his part, will point out that every government that ever has existed has gone far beyond this, and is likely to do so in the future. The limited-government libertarian will simply agree, but emphasize that this is no refutation of his view, since his allegiance to government goes only so far as the limited function of protection of rights, and the adequate enforcement of the laws which do this.

At this point there is one argument that is commonly used which if not examined may cause confusion: "We live in a democracy, and in a democracy we rule ourselves; that is, *we* decide who our president, congressmen, etc., shall be, by means of the vote." But this is the collective "we"; it is not true that each individual has made such a decision. Each individual who is of voting age, and not disqualified for reasons of being insane or a felon, etc., is given a choice on the ballot—the system of voting, the whole procedure, and the governmental structure within which he has to exercise his choice, is not itself chosen by him; and the candidates between whom he chooses may neither of them be the ones he would have chosen himself if he'd had anything to say about it—the candidates were chosen by the Republican or Democratic Party convention, not by him. Besides, a large percentage of the electorate must put up with a man they did not vote for; it cannot be said that *they* chose him. And even those who voted for a winner, even if they approved him enthusiastically and not as the lesser of two evils, could hardly know what legislation he would approve or to what pressure-groups he would respond once he got into office—nor would he be bound to act in a certain way even if he knew that every member of his electorate wanted it so.

In addition to all this, is it not inevitable that democracy must violate some people's rights? Even if a government starts out limited, it becomes less limited as time passes. When one pressure-group induces Congress to enact a tax on another group, are not the rights of each member of the second group violated? When a president decides that some men shall fight and die in Vietnam, are not their rights violated? Are not the rights of every citizen violated when they must have part of their weekly paycheck deducted in order to pay for a federal dam in Arkansas or Tennessee? If it is wrong for one man to impose his wishes on another by force, is it not equally wrong for a thousand or a million or fifty million men to impose their wishes on another by force, via government? If a holdup man is violating your rights when he robs you, why is it any less a violation of your rights when many men do so, through acts of legalized plunder? Isn't the principle exactly the same—the taking by force of your life or a product of your labor and using it against your will, for causes you do not approve and to which you would not contribute voluntarily? If a million men rather than one man violated your rights, does this make it any less of a violation?

Moreover, what is to determine the size of the group to which one is supposed to profess allegiance?

Does democracy majority rule over a large, or over a smaller, area? In short, *which* majority should prevail? The very concept of a national democracy is, in fact, self-contradictory. For if someone contends that the majority in Country X should govern that country, then it could be argued with equal validity that the majority of a certain district within Country X could be allowed to govern *itself* and secede from the larger country, and this subdividing process can logically proceed down to the village block, the apartment house, and finally, each individual, thus marking the end of all democratic government through reduction to individual self-government.[2]

But this is precisely the point made by the no-government libertarians: each man is the ruler of himself, and no one should be in a position to rule him. But that is just what political power is—one man or group of men ruling over the others. And this is a clear violation of rights. In any enterprise involving a number of persons, there must be the voluntary consent of every member—if some member has not consented but is forced to belong anyway, his rights are being violated because force is being used against him. Well, government is something that involves a large number of people—all the people in the geographical area bounded by the nation in question. And it is certain that not all of these people (democracy or not) consented to the laws by which they are governed, nor the men who administer these laws. *By what right, then, do the rulers rule the non-consenters?* This has been a troublesome point all along, and the no-government libertarian's answer is clear: no one should be governed by another without his consent. I may do whatever I please with my life as long as I do not use force or threat of force against anyone else, and everyone else has the same right in relation to me.

The advocate of limited government, however, will reply: "You are only condemning something I never approved of in the first place. I approve only of limited governments—limited in the very strict way which I specified. Democracy is unlimited rule by the majority; democracies typically bargain away individual rights by majority vote, so I don't favor them any more than you do: I favor a constitutional republic, whose laws have only one function: the retaliatory use of force against those who initiate the use of force. And as for the point about how large the geographical subdivision should be, this is really a point of administrative detail—it wouldn't really matter how large or how small a nation was, since it wouldn't initiate force against you in any case. Once again, you wouldn't need to take cognizance of its existence unless you violated someone's rights. So it wouldn't matter how big the geographical unit was: you wouldn't be subservient to any laws other than the fundamental one that you do not initiate force against others. And as long as the government didn't initiate force against you, the size of the political unit would make no difference."

A limited government, then, could not be accused of violating rights. There is, however, another argument which the no-government libertarian employs, which is in fact the principal arena on which the controversy has been waged:

3. *The pragmatic argument.* The no-government libertarian contends that, whatever may be concluded about consent and about rights, the "laissez-faire society" operating without government, would work better: it would be more efficient, less wasteful, less corrupt, and less likely to get out of hand than any society that has a government. We shall now examine, point by point, how, according to its advocates, a no-government (laissez-faire) society would function, how individuals could be protected without the instrumentality of government, and how justice would be done in cases of aggression against life, liberty, and property.

At the outset, the no-government libertarian would say, government should be viewed with suspicion on the basis of the historical record: for however limited they may have been when they began, they have always tended to become *un*limited—witness the case of the American government in the twentieth century. And since government already possesses the physical force to implement its decrees, there is no way short of armed revolution in which the power can be taken from its hands, once the power has been lodged there. Prima facie, therefore, any political theory which can do without government is more plausible than one with it. If you have it, you have on your hands a time-bomb which may, and probably will, explode; without it, you don't have that danger.

And lest we be deterred by the thought that "after all, government protects us," we could point out that government in fact doesn't protect very much: only a few individuals, such as the President of the United States, are protected (at the tax-payers' expense), and even when he is, all the secret service agents in the world can't guarantee that he won't be assassinated. What government typically does is to try (often not very hard) to find and try the culprit *after* the crime has been committed. Even if he is found and convicted, if he's a thief you don't get your money back (you only have the satisfaction of seeing him in prison), and if he's a murderer and you are the one murdered, his conviction does you no good at all.

Indeed, present governments are usually more interested in threats to *themselves* than in threats to *you*:

Which categories of crime does the State pursue and punish most intensely—those against private citizens or those against *itself*? The gravest crimes in the State's lexicon are almost invariably not invasions of person and property, but dangers to its *own* contentment: e.g., treason, desertion of a soldier to the enemy, failure to register for the draft, conspiracy to overthrow the government. Murder is pursued haphazardly unless the victim be a *policeman,* or . . . an assassinated Chief of State; failure to pay a private debt is, if anything, almost encouraged, but income tax evasion is punished with utmost severity; counterfeiting the State's money is pursued far more relentlessly than forging private checks, etc. All this evidence demonstrates that the State is far more interested in preserving its own power than in defending the rights of private citizens.[3]

Let us see, then, how the no-government libertarian's program for society works out in detail. (It has been most thoroughly worked out in the book, *The Market for Liberty*, by Morris and Linda Tannehill.)

First, let us consider how the *arbitration of disputes* would occur in a no-government (or "laissez-faire") society. Anyone who had any dealings with anyone else—which would include virtually everyone except a hermit in the hills—would be a party to numerous contractual relations: in paying for merchandise on time, in dealing with lawyers and physicians, and so on —even one's dealing with a merchant on a cash basis is an implicit contractual relation: the merchant contracts to exchange a certain amount of goods for a certain amount of cash. It would, accordingly, be to everyone's interest, in the absence of a government system of courts, to subscribe to an *arbitration agency*. (For those who didn't, there would be no means to collect in case of a dispute.) Since there would be a demand for such a service, arbitration agencies would arise, each competing for the customer's payment of his fees in return for the service of arbitration.

Arbitration agencies would employ professional arbiters, instead of using citizen-jurors as governmental courts do. A board of professional arbiters would have great advantages over the present citizen-jury system of "ignorance times twelve." Professional arbiters would be highly trained specialists who made a career of hearing disputes and settling them justly. They would be educated for their profession as rigorously as engineers or doctors, probably taking their basic training in such fields as logic, ethics, and psychology, and further specialization in any field likely to come under dispute. While professional arbiters would still make errors, they would make far fewer than do the amateur jurors and political judges of today. Not only would professional arbiters be far better qualified to hear, analyze, and evaluate evidence for the purpose of coming to an objective judgment than are our present citizen-jurors, they would also be much more difficult to bribe. A professional arbiter who tried to "throw" a case would be easily detected by his trained and experienced colleagues, and few men would be so foolish as to jeopardize a remunerative and highly respected career, even for a very large sum of money.[4]

The parties to a contract would indicate in writing that in case of a dispute, a certain arbitration agency would be agreed upon by them to hear the case; and in the event that one of the parties was not satisfied with the arbitration agency's decision, and wished to appeal the case, the contract could provide for other such agencies to hear the case and render a decision. There could be a hierarchy of such agencies (to be used if the complaining party felt it was worth the money to use them) written into the contract, up to the final court of appeal. There would not have to be one final court of appeal for the entire society, such as the U.S. Supreme Court; there need only be an arbitration agency agreed upon by the parties to the contract as the one whose decision they would agree in advance to accept.

Moreover, insurance companies would arise to handle contract insurance, a service which most firms would probably use. The insurance company would indemnify the insured party for a loss, but probably not before the case had been submitted to the arbitration agency.

Since the debtor is in actual or potential possession of a value(s) which rightfully belongs to the creditor, the creditor has the right to repossess it by any means that will not take or destroy values which are the rightful property of the debtor. If the creditor, in the process of collecting his property, does deprive the debtor of values which rightfully belong to the debtor, the creditor may well find that he has reversed their roles, that he is now the one in debt.[5]

So the insurance company would have the right to collect the debt (or whatever), making arrangements with the debtor of such payment.

What if the debtor refused to make payment? The insurance company could then make arrangements with other individuals or firms, such as the debtor's bank (to attach part of his bank account) or his employer (to attach a portion of his wages). The bank and the employer would not, of course, be forced to cooperate in this, but they would probably do so out of self-interest:

Most banks would no doubt have a policy of cooperating with insurance companies in such matters, since a policy of protecting bank accounts from just claims would tend to attract customers who were undependable, thus increasing the cost of banking and forcing the bank to raise its charges. The same would be true of employers, only more so. Most employers would hesitate to attract undependable labor by inserting a clause in their employment contracts guaranteeing protection from just claims against them.[6]

But the debtor would usually pay his debt without such measures, since he would find that insurance companies would refuse to do business with him thereafter if he did not. And if this happened, he would be unable to purchase protection or enter into contracts, or even buy a car on time. Other business houses would also look up his rating and hesitate before doing business with him. He might well be driven entirely out of business, unable even to hold a position.

Even the poorest and most irresponsible man would think twice before putting himself in such a position. Even the richest and most powerful man would find it destructive of his interests to so cut himself off from all business dealings. In a free society, men would soon discover that honesty with others is a selfish, moral necessity.[7]

Next, what about the *protection of life and property?* Since the protection of these things is a value to virtually everyone, it would be worth something to have it protected; and it would be your right to have it protected as you choose, just as you now take measures to protect your health by consulting a physician. A person could attempt to do this himself if he felt able, but more likely he would subscribe to a *defense agency* whose task it was to provide the protection. He would not be forced to pay for protection as he is now, by paying taxes for the maintenance of a police force, which may or may not be inefficient or corrupt and may or may not protect him. (And lest anyone say he might not be able to pay the fee for the protection agency, consider that he would no longer be paying taxes to the government to support the police force—nor to a thousand and one other things, for most of which he gets nothing in return.)

In a laissez-faire society, there would be no governmental police forces, but this does not mean that people would be left without protection except for what they could furnish for themselves. The market always moves to fill customers' needs as entrepreneurs look for profitable innovations. This means that private enterprise defense agencies arise, perhaps some of them out of the larger private detective agencies of today. These companies have already proved their ability to provide efficient and satisfactory service, both in protection of values and the detection of crooks.[8]

But what if the defense agency, in order to protect you, started to use force against others, such as innocent persons with the "wrong look in their eye" who they think for some fanciful reason might agress against one of their customers?

The function of a private defense service company is to protect and defend the persons and property of its customers from initiated force or any substitute for initiated force. This is the service people are looking for when they patronize it, and, if the defense agency can't provide this service as well or better than its competitors, it will lose its customers and go out of business. A private defense service company, competing in an open market, couldn't use force to hold onto its customers—if it tried to compel people to deal with it, it would compel them to buy protection from its competitors and drive itself out of business. The only way a private defense service company can make money is by protecting its customers from aggression, and the profit motive guarantees that this will be its only function and that it will perform this function well.[9]

But what if the defense agency committed aggressions anyway? Who would stop them? And it might even pay them to do so (one might say)—they might so terrorize non-subscribers that many people would become subscribers to their agency, seeing what would happen to them if they didn't, and how efficiently the defense agency was operating (via terror). Couldn't this happen?

The no-government libertarian replies in the negative. Defense agencies would be closely connected with *insurance companies,* whose function it would be to insure people against aggressive acts by others. A defense company might not want to take on a customer if he were not insured against loss—or, the defense company might take on the insurance itself (or the insurance company take on the defense). Insurance companies would be interested in keeping aggression down to a minimum, since they would have to pay out less in claims, the less aggression took place; besides, in a peaceful society more things would arise for which people would want insurance coverage, hence more sales of insurance. Insurance companies would sell policies covering the individual against loss resulting from aggression.[10] To reduce the risks, they would probably insist that the customer install (or would themselves install) protection devices, such as burglar alarms connected to the defense company's office. Indeed, there would be much more in the way of *protection against* aggression (such as safety devices of various sorts), for it would be to the interest of the insurance company not to let the aggres-

sive acts occur. Police at present are far less concerned with
the prevention of crime than they are with punishing the offender after the crime has occurred; if the crime hasn't occurred yet, they will tell you they can do nothing until it has.
But the defense insurance company, acting strictly from the
profit motive, would find it to its interest to reduce aggressive
behavior to a minimum—and would finance the invention
and distribution of many devices not now even thought of, to
protect people's houses and persons against aggressive activity
by others.

This fact provides the solution to the problem about the defense agency overstepping its bounds.

This close affinity between insurance and defense would provide a
very effective check on any defense agency which had an urge to over-
step the bounds of respect for human rights and to use its force coercively—i.e., in a non-defensive manner. Coercive acts are destructive of
values, and value-destruction is expensive for insurance companies. No
insurance company would find it in its interest to stand idly by while
some defense agency exercised aggression, even if the values destroyed
were insured by a competing company; eventually the aggressors
would get around to initiating force against their own insureds—with
expensive results!

Insurance companies, *without any resort to physical force,* could
be a very effective factor in bringing an unruly defense agency
to its knees via boycott and business ostracism. In a laissez-faire,
industrialized society, insurance is vitally important, especially to
business and industry, which are the most important segment of the
economy and the biggest customers for any service. It would be difficult, indeed, for any defense company to survive if the major insurance
companies refused to sell insurance not only to it, but to anyone who
dealt with it. Such a boycott would dry up the major part of the defense company's market in short order; and no business can survive for
long without customers. There would be no way for a defense agency
to break such a boycott by the use of force. Any threatening or aggressive actions toward the insurance companies involved would only

spread the boycott as other businesses and individuals attempted to stay as far from the coercive agency as possible.[11]

In general, how does the no-government libertarian deal with cases of *coercion* used against you? In limited government, the government is considered the agent of the citizens— but the individuals in question have never signed a contract naming the government as their agent. So there is no reason why government officials should be the arbiters of disputes and rectifiers of injustice.[12] You have, in a no-government society, the right to deal with coercion yourself, *or* delegate a person or agency to do so.

You would probably choose to belong to a defense agency whose business it was to collect from the aggressor. There would also be insurance companies, which would sell policies covering the individual against loss of value via aggression. When they got hold of the aggressor,[13] the insurance company's representatives would give him a bill for damages and costs. A voluntary settlement would be attempted. "Legislation forcing the parties to submit to binding arbitration would be unnecessary, since each party would find arbitration to be in his own self-interest."[14]

The insurance company would not dare to bring charges against a man unless it had very good evidence of his guilt, nor would it dare to ignore any request he made for arbitration. If the insurance company blundered in this manner, the accused, especially if he were innocent, would bring charges against the company, forcing it to drop its original charges and/or billing it for damages. Nor could it refuse to submit to arbitration on his charges against it, for it would do serious damage to its business reputation if it did; and in a free-market context, in which economic success is dependent on individual or corporate reputation, no company can afford to build a reputation of carelessness, unreliability, and unfairness.[15]

If the insurance company and the accused cannot agree on

terms, they could choose an arbitration agency to handle the case and render a decision (or in case they could not agree on one, two agencies meeting jointly). But what if they could not get the aggressor (who doesn't want the case arbitrated) to appear for the hearing? In such case, the insurance company could order its defense agency to incarcerate the accused aggressor before and during arbitration (which would probably be only a matter of a few days, since the market is always more efficient than the bumbling government); but in doing so, they would have to take two factors into consideration. First, if the accused were shown to be innocent, the insurance company and defense agency would owe him reparations for holding him against his will. Even if he were judged guilty, they would be responsible for making reparations if they had treated him with force in excess of what the situation warranted; not being government agents, they would have no legal immunity from the consequences of their actions. Second, holding a man is expensive—it requires room, board, and guards. For these reasons, the defense company would put the accused aggressor under no more restraint than was deemed necessary to keep him from running off and hiding.[16]

How does the man get incarcerated against his will? Presumably, a member of the defense agency picks him up and takes him in, by force if necessary, to insure that he will be present at the arbitration of this case. The representative of the defense agency does not *know* at the time of apprehending the suspect that he is guilty. He simply takes him to an arbitration agency that decides his case. If the suspect is found to be innocent, he can collect damages (loss of time from work, plus inconvenience, and so on) from the defense agency that arrested him; for this reason the agency would not go about arresting suspects idly or at random, but would have clear evidence against him first. If the suspect is judged guilty, he would pay a fine by way of restitution to the victim (the victim, not the government) and/or be incarcerated for a period specified by the arbitration agency, during which he would work off his debt to the victim.

Another solution has been suggested: a man accused of a crime need not appear for trial if he does not choose to. But if he is accused and does not appear, his name and a description of the case against him will be published in the newspapers and announced on television stations, with possibly embarrassing consequences for himself if he fails to appear; in addition, businesses and credit companies will refuse to deal with him until the case is tried—they don't want to do business with undependables, and his good name (in a free society) is his most precious possession. A rational man will wish to preserve this, and will ignore it at his own peril. He will probably be unable to get a job, or protection from any defense agency (which would consider him too much of a risk), until his case is tried by an arbitration agency. It would usually, but perhaps not always, be to his interest to appear for trial, and clear his name (or if guilty, do his time), rather than risk such total ostracism. In an industrialized society, it is very difficult to continue for long without having dealings with anyone else.[17]

Evaluation of the No-Government View

The world does not consist of no-government societies—or of *a* no-government society (it is not clear what the difference would be since there would no longer be national boundaries). Under the circumstances it is difficult to form an exact conception of how it would function. Nevertheless, a number of questions arise which can be put to its advocates by the libertarians who champion limited constitutional government. Most of these questions would fall under the general heading, "How do you know it would work out the way you say?" Here are a few such questions:

1. Advocate of limited government: "In your laissez-faire society, nobody *has* to belong to a defense agency. He may be his own protector if he wishes. If someone has assaulted him, he can act in entire independence of whatever protection agencies or arbitration boards there may be, and, as the saying goes, 'take the law into his own hands.' But to such an alternative there is an objection that has been well known for thousands of years: a man is not likely to be the best judge of his own case; he will usually overestimate the aggression against him. He may consider death-by-a-thousand-cuts to be the appropriate punishment for someone who stepped on his toe. But surely, in a non-government society, if he chooses to take over the role of his own defender, he can, can't he? If others can defend his rights, surely he can himself if he so chooses."

Advocate of no government: "Of course. He may defend his rights, but not aggress against the rights of others. The moment he himself becomes an aggressor, the person aggressed against (or his defense agency) has the right to retaliate against *him*."

L: "But he might say that he was only defending himself—the other person did initiate the aggression by stepping on his toe. He just takes a stronger view of what defending himself consists of than other people might. That's the whole problem: since there is no such thing as the law of the land, anyone can take whatever defensive measures he wants to—and any definition of defense! This is what existed in the pre-law days in the Wild West—and why this anarchic state of affairs was fortunately replaced by a government under the rule of law. It is this *rule of law* that I find missing in your theory. Yours is a "rule of men"—each defending himself according to his own convictions, his own impulses, or his own whims. I would certainly feel more secure in a government by law, with the laws clearly defined in advance, and so formulated as not to permit an aggrieved party to do just anything he wishes, than I would in your anarchical society where each man is (or can be if he wishes) his own private avenger."

N: "Even in the Wild West, if a man tortured someone for aggressing against him, the victim's friends and neighbors would punish him to see to it that he never did it again. There was a code of ethics even though it didn't have the status of law."

L: "Just one? and suppose someone else had a different one? *How* for example would the friends and neighbors punish the culprit? By killing him? By torturing him in turn? And would they necessarily use carefully formulated rules of evidence and procedue? No—if they thought he was guilty they'd just hang him, wouldn't they? (Remember 'The Ox-Bow Incident.') They would just 'take care of him' according to their collective whim. And if the group that did this aroused the hostility of another group, then the second group would 'take care of' the first group—and so on, with might makes right and the strongest gang or group of gangs winning in the end. Hardly a formula for security of life and limb!"

N: "But in fact it wouldn't work out that way in an industrialized society, however things might have been in the Wild West. It is simply uneconomic for a person doing a full-time job at production to be also a specialist in defense; he would surely delegate such a task to a defense agency."

L: "Perhaps, but since no one *has* to do this, the anarchical society of individuals, each of whom is his own avenger with his own code, is still a possible one, and so it must represent at least one possible version of your no-government society—one to which I have just voiced my strong objections. What is miss-

ing from that society is protection by government against aggression, as embodied in the law of the land; and what is substituted for it is the individual or collective whims of whatever
person or group has the power to retaliate (or to initiate aggression for that matter)—not according to law, but according to its own views (often distorted views) of justice.

2. *L:* "Now to defense agencies. They have to apprehend
suspects if they are to be able to function. A man is appre-
hended by another who is a member of the X Defense Agency.
And the suspect says, 'I don't belong to the X Agency, and so
you have no jurisdiction over me. You have no right to apprehend me.' (Even if the suspect did belong to the X Agency, he
could say, 'I hired you to protect me, not to arrest me!') How
do you answer him?"

N: "If the suspect is guilty of aggression against someone,
any other individual has the right to exercise the retaliatory
use of force to take him in, until he makes restitution to the
victim."

L: "This seems to me far more chaotic than the limited-
government arrangement whereby only a policeman is empowered to make arrests. If anybody can take anyone else in,
snoopy neighbors could really have a ball, couldn't they?"

N: "But they would be subject to being sued if they took the
wrong person in. Usually, at any rate, it would be the injured
party himself who would do this, or (more likely) his delegated representative, his defense agency, whose paid job it would
be to do such things."

L: "But if he did it himself, he could do it according to his
own code of retaliatory ethics, couldn't he? And if a member
of the defense agency he belonged to did it, then it would be
done according to the representative's (or the defense agency's) code of ethics—which might be anything at all from
pacifism to torture of suspects."

N: "If the defense agency used torture or even violence on apprehending suspects, it would be boycotted by all its customers, and would have to go out of business."

L: "Not by its aggressively-minded customers, as long as the same methods wouldn't be used against *them* by other agencies. For that matter, the defense agencies, for a price, would surely be willing to take on many matters other than defense—there would be no law to stop them, would there? Your laissez-faire society would work out as you predict only if the vast majority of people in the society had your moral convictions, and didn't believe in brutal police methods (that is, brutal defense-agency methods), and believed that these agencies should exist only for the purpose of defense. But I don't see how you could keep the agencies from handling all sorts of things, depending on the whims of their members. If a group of rich men were willing to pay enough to a defense agency to have their enemies eliminated by a bunch of killers hired by the agency, I am sure there would be agencies that would be happy to take on that job. You say they'd be boycotted by others; maybe. But if they got enough money doing killing for this wealthy group, why should they care? They might even get more business from other people who wanted their enemies killed. Nor do I believe that everyone else would cease to do business with them; they would do business with them for money, just as people do now with the Mafia. The Mafia after all acts as a defense agency for many criminals, partly by eliminating their enemies; and for the members it seems to work pretty well. Under government the Mafia is illegal, and subject to prosecution by law; but in your no-government society it wouldn't even be that. If there were defense agencies who behaved like the Mafia, then other defense agencies (or private citizens) would have to make open war on them. In the absence of law, there would simply be war—civil war—among various groups holding different convictions."

N: "It's true that things would work out as I recommended only if the majority of people shared my convictions. But I am quite confident that this would be the case: once government, the chief coercive force in men's lives, is eliminated, people would behave much more rationally than they now do. They would see, for example, that peace is to their mutual self-interest."

L: "Perhaps, though I tend to doubt this. I do not antici-pate any drastic change in human nature as the result of a re-formed political or social system. And even if there were, there would still be *some* aggressors, and there would have to be some procedure for handling them—some procedure, I might add, other than the policies of competing defense agencies, who in order to get one aggressor might apprehend and detain (and even torture) a hundred suspects, which they would have the power to do, since, being in the business of defense for a living, would presumably possess most of the artillery. And this leads to my main question: The defense agency rep-resentative doesn't yet *know* that the man is guilty. Suppose they just want to check him out. The suspect may turn out to be innocent; and in that case, by what right does the other man arrest him? What if the suspect is innocent and doesn't want to go to the inconvenience of 'being checked out'? By what right does the defense agency representative take him in anyway, by force?"

N: "You are in no position to press this problem—you are hoist by the same petard. In your limited-government society, an innocent person may be arrested by the police, taken in for questioning, and even kept in jail for forty-eight hours (or whatever) to make sure that he won't skip town before ap-pearing before the judge. How do you justify *that*?"

L: "I would say that if crimes are to be solved, there has to be a *procedure* for solving them; and you can't solve them without evidence and without witnesses. If you want protection in a society, cooperation with those who afford that protection is the price you have to pay for it, even though it may involve your interrogation and detention. Police cannot be omniscient; they cannot be expected to know at the time of a man's arrest whether he is guilty. If I am working late and come out of my office building at 2 A.M., the police may be suspicious seeing me about at that hour, demand my identification, and even take me to the station house. I'm quite willing to put up with this as the price for having the building efficiently guarded against aggressors. If I owned the building I'd certainly want the police to check out all such persons! Since the only alternative is their *not* having that power, with the result that crimes would remain unsolved (followed by a sharp rise in the crime rate), my temporary detention is a small price to pay for the discouragement of aggression."

N: "But isn't it a violation of your rights, at least if you are innocent?"

L: "I would say that it's a part of my implicit contractual agreement in dealing with others at all: in consenting to a rule of law that punishes only the initiation of force, I am consenting at the same time to the necessary *implementation* of that law that would discourage the initiation of force. You can't have a rule of law for long without the implementation of that law. If you have the first, you've got to have the second."

N: "But on my system you have the second too: the defense agencies take care of matters of defense, and being competitive they would do it more efficiently than the police now do—as always happens when you leave things to private enterprise rather than government. That is my main contention, and one which I challenge you to rebut."

L: "I agree that most police forces aren't very efficient now, and that there's nothing like competition to put and keep hired service-groups on their toes. But the point on which I insist is that there has to be a rule of law—one law for the entire land —and not a decentralized system of defense agencies, each with its own law."

3. *L:* "What of family relations? Ordinarily parents are the proper guardians of their children, without coercion from government. But what if they mistreated their children? There was a recent newspaper article about a married couple who were about to burn their eighteen-month-old baby to death when the police entered and arrested them. What would have happened in a no-government society?"

N: "Any member of a defense agency would have been equally entitled in a no-government society to do what the police did; in fact any private person could have done so and then phoned the defense agency. Coercion would be a matter for defense agencies to handle, just as it now is for the police to handle. And a private agency could do it more effectively than the police now do."

L: "But who would be interested in the matter?"

N: "Neighbors, friends, relatives, people who suspected the parents—just as many as are interested now in calling the matter to police attention; only they'd be calling it to the attention of a defense agency, who would then publicize the incident, and all business houses, insurance companies, etc., would probably cease dealing with such parents."

L: "Perhaps—unless they could pay hush money. Today a mistreated child becomes a 'ward of the state' when the parents have violated the child's rights, the government undertakes to protect those rights against the violating parents; but what would happen to the child when there is no government?"

N: "There would be charitable foundations, probably much better endowed than ours are now because of the heavy taxes we have to pay out of our earnings. There would be people trained in child care who would usually find the child a good home. And they would receive their pay from the charitable foundation, out of funds voluntarily given to support it."

L: "But who would make sure that parents could not recapture the children they were mistreating, so as to mistreat them again? Who would have the authority to do this?"

N: "Any individual or agency, perhaps the one that witnessed the mistreatment in the first place."

L: "What would it be worth to them to do it? What would motivate them to do it at all?"

N: "Their moral indignation against cruelty, plus the reputation and good name they would receive from performing such deeds, as a byproduct of their regular profit-making activities. And perhaps the fact that more people would become paid members of such agencies."

L: "They might—and then again they might not. I suspect that if not going in for these byproducts resulted in cheaper rates for members, people would take the cheaper rates. Cheaper rates for the same product or service in an economic situation are just fine, and the lowest-price and highest-quality service should win in the open market. But not all goods are economic goods; and here we are dealing not with economic goods but with justice. And the best chance for justice, it seems to me, is under a rule of law. Cruelty to children by parents should be *illegal*—and of course nothing can be illegal when there is no law."

4. *L:* "Here is a very troublesome objection that was ready to surface in my previous objection: Since there is no government, there is no law. What *criteria,* then, would a defense agency use in picking up suspects? And by what *rules* and *procedures* would arbitration agencies adjudicate a case?"

N: "In order to get new members and tell them in advance

just what they were getting, an arbitration agency would find it to its own interest to state its rules and procedures in writing, in advance. These rules would be very explicit, and they would probably be very much like our present 'law of the land,' except of course that they would deal with matters of aggression only and not concern themselves as the law now does, with voluntary relations among individuals."

L: "I don't know how you would insure that they would deal only with that. Why would they *have* to limit themselves to such things? Suppose there were lots of people who were sufficiently incensed against pornography to get together and pay a defense agency to 'protect them against the pornographers.' They could surely find a defense agency that would accept money to do this; since this was their wish, and they'd be paying the agency to have their wish carried out, the agency would surely say yes and do it. They would hire the defense agency not only to protect their lives but to protect them against pornography of all kinds, or whatever constituted pornography according to their definition. The defense agency, following its members' instructions, would raid the pornographic bookstores, smash the windows, and burn all the books and magazines."

N: "If they did that, the store-owners would sue for damages, and win."

L: "There would be no courts to sue in; the owners, if they didn't take out after the anti-pornographers themselves (there'd be no law to stop them if they did), would go to their arbitration agencies. And the store-owners would probably win in *their* 'courts'—the arbitration agencies *they* belonged to—but not in the arbitration agencies of their opponents. Each group of course could contact its defense agency (which has the guns) to back up the decision of its own arbitration board, and then it would be a war of one defense agency against another. Which side won would depend on whether the pornographers or the anti-pornographers were the more numerous. Without a single 'rule of law,' we revert to a Hobbesian 'state of nature.' "

N: "But it wouldn't be to the interest of either group to go to war over the issue."

L: "That would depend on how strongly each group felt about pornography. The point is that there is *no one* agency, no highest court of the land, to decide the matter once and for all. When there is, its decision may not always be right, but it *is* the final decision and when the Supreme Court makes it, that's the end of the matter. But in your decentralized, no-government society, there is no such thing as the highest *court* in the land, just as there is no such thing as the *law* of the land: there's just different rules of different defense and arbitration agencies, with disputants sometimes able and sometimes unable to agree on a 'higher' agency to resolve the case. And if one party chose not to use an arbitration agency, or not to abide by its decision if it did use one, there would be no law of the land to make him do so, or to prevent him or his group from taking matters into their own hands, either themselves or through their defense agencies."

N: "But you forget that it wouldn't be to their interest to do so: a man who refused to accept the decision of the arbitration agency he'd agreed to, would be boycotted in all his dealings with others thereafter; and he would lose his most valuable asset in human relations, his good name."

L: "Perhaps, and perhaps not. A business firm has to preserve its good name to some extent if it wants to continue having lots of customers; but an individual can often get along quite well without it; for money, lots of people and organizations will deal with him gladly and close their eyes to his ethics while having their palms greased. Besides, he might not even lose his good name: if the society were primarily anti-porno-graphic, he wouldn't lose his good name by raiding the shops and burning the books—he might even lose his good name if he didn't! It would all depend on which was the prevailing sentiment in the society. Take another example: I write a book, and after it's published you decide to pirate it and sell the copies yourself, pocketing the income. Suppose you even change some of its contents to suit your tastes while keeping my name on the title page. Now since there is no law of the land, there is no copyright law to protect me as the author. I go to my defense agency, which I've chosen to belong to be-cause it does believe in copyright protection, and tell the men in the agency to go apprehend the culprit (and punish him—by what law?). They locate the man who's pirating my work, and he says, 'You don't have the right to apprehend me. I don't believe in copyright protection, and I belong to a de-fense agency that doesn't either.' Now where do we go from there? We have two different defense agencies with two in-compatible positions on the matter. So do we say: Here ends the argument and begins the fight? You see, there isn't any *one* law or any *final* court to decide the matter: there is the ar-bitration agency you belong to, which doesn't respect copy-right, and the agency I belong to, which does. Now—you take it up from there! If I feel strongly enough about the matter, I'll fight rather than let you get away with your piracy. I don't ac-cept the jurisdiction of your 'court' and you don't accept the jurisdiction of mine, so we're at an impasse. What alternative is left, under anarchy, but the use of force against each other, either ourselves or via our defense agencies? If *my* arbitration agency says that the boundary between your yard and mine is ten feet from my house and your arbitration agency says no, it's only five feet from my house (or that the house isn't even mine), what happens next? It's to our interest to work it out, you say; perhaps it is; but suppose we don't, or that it's to our interest but we don't see it. Since there's no court whose verdict we have to accept, isn't that where the fight begins—or could very easily begin? You see, even with arbitration agencies, it's not so far from the Wild West after all. Since the arbitration agencies aren't compulsory, and have no binding jurisdiction over non-members (or even members if they choose to ignore it, or cancel their membership), in case of disagreements which the disputants feel strongly about, the anarchic Wild West situation is always on the verge of breaking out. And I don't see why it wouldn't break out—quite often. Your no-government society is always trembling on the verge of chaos."

5. *L:* "I'm worried about the debtors' prisons and other places of detention in which aggressors would be kept to work off their debt to the aggrieved parties: you seem quite confident that they wouldn't abuse prisoners, but I don't see why. Both courts and prisons are supposed to dispense *just* treatment—but in the laissez-faire society (assuming that it *would* work out that way, which is a large assumption) I see no reason why this treatment would turn out to be just. As for the courts, it seems to me that they would be inclined to render the *most popular* verdicts—that is, those that would gain the arbitration agency the most paid members—and the most popular decisions aren't necessarily the most just ones. What would make their decisions just, as opposed to simply popular, if their incomes increased in proportion to their paid membership? If it was popular with the white majority to lynch black prisoners, what would prevent arbitration agencies from approving this?

"As for the prisons, wouldn't the prison officials want to cut costs so they could gain more profit from running the prison? True, if they let the prisoner die of malnutrition, or even gave him grossly substandard rations, he wouldn't be able to work as hard or at all, and then he could never pay off his debt; but still they could make conditions pretty grim while yet enabling him to work (as in some of the Southern chain gangs). What would prevent this? I can easily see how, in economic activities, profit should rule, and the most profits would and should go to the soap-manufacturer who sells the most soap; but it doesn't follow that the most income should go to the arbitration agency that renders the most popular decisions, or that a prison should be run for profit at all. That's the difference between economic activities and those having to do with justice.

"Besides, how would a prisoner who has been abused by an inmate or a jailor find the money to sue through arbitration? For that matter, how could he ever get *to* the arbitration agency to make his grievances known? And why should the arbitration agency care about his condition? Would they care enough to run a careful investigation, which would probably cost them more money than they could ever get out of him?

"And as for losing their good name if they didn't, I consider this most improbable. Most people don't really care that much what goes on in prisons. As between Defense Agency A which charges customers less but underfeeds or abuses its prisoners, and Agency B which treats them well but charges its customers more, most people would probably select Agency A.

"Besides, what about people who refused to work—who preferred continued incarceration to work? What could the prison get out of them? Or would they use the whip to make them work? And what of people who are unable to work? Or the old and infirm? Who would pay the expenses of such people in a prison run for profit? Or would such people just be let go? And what of the criminally insane? Who would keep them, and for what reason? Or would they just be free to roam the streets as they liked, since no one could make a profit out of their labor?"

6. *L:* "A man or organization contracts with a defense agency to protect him; and for this purpose of course the defense agency must possess arms. (The individual, of course, may also possess arms if he wants to.) But now suppose the defense agency, which has most of the arms in a given region, becomes very powerful and gets the physical force to rob him of all he has? That's easier than offering him services, isn't it?"

N: "But there are other defense agencies. They would gang up on such an aggressor, and the aggressor could never again get insurance, since he'd be too much of a bad risk. It just wouldn't be worth his while to try."

L: "Yes, there are other agencies—but they might get the idea and do the same thing as the first agency. Not only that: they might band together and form a huge merger, and expand their geographical limits until the entire geographic area is protected by just one big agency, with the people having no recourse but to do their business with that agency. Thus the element of competition is now gone, together with the motivation for efficiency. Worst of all, our huge merged agency now has a virtual monopoly of arms, and can gang up on the individuals in the entire area—they would be defenseless against it. The agency doesn't *need* to offer a service now—it can get what it wants for nothing via robbery. And what is to stop the defense and insurance companies from joining in collusion and returning to a state of government (a plundering government), since they have the guns? They could literally take over the entire area in which they operate, and perhaps conquer other areas as well. In short, it would be like wars waged by governments all over again!"

N: "I suppose I have to admit this is a possibility—but I doubt if it could get very far, considering how many individuals would retain arms of their own, and would join forces once they got the drift of what was happening. Anyway, a take-over of the United States or any other government is a real possibility *now*: if the army doesn't like the government policies, the army can always stage a coup and take over. In fact this is a stronger possibility—with governments holding a legalized monopoly of force—than the possibility you describe of all the competitive agencies merging into one and taking over. Both are possibilities, but the chances with a government are worse."

L: "*Any* group that owns lots of guns is dangerous—granted. But in a proper government, with the civilian traditionally in control of the military, there is surely much less danger than there is when there is no final legal authority, with the consequent possibility of different agencies (and individuals) breaking out into civil war whenever there's a major disagreement in which the disputants don't accept the jurisdiction of the agency that returns the verdict, or choose to ignore it."

No-Government Society and War

If the entire world consisted of no-government (laissez-faire) societies, or were one no-government society (which would be the same thing), there would be no nations to make war on one another. But the problem facing us in the foreseeable future, if a no-government society came into existence, would be that of such a society facing the armed hostility of armed governments. If the territory now occupied by the United States became "decentralized" into a no-government society, what would happen in the event of aggression, or even nuclear attack, from a foreign nation?

One thing to remember at the outset is that economic freedom brings tremendous economic strength—more than we can easily imagine.

Because of its economic strength, a laissez-faire society would exercise a profound effect on the nations of the world even though it would have no government to formulate and carry out a foreign policy. First, the existence of a free area would cause the rest of the world to experience a brain drain of such tremendous proportions as to make the brain drain which currently worries the British look laughable by comparison. As the economy of the laissez-faire society expended almost explosively in response to freedom, it would be able to offer such men more—in terms of money, ideal working conditions, opportunity to associate with other men of ability, and (most important) freedom—than would any governmentally controlled society. Producers in every nation would want to move to the laissez-faire society. Many might decide to move not only themselves but their entire businesses to the free area. They would see that, by escaping taxation and regulation, they could make greater profits even if they had to pay additional shipping costs and higher wages. Such an influx of business would cause a high demand for competent labor in the free area, which would raise wages. It would also tend to make the nations which lost producers and businesses economically dependent on the laissez-faire society for necessary goods and services and, therefore, reluctant to attack it.

Governments wouldn't be able to offer the men of ability in their countries enough to keep them from flocking by the thousands to the exciting opportunities in the laissez-faire society. If they wanted to hold such men, the governments would have to hold them by force, as the iron curtain countries do now, and the experience of these iron curtain countries has shown that men of ability do not function well under constraint. A brain drain of this magnitude would constitute a crippling hemophilia for the nations of the world, and the only response the governments could make to it would be to institute restrictive measures—a move toward tyranny which would also be crippling—or to disband (which is unlikely, considering the nature of politics).

But a brain drain is not the only hemophilia which the governments of the world would experience as their citizens became aware of the opportunities in the free area—there would also be a capital drain. Investors always try to place their capital in areas of maximum profit and minimum risk (that is, minimum future uncertainty), and one of the greatest sources of future uncertainty is the power of bureaucrats to issue directives and regulations on any whim. This means that business in a laissez-faire society would be tops on the list of attractive investments for investors all over the world. Like the brain drain, the capital drain would strengthen the free area at the expense of the nations; and again, the only response their governments could make would be further restrictive legislation—which would further weaken their economies—or to disband.[18]

Nor is this the end. Most governments sustain their endless programs by inflationary policies, a practice which always weakens the value of their currencies. But in a laissez-faire society, with private minting of money and paper money trusted only to the extent that it was backed by more than paper, there could be no such inflation: inflated currencies would be driven off a free market by sound currencies. The effect on the holders of capital is obvious: they would invest in the area where the currency was sound. There would be a severe financial crisis in the nations of the world. "Thus, a government would have to choose between maintaining a sound currency (necessitating a strict limitation of government functions) or attempting to hedge its currency about with a wall of restrictive legislation which would paralyze its economy and, at best, would do little more than postpone its collapse."[19] Without the use of coercion against them, without firing a shot, the nations of the world would have to amend their policies or face internal collapse. The mere *existence* of a laissez-faire society would have this effect, without the use of force or arms. (In a limited government that was really limited, the effect on unfree nations would be much the same.)

Keeping this background in mind, let us see what might happen in the case of foreign aggression against the laissez-faire society. What might happen to it when confronted by the armed nuclear might of a nation like the Soviet Union?

"Totalitarian governments, in spite of their outward appearance of unconquerably massive solidarity, are inwardly rotten with ineptitude, waste. corruption, fear, and unbeliev-able mismanagement."[20] In addition, free men will produce ideas as enslaved men will not, and free men have enormous values to protect which slaves do not have. All these factors operate in favor of the strength of the free society. Still, isn't it possible that a nuclear power could attack the United States (or the territory which formerly comprised this nation)? and wouldn't it be likely to do so once it was clear that there was no *nation* to retaliate?

Surely it is possible; but let us see how the laissez-faire soci-ety would be defended. Defense of a laissez-faire society would be undertaken by defense companies, in conjunction with insurance companies.

Competition between the defense companies . . . would foster the development of the most powerful and efficient defense system ra-tionally warranted. Technological innovations which are at present un-foreseeable would constantly upgrade its safety and effectiveness. No governmental system, with its miles of red tape and built-in politicking, pork barrelling, wirepulling, and power-grabbing could even remotely approximate the potency and efficiency naturally generated by the free-market forces (which are always moving to meet demand).[21]

The main cost of such defense would be borne by business and industry, which have the most to lose from attack. But to keep going they would have to pass much of the cost of this to the consuming population in the form of increased prices for the duration of the crisis. This would make it impossible for "freeloaders" to get along without paying for their own de-fense, and spread the cost of defense among the entire con-suming population. And, as indicated earlier (p. 412 ff.), a society of businessmen and traders would not want to increase aggression—they stand to lose too much by having their prop-erty bombed, not to mention themselves and their families.

How much would each person contribute to the common defense? He would have to pay higher prices for products

bought, for the reason already given; and he would not have
to be a soldier, since there would be no draft, but only an efficient group of defenders hired by the defense agencies and insurance companies. But

... such a defense network would not obligate any individual to
contribute money or effort to any defensive action in which his values
were not threatened. Under the present governmental system of collectivistic defense within arbitrary boundaries, a Californian would be
forced to sacrifice his values and possibly his life in order to defend
the State of Maine, even though he had no interest at all in the matter.
At the same time, a man a few miles away in Quebec, because he was
on the other side of a particular river, would have to sit idly by unless
his own government decided to take some action. This is because governmental defense, like any other governmental action, is and must be
collectivistic in nature. With a free-market defense system, each man
acts to defend his own values to the extent he wishes to have them
defended, regardless of what piece of real estate he happens to be occupying. No man is forced to sacrifice for the defense of the collective
system of a coercive gang called government.[22]

Another point worth noting is that there would be no national government that could capitulate:

A free-market defense system would also make it very difficult for
an attacker to obtain a surrender. Just as a laissez-faire society would
have no government to start a war, it would have no government to capitulate. The defenders would fight as long, and only as long, as they
believed was in their self-interest. Even the insurance companies and defense agencies couldn't negotiate a surrender, because their agreements
could bind no one but the persons who actually signed them. It is interesting to speculate on what an aggressive foreign nation would do if
confronted with such a situation.[23]

It is true, of course, that armed governments do constitute a
threat. The longer a truly free sector of the world existed, the
more of a drain of ability there would be from the other sectors
to it, and the more strength the economy of the free sector
would have with every passing year—so much that even an expensive series of defense organizations with retaliatory weap-

ons could be afforded without great loss of prosperity. And without assistance from and trade with the free sector, it is questionable how long the totalitarian or semi-totalitarian regimes could last. It would be the early period that would be the most hazardous.

It is true that the missiles, the deadly chemicals, and the plagues of modern warfare constitute a very real threat. But these implements of mass destruction were ordered to be constructed by governments, and these same governments are continually bringing new and more deadly weapons into existence. To say that we must have a government to protect us as long as these products of government are around is like saying that a man should keep his cancerous tumor until sometime in the future when he gets better, because it would be too dangerous to remove it now![24]

The limited-government libertarian would agree with virtually all of the above, except the recommendation of the complete abolition of governments. He would say that a national government which kept its hands off the economy and was free of inflation and committed no aggression against its own citizens would be so strong, so free, so much an object of envy to the citizens of other nations of the world, that the same effects described above in connection with the laissez-faire society would occur with a limited government also.

One claim of the no-government libertarian, however, is that *"limited" governments never remain limited*. Once a monopoly of physical force exists, the powers become wider and wider, until, like the government of the United States, which was comparatively limited at its beginning (though not limited enough, even then), a government ends up interfering in every aspect of the citizen's life, and charging every citizen confiscatory taxes for this privilege. In the light of the historical record, this charge is very difficult to rebut.

If a limited government is to remain limited, there would seem to be no way to keep it that way other than through the diligence of every citizen in guarding such a priceless treasure: "Constant vigilance is the price of freedom." And that diligence could occur and continue through time only through the *education* of citizens in the inestimable advantages in keeping the government limited—so much that they would unfailingly resist every temptation to pass a law by which they could get something out of government at someone else's expense. It is obvious that the American citizen has no such education now: on the contrary, he is told on all sides that he needs government to help and protect him against profiteers, that the government should own lands and license professions and supervise the schools, that charity requires that many millions of the population be supported on welfare, and so on without end.

If either the limited-government or the no-government ideal were to be realized, both types of libertarians would be relatively satisfied: the points of agreement between them are so much greater than the points of difference that they would be more content with one another's company than with that of any other group. And it surely seems that the possibility of government in the United States becoming limited, small though it is, is still greater than that of its ceasing to exist entirely.[25]

From Here to Libertarianism

Whether the libertarian in question advocates a limited government or no government at all, there is a tremendous stretch of distance between this ideal and our present situation. And how do we get from here to there? The trend toward statism increases with every year that passes. Can it be reversed at all? Can it be reversed enough to take us even so far as a limited government?

It is possible that in the next few decades a few well-placed missiles from Russian or Chinese submarines may devastate a few dozen American cities. In that event totalitarianism (statism), which is always accelerated by war, will probably win the day and be tolerated by the majority of people in the name of survival.

More probably, there will be an economic crisis of major proportions in the United States, the result of the insane (if this is not too mild a word) economic policies of the past generation. If this happens, calls for massive federal expenditure will again be heard, depression and perhaps hunger will stalk the land, and government will once again be called upon to rectify a condition which government brought on in the first place. If this happens, fascism in America will be so well solidified, and the government so omnipotent in the lives of citizens, as to preclude any real chance that the trend can be reversed in the foreseeable future.

But assuming that neither of these eventualities occurs, what measures can be taken now to make possible the realization of the libertarian idea, with its severe limitations on the powers of government (or, the no-government advocates would say, the abolition of government)?

Some have said that *revolution*, armed revolution, is the only way to effect the change. But this is not a means that a libertarian could advocate. First, armed revolution would almost surely involve the destruction of life and property of many innocent people—innocent in the sense that they had committed aggression against no one. Second, the government is more thoroughly armed than any revolutionary group or combination of such groups is likely to be, and defeat would be extremely likely. Third, the more such destruction the revolutionists cause, the more the vast majority of the population who may have been indifferent before will align themselves on the side of the government to squelch the revolutionaries—not only their armed forces, but everything about them, including their ideas. The attempt would be self-defeating. Even with tiny revolutionary movements today, with just a bit of violence here and there, it is noticeable how strongly the public lines up in favor of "the forces of law and order," including many unjust repressive actions.

Suppose that one simply *refused to obey* the law—not the laws prohibiting aggressive activity against others, which are perfectly proper laws, but the vast multitude of other laws that are not: welfare laws, draft laws, tariffs, subsidies, and so on. Suppose one just refused to pay taxes that went for these things. The result is predictable: one would be fined and jailed for tax evasion; and similar punishments would result from refusing to register for the draft. The strong arm of the government would bring rebellion to an end. It would take *very large* numbers of dissenters for the result to be otherwise: if fifty million people refused to pay their income taxes, there would not be enough enforcement officials left (or the money to pay them) to round them all up and imprison them (prisons are overcrowded as it is). But there would first be a long bloody struggle, with many innocent people killed and wounded, much property confiscated and destroyed, and a great deal of suffering with uncertain outcome.

The only safe and sure way, a peaceful though not a quick one, is *education*—education in the need for restricting the powers of government. As the libertarian Albert Jay Nock wrote in 1928,

Inaction is better than wrong action or premature right action, and effective right action can only follow right thinking. "If a great change is to take place," said Edmund Burke, in his last words on the French Revolution, "the minds of men *will be fitted to it.*" Otherwise the thing does not turn out well; and the processes by which men's minds are fitted seem to me untraceable and imponderable, the only certainty about them being that the share of any one person, or any one movement, in determining them is extremely small. Various social superstitions, such as magic, the divine right of kings, the Calvinist theology, and so on, have stood out against many a vigorous frontal attack, and thrived on it; and when they finally disappeared, it was not under attack. People simply stopped thinking in those terms; no one knew just when or why, and no one even was much aware that they had stopped. So I think it very possible that while we are saying, "Lo, here!" and "Lo, there!" with our eye on this or that revolution, unsurpation, seizure of power, or what not, the superstitions that surround the State are quietly disappearing in the same way.

. . . Mr. Jefferson said that if a centralization of power were ever effected at Washington, the United States would have the most corrupt government on earth. Comparisons are difficult, but I believe it has one that is thoroughly corrupt, flagitious, tyrannical, oppressive. Yet if it were in my power to pull down its whole structure overnight and set up another of my own devising—to abolish the State out of hand, and replace it by an organization of the economic means—I would not do it, for the minds of Americans are far from fitted to any such great change as this, and the effect would be only to lay open the way for the worse enormities of usurpation—possibly, who knows? with myself as the usurper! After the French Revolution, Napoleon![26]

It may be that the climate of the 1970s is different in this respect from that of the 1920s. There is much less of a detached sheeplike attitude toward government, particularly among the young. Many of the younger generation are so skeptical of the word of government, all government, that they will refuse to believe even the most "factual" items presented on a television news report, as long as it has its source in government. Unfortunately, the conclusion many of them draw is that "one government is as bad as another," specifically, the governments of Communist China and Soviet Russia are no worse than that of the United States; and this may yet lead to such a strengthening of those governments in relation to ours that the residents of the United States may be subjected to a nuclear attack from one of those governments—after which statism will rule the ruins and it will be too late for any libertarian movements to be permitted to flourish in the United States.

But if the facts can be sorted out and communicated to enough people, that the United States government is not as tyrannical as most others, but that *no* government that initiates force against its citizens deserves our wholehearted allegiance, then perhaps the next decades will be witness to a new concept in political philosophy whose time has come.

Notes

Chapter 1

1. See Friedrich von Hayek, *The Constitution of Liberty* (Chicago: University of Chicago Press, 1960), Chapter 1.
2. Ayn Rand, *Atlas Shrugged* (New York: Random House Inc., 1957), p. 1024. (All page-references are to the clothbound edition.)
3. Henry Hazlitt, *Time Will Run Back,* pp. 83–85. (Originally published by Appleton-Century-Crofts, 1952, under the title *The Great Idea.* Published in Great Britain as *Time Will Run Back,* and also reprinted under this title by Arlington House Inc., New Rochelle, N.Y. Page references are to the British edition.)
4. John Stuart Mill, *On Liberty* (first published in 1859), Chapter 1.
5. See Ayn Rand, "Man's Rights," in *The Virtue of Selfishness* (New York: New American Library, Inc., 1964), pp. 97–99.
6. See, for example, G. Warren Nutter, *The Strange World of Ivan Ivanov* (Cleveland: World Publishing Co., 1969), from which some of the following data are taken.
7. David Dallin, *Forced Labor in Soviet Russia* (New Haven, Conn.: Yale University Press, 1948 and succeeding editions).
8. See von Hayek, *op. cit.,* Chapter 5.
9. Herbert Spencer, *The Man Versus the State,* pp. 181, 182. (First printed 1884. Reprinted by Caxton Printers, Ltd., Caldwell, Idaho, 1940.)

10. *Ibid.*, pp. 183–84.

11. Spencer, "Railway Morals and Railway Policy," *Edinburgh Review*, October 1854.

Chapter 2

1. Herbert Spencer, *Social Statics*, p. 69. (First published in 1851. Reprinted by The Robert Schalkenbach Foundation, New York, 1970.)

2. *Ibid.*, p. 95. There are certain ambiguities and redundancies in Spencer's formulation, which are pointed out in Murray Rothbard, *Power and Market*, pp. 159–60 (Menlo Park, Calif.: Institute for Humane Studies, 1970).

3. H. L. A. Hart, "Are There Any Natural Rights?" in *Human Rights*, ed. A. I. Melden (Belmont, Calif.: Wadsworth Publishing Co., Inc., 1970).

4. Murray Rothbard, *Power and Market* (Menlo Park, Calif.: Institute for Humane Studies, 1970), p. 180.

5. Ayn Rand, "The Objectivist Ethics," in *The Virtue of Selfishness* (New York: New American Library, Inc., 1964), p. 24. In the formulation of the philosophy of libertarianism, I am more indebted to the works of Ayn Rand than to those of any other writer.

6. Rand, *Atlas Shrugged* (New York: Random House Inc., 1957), p. 1023.

7. Jarrett Wollstein, "Economic Freedom and Monopoly Power," *The Individualist* 2, nos. 3 and 4 (March-April 1970): 8.

8. Herbert Spencer, *The Man Versus the State*, p. *191*. (First printed 1884. Reprinted by Caxton Printers, Ltd., Caldwell, Idaho, 1940.)

9. *Ibid.*, pp. 195–96. Italics mine.

10. *Ibid.*, p. 203.

11. Nathaniel Branden, *Who Is Ayn Rand?* (New York: Random House, Inc., 1962), p. 47.

12. For a precise and detailed discussion of the issue of rights see Rand, "Man's Rights," in *The Virtue of Selfishness*, pp. 92–100.

13. Rothbard, "The Great Ecology Issue: Conservation and the Free Market," *The Individualist* 2, no. 2 (February 1970): 5.

14. See Branden, "Inherited Wealth," in Ayn Rand, *Capitalism: the Unknown Ideal* (New York: New American Library, Inc., 1967), pp. 92–94.

15. See Rand, "Patents and Copyrights," in *Capitalism: the Unknown Ideal*, pp. 130–34.

16. See Rand, "The Property Status of Airwaves," in *Capitalism: the Unknown Ideal*, pp. 122–29.

17. See Rand, *The Virtue of Selfishness*, pp. vii–viii. See also Branden, "Rational Egoism," *The Personalist* 51 (spring 1970): 196–211.

18. Rand, *The Virtue of Selfishness*, p. 96.

19. *Ibid.*, p. 97.

20. Rand, "Collectivized Ethics," in *The Virtue of Selfishness*, pp. 84–85.

21. William W. Bayes, "What Is Property?" *The Freeman*, July 1970, p. 398. Italics mine.

22. For a detailed discussion of his point, see Isabel Paterson, *The God of the Machine* (New York: G. P. Putnam's Sons, 1943. Reprinted by Caxton Printers, Ltd., Caldwell, Idaho, 1964), Chapter 17.

23. Rand, "Racism," in *The Virtue of Selfishness*, pp. 126–67.

24. *Ibid.*, p. 127.

25. *Ibid.*, p. 133.

26. Rand, "What Is Capitalism?" in *Capitalism: the Unknown Ideal*, p. 30.

27. Rand, "Collectivized Ethics," in *The Virtue of Selfishness*, p. 83. See also: *The Fateful Turn from Individualism to Collectivism, 1880–1960* by Clarence B. Carson. (Irvington-on-Hudson, N.Y.: Foundation for Economic Education, 1963.)

28. Friedrich von Hayek, *The Road to Serfdom* (Chicago: University of Chicago Press, 1944), p. 149.

29. Robert Payne, *The Life and Death of Lenin* (New York: Simon and Schuster, Inc., 1964), p. 631.

30. Rand, "Collectivized Ethics," in *The Virtue of Selfishness*, p. 84.

Chapter 3

1. Henry G. Weaver, *The Mainspring of Human Progress* (Irvington-on-Hudson, N. Y.: Foundation for Economic Education, 1947), p. 11–12.

2. Henry Hazlitt, *Economics in One Lesson* (New York: Harper and Row, Publishers, 1946), p. 44.

3. See Friedrich von Hayek (ed.), *Capitalism and the Historians* (Chicago: University of Chicago Press, 1954), p. 44.

4. Clarence B. Carson, *The War on the Poor* (New Rochelle, N.Y.: Arlington House, Inc., 1969), p. 226.

5. Hazlitt, *Economics in One Lesson*, pp. 111–112.

6. Leonard Read, in *Clichés of Socialism* (Irvington-on-Hudson, N. Y.: Foundation for Economic Education, 1970), pp. 165–66.

7. Milton Friedman, column in *Newsweek*, September 29, 1969, p. 94.

8. Rothboard, *Power and Market* (Menlo Park, Calif.: Institute for Humane Studies, 1970), p. 176.

9. *Ibid.*, p. 168.

10. *Ibid.*

Chapter 4

1. Frederic Bastiat, *Selected Essays on Political Economy* (Princeton, N. J.: D. Van Nostrand Co., 1964), p. 2.

2. *Ibid.*, pp. 2–4.

3. *Ibid.*, pp. 5–7.

4. *Ibid.*, pp. 7–8, 9.

5. *Ibid.*, pp. 16–17.

6. *Ibid.*, pp. 32–34.

7. *Ibid.*, p. 40.

8. John C. Sparks, in *Clichés of Socialism* (Irvington-on-Hudson, N. Y.: Foundation for Economic Education, 1970), pp. 180–81.

9. See Milton Friedman, "Myths That Keep People Hungry," *Harpers Magazine*, July 1967.

10. See Henry Hazlitt, *Economics in One Lesson* (New York: Harper and Row, Publishers, 1946). Each chapter deals with a different kind of government interference in the economy, including many for which space does not permit treatment here.

11. Ludwig von Mises, *Socialism* (New Haven, Conn.: Yale University Press, 1951), pp. 533–34.

12. Hazlitt, *Man Versus the Welfare State* (New Rochelle, N.Y.: Arlington House, Inc., 1968), p. 102.

13. *Ibid.*, p. 25.

14. These three quotations are taken from a news release from the National Federation of Independent Business, August 14, 1967, p. 15. They are reprinted in Clarence B. Carson, *The War on the Poor* (New Rochelle, N. Y.: Arlington House, Inc., 1969), pp. 152–53.

15. Friedman, column in *Newsweek*, July 27, 1970, p. 60.

16. Bastiat, *op. cit.*, p. 37.

17. Hazlitt, *Economics in One Lesson*, pp. 35–36 and pp. 37–38.

18. Abraham Ellis, *The Social Security Fraud*, p. 159. Also pp.

70–1, 199–200 and *passim.* (New Rochelle, N.Y.: Arlington House, 1971.)

19. See Hazlitt, *Economics in One Lesson,* Chapter 11.

20. Clarence B. Carson, *The War on the Poor* (New Rochelle, N. Y.: Arlington House, Inc., 1969), p. 87.

21. *Ibid.,* pp. 88–89.

22. Hazlitt, *Economics in One Lesson,* pp. 41–42.

23. *Ibid.,* p. 49.

24. See Jarrett Wollstein, "Economic Freedom and Monopoly Power," *The Individualist* 2, nos. 3 and 4 (March-April 1970): 7–18.

25. Robert Masters, "An Alternative Concept of Competition," *The IREC Review* 2, no. 5: 4–5.

26. Armen Alchian and William Allen, *University Economics* (Belmont, Calif.: Wadsworth Publishing Co., Inc., 1964), pp. 320–22.

27. John Chamberlain, *The Enterprising Americans* (New York: Harper and Row, Publishers, 1961), p. 149.

28. *Ibid.,* p. 151.

29. John S. McGee, "Predatory Price-Cutting: the Standard Oil (N. J.) Case," *The Journal of Law and Economics* 1 (October 1958): 137–169.

30. Alchian and Allen, *op. cit.,* p. 320.

31. Chamberlain, *op. cit.,* p. 147.

32. Carl Snyder, *Capitalism the Creator* (New York: Macmillan Company, 1940), p. 250.

33. The above points are all made in Jarrett Wollstein's articles, "The Myth of Monopoly Power," *The Individualist* 2, no. 2 (February 1970): 13, 19; and "Market Limitations on Monopoly Power," *The Individualist* 2, no. 5 (May 1970): 18–25.

34. Carson, *op. cit.,* p. 137.

35. Patrick Boarman, *Union Monopolies and Antitrust Restraints* (Washington, D. C.. Labor Policy Association). pp. 162–63.

36. Carson, *op. cit.,* pp. 150–41.

37. *Ibid.,* p. 151.

38. *Ibid.,* p. 150.

39. Hazlitt, "Nobody Wins at Leapfrog," *National Review,* January 26, 1971, p. 83.

40. See Dick West, "In Defense of the Drug Industry," *Human Events,* November 28, 1970, p. 936.

41. West, "The Doctor Will Give You Six Minutes," *Human Events,* April 3, 1971, p. 289.

42. Ayn Rand, *Atlas Shrugged* (New York: Random House Inc., 1957), p. 744. See also Matthew Lynch and Stanley Rathael, *Medicine and the State* (Springfield, Ill.: Charles C. Thomas, Publisher, 1963).

43. Carson, *op. cit.*, pp. 176–77.

44. *Ibid.*, pp. 179–80.

45. Cornelius P. Cotter, *Government and Private Enterprise,* (New York: Holt, Rinehart and Winston, Inc., 1960), pp. 295–96.

46. Carson, *op. cit.*, p. 185.

47. Rand, "America's Persecuted Minority: Big Business," in *Capitalism: the Unknown Ideal* (New York: New American Library, Inc., 1967) p. 49.

48. Alan Greenspan, "Anti-Trust," in Rand, *Capitalism: the Unknown Ideal*, p. 66.

49. *Ibid.*

50. A. D. Neale, *The Anti-Trust Laws of the U. S. A.* (Cambrige: (Cambridge University Press, 1960), p. 114.

51. Rand, *Capitalism: the Unknown Ideal*, p. 114.

52. On inflation, see, for example, Hazlitt, *Economics in One Lesson,* Chapter 22, and *What You Can Do About Inflation* (Princeton, N. J.: D. Van Nostrand Co., 1960); also Murray N. Rothbard, *Man, Economy, and State* (Princeton, N. J.: D. Van Nostrand Co., Inc., 1962; new edition by Nash Publishing Co. in press), *passim.*

53. Morris and Linda Tannehill, *The Market for Liberty* (Privately printed; available from Morriss Tannehill, Box 1383, Lansing, Mich.), 6. 22.

54. Rothbard, *Power and Market* (Menlo Park, Calif.: Institute for Humane Studies, 1970), p. 195.

Chapter 5

1. *U.S. News and World Report,* March 5, 1962, pp. 60–61.

2. Ludwig von Mises, *Planning for Freedom* (South Holland, Ill.: Libertarian Press, 1952), p. 121.

3. *Ibid.*, pp. 122,123.

4. Dean Russell in *Clichés of Socialism* (Irvington-on-Hudson, N. Y.: Foundation for Economic Education, 1970), p. 186.

5. This is not to say that he earned all he did on the open market. He has undoubted entrepreneurial abilities, but many of his opportunities were opened to him by means of political pull.

6. As quoted by John T. Flynn, *The Road Ahead* (New York: Devin-Adair Co., 1955), p. 36.

7. *Ibid.*, p. 49.

8. *Ibid.*, p. 41.

9. Percy L. Greaves, "How Wages Are Determined," *The Freeman*, July 1970, p. 423.

10. *Ibid.*, p. 424.

11. Carl Snyder, *Capitalism the Creator* (New York: Macmillan Co., 1940), p. 172.

12. *Ibid.*, p. 171.

13. Greaves, *op. cit.*, p. 425

14. Friedrich von Hayek, *Capitalism and the Historians* (Chicago: University of Chicago Press, 1954), pp. 15–17.

15. Murray Rothbard, *Power and Market* (Menlo Park, Calif.: Institute for Humane Studies, 1970), p. 169.

16. *Ibid.*, pp. 170–71.

17. Albert Jay Nock, *Anarchist's Progress.* Quoted in William F. Buckley, Jr. (ed.), *Did You Ever See a Dream Walking? American Conservative Thought in the Twentieth Century* (Indianapolis: Bobbs-Merrill Co., Inc., 1970), p. 138.

18. Ayn Rand, *Atlas Shrugged* (New York: Random House Inc., 1957), pp. 1048–49, 1064–65.

Chapter 6

1. Henry Hazlitt, *Time Will Run Back*, p. 95. (Originally published by Appleton-Century-Crofts, 1952, under the title *The Great Idea*. Published in Great Britain as *Time Will Run Back*, and also reprinted under this title by Arlington House, New Rochelle, N. Y. Page references are to the British edition.)

2. Harold Laski, *Democracy in Crisis*, p. 87 (Chapel Hill: University of North Carolina Press, 1933.)

3. Sidney and Beatrice Webb, *Soviet Communism: A New Capitalism?*, p. 1038. (New York: Scribners, 1936.)

4. Hazlitt, *Time Will Run Back*, p. 96.

5. Benpamin R. Rogge, "The Case for the Free Market," *The Freeman*, September 1963.

6. See Ludwig von Mises, *Socialism* (New Haven, Conn.: Yale University Press, 1951). This monumental work is probably the best and most through treatment of the consequences of socialism to be found anywhere.

7. *Hazlitt, Time Will Run Back*, pp. 86–90. Reprinted from *Time Will Also Run Back* by Henry Hazlitt, published by Arlington House and used with their permission. Copyright © 1951, 1966 by Henry Hazlitt.

8. Frederic Bastiat, "The Law," in *Selected Essays on Political*

Economy (Princeton, N. J.: D. Van Nostrand Co., Inc., 1964), p. 95.

9. Herbert Spencer, *Man Versus the State* (Caldwell, Idaho: Caxton Printers, Ltd., 1940), p. 122.

10. *Ibid.*, pp. 69–71.

11. *Ibid.*, pp. 41–43. Italics mine.

12. Carl Snyder, *Capitalism the Creator* (New York, Macmillan Co., 1940), p. 241.

13. Albert Jay Nock, *Anarchist's Progress.* Quoted in William F. Buckley, Jr. (ed.), *Did You Ever See a Dream Walking? American Conservative Thought in the Twentieth Century* (Indianapolis: Bobbs-Merrill Co., Inc., 1970), p. 140.

14. Isabel Paterson, *The God of the Machine* (New York: G. P. Putnam's Sons, 1943. Reprinted by Caxton Printers, Ltd.: Caldwell, Idaho, 1964,) pp. 253–54.

15. Von Mises, "The Elite Under Capitalism," *The Freeman* 12, no. 2 (January 1962): 8.

16. Murray Rothbard, *Power and Market* (Menlo Park, Calif.: Institute for Humane Studies, 1970), p. 172.

17. See Rothbard, *Power and Market.* pp. 172–73.

18. *Life* magazine, September 14, 1970, p. 64.

19. See Richard Grant's excellent book, *The Incredible Bread Machine.* (Privately printed, 1966.)

Chapter 7

1. James Madison in *The Federalist,* No. 83.

2. Letter from Thomas Jefferson to Albert Gallatin, 1817.

3. *U. S. News and World Report,* February 8, 1971, p. 30.

4. *Ibid.*, p. 32.

5. *Newsweek,* February 8, 1971, p. 22.

6. Quoted in *Human Events, January 30, 1971.*

7. Governor Ronald Reagan, in an interview printed in *U. S. News and World Report,* March 1, 1971, p. 39.

8. *Ibid.*, p. 40. (Also spoken by Governor Ronald Reagan.)

9. Shirley Scheibla, *Poverty Is Where the Money Is* (New Rochelle, N. Y.: Arlington House, Inc., 1968), p. 48. Reprinted from *Poverty Is Where the Money Is* by Shirley Scheibla, published by Arlington House and used with their permission. Copyright © 1968 by Arlington House, New Rochelle, New York.

10. *Ibid.*

11. *Ibid.*, p. 58.
12. *Ibid.*, p. 58.
13. *Ibid.*, pp. 58–59.
14. Ibid., pp. 59–60. Also quoted in *U. S. News and World Report,* May 16, 1966, p. 67.
15. Scheibla, *op. cit.*, p. 100.
16. *Ibid.*, p. 88.
17. *Ibid.*, p. 102.
18. *Ibid.*, pp. 103–104.
19. Clarence B. Carson, *The War on the Poor* (New Rochelle, N. Y.: Arlington House, Inc., 1969), pp. 270–71. Reprinted from *The War on the Poor* by Clarence B. Carson, published by Arlington House and used with their permission. Copyright © 1969 by Arlington House, New Rochelle, New York.
20. *Ibid.*, p. 280.
21. Henry Hazlitt, *Man Versus the Welfare State* (New Rochelle, N. Y.: Arlington House, Inc., 1968), p. 76. Reprinted from *Man vs. the Welfare State* by Henry Hazlitt, published by Arlington House and used with their permission. Copyright © 1969 by Arlington House, New Rochelle, New York.
22. Ayn Rand, *Atlas Shrugged* (New York: Random House, Inc., 1957), p. 1031.
23. See Hazlitt, *Man Versus the Welfare State,* Chapter 2.
24. John Stuart Mill, *Principles of Political Economy,* Book 1, Chapter 2.
25. Carl Snyder, *Capitalism the Creator* (New York: Macmillan Company, 1940), pp. 294–95. Italics mine.
26. For an excellent account of what government building programs have done to the people they were supposed to help, see Martin Anderson, *The Federal Bulldozer* (Cambridge, Mass.: M. I. T. Press, 1964).
27. Carson, *op. cit.*, p. 19.
28. *Ibid.*, p. 33.
29. *Ibid.*, p. 64.
30. Herbert Spencer, *Man Versus the State* (Caldwell, Idaho: Caxton Printers, Ltd., 1940), pp. 34-35, 37.
31. *Ibid.*, pp. 37–39.
32. *Ibid.*, p. 133.
33. *Ibid.*, pp. 116–17.
34. *Ibid.*, p. 123.
35. *Ibid.*, pp. 126–27.

36. Isabel Paterson, *The God of the Machine* (New York: G. P. Putnam's Sons, 1943. Reprinted by Caxton Printers, Ltd.; Caldwell, Idaho, 1964), pp. 255–57, 258–59.
37. Paul L. Poirot, in *Clichés of Socialism* (Irvington-on-Hudson, N.Y.: Foundation for Economic Education, 1970), p. 265.

Chapter 8

1. Herbert Spencer, *Man Versus the State* (Caldwell, Idaho: Caxton Printers, Ltd., 1940), pp. 15–16.
2. Alexis de Toqueville, *Democracy in American,* pp. 579–90 (ed. Henry Steele Commager, 1946).
3. Raymond Moley, in *Newsweek,* September 2, 1963, p. 84.
4. Isabel Paterson, *The God of the Machine* (New York: G. P. Putnam's Sons, 1943. Reprinted by Caxton Printers, Ltd., Caldwell, Idaho, 1964), pp. 38–40.
5. Richard Grant, *The Incredible Bread Machine* (Privately printed, 1966), pp. 25–27.
6. In the material in the preceding pages I have drawn on a series of taped lectures composed and delivered by Alan Greenspan. The analogy of government intervention with the electrical system in the fuse box is his.
7. Amoury de Riencourt, *The Coming Caesars* (New York: Coward-McCann, Inc., 1957), pp. 236–37.
8. John T. Flynn, *The Roosevelt Myth* (New York: Devin-Adair Co., 1956), pp. 428–29.
9. *Ibid.,* pp. 412-17.
10. *U. S. News and World Report,* January 6, 1969, p. 14.

Chapter 9

1. See "Can Free Enterprise Endure?" *Freedom,* October-November-December, 1968, pp. 9–10.
2. Jarrett Wollstein, *Public Services Under Laissez Faire* (Pamphlet published by the Society for Individual Liberty, 400 Bonifant Road, Silver Spring, Md. 20904), p. 7.
3. See Harold Hughes, "Public Utilities," *Encyclopedia Americana* XXII (1959).
4. Wollstein, *Public Services Under Laissez Faire,* pp. 30–31.
5. *Ibid.,* pp. 42–43.
6. *Ibid.,* p. 40.
7. Stan Lehr and Louis Rossetto, Jr., "The New Right Credo—Libertarianism," *The New York Times Magazine,* Sunday, January 10, 1971, p. 93. See also Clarence B. Carson, *Trottl-*

ing the Railroads. Irvington-on-Hudson, N. Y.: Foundation for Economic Education, 1971.

8. Murray Rothbard, *Power and Market* (Menlo Park, Calif.: Institute for Humane Studies, 1970), p. 34.

9. *Ibid.,* pp. 34–35.

10. Leonard A. Read, "A Conservationist Looks at Freedom," *The Freeman,* November 1970, pp. 670–71.

11. *Ibid.,* p. 669.

12. Rothbard, "The Great Ecology Issue: Conservation and the Free Market," *The Individualist,* February 1970, p. 3.

13. *Ibid.,* pp. 3–4.

14. *Ibid.,* p. 4.

15. Rothbard, *Power and Market,* p. 60.

16. *Ibid.*

17. David F. Nolan, "Free Market Education: a Radical Proposal," *The Rational Individualist* 2, no. 1 (January 1970): 15.

18. *Ibid.,* p. 16.

19. *Ibid.,* p. 17.

20. Wollstein, *Public Services Under Laissez Faire,* p. 13.

21. Ayn Rand, "Government Financing in a Free Society," in *The Virtue of Selfishness* (New York; New American Library, Inc., 1964), p. 118.

22. David Walter, "Taxation Is Theft" (pamphlet issued by the Society for Individual Liberty, Silver Springs, Md.).

Chapter 10

1. David Dallin, *Forced Labor in Soviet Russia* (New Haven, Conn.: Yale University Press, 1948), pp. 128–29.

2. Werner Keller, *East Minus West Equals Zero* (New York: G. P. Putnam's Sons, 1962).

3. George N. Crocker, *Roosevelt's Road to Russia* (Chicago: Henry Regnery Co., 1959).

4. Anthony Kubek, *How the Far East Was Lost* (Chicago: Henry Regnery Co., 1963).

5. Murray Rothbard, "War, Peace, and the State," in *The Libertarian Forum.*

6. Erik von Kuehnelt-Leddihn, "The Woes of the Underdeveloped Countries," *The Freeman,* January 1971, p. 30.

7. *Ibid.,* p. 31.

8. R. Daniel McMichael, *The Journal of David Q. Little* (New Rochelle, N. Y.: Arlington House, Inc., 1967), pp. 103–104. Reprinted from *The Journal of David Q. Little* by R. Daniel

McMichael, published by Arlington House and used with permission. Copyright © 1967 by Arlington House, New Rochelle, New York.

9. Ludwig von Mises, *Omnipotent Government: the Rise of the Total State and Total War* (New Haven, Conn.: Yale University Press, 1944).

10. Ayn Rand, "The Roots of War," in *Capitalism: the Unknown Ideal* (New York: New American Library, Inc., 1967), p. 38.

11. *Ibid.*, p. 40.

Chapter 11

1. Nathaniel Branden, *Who Is Ayn Rand?* (New York: Random House, Inc., 1962), p. 49. See also vol. 13 in his *Basic Principles of Objectivism* (Series of twenty lectures recorded by Nathaniel Branden Institute, now available from Academic Associates, Los Angeles).

2. Murray Rothbard, *Power and Market* (Menlo Park, Calif.: Institute for Humane Studies, 1970), p. 142.

3. Rothbard, "War, Peace, and the State," in *The Libertarian Forum*, p. 16.

4. Morris and Linda Tannehill, *The Market for Liberty* (Privately printed; available from Morris Tannehill, Box 1383, Lansing, Mich.), p. 68.

5. *Ibid.*, p. 72

6. *Ibid.*, p. 72.

7. *Ibid.*, p. 73.

8. *Ibid.*, p. 80.

9. *Ibid.*, p. 80–81.

10. *Ibid.*, p. 85.

11. *Ibid.*, p. 86.

12. *Ibid.*, p. 89.

13. *Ibid.*, p. 92.

14. *Ibid.*, p. 92.

15. *Ibid.*, pp. 92–93.

16. *Ibid.*, p. 94.

17. This suggestion was made by Murray Rothbard in an unpublished lecture.

18. Tannehill, *op. cit.*, pp. 141–42.

19. *Ibid.*, p. 142.

20. *Ibid.*, pp. 143–44.

21. *Ibid.*, p. 130.

22. *Ibid.*, p. 132.

23. *Ibid.*, p. 132.
24. *Ibid.*, p. 135.
25. There has been some speculation that a no-government society might first appear in Eastern Europe. See Michael Gamarnikow, *Economic Reforms in Eastern Europe* (Detroit, Wayne State University Press, 1967).
26. Albert Jay Nock, *Anarchist's Progress.* Quoted in William F. Buckley, Jr. (ed.), *Did You Ever See a Dream Walking? American Conservative Thought in the Twentieth Century* (Indianapolis: Bobbs-Merrill Co., Inc., 1970), pp. 142–43.

Selected Reading Lists

I. Books

Items marked with an asterisk (*) are concerned primarily with economic matters.

*Adam Smith. *The Wealth of Nations*. 1776 (Many editions).

*Frederic Bastiat (1801–1850). *Selected Essays on Political Economy*. Princeton, N.J.: D. Van Nostrand Co., 1964.

*———. *Economic Sophisms* and *Economic Harmonies*. Princeton, N.J.: D. Van Nostrand Co., 1964.

———. *The Law*. 1850. Irvington-on-Hudson, N.Y.: Foundation for Economic Education, 1962 (Paperbound).

Herbert Spencer. *Social Statics*. 1851. New York: Robert Schalkenbach Foundation, 1970.

Herbert Spencer. *The Man versus the State*. 1884. Caldwell, Idaho: Caxton Printers, Ltd., 1940.

*Eugen von Böhm-Bawerk (1851–1914), *Capital and Interest*. 3 volumes. South Holland, Ill.: Libertarian Press, 1959.

*———. *The Exploitation Theory* and *Value and Price*. (Extracts from the three-volume work.) South Holland, Ill.: Libertarian Press, 1960 (Paperbound).

*———. *Shorter Classics of Böhm-Bawerk*. 2 volumes. South Holland, Ill.: Libertarian Press, 1962.

*Ludwig von Mises. *Human Action.* New Haven, Conn.: Yale University Press, 1951. Revised edition, Chicago: Henry Regnery Co., 1963.

*————. *Socialism.*, New Haven, Conn.: Yale University Press 1951.

*————. *Theory of Money and Credit.* 1924. Irvington-on-Hudson, N.Y.: Foundation for Economic Education, 1971.

————. *Omnipotent Government: the Rise of the Total State and Total War.* New Haven, Conn.: Yale University Press, 1944.

————. *Theory and History.* New Haven, Conn.: Yale University Press, 1957. Reprinted, New Rochelle, N.Y.: Arlington House, Inc., 1969.

*————. *Bureaucracy.* New Haven, Conn.: Yale University Press, 1945.

*————. *Planning for Freedom.* South Holland, Ill.: Libertarian Press, 1952 (Paperbound).

*————. *The Anti-Capitalist Mentality.* South Holland, Ill.: Libertarian Press, 1956 (Paperbound).

Isabel Paterson. *The God of the Machine.* New York: G. P. Putnam's Sons, 1943. Reprinted, Caldwell, Idaho: Caxton Printers, Ltd., 1964.

Ayn Rand. *Atlas Shrugged.* New York: Random House, Inc., 1957 (Hardbound and paperbound editions).

————. *The Virtue of Selfishness.* New York: New American Library, Inc., Signet Books, 1964 (Paperbound).

*————. *Capitalism: the Unknown Ideal.* New York: New American Library, Inc., 1967 (Hardbound and paperbound editions).

Friedrich von Hayek. *The Constitution of Liberty.* Chicago: University of Chicago Press, 1962.

*Henry Hazlitt. *Economics in One Lesson.* New York: Harper & Row, Publishers, 1946 (Paperbound edition, Macfadden Books).

*————. *Time Will Run Back* (A Novel). New Rochelle, N.Y.: Arlington House, Inc., 1970. (Originally published as *The Great Idea* by Appleton-Century-Crofts, 1952.)

*————. *Man Versus the Welfare State.* New Rochelle, N.Y.: Arlington House, Inc., 1969.

*————. *The Conquest of Poverty*. New Rochelle, N.Y.: Arlington House, Inc., 1971.

*Murray Rothbard. *Man, Economy, and the State*. 2 volumes. Princeton, N.J.: D. Van Nostrand Co., 1962. New edition by Nash Publishing in press.

*————. *Power and Market*. Menlo Park, Calif.: Institute for Humane Studies, 1970.

Jerome Tuccille. *Radical Libertarianism*. Indianapolis, Ind.: Bobbs-Merrill Co., 1970.

II. Periodicals

The following magazines, though differing from one another widely on particulars, all contain articles on aspects of the libertarian moral and political philosophy, on the economics of liberty, and comments on current national and international issues:

The Freeman. Monthly. Published by the Foundation for Economic Education, Irvington-on-Hudson, N.Y. Primarily on free-enterprise economics.

The Objectivist. Edited by Ayn Rand. Monthly. Published at 201 East 34th St., New York, N.Y. 10016.

Reason. Monthly. Box 6151, Santa Barbara, Calif. 93105.

The Libertarian Forum. Monthly. Box 341, Madison Square Station, New York, N.Y. 10010.

The Individualist. Monthly. 400 Bonifant Road, Silver Spring, Md. 20904.

RAP. Quarterly. Pine Tree Publications, 104 West Fourth St., Santa Ana, Calif. 92701.

Index

483